# INSIDERS' GUIDE® TO

# LOUISVILLE

## HELP US KEEP THIS GUIDE UP-TO-DATE

We would love to hear from you concerning your experiences with this guide and how you feel it could be improved and kept up-to-date. Please send your comments and suggestions to:

editorial@GlobePequot.com

Thanks for your input, and happy travels!

INSIDERS' GUIDE® SERIES

# INSIDERS' GUIDE® TO

# LOUISVILLE

## FIRST EDITION

**DAVID DOMINÉ**

**INSIDERS'** GUIDE

GUILFORD, CONNECTICUT
AN IMPRINT OF GLOBE PEQUOT PRESS

All the information in this guidebook is subject to change. We recommend that you call ahead to obtain current information before traveling.

# INSIDERS' GUIDE ®

Editor: Amy Lyons
Project Editor: Lynn Zelem
Layout Artist: Kevin Mak
Text Design: Sheryl Kober
Maps: Design Maps Inc. © Morris Book Publishing, LLC

Library of Congress Cataloging-in-Publication Data is available on file.
ISBN 978-0-7627-5695-7

Printed in the United States of America
10 9 8 7 6 5 4 3 2 1

# CONTENTS

## Directory of Maps

# ABOUT THE AUTHOR

David Dominé didn't know what he was getting himself into when he moved to Kentucky in 1993. He had only planned on staying a year, but Louisville, the bustling river city with the split personality—is it northern or southern?—quickly won him over. It had wonderful restaurants, a vibrant art scene, great architecture, historic neighborhoods, and more. He became one of its biggest fans and began writing travel pieces extolling the virtues of his adopted hometown for local and national publications. Several years later he won acclaim for his first book, *Ghosts of Old Louisville: True Stories of Hauntings in America's Largest Victorian Neighborhood*, which he wrote after a series of unexplained occurrences in his Victorian house led him to research the haunted history of the neighborhood. Since then he has authored several more books, including his first cookbook, *Adventures in New Kentucky Cooking*, and a series about the haunted history of his adopted city. His most recent project, *Splash of Bourbon, Kentucky's Spirit*, was released in early 2010.

Travel has always been a great passion for David, and he has lived in the Philippines, Mexico, Spain, Italy, Austria, and Germany—all places that allowed him to indulge his passion for food, wine, and adventure. He holds postgraduate degrees from the University of Louisville, the University of California at Santa Barbara, and Karl-Franzens-Universität in Graz, Austria. When not writing or teaching, he likes to sneak off with his dogs and look for interesting places to write about and good places to eat. He also writes a monthly food column, The Bluegrass Peasant, for *Kentucky Monthly* magazine.

# ACKNOWLEDGMENTS

First, I'd like to say thank you to the people at Estes Public Relations and my agent, Julie Hill, without whose assistance this book never would have been a reality. I'd like to thank James Nold Jr. and Bob Bahr as well, for their work on the *Insiders' Guide to Louisville and Southern Indiana*, which first came out in 1995. Their diligence and research helped me lay the groundwork for this, the most recent and up-to-date travel guide for Louisville, Kentucky. In addition, my gratitude goes out to the many such as Nancy Stephen and Doris Sims at the Louisville Convention and Visitors Bureau who answered my questions and steered me in the right direction when I was looking for the facts and figures about Louisville tourism and demography that would bolster my conclusions about why the Derby City is such a great place to live, work, and play.

I need to thank historians and fellow writers such as Dr. Clyde Crewes, Wade Hall and George Yater as well, because their scholarship in the field of local history proved invaluable in writing parts of this book; in particular, I owe a debt of gratitude to John E. Kleber and the many contributors who made the *Encyclopedia of Louisville* the wonderful resource that it is.

A big thank you also goes to Amy Lyons, my editor, and all the others at Globe Pequot Press who helped put this guide together. Finally, thank you to the friends and helpers like Wendy Flowers, Ramon Garcia, Laura Horan and Beth Schott who did the proofing and fact checking for me.

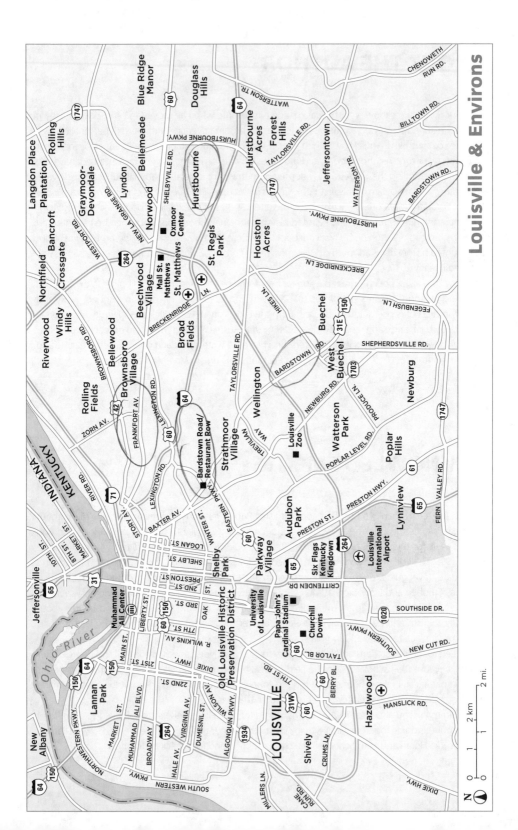

N

KENTUCKY
INDIANA

Ohio River

New Albany

Jeffersonville

Lannan Park

LOUISVILLE

Muhammad Ali Center

Old Louisville Historic Preservation District

University of Louisville

Papa John's Cardinal Stadium

Churchill Downs

Six Flags Kentucky Kingdom

Audubon Park

Parkway Village

Shelby Park

Strathmoor Village

Bardstown Road/ Restaurant Row

Louisville Zoo

Wellington

Bardstown

West Buechel

Buechel

Watterson Park

Newburg

Poplar Hills

Lynnview

Louisville International Airport

Hazelwood

Shively

Rolling Fields

Brownsboro Village

Bellewood

Windy Hills

Riverwood

Crossgate

Northfield

Bancroft

Langdon Place

Rolling Hills

Graymoor-Devondale

Lyndon

Norwood

Bellemeade

Blue Ridge Manor

Douglass Hills

Hurstbourne

Hurstbourne Acres

Forest Hills

Jeffersontown

Houston Acres

St. Regis Park

Beechwood Village

Broad Fields

Mall St. Matthews

Oxmoor Center

St. Matthews

ZORN AV.

RIVER RD.

FRANKFORT AV.

BROWNSBORO RD.

WESTPORT RD.

NEW LA GRANGE RD.

SHELBYVILLE RD.

HURSTBOURNE PKWY.

WATTERSON TR.

CHENOWETH RUN RD.

BILLTOWN RD.

TAYLORSVILLE RD.

WATTERSON TR.

HURSTBOURNE PKWY.

BARDSTOWN RD.

FEGENBUSH LN.

BRECKENRIDGE LN.

SHEPHERDSVILLE RD.

PRODUCE LN.

POPLAR LEVEL RD.

NEWBURG RD.

FERN VALLEY RD.

PRESTON HWY.

PRESTON ST.

CRITTENDEN DR.

SOUTHSIDE DR.

NEW CUT RD.

SOUTHERN PKWY.

TAYLOR BL.

BERRY BL.

7TH ST RD.

MANSLICK RD.

CRUMS LN.

MILLERS LN.

CANE RUN RD.

DIXIE HWY.

DIXIE HWY.

HALE AV.

ALGONQUIN PKWY.

DUMESNIL ST.

VIRGINIA AV.

WILSON AV.

BROADWAY

MUHAMMAD ALI BLVD.

MARKET ST.

SOUTH WESTERN PKWY.

NORTHWESTERN PKWY.

MAIN ST.

LIBERTY ST.

MARKET ST.

8TH ST.

10TH ST.

21ST ST.

22ND ST.

3RD ST.

7TH ST.

R. WILKINS AV.

OAK ST.

2ND ST.

PRESTON ST.

SHELBY ST.

LOGAN ST.

WINTER ST.

STORY AV.

BAXTER AV.

LEXINGTON RD.

EASTERN PKWY.

TAYLORSVILLE RD.

TREVILIAN WAY

HIKES LN.

BRECKENRIDGE LN.

BARDSTOWN RD.

LEXINGTON RD.

150

64

65

31

111

60

150

60

150

31W

60

1934

264

65

65

264

1020

61

747

703

150

31E

64

747

1747

1747

264

42

71

60

64

0   1   2 km

0   1   2 mi.

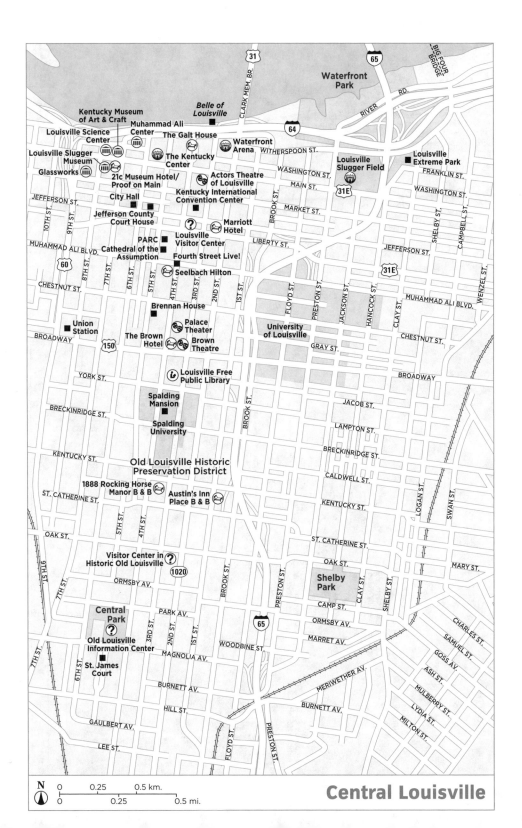

Kentucky Museum of Art & Craft
Muhammad Ali Center
Louisville Science Center
The Galt House
Belle of Louisville
Waterfront Park
Louisville Slugger Museum
The Kentucky Center
Waterfront Arena
Louisville Extreme Park
FRANKLIN ST.
Glassworks
21c Museum Hotel/Proof on Main
Actors Theatre of Louisville
Louisville Slugger Field
WASHINGTON ST.
WITHERSPOON ST.
MAIN ST.
MARKET ST.
WASHINGTON ST.
City Hall
Kentucky International Convention Center
JEFFERSON ST.
Jefferson County Court House
Marriott Hotel
LIBERTY ST.
JEFFERSON ST.
PARC
Louisville Visitor Center
MUHAMMAD ALI BLVD.
Cathedral of the Assumption
Fourth Street Live!
MUHAMMAD ALI BLVD.
CHESTNUT ST.
Seelbach Hilton
CHESTNUT ST.
Brennan House
Union Station
Palace Theater
The Brown Hotel
Brown Theatre
University of Louisville
GRAY ST.
BROADWAY
BROADWAY
YORK ST.
Louisville Free Public Library
Spalding Mansion
JACOB ST.
BRECKINRIDGE ST.
Spalding University
LAMPTON ST.
BRECKINRIDGE ST.
KENTUCKY ST.
Old Louisville Historic Preservation District
CALDWELL ST.
1888 Rocking Horse Manor B & B
ST. CATHERINE ST.
Austin's Inn Place B & B
KENTUCKY ST.
OAK ST.
ST. CATHERINE ST.
Visitor Center in Historic Old Louisville
OAK ST.
MARY ST.
ORMSBY AV.
Shelby Park
Central Park
PARK AV.
CAMP ST.
CHARLES ST.
SAMUEL ST.
Old Louisville Information Center
ORMSBY AV.
MARRET AV.
GOSS AV.
St. James Court
MAGNOLIA AV.
WOODBINE ST.
ASH ST.
BURNETT AV.
MULBERRY ST.
HILL ST.
BURNETT AV.
LYDIA ST.
GAULBERT AV.
MILTON ST.
LEE ST.

RIVER RD.
BIG FOUR BRIDGE

N
0          0.25          0.5 km.
0          0.25          0.5 mi.

**Central Louisville**

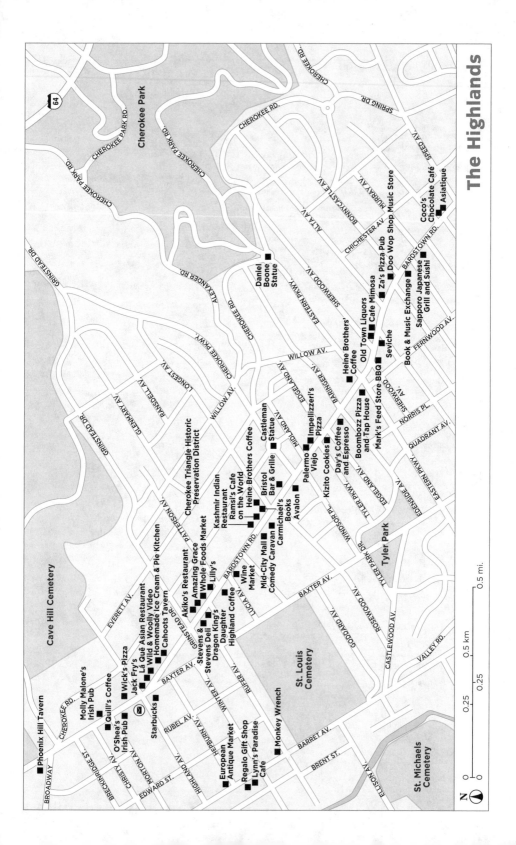

# The Highlands

**Cave Hill Cemetery**

**Cherokee Park**

**St. Louis Cemetery**

**St. Michaels Cemetery**

**Tyler Park**

Cherokee Triangle Historic Preservation District

64

Phoenix Hill Tavern
Molly Malone's Irish Pub
Quill's Coffee
O'Shea's Irish Pub
Wick's Pizza
Jack Fry's
Là Quê Asian Restaurant
Wild & Woolly Video
Homemade Ice Cream & Pie Kitchen
Cahoots Tavern
Akiko's Restaurant
Amazing Grace
Whole Foods Market
Lilly's
Stevens & Stevens Deli
Dragon King's Daughter
Highland Coffee
Starbucks
European Antique Market
Regalo Gift Shop
Lynn's Paradise Cafe
Monkey Wrench
Wine Market
Mid-City Mall
Comedy Caravan
Carmichael's Books
Avalon
Kizito Cookies
Kashmir Indian Restaurant
Ramsi's Cafe on the World
Heine Brothers Coffee
Bristol Bar & Grille
Castleman Statue
Palermo Viejo
Impellizzeri's Pizza
Day's Coffee and Espresso
Boombozz Pizza and Tap House
Mark's Feed Store BBQ
Seviche
Heine Brothers' Coffee
Old Town Liquors
Cafe Mimosa
Za's Pizza Pub
Daniel Boone Statue
Book & Music Exchange
Sapporo Japanese Grill and Sushi
Doo Wop Shop Music Store
Coco's Chocolate Café
Asiatique

N

0    0.25    0.5 km
0    0.25    0.5 mi.

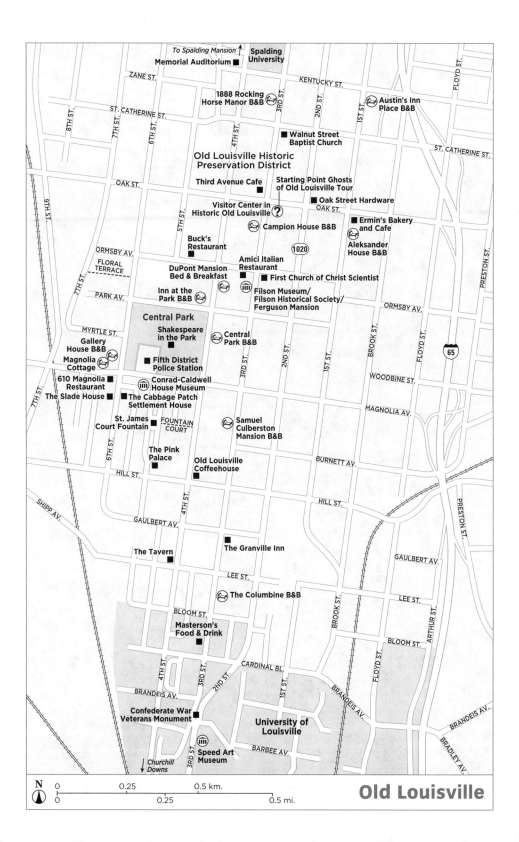

To Spalding Mansion →

Spalding University

Memorial Auditorium ■

ZANE ST.

KENTUCKY ST.

FLOYD ST.

8TH ST.

ST. CATHERINE ST.

7TH ST.

6TH ST.

3RD ST.

2ND ST.

1ST ST.

1888 Rocking
Horse Manor B&B

Austin's Inn
Place B&B

4TH ST.

Walnut Street
Baptist Church

ST. CATHERINE ST.

Old Louisville Historic
Preservation District

OAK ST.

9TH ST.

5TH ST.

Third Avenue Cafe ■

Starting Point Ghosts
of Old Louisville Tour ■

Oak Street Hardware ■

OAK ST.

Visitor Center in
Historic Old Louisville ?

Ermin's Bakery
and Cafe ■

Campion House B&B

PRESTON ST.

Buck's
Restaurant

Aleksander
House B&B

1020

Amici Italian
Restaurant

ORMSBY AV.

FLORAL
TERRACE

DuPont Mansion
Bed & Breakfast

First Church of Christ Scientist ■

PARK AV.

Inn at the
Park B&B

Filson Museum/
Filson Historical Society/
Ferguson Mansion

ORMSBY AV.

7TH ST.

Central Park

BROOK ST.

FLOYD ST.

MYRTLE ST.

Shakespeare
in the Park

Central
Park B&B

65

Gallery
House B&B

Fifth District
Police Station ■

3RD ST.

2ND ST.

1ST ST.

WOODBINE ST.

Magnolia
Cottage

610 Magnolia
Restaurant ■

Conrad-Caldwell
House Museum

MAGNOLIA AV.

The Slade House ■

The Cabbage Patch
Settlement House

St. James
Court Fountain ■

FOUNTAIN
COURT

Samuel
Culberston
Mansion B&B

6TH ST.

The Pink
Palace ■

BURNETT AV.

Old Louisville
Coffeehouse

HILL ST.

4TH ST.

HILL ST.

PRESTON ST.

SHIPP AV.

GAULBERT AV.

The Granville Inn ■

GAULBERT AV.

The Tavern ■

LEE ST.

LEE ST.

BROOK ST.

ARTHUR ST.

The Columbine B&B

BLOOM ST.

Masterson's
Food & Drink ■

BLOOM ST.

4TH ST.

3RD ST.

2ND ST.

CARDINAL BL.

1ST ST.

FLOYD ST.

BRANDEIS AV.

Confederate War
Veterans Monument ■

BRANDEIS AV.

University of
Louisville

BRANDEIS AV.

Churchill
Downs ↓

3RD ST.

Speed Art
Museum

BARBEE AV.

BRADLEY AV.

**N**

0        0.25        0.5 km.

0        0.25        0.5 mi.

# Old Louisville

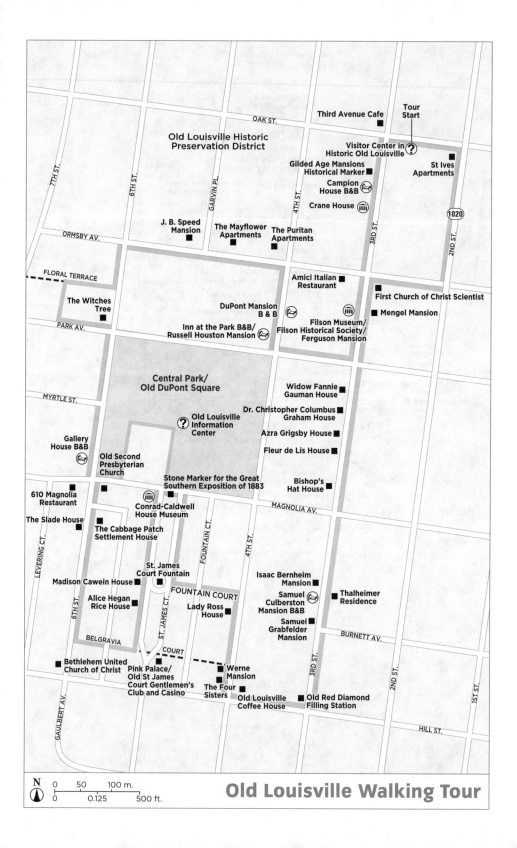

# Old Louisville Walking Tour

**N** 0 50 100 m.
0 0.125 500 ft.

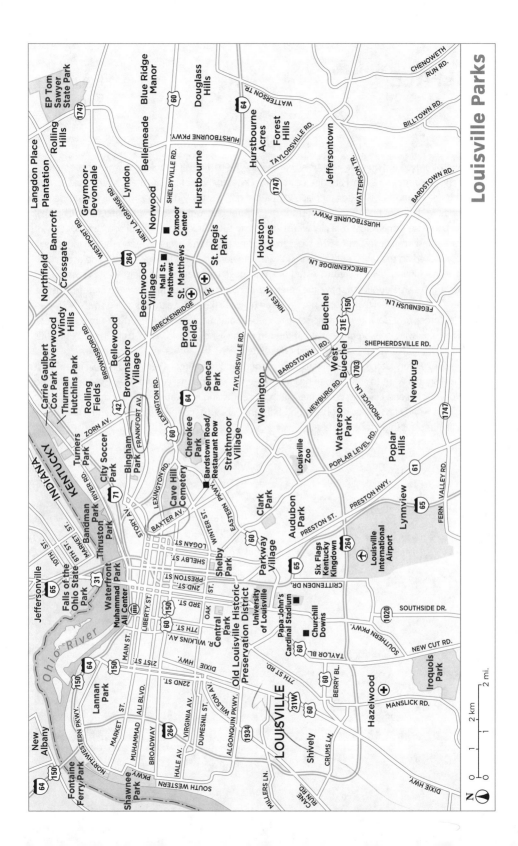

# Louisville Parks

# PREFACE

When I first arrived in Louisville, Kentucky, in the early 1990s, I never imagined it would become one of my favorite places on Earth. Far from a cultural backwater, the vibrant city that awaited me was one rich in tradition and full of history, a place with a distinct identity where the arts thrived and people took pride in the local team. From its historic neighborhoods to the legendary racetrack at Churchill Downs, Louisville came across as a city with a story to tell. Racetrack royalty, bourbon barons, titans of tobacco—these were just some of the types that helped shape this river town, and their mark was still indelibly etched on the fabric of the community. In addition, the people were friendly and accommodating—unassuming, even—yet possessed of an unspoken assurance that theirs was a town indeed worth living in. Large enough to have the amenities of most major cities in the United States, Louisville still had a small-town feel to it. People nodded their heads in passing, waitresses called you "hon" when taking an order, and downtown traffic seemed to be manageable to even the most timid of drivers. Given that Louisville consistently ranked at the top of the list of "most livable" cities in the nation, it's hardly surprising that I chose to make my home here.

Almost 20 years later, Louisville is still telling stories and revealing its secrets to me. So it's only fitting that I should want to share the things that make this exceptional city worth a visit—or a lifetime stay. Horse racing and college sports, interesting museums and innovative stage productions, historic homes and world-class parks, neighborhood bars and fabulous independently owned restaurants— Louisville has something for every taste.

# HOW TO USE THIS BOOK

Like most American cities, Louisville suffered the disastrous effects of urban renewal, and the subsequent flight to the suburbs proved to be the undoing of the quintessential downtown that our parents and grandparents used to know. Find a parking lot in the city center, and chances are, something of architectural interest stood there at one time. The town square with its main shopping artery and surrounding districts is, unfortunately, a thing of the past. But, compared to many towns across the nation, Louisville has managed to preserve a great portion of its historic structures, and efforts are under way to make the downtown area an attractive place to live again. This, coupled with recent endeavors to revitalize local business corridors, has slowly lured people back to the heart of the city, and prospects for a thriving center are looking good.

Louisville is nonetheless a city of neighborhoods. While making sure that you can find your way around the downtown area, this book will also get you to these neighborhoods and help you discover all that Louisville has to offer. It will also let you know what's available in the city environs, and what nearby destinations might be worth a day trip or a weekend getaway. Items of particular interest to tourists or first-time visitors—such as ways of getting around and places to stay, shop, eat, and visit—tend to appear in the front of the book. Moving to Louisville or already live here? Be sure to check out the blue-tabbed pages at the back of the book, where you will find the **Living Here** appendix that offers sections on relocation, health care, education, child care, worship, retirement, and the media. In addition, readers will learn something about the history and demographics of Kentucky's largest city and how it relates to the rest of the state.

All in all, this Insiders' Guide strives to capture the essence of an entire city by touting its virtues and steering newcomers to its most interesting, significant, and useful places, without glossing over its downsides and shortfalls. Given the magnitude of this scope and the inherently subjective nature of reviews and recommendations, this is indeed a daunting task to fulfill. For this reason, this book breaks down each area of interest—accommodations, restaurants, attractions, etc.—into the particular parts of town that locals and outsiders tend to frequent. And although its most noteworthy attractions and points of interest are featured, it still tries to mention places that will get visitors to Louisville off the beaten track and out among the natives.

That having been said, the best way to use this book is as a reference tool to help plan your visit to or stay in the Derby City. Organize your travel here and use it to find the bed-and-breakfast inn or hotel that best suits you. Once you've checked in, fill in your itinerary with must-see sights and eateries that will introduce you to our regional flavors. (And don't forget to leave room for coffee as you read a book in the afternoon, and a bourbon nightcap before you go to bed.)

By all means, don't let this book bind you to a rigid schedule that could curtail the spontaneous joys of travel; be adventuresome, and remember that a city is the sum of its parts, the most important being its people. So ask the person next to you at the bar where they like to go for their favorite hot brown, or what the best local bluegrass band is. Find out from the hotel concierge if there's a local festival taking place and where the best walking tours are. See if the lady behind the counter at the drugstore has a recommendation for a good breakfast spot or if she knows of some out-of-the-way shop with great souvenirs. Whatever it is you're looking for, it's most likely out there; but how you go about finding it is up to you. Enjoy yourself in Louisville and remember that it's full of insiders willing to be your guide.

# AREA OVERVIEW

**W**elcome to Louisville, recently rated one of the top 20 cities in America to live by *Outside* magazine. But the accolades don't stop there. In 2008, Louisville was recognized as the Most Livable Big City in America by the U.S. Conference of Mayors, and it has been consistently ranked by *Places Rated Almanac* as one of the best places to live in the United States. Louisville has always scored high on "livability" rankings, but it's also a great place to visit. It's a community on the move, with big-city amenities like world-class performing arts, great sports, and a nationally acclaimed parks system, yet visitors find hospitality, warmth, and smaller-city advantages like shorter commutes and a lower cost of living. Whether planning a visit for pleasure or business, you'll discover there's a lot to see and do.

## LOCATION

Louisville is situated between Cincinnati and St. Louis on the banks of the scenic 981-mile-long Ohio River. Located at the northern edge of the South and the southern edge of the Midwest, its central location puts Louisville within a day's drive of half the nation's population. Three major interstates—I-64, I-71, and I-65—intersect here, directly connecting the city to metropolitan centers such as Indianapolis, Nashville, Cincinnati, St. Louis, Chicago, Columbus, Cleveland, and Birmingham.

**i** Louisville operates on Eastern Standard Time (EST) from the first Sunday in November to the second Sunday in March, and on Eastern Daylight Saving Time the rest of the year.

## WEATHER

By most accounts Louisville's weather is temperate, but it's still a place where you can enjoy four distinct seasons. Summers tend to be hot with warm evenings; in the spring, the evenings can get cool, so bring along a light jacket. Although rainfall is fairly constant year-round, there seems to be more precipitation in the early fall and spring, and snow usually falls in winter, even if it doesn't always accumulate. Winter temperatures range from 27 to 43 degrees, and in summer it varies between 66 and 86 degrees. Most agree that spring and fall are the most scenic times of year to visit the Derby City. In the spring, buds on the trees suddenly come to life, and an explosion of dogwood blossoms, azaleas, and redbuds can make a simple drive along a neighborhood street an enchanted experience; in the fall, pleasantly cool days and colorful autumn leaves make the region as spectacular as any New England forest.

## CRIME

Louisville is consistently ranked as one of the safest cities in the country and has been ranked as one of the Top 10 safest large cities by Morgan Quitno Press in the past four years. In the 2005 Morgan Quitno survey, Louisville was rated as the seventh-safest large city in the United States. The 2006 edition of the survey ranked Louisville eighth. To put this in more tangible terms, in 2006, Louisville-Jefferson County recorded only 50 murders, compared to over 100 murders in the similarly sized cities of Cincinnati, Columbus, Indianapolis, Kansas City, Memphis, and Nashville. Louisville's total crime rate is generally less than half of most surrounding cities of a comparable size. In 2008, Louisville recorded 79 murders, that number being up from previous years, although still staying slightly lower than Cincinnati and Memphis.

That having been said, Louisville still has its problems, and some parts of town are con-

## Free Wi-Fi

Hotspots for free wireless access are available at many private businesses and all public libraries throughout Louisville. Downtown you'll also find free Wi-Fi at Fourth Street Live! and on all 85 acres of Waterfront Park. In Old Louisville, St. James Court is a Wi-Fi hotspot, and in the Highlands so are portions of Baxter Avenue from East Breckinridge Street to Highland Avenue. In addition, Louisville International Airport, the University of Louisville, and Papa John's Cardinal Stadium are all wireless hotspots. The Louisville Wireless Hotspots campaign identifies all the wireless points in the metro area. You can find a listing of access points, including free access, at their Web site at www .louisvillehotspot.com.

## Hotel/Motel Safety

- Pay attention to the most direct route from your room to the fire escape, elevators, and nearest telephone.
- Use all auxiliary locking devices on doors and windows.
- Use the door peephole to identify anyone requesting entry to your room.
- Never leave money, checks, credit cards, jewelry, extra room keys, car keys, or other valuables in the room. Take valuables with you or leave them in the hotel safety deposit box.
- Always report lost or stolen items to hotel management and the police.

## Personal Safety

- When in town for a convention, always remove your name badge when leaving the convention area.
- Carry your cash separately from your ID and credit cards.
- Never leave your purse, wallet, or valuables on a store counter or in a shopping cart unattended. Do not leave valuables in plain sight in your car. Purse, cell phones, laptop computers, wallets, and shopping purchases should be stored in the trunk of your car, or in another secure location.
- Park and walk in well-lit areas, and with a companion, if possible.
- If you encounter a panhandler, just say "no" and walk away. Do not place yourself in a compromising position by opening your purse, reaching for your wallet, or pulling money from your pockets.

sidered less safe than others. Traditionally, the West End has been considered the neighborhood with the highest number of shootings and gang-related violence, but as with any city, you'll find random shootings, break-ins, and burglaries scattered throughout its different neighborhoods. Downtown generally doesn't present many problems, but it's always better to be on the safe side and not be out alone after dark in unpopulated areas if you can avoid it. Panhandlers are not uncommon on streets in the center city area, along Bardstown Road, and along Oak Street in Old Louisville.

The Louisville Convention and Visitors Bureau makes the following suggestions to help ensure that your stay in the Derby City is a safe one, whether you're planning to visit for pleasure, business, or to attend a meeting or convention:

# NEIGHBORHOODS AND SUBURBS

Like many older cities across the country, Louisville has a large number of well-defined neighborhoods, in addition to suburbs and unincorporated communities. The areas of downtown Louisville and Portland constitute the oldest neighborhoods, highlighting the early role the Ohio River played as the most important form

## What *Is* Kentuckiana?

Watching local TV in your hotel room or traveling around town, you'll most likely discover a range of businesses with "Kentuckiana" in their names. It's easy enough to figure out. According to the *Encyclopedia of Louisville,* the *Courier-Journal* and *Louisville Times* coined the word sometime in the 1940s to briefly describe the Kentucky and Indiana areas surrounding Louisville. Bisected by the Ohio River, Kentuckiana encompasses counties on both sides, and over the last few decades the term has come to include the larger areas of southern Indiana and north-central Kentucky. Today, many residents commute back and forth across the river, and economic and population changes in Louisville proper tend to affect both sides of the river in the same way.

of transportation and commerce in the region. As the downtown expanded, neighborhoods such as Butchertown, Shelby Park, Phoenix Hill, Russell, and Smoketown sprang up to house and employ growing numbers of residents. To the south Old Louisville emerged as a bastion for the city's elite, who populated the new suburb with hundreds of grand mansions and well-built homes. The advent of the streetcar allowed suburbs to be developed in other parts of the city—in neighborhoods now known as Beechmont, Shawnee and the Highlands—and in the early 1900s an interurban rail line resulted in communities to the east like Anchorage and Glenview becoming year-round homes for the rich. As the city grows today, new communities joining the ranks of dozens of established ones, neighborhoods continue to define Louisville and its character. There are

too many neighborhoods to list, but read on for some names you will most likely hear during your stay in Louisville.

## Butchertown

Butchertown was established in 1796 by a gristmill owner, Henry Fait, and lies just east of downtown. Aside from the Edison House, it is also home to two of the city's most popular sports venues. For bike, board, and blade enthusiasts, there is Louisville's outdoor Extreme Park, open 24 hours a day, seven days a week. Fans of America's favorite pastime will enjoy Slugger Field, home to the Louisville Bats, the Triple-A affiliate of the Cincinnati Reds. Award-winning Louisville Waterfront Park links the downtown central business district to Butchertown and includes a 14-acre great lawn, a children's play area, picnic areas, and two restaurants. Home to free concerts six months out of the year, this popular park was designed by the renowned firm of Hargreaves Associates, the architect for the 2012 Summer Olympics in London.

## Downtown

In the last few years, Louisville's downtown area has really turned around, and once again it's a place to live, work, and play. Although some work is still needed to get it back to its glory days of the 1940s and '50s, developers are building lofts and condos in older buildings that were previously vacant, and new restaurants and clubs have added extra incentive for the locals to come out after dark. Modern hotels are drawing more and more overnighters, and regular conventioneers comment favorably on the city center's accessibility and ease of getting around.

Downtown Louisville is bounded by the Ohio River to the north, and, generally speaking, by Broadway to the south; Ninth Street constitutes its border to the west, and to the east, it ends where Butchertown begins and Baxter Avenue leads up to the Highlands. Although you'll find businesses and sites of interest scattered throughout the downtown area, most attractions are grouped in three major areas of downtown

# ⊙ Close-up

## The Place Where Blue-Sky Thinking Meets Grassroots Can-Do

Louisville recently embarked on a multimillion-dollar ad campaign that branded itself as the *Possibility City*. "It isn't just a place to live—it's a place to really live. It's a town without excuses, blissfully free of the hang-ups and holdups that keep things from happening. It's a place where blue-sky thinking meets grassroots can-do. It's a city without limits. Anything's possible here in Louisville. Especially you." To promote this idea, Louisville-based marketing and advertising firm Red7e was hired to create publicity for the campaign, which, in the end, garnered a good deal of national attention for the city. Whether the attention was good or bad hasn't been decided yet, but the firm maintains that the overwhelming majority of the responses it received from its ads were positive. Aside from touting the high number of "butt tattoos" in Louisville, a series of tongue-in-cheek television spots spoofed erectile dysfunction commercials in an attempt to lure people to Possibility City. Go to www.possibilitycity.com to watch the commercials and find out more about the "Possibility City" campaign.

As part of the campaign, they came up with The Top 10 Reasons that Louisville is a Top-Tier Town:

1. 21c Museum Hotel was selected as the number-one hotel in the United States, and the number-six hotel in the world, in the prestigious *Condé Nast* Traveler Readers' Choice Awards for 2009.

2. Louisville has been voted all the way to Number Two as a "Top-25 City" according to a Kiplinger.com poll.

3. Louisville is one of the top-three winners for "Most Improved Cities for Cycling" by *Bicycling Magazine.*

4. Louisville was voted the fourth-most "Photo-Friendly City" in the country by pop-photo.com.

5. *Bon Appetit* magazine chose Louisville as one of the five finalists for "America's Foodi-est" city.

6. *AmericanStyle Magazine* recently selected the St. James Court Art Show as one of the best art fairs in the country.

7. Louisville was ranked seventh in the "Best Towns of 2008" by *Outside* magazine.

8. It was "Just Eight More Miles to Louisville" in Willie Nelson's 1995 hit by the same name.

9. Heck, nobody wants to be ninth in anything, so how about this instead: Last year we finished first for having the "Best-Tasting Water in America."

10. And rounding out the list, West Main Street was ranked the 10th-best Main Street in the nation by the American Planning Association, based in Washington, D.C.

Louisville: the East Market District, Fourth Avenue, and West Main Street.

## East Market District

The East Market District, anchored by Baxter Avenue on the east and Preston Street on the west, comprises some 14 city blocks in parts of the Butchertown and Phoenix Hill neighborhoods. Another of those areas that has been enjoying a rebirth, East Market is a focal point for new businesses and residences alike. With more than 200 businesses, it's a popular place for boutiques and shops specializing in antiques, home furnishings, and gifts. This is the location of Joe Ley's Antiques, known for its dizzying array of collectibles and carnival atmosphere; it's also where you'll discover Louisville's oldest candy store, Muth's, a place that still hand-dips its chocolates. In addition, some of the region's finest galleries have chosen to locate here, and their artists represent many mediums, including glassblowing, which can be seen at Flame Run. The area also boasts a number of fine dining establishments such as White Oak and Mayan Café.

East Market isn't short on history, either. St. Martin of Tours Catholic Church provides a glimpse of what the area looked like in the middle of the 19th century, and several old temples and synagogues hint at the city's Jewish past. In nearby Butchertown is a house where famed inventor Thomas Edison resided when he was a young Western Union telegraph operator in Louisville in the 1860s.

## Fourth Avenue

Fourth Avenue—an early designation for today's Fourth Street—has been enjoying a resurgence after a recent $70 million entertainment district revitalized much of the downtown by adding a variety of restaurants and entertainment venues that reconnected the city's riverfront to its main east/west thoroughfare, Broadway. It's been a hit with diners, shoppers, theatergoers, and urbanites who are slowly breathing life back into a space that many people had given up on. This is where you'll find two of the city's grandest hotels—the Brown and the Seelbach

Hilton—and on the Ohio River is the city's only waterfront hotel, one of the Southeast's largest, with 600 suites and 700 guest rooms. The Galt House Hotel & Suites recently underwent a $60 million renovation, and today visitors can use a glass-enclosed sidewalk that takes them from the hotel to the Kentucky International Convention Center nearby.

On the other end of Fourth Avenue, where the Brown Hotel is located, you'll be in the city's original theater district. Although most of the grand old movie houses were torn down in the '60s and '70s, several of them remain, giving an inkling of what the area must have been like in its heyday. One of the surviving structures, the Louisville Palace, which opened in 1928, showcases the lavish Spanish Baroque Revival style with fountains, statues, tapestries, and a "Ceiling of Celebrities" in the foyer, with scores of medallion faces of famous men, including the architect himself, John Eberson. Nearby, in a wonderfully rehabbed old building, you'll find the studios for Louisville's three public radio stations; and across the street from that is Cunningham's, one of the oldest restaurants in town and known for its fish sandwiches.

In the middle of Fourth Avenue is Fourth Street Live!, the Kordish-designed entertainment complex that features a variety of restaurants, pubs, nightclubs, retailers, and live-music venues. One of the most popular destinations is the Maker's Mark Bourbon House and Lounge, a hip nightspot that showcases one of the state's most famous whiskeys in several different forms.

## West Main Street

West Main Street—specifically the stretch between Fifth Street and Eighth Street—combines historic buildings and striking contemporary architecture with a wonderful collection of Victorian cast-iron facades. Here you'll find the largest collection of such facades outside of the famed SoHo District in New York City, making it one of the most creative and arts-inspired cultural districts in the region. With its unique streetscape program, museums, and cultural institutions, West Main has become a destination for both residents and visitors who enjoy its architecture and energy. The architecture reveals Louisville's roots as a river port and distribution center, seeing that many of the original buildings served as hardware stores or manufacturing houses. This is the area where two of Kentucky's most famous exports—tobacco and bourbon whiskey—would leave their mark on the city. In fact, West Main Street was once known as "Whiskey Row" because at one time there were as many as 50 distilleries and other whiskey-related businesses located along Main Street.

Home to one-of-a-kind museums and attractions such as the Louisville Slugger Factory and the Frazier International History Museum, West Main Street has become known as Louisville's Museum Row. Other popular destinations include the Glassworks Gallery, Louisville Science Center & IMAX Theatre, Kentucky Museum of Art and Craft, 21c Museum Hotel, the Muhammad Ali Center, and the Kentucky Show.

## East End

For the most part, this section of town sprang up in the years following World War II when American city dwellers migrated to the suburbs, and today you'll find a number of stores and restaurants, many of them chain, along the Hurstbourne Lane commercial corridor. One of the city's most historic properties, Locust Grove, the 1790s home where Louisville founder George Rogers Clark spent the last years of his life, is located here, and so is the home of former president Zachary Taylor, although it's a private residence today. This is also where three of Louisville's largest shopping malls—Oxmoor Center, Mall St. Matthews, and the Summit—are located.

The East End is a designation that loosely describes a handful of the city's suburbs, most of which are located between the Watterson Expressway (I-264) and the Gene Snyder Freeway (I-265). Named for influential men in Louisville's development, these interstates provide beltways around the city center and serve as connectors to two of the East End's main population centers, Jeffersontown and Middletown.

## Frankfort Avenue

Just minutes from downtown, historic Frankfort Avenue is a vibrant area that stretches from the old Clifton neighborhood to Crescent Hill, home of the Peterson-Dumesnil House that was built in 1869 as a summer residence for prominent tobacco dealer Joseph Peterson. Also situated in this neighborhood is the American Printing House for the Blind, the world's largest company devoted solely to researching, developing, and manufacturing products for those who are blind or visually impaired. Founded in 1858, it is the oldest organization of its kind in the United States, and its Callahan Museum offers hands-on interactive exhibits that explore the chronology of the printing house and its accomplishments over the years. On display is a rare collection of artifacts related to the educational history of blind people in this country.

Another draw to this part of town is that you'll find some of the city's best shopping and dining here. Popular local hangouts such as Porcini's, the Irish Rover, Bourbons Bistro, and L&N Wine Bar line Frankfort Avenue, and deals on designer clothing can be found in the area's upscale consignment shops. In addition, specialty and antiques shops offer items that cannot be found anywhere else in the city. This is also where branches of local favorites like Heine Brothers' Coffee and Carmichael's Books can be found. Nearby is the Mellwood Arts and Entertainment Center, a former meat-packing plant that is home to some 200 artists and entrepreneurs, as well as cafes and event space.

## Germantown

Located several miles southeast of downtown Louisville, the Germantown neighborhood is bounded by Eastern Parkway, Barret Avenue and the south fork of Beargrass Creek. As a general term, it applies to the area of Louisville from the Original Highlands to the Bradley and St. Joseph neighborhoods—areas settled predominantly by Germans. It was heavily developed during the 1890s, and many of the original shotgun structures still remain. The neighborhood's most famous restaurant, Lynn's Paradise Cafe, is often featured on national food shows for its quirky decor and spunky diner fare.

## Highlands

Bardstown Road and Baxter Avenue form the main thoroughfares of the area known as the Highlands. Long considered one of the most progressive parts of town, this area comprises 15 neighborhoods, including the picturesque historic preservation district known as Cherokee Triangle. A jaunt through the Highlands will reveal a great deal of local charm in the number of lovingly preserved homes and turn-of-the-20th-century architecture on display. It is also the spot to go for shopping, people-watching, and dining.

Known as "Restaurant Row," Bardstown Road slices through the middle of the Highlands and is home to a large variety of eclectic eateries, pubs, and coffeehouses. Award-winning chefs are always cooking up a storm at popular restaurants such as Jack Fry's, Lilly's, Asiatique, Seviche, and Avalon, and casual yet upbeat eateries like the Bristol and Ramsi's Café on the World have become local institutions. The Highlands is also known for its nightlife, and live, local music and artists are featured at different venues. In addition to being the ideal spot to take a date out for dinner and drinks, it's the place to enjoy a good laugh at Comedy Caravan or catch a foreign film at Baxter Avenue Theaters.

Among the many galleries, boutiques, specialty stores, and antiques shops that dot this diverse neighborhood, you'll find a local gem known as ear X-tacy, an independent music store founded by John Timmons. More than just CDs and vinyl records, this popular music venue is always hopping, and has become a home away from home for music lovers of all types. This is also where you'll find WHY Louisville, a small shop that bills itself as "a fan club for the city." The store features clothing and accessories designed by local artists, and Louisville's symbol, the fleur-de-lis, can be found on T-shirts, hats, bags, and more.

Nearby is the city's most popular green space, Cherokee Park, another of the famous parks designed by landscape architect Frederick Law Olmsted in the 1890s. With its many miles of pathways and hidden trails, it's a popular spot for joggers and dog walkers.

**i** Now in its fourth decade, the Bambi Walk is a Louisville tradition that showcases some of the most popular bars along Bardstown Road. To do this pub crawl, revelers start the night with a drink at the Bambi Bar (2701 Bardstown Rd., 502-456-9635) and then head north, stopping for a drink at each watering hole along the way. If you make it all the way to Phoenix Hill Tavern, you've undergone a Lousiville rite of passage. Have fun, but make sure to nominate a designated driver/walker before you start.

## Jeffersontown

Known as J-town to the locals, Jeffersontown was founded in 1797 and covers 10 square miles today. More than 25,000 residents call it home, and it is the site of Bluegrass Industrial Park and its nearly 900 companies. With more than 38,000 people employed there, it counts as one of the largest employers in the state. Easily accessible and strategically located, Jeffersontown has over 3,500 hotel rooms and 125 restaurants.

In addition, J-town is home to Veterans Memorial Park, 25 acres of green space dedicated to all those who served or are currently serving in the United States Armed Forces, which opened in 1997. On display at the park's entrance is an assortment of military equipment, including M60 tanks and Huey helicopters.

Among the sites of tourist interest is the Jeffersontown Historical Museum, located at the rear of the Jeffersontown branch of the Louisville Free Public Library. The "Dolls of the World" exhibit has on view some 1,250 dolls representing the dress and culture of people around the globe, and is rumored to be the largest doll collection in the Midwest.

## Middletown

Take Shelbyville Road (US 60) 12 miles east out of downtown Louisville and you'll reach Middletown, a suburb that began as one of the oldest communities in the state. The site of an old stagecoach stop, the town was chartered in 1797, and the town prides itself on its small historic district today. Nine National Register buildings, including the Captain Benjamin Head House, the Middletown Inn, the Beynroth House, Davis Tavern, Frank House, the Joseph Abell House, and the Middletown Methodist Church, are located here, and visitors can relive the past at the Middletown Historic Museum. The heart of the Historic District is located in a three-block area of Main Street, where you'll also find antiques shops, jewelry and collectible shops, pottery, and fashions. Many of these businesses, including a couple of cafes and delis, are located in restored old homes. Middletown can claim that history is still being made today, since it is home to the Valhalla Golf Club, the PGA-owned course where the United States dramatically retook the Ryder Cup from the European team in 2008.

## Okolona

Located in southern Jefferson County and centered around the intersection of Preston Highway and the Outer Loop, Okolona claims about 20,000 residents. In the late 1700s farmers from Virginia and Pennyslvania settled the area and later called it Lone Oak. A town in the western part of the state had already claimed that name, however, so the city fathers reformulated the name into Okolona. Although it sits 10 miles from downtown Louisville, it is at exactly the same elevation and is therefore prone to flooding. Several square miles of wetlands needed to be drained to make development possible. Okolona is home to Jefferson Mall, the largest shopping center in Louisville's South End.

## Old Louisville

Mention Victorian architecture and Louisville, Kentucky, doesn't come to mind. Most people think of San Francisco and its colorful painted ladies or quaint New England towns. Louisville, however,

is home to an enviable collection of Victorian homes and boasts three National Register Historic Preservation Districts. One of them is Old Louisville, which is located directly south of the downtown area. Roughly bounded by Kentucky Street to the north, U of L to the south, and I-65 and Ninth Street to the east and west, respectively, Old Louisville is a veritable treasure trove of late-19th- and early-20th-century architecture that can rival most historic neighborhoods across the nation. With some 45 square blocks and a total of more than a thousand historic structures, Old Louisville is an architectural feast for the eyes. Once the redheaded stepchild of Louisville neighborhoods, Old Louisville has undergone a remarkable transformation since the 1970s; today, most of the old mansions and quaint townhomes have been restored or rehabilitated and are now occupied by families and community-minded individuals. Although some problem areas remain—most notably the corridor along Oak Street, which is frequented by panhandlers and loiterers, and the blocks closest to the University of Louisville—Old Louisville has emerged as a shining example of historic preservation in the heart of Kentucky's largest city.

Olmsted-designed Central Park and elegant St. James and Belgravia courts comprise the heart of Old Louisville, which evolved as the city's first suburb after the conclusion of the famous Southern Exposition of 1883. After the main exhibit hall—a huge wooden structure that measured 600 by 900 feet in dimension—was dismantled, the resulting grid served as the footprint for a spectacular neighborhood of elegant mansions and quaint townhomes. Most of the city's bed-and-breakfasts are located here, and it's a popular tourist stop for its architectural walks and haunted history tours. The opulent Conrad-Caldwell House, one of the city's historic house museums, is located here, as is the region's premier art museum, the Speed Art Museum.

## Pleasure Ridge Park

First settled by German and French Catholics in the mid 1800s, this area of southwest Louisville had a resort hotel on a shaded ridge of Muldraugh Hill that made it a popular leisure destination up until World War I. Rapid expansion took place in the years after World War II as subdivisions were built, attracting blue-collar homeowners in search of cheap land and proximity to Fort Knox and downtown Louisville. Most often referred to as PRP by the locals, this is the home of the Pleasure Ridge Park High School that made national headlines in 2009 when football coach, David Jason Stinson, was indicted for reckless homicide—and later acquitted—in the death of lineman Max Gilpin, who collapsed during practice the previous summer. Members of the school played for The Valley Sports American Little League of Louisville in 2002 when the team defeated Sendai Hagashi Little League of Sendai, Japan, in the championship game for the 56th Little League World Series.

## Shively

Centered around the junction of US 60 and the Dixie Highway to the southwest of Louisville, the Shively area was first settled and farmed around 1780, like much of Jefferson County. It was named for early landowner Christian William Shively, who settled there in 1810 and established a mill. The area came to be known as the Shively Precinct after he donated land for a church in 1816. Shortly before the Civil War, German immigrants began moving to the area and operating truck farms, many of which continued up through the 1930s.

After Prohibition, eight distilleries opened there, and this would lead to its incorporation as its own city when Depression-weary Louisville tried to annex the area for the tax dollars that would be generated. To avoid annexation by its much larger neighbor, Shively incorporated as a city in 1938 and annexed the distilleries, acquiring a $20 million tax base in the process. As a result, Shively entered a period of prosperity and became a favorite location for many families leaving the West End to the north as it became racially integrated.

The all-white suburb made national headlines in 1954 when activists Carl and Anne Braden

bought a house there and sold it to a black family. After the family moved in, shots were fired into the house, and a bomb exploded. No one was harmed, and no one was ever convicted of the crime. Many of the distilleries closed in the 1960s, and the area entered a period of decline; however, recent public works projects and more businesses moving to the area have improved local fortunes. Today, the area around Seventh Street north of Dixie is known for its seedy adult entertainment businesses, something that has earned it the nickname of "Lively Shively."

## South Louisville/Beechmont

In recent years, the Beechmont neighborhood has experienced a renaissance of sorts. New, young families have moved in and taken up residence alongside second- and third-generation occupants. Many of the new neighbors come from all corners of the globe, and the mix of old and new has transformed Beechmont into a multicultural neighborhood with a rich and diverse population that can be seen in its restaurants, churches, schools, and shops. Take a trip to the Iroquois Manor shopping center, home to a number of immigrant-owned businesses, and you'll see for yourself.

This South End neighborhood has a rich history that goes back to its development in the late 1800s, when the neighborhood was touted as "Beechmont the Beautiful" and "The Grand Dame" of Louisville's South End. One of the highlights of this part of town is Iroquois Park, a masterpiece of urban landscaping and natural architecture by renowned park designer Frederick Law Olmsted. One of the crown jewels in the Louisville park system, it is a popular gathering spot for outsiders and South End residents alike. The park also hosts frequent concerts and musical theater productions at the outdoor amphitheater, and sends 8,000 runners on their way as the official start of the Kentucky Derby Festival's annual marathon. Nearby you will find the Little Loom House and the wooded grounds that were once home to renowned textile artist Lou Tate.

**i** Some famous people who were born in Louisville or have called it home include actors Irene Dunne, Lillian Gish, Victor Mature, Tom Cruise, and Ned Beatty; Supreme Court justice Louis Brandeis; filmmakers Tod Browning and D. W. Griffith; singers Joan Osborne and Mary Travers; writers Sue Grafton, Sena Jeter Naslund, and Hunter S. Thompson; and magician Lance Burton.

## The Sunny Side

"The Sunny Side of Louisville" is what the folks at the Clark-Floyd Counties Convention & Tourism Bureau have optimistically dubbed the three communities located across from Louisville in southern Indiana.

### Clarksville

Immediately across from downtown Louisville, and east of I-65, lies Clarksville, Indiana, home to the Colgate clock, one of the world's largest, and the huge fossil beds at the Falls of the Ohio State Park. Founded in 1783 and named after George Rogers Clark—he was a celebrated figure of the American Revolutionary War, and his brother William gained renown as one of the leaders of the famed Lewis and Clark Expedition—Clarksville has more than 20,000 residents. Although it was the oldest town in the former Northwest Territory, you wouldn't know it today to look at the busy chain store–riddled commercial strip that defines the community today.

### Jeffersonville

Jeffersonville is situated across from Louisville and to the west of I-65 along the banks of the Ohio River. Commonly abbreviated as "Jeff" by the locals, it is the county seat of Clark County and has a population of some 30,000. A community arose there in the 1780s when soldiers erected a fort to protect settlers from Indian attacks, but it wasn't until 1802 that the town was actually laid out. Residents used a grid pattern designed by Thomas Jefferson, the city's namesake, making it the only city ever designed by Jefferson. A small-town feel remains today, due largely in part to an intact center and many historical structures.

### New Albany

According to the most recent census, nearly 40,000 residents call the Floyd County seat home. Bounded by I-265 to the north and the Ohio River to the south, the town was founded in July 1813 when three brothers—Joel, Abner, and Nathaniel Scribner—arrived at the Falls of the Ohio and named the site after their home, Albany, New York. A thriving steamboat industry fueled the city's economy during the mid-19th century, when at least a half-dozen shipbuilders were in operation and turned out great numbers of packet boats and steamboats including the famed *Robert E. Lee*. Today Main Street features a collection of 19th-century mansions from the city's heyday as a shipbuilding center. A major attaction is the Culbertson Mansion, a three-story French Second Empire style structure that is an Indiana state memorial. Every October, New Albany hosts the Harvest Homecoming festival, one of the largest annual events in the region.

**i** For more information about Louisville's "Sunny Side," contact the Clark-Floyd Counties Convention & Tourism Bureau at 305 Southern Indiana Ave., Jeffersonville, IN 47130-3218; (812) 280-5566; sunnysideoflouisville.org.

## West End

Although many residents who live in other parts of the city tend to lump them all together, there are several distinct neighborhoods in the western part of the city. One of them, Portland, is a historic neighborhood that was founded in 1811. Located west of downtown Louisville and bounded on the north by the Ohio River, Portland at one time bustled with river activity centered around its own wharf. By the 1830s, however, the shipping trade that had made it its own, independent city shifted to Louisville when a canal was built on the river. Listed on the National Register of Historic Places, the Portland Historic District includes notable historic sights such as Notre Dame du Port Church, which was completed in 1841 and is one of the oldest Catholic churches in the city. The U.S. Marine Hospital, built in 1852, is considered the best example of antebellum-era hospitals in the United States today, and it's the only surviving structure built by the federal government for inland soldiers.

Another West End neighborhood is the Russell neighborhood. Located north of Muhammad Ali Boulevard and west of Ninth Street downtown, this vibrant community was the city's premier African-American neighborhood in the 1940s. Its namesake was the renowned black educator Harvey C. Russell, and the area became the home to many well-to-do African Americans. Its main thoroughfare, Walnut Street—today's Muhammad Ali Boulevard—bustled with night-clubs in its heyday when local audiences flocked there to hear the jazz greats of their age.

Today, grand Victorian and Italianate homes, historic churches, and public buildings dot the predominantly black area, which was listed on the National Register of Historic Places in 1980. Among the historic structures that survive today is the Doerhoefer-Hampton House from 1887 at 422 West Chestnut Street. Named for previous occupants, Basil Doerhoefer and Sarah and G. Wade Hampton, the home is now used for community events. Another significant site is the Western Colored Branch of the Louisville Free Public Library, which was built in 1908. The nation's first public library for African Americans, it is located at 604 South Tenth Street and is the home of the library's African-American archives and resource center.

# GETTING HERE, GETTING AROUND

During the early days, as the country began extending its tendrils to the Pacific Ocean, Louisville was a gateway to what would become known as the Wild West. Adventurers returning from those far-flung territories saw it as the portal to the East and the civilization it represented. After that, as its reputation as a manufacturing center became solidified, people started referring to Louisville as the Gateway to the South or the Gateway to the North, depending on their cultural and geographic leanings. Louisville, it seems, was always in the middle of things. Today, its geographic location makes it easily accessible from most parts of the country, and visitors find it a convenient destination whether traveling by plane, bus, or car. With its basic grid pattern and lack of urban sprawl, Kentucky's largest city is also easy to navigate once you get here.

## GET YOUR BEARINGS

The Louisville visitor center downtown at the corner of Fourth and Jefferson Streets, adjacent to the Hyatt Regency, can help you find your way around the Derby City. In addition to a supply of maps and brochures, the 2,950-square-foot center has clothing, souvenirs, and a skilled staff that can assist with many services:

*Need to know where to go?* Here you can purchase attraction tickets or have a customized itinerary of places to visit created just for you.

*Need to know how to get there?* Friendly staffers will map it out for you.

*Need a ride?* This is the place to arrange a taxi pickup or plan a bus or trolley route.

*Need a bite to eat?* Knowledgeable volunteers will tell you where the locals eat and where to find their favorite restaurants. They'll even make reservations at a restaurant that suits your tastes.

## AIRPORTS

### LOUISVILLE INTERNATIONAL AIPORT
**600 Terminal Drive**
**(502) 367-4636 (Airport Information)**
**(502) 368-6524 (Airport Authority)**
**www.flylouisville.com**
Chicago and New Orleans are an hour's flight from Louisville, and cities such as New York, Miami, and Houston are about two hours away, so it's apparent that Louisville is an easy trip from most points in the South, Midwest, and Northeast. Stop and change planes once or twice, and most points in the West can be reached in a morning or afternoon. Louisville International Airport (SDF) serves all the major American airlines, although it's only a spoke for most. And despite its "international" status, the only country served directly is Canada.

Louisville International Airport is located in the southern part of the city and is situated on 1,200 acres. The passenger terminals comprise more than 360,000 square feet and have 23 boarding gates. There are 5,625 public parking spaces, including a four-level parking garage, with three levels under cover. The airport consists of two parallel runways, one crosswind runway, and more than 62,000 linear feet of taxiways.

Apart from commercial passenger and general aviation activities, Louisville International Airport is also home to the Kentucky Air National Guard and UPS, Kentucky's second-largest private-sector employer. Louisville International Airport currently has one terminal with two concourses; Concourse A houses Delta, Continental, and Northwest Airlines, in addition to American Airlines and Midwest Airlines. You'll find United Airlines, US Airways, Frontier Airlines, and Southwest in Concourse B. The terminal is very small and easy to navigate; to claim your luggage, follow the signs to the main hallway, jump on a moving sidewalk, and at the main lobby, take the escalator to the bottom level, where you'll also find kiosks for all the major car-rental agencies. This is where taxis and limos will be waiting as well; arriving passengers come in through the entrances on the second level. The trip to downtown Louisville takes about five minutes from the airport.

May is by far the busiest time to visit Louisville, thanks to the Kentucky Derby. If you hold tickets to the annual races, arrange your flights and make accommodations well in advance. Aside from the Kentucky Derby, spring is a lovely time to visit Louisville, when the weather is warm and the dogwoods, redbuds, and azaleas are blooming. Winters in Louisville can get cold, and snow is likely from December to February, although it usually doesn't stay on the ground for very long. If you don't mind the cold, inexpensive flights to Louisville and discount accommodations are likely to be found in the off-season.

i Louisville International ranks third in North America—and ninth in the world—in the total amount of cargo handled as home of UPS's international air-sorting hub. The airport handles 4.3 billion pounds of cargo, freight, and mail in an average year.

## "THANKS FOR CALLING LOUISVILLE!"

Call the Louisville Convention and Visitors Bureau's Call Center at (888) LOUISVILLE and that's what you'll hear. The friendly staff is knowledgeable and always happy to answer any questions you may have. In addition to requesting information to assist in preplanning their visits, callers may book hotel rooms or ticket packages as well. The Louisville Convention and Visitors Bureau also offers discounted hotel accommodations and attraction tickets throughout the year, so this is the number to call to get reduced prices

to help customize your own Louisville adventure on a budget.

Or if you prefer to surf the Web for information, go to www.gotolouisville.com any time of the day or night and you'll find useful information about attractions, accommodations, restaurants, and more. You'll also discover a searchable calendar of events and links to monthly podcasts. The Web site also offers the convenience of one-stop shopping because you can create your own vacation package with specially priced admission tickets and hotel accommodations.

## HELPFUL INFORMATION

Tune your radio dial to 1610 AM for up-to-date traffic reports and 530 AM for visitor information.

### Important Phone Numbers

AAA Emergency Road Service: (502) 423-8222
Baptist Hospital East: (502) 897-8100
Clark Memorial Hospital: (812) 282-6631
Federal Express: (800) 238-5355
Greater Louisville, Inc.
   (Chamber of Commerce): (502) 625-0000
Jewish Hospital: (502) 587-4011
Jewish Southwest: (502) 955-2400
Kentucky Department of Travel: (800) 225-TRIP
Kentucky Relay Service: (800) 648-6056
Kosair Children's Hospital: (502) 629-6000
Local Directory Assistance: 4-1-1
Louisville Convention and
   Visitors Bureau: (502) 584-2121
Louisville Free Public Library: (502) 574-1611
Metro Police Dispatch: (502) 574-7111
Norton Audubon Hospital: (502) 636-7111
Norton Hospital: (502) 629-8000
Norton Suburban Hospital: (502) 893-1000
Poison Center: (502) 589-8222
Police, Fire, Ambulance: 9-1-1
Sheriff's Department: (502) 574-5400
Time & Temperature: (502) 585-5961
Transit Authority of River City (TARC): (502) 585-
   1234
Translation Service (Red Cross): (502) 589-4450
United Parcel Service (UPS): (800) 742-5877
United States Postal Service: (502) 454-1837

# Close-up

## The Louisville Clock

On the other side of Bowman Field, behind a chain-link fence off Dutchman's Lane, you'll find the Louisville Clock, often called the Derby Clock by the locals. The ornamental timepiece is 40 feet high and was once located downtown on Fourth Street, but through a spate of bad luck, mechanical issues, and mismanagement by the powers that be in city government, it ended up stored away in pieces until Adam Matthews got the idea to put it back together. With the help of many generous donors, volunteers, and supporters, the clock is now coming back to life as the grand piece of public art that it is, and it is poised to rejoin the ranks of cherished Louisville icons.

Officially dedicated in 1976, the mechanized work of art arose as a collaboration between the city of Louisville, former Kentucky governor Wyatt Wilson, and entrepreneur Henry Vogt Heuser. Louisville artist Barney Bright won the bid to design the timepiece, and he chose to emphasize Kentucky cultural figures in a larger-than-life toy. Whimsical to say the least, it is a wonderful piece of folk art that is a sight to behold. A tribute to the Kentucky Derby, it has eight ornamental columns supporting an elevated track. At noon each day, a bugle announced the beginning of a race between five hand-carved statues of figures of local significance: George Rogers Clark, Daniel Boone, Thomas Jefferson, King Louis XVI of France, and the Belle of Louisville. From above, in a Victorian gazebo, mechanized sculptures of notable past Louisvillians looked on: Mary Anderson, D. W. Griffith, Zachary Taylor, Henry Watterson, and Oliver Cooke.

In March of 2004 the Adam Matthews Foundation started restoring the landmark, and with the help of the artist's son, Jeb, it has been reassembled and is nearing completion. Once the project has been finished and the clock can run without further work or repairs, the timepiece will be moved to the Louisville Zoo for the public's enjoyment. In the meantime, visitors are encouraged to stop by and see the progress. More information about the Adam Matthews Foundation and its restoration of the Louisville clock can be found at www.louisvilleclock.com.

University of Louisville Hospital: (502) 562-3000

Weather Forecasts: (502) 968-6025

Western Union: (800) 225-5227

## BOWMAN FIELD

Bowman Field, the city's first airport, was established in 1919 and counts as the longest continuously operating, general aviation airport in the United States. It is conveniently located approximately 5 miles from downtown Louisville. Bowman Field is situated on 426 acres, with 17 buildings, including the historic art deco Administration Building that was built in 1929. Bowman Field is located at 2900 Taylorsville Road. Call (502) 458-8605 for more information.

At Bowman Field you'll find Louisville Executive Aviation, a family-owned company that offers a large number of services, including 24-hour flight operation, aviation fuels, sales, corporate hangar, office leasing, and worldwide charters. Call (502) 292-4800, or contact them at info@louisvilleexecutive.com for more information.

**i** The lovely art deco Administration Building at Bowman Field is home to Louisville's favorite French restaurant, Bistro Le Relais. Aside from elegant dining inside, there's also an informal terrace at the rear with a wonderful view of the landing strip, where wingnuts can sip a glass of wine and enjoy an appetizer. For more information, call them at (502) 451-9020, or visit www.lerelaisrestaurant.com. Read more about Bistro Le Relais on page 94.

## GENERAL AVIATION SERVICES

Atlantic Aviation Services at Louisville International (SDF) is a comprehensive facility that offers complete line service. In addition to the convenience of a new terminal and corporate hangar, AvPorts has developed an exclusive handheld fuel management technology to handle quick-turn requirements. For more information, call (502) 368-1515, or visit www.atlanticaviation.com/Locations/SDF.aspx.

## BUSES

Interstate buses leave daily from the Greyhound Terminal at 720 West Muhammad Ali Boulevard. The terminal is open 24 hours a day. Most buses travel north and south, especially to Cincinnati, Indianapolis, and Nashville, and those headed west usually go to St. Louis first; Lexington is the first major stop to the east. The number for the terminal is (502) 561-2805. For schedule and fare information, call (800) 231-2222, or go online at www.greyhound.com/home. For information about Louisville's public bus system, see the TARC section below.

## TARC

Louisville is a city for car owners—there's no way around it. Although the number of users has steadily been on the rise in recent years—thanks to the fluctuation of gasoline prices and growing concern for the environment—its public transportation options are rather limited compared to larger cities. That's not to say a visitor cannot get around using its public buses; it's just that a bit of planning might be required if you're going to use routes other than the main ones in the downtown area, or along business corridors such as Bardstown Road.

TARC, or the Transit Authority of River City, is the major provider of public transportation in the Louisville metro area, which has been nicknamed the "River City," and includes areas that are also located across the river in Indiana. Although the TARC system consists of over 7,000 bus stops,

---

### Downtown Trolleys

TARC operates two circulators to help visitors access the main sights and shopping attractions in the center of Louisville. One, TARC Route #1, travels up Fourth Street from the Galt House to Theater Square and back from 7 a.m. to 8 p.m. during the week and from 10 a.m. to 6 p.m. on Saturdays; trolleys go every 15 or 20 minutes. At certain times, it also continues south to Breckenridge Street before turning back. The other, TARC Route #77, makes scheduled stops along Main and Market between Slugger Field and the Louisville Slugger Museum every 15, 20, or 25 minutes, depending on the time of day. On weekdays, the trolleys run from 6 a.m. to 8 p.m., and on Saturdays times are from 10 a.m. to 6 p.m. On nights when ball games take place, they go from 8 p.m. till the end of the game. The cost to board the trolleys is 50 cents.

---

only about 200 of them have benches and rain shelters; the rest simply have signs—very often posted on utility poles—designating the location as a bus stop. These stops are served by a total of 51 total routes, and daily routes are named for the primary roads they serve. On some daily routes, there might be up to an hour between scheduled buses at any stop, although scheduled stops on the busiest routes tend to be much more frequent.

Cash fare for an adult is $1.50 per ride, and discounted tickets for seniors and younger students cost 75 cents. It is possible to make two transfers in two hours. Monthly passes cost $42, and a strip of 10 regular tickets costs $12.50. Ten special tickets for seniors 65 and over, students

# Close-up

## Union Station

TARC's Administrative Offices are housed at the corner of Ninth and Broadway in beautiful Union Station, which was dedicated on September 7, 1891. The total cost of the majestic Richardsonian Romanesque structure was $310,056, and at the time it was the largest station in the South. With the exception of Seth Thomas, who supplied the timepieces, and the Kendell Company, who manufactured the skylights, all of the station's contractors and craftsmen came from Louisville. Faced in limestone quarried in Bowling Green, the building is trimmed in Bedford stone, and the slate roof is trussed with a combination of ornate iron and wood. Large rose stained-glass windows illuminate the interior, where original ceramic tile floors and marble wainscoting have been restored, and an enormous stained-glass skylight causes the abundance of oak and pine trim to glow. It was the point of entrance for practically every immigrant to Louisville, and presidents such as Franklin D. Roosevelt, Harry S. Truman, and Dwight D. Eisenhower made their arrivals in the Derby City through the doors of Union Station.

Although its last train left for Nashville on October 31, 1976, Union Station is still an important landmark in the community, and it's a favorite stop for railroad aficionados in the Derby City. Restoration of the building began in 1979 and was completed a year later, at a cost of some $2 million. At that time, the Transit Authority of River City became the new occupant of the building. Today, the public is welcome to view the first floor of Union Station, where an original mule-drawn trolley built in 1865 for the Louisville Railway Company—one of only two original mule-drawn trolleys left in the United States—is on display. Union Station is open Monday through Friday from 8 a.m. to 5 p.m.

6–17, and disabled persons go for $7.50. For more information, use the automated phone system at (502) 585-1234, or visit them at www.ridetarc.org.

## BICYCLES

When, after two years of successful events in Louisville, USA Cycling and the Louisville Sports Commission announced the return of the USA Cycling Masters Road National Championships to Louisville in 2010, many enthusiasts saw it as a testament to the Derby City's appeal for hosting world-class cycling events. It was also seen as a sign of cycling's increasing popularity, something that came on the heels of the 2005 Louisville Bike Summit and the ensuing Louisville bike program. Developments are occurring quickly, and there are significant improvements on the horizon, but for the time being, Louisville's growing affinity for two wheels as opposed to four can be seen in the proliferation of downtown bike racks and the increasing number of bike lanes being added

to city streets. In addition, more than 5,000 people participate in the semiannual Hike and Bike event, in which streets are closed to cars in favor of hikers and bikers.

### Bicycling for Louisville

If you want more information about cycling in the Derby City, contact the folks at Bicycling for Louisville, the region's only bicycle advocacy organization with a paid staff that dedicates the time, energy, and resources needed to make Louisville and the surrounding region a safe, fun place to be a bicyclist. Call (502) 582-1814, or go online at www.bicyclingfor louisville.org.

## Hike and Bike

TARC has a Bikes-On-Board program, which makes it easy for bikers to get around the Derby City. Every single TARC bus is equipped with bike racks so you can connect to your destination, no matter where you're going. The bike racks are very easy to use, and it takes less than 10 seconds to load your bike. Although there is no additional charge for your bike, you should keep these things in mind as you stash your wheels:

- Bikes are mounted at your own risk.
- TARC is not responsible for theft or damage while the bike is on the rack.
- Each bike rack can carry only two bikes.
- For safety reasons, the driver cannot get off the bus to assist you.

If you want more information about the city's involvement in promoting cycling in the community, or for a list of bike shops, rentals, and regional organizations, contact Dirk Gowin at Bike Louisville at (502) 574-5925, or Jonathan Villines at jonathan.villines@louisvilleky.gov. You can also visit the Web site at www.louisvilleky.gov/bikelouisville.

**CYCLER'S CAFE**
**2295 Lexington Rd.**
**(502) 451-5152**
**www.cyclerscafe.com**
Located near Cherokee Park and a variety of good bike paths, Cycler's Cafe is a favorite spot for serious cyclists wanting to begin or end their long ride. Cycler's carries a complete line of top-quality

**i** "Dedicated to promoting the sport of bicycling and advocating for the rights of all cyclists," the Louisville Bicycle Club is one of the country's oldest cycling clubs and one of the most active and progressive in the Midwest. Founded in the 1890s, it serves the greater Louisville metropolitan area, including parts of Southern Indiana. For more information, contact them at www.louisvillebicycleclub.org.

bicycles, frame and wheel sets, and cycling gear featuring names such as Felt, BMC, Kona, Salsa, and Santa Cruz, and a professional workshop also offers tune-ups, wheel building, and complete fittings to get you back on the trail in no time. In addition, you can stop by for lunch or dinner anytime, where you'll find an assortment of inexpensive sandwiches, salads, and burritos at the cafe. Or you can just grab a quick espresso at the drive-through as you head out for the open road. Open every day except Sunday.

## HIGHWAYS AND ROADS

Louisville streets are laid out in a grid pattern in the downtown area and in a wheel-and-spoke system in the areas farther out. Streets such as Bardstown Road, Lexington Road, Shelbyville Road, etc., let you know they were named for the outlying towns they lead to. One-way streets in some urban neighborhoods, most notably Portland, Germantown, and the Highlands, can be confusing for first-timers; however, most Louisville neighborhoods are quite safe, and locals will be happy to help you out. Louisville is encircled by two beltways: I-264, or the Henry Watterson Expressway ("the Watterson"), and I-265, or the Gene Snyder Freeway ("the Snyder"), and traffic is generally moderate. Peak hours can get congested, however, especially in the downtown area where Interstates 64, 71, and 65 all merge in a tangled mess the locals call "Spaghetti Junction."

Louisville is a relatively compact city, and car owners from comparable urban centers in other parts of the country who drive here are often

## The Louisville Loop

In the past few years, ride-happy residents have been pushing for a bicycle-friendlier Louisville. In response, not only has the city installed more than 50 bike lanes on city streets so cyclists can pedal away without sharing space with cars, but it has also started construction on the Louisville Loop. This partially completed hiking and biking path will eventually extend more than 100 miles and connect many of Louisville's neighborhoods and parks. Currently about 25 percent complete, the Loop connects the Ohio River Levee Trail and the downtown RiverWalk, making it possible for bicyclists and pedestrians to travel nearly 25 miles from Chickasaw Park to Riverside, the Farnsley-Moremen Landing, along paved, multiuse paths. Along stretches of the existing trail, cyclists will find mileage markers every tenth of a mile, as well as plaques giving information on 19th-century river culture For more information about progress on the Louisville Loop, visit the city's Metro Parks Web site at www.louisvilleky. gov/MetroParks and click on the appropriate link.

### Things to Know about Driving in and around Louisville

- There is a mandatory seat-belt law in Kentucky.
- The speed limit is 70 miles per hour on rural sections of interstate highways in Kentucky. Within city limits, the speed limit on interstates and on primary and secondary highways is 55 mph, unless otherwise posted.
- Kentucky has a permissive "right turn on red" law unless otherwise posted at the intersection.

## Take the Scenic Route

To get a good look at our city's neighborhoods, take the six tree-lined parkways and byways when you're traveling around Louisville. Each provides a glimpse of our local historic homes, landmarks, and user-friendly parks designed by the world-famous Frederick Law Olmsted; there are over 30 miles of bike lanes as well. Apart from Eastern Parkway, the most popular of the scenic drives, you'll find parkways with names such as Southern, Algonquin, Northwestern, and Southwestern. Started in the early 1890s and completed in the 1930s, the 26-mile system was initially owned by a state-level parks commission and passed to the city's control in 1942. Origially, the parkways were intended for light pleasure vehicles traveling between the Louisville's major green spaces, and heavier commercial vehicles were denied access. In 1958 the city opened up the parkways to commercial and passenger traffic alike.

impressed by how easy it is to get around. In most cases, a half-hour's trip by automobile will get you from one end of the metro area to the other, and most points are no more than 15 minutes from downtown Louisville. Drivers generally do not use their horns in Louisville unless it is to get someone's attention or if danger seems imminent; using your horn too often or laying on the horn too long will be seen as aggressive behavior.

**i** TRIMARC is an Intelligent Transportation System (ITS) designed to improve the performance of the freeway system in the metropolitan Louisville and Southern Indiana area. It includes an integrated system of sensors, cameras, dynamic message signs, highway advisory radio, and computers that monitor more than 60 miles of interstate traffic in the greater Louisville area. Northrop Grumman operates the system for TRIMARC, which disseminates information to motorists via dynamic message signs and highway advisory radio. For more information, including interactive travel maps, travel times, and construction reports, go online at www.trimarc.org/perl/home.pl.

## PARKING

### PARKING AUTHORITY OF RIVER CITY
120 South Sixth Street
(502) 574-2602
www.louisvilleky.gov/PARC

The Parking Authority of River City (PARC) has 13 garages and 6 lots in and around the central business district, with a total of more than 10,000 off-street and 5,000 on-street spaces. Here are some of their tips and useful information for "parking smart" in Louisville:

- Use a parking meter for short-term parking such as running errands or grabbing a quick bite to eat. Use a parking garage or surface lot for longer stays.
- Operating hours for all meters are Monday through Saturday, 7 a.m. to 6 p.m. This means free parking after 6 p.m. Monday through Saturday and free all day Sunday!
- Parking meter rates range from 50 cents/hr to 75 cents/hr, and are limited from one hour to four hours of parking. Look for signs that have this information.
- You may pay parking meters with nickels, dimes, quarters, and dollar coins, or by using the SmartCard on newer meters. To find locations to purchase a SmartCard, visit their Web site listed above.

- Depending on the area and roadway, there may be specific parking restrictions to be aware of. Some common restrictions are: No parking 7 a.m. to 9 a.m.; no parking 3 p.m. to 6 p.m.; no parking in bus zone; no parking in fire lane; and no stopping anytime.
- Many parking meters are two-space meters, which allows for fewer meters on the streets and creates efficiency in maintaining and collecting. If you are using a two-space meter, make sure you designate the left or right parking space after depositing your payment. Arrows will indicate which button you should press for the left or the right side.

**i** One unique traffic system you may encounter in Louisville is on a stretch of Baxter Avenue and Bardstown Road, where reversible lanes can be confusing at times. During non-rush hours you'll find street parking on either side of Bardstown Road, with one lane of traffic in each direction; however, no parking is allowed during rush hour. Posted signs at frequent intervals will let you know the exact times. In addition, hanging lighted signs with green arrows and red or yellow "X"s will let drivers know which lanes to use.

## TAXIS AND LIMOUSINES

Once again, Louisville is a typical American city when it comes to public transit—i.e., it is underdeveloped and underutilized—and this extends to private car services. This is a city for drivers, and cabs and limos are generally used by out-of-towners, or else when locals need a lift to the airport or to their houses in the early hours after they've been out on the town. If you find yourself getting the urge to step to the corner in downtown Louisville and wave down a taxi, don't. You don't hail a passing cab in Louisville; instead, you'll have to call Dispatch, or find one at the few marked cab stands around town. You'll find taxi stands outside the terminal of Louisville International Airport, at the Greyhound terminal, in front of the Levy's building at 235 West Market,

## Close-up

### The Environmentally Friendly Choice

Derby City Pedicabs

1402 Elm Rd.

(502) 338-0877

www.derbycitypedicabs.com

If you can't resist the big-city urge to hail a taxi, wave down a Derby City Pedicab. Pedicabs are red, open-air carts for two powered by the driver's foot power. They operate around Fourth Street Live!, Slugger Field, the Waterfront, and up and down Bardstown Road. They're easy to use: Just flag one down and take a ride, or call and reserve one. No matter if you want to enjoy a leisurely ride to enjoy the sights or if you need to get back to that business meeting, they do all the pedaling. The best part—you determine the price. "We pedal for tips!" is their motto.

and at Churchill Downs during racing season. In addition, cabs can usually be found outside some hotels like the Galt House, the Seelbach Hilton, and the Brown.

> **i** Taxi fare from the airport to downtown is regulated by Metro Government. As of September 2008, the rate is $19.55, but the rate may fluctuate with rising gas prices.

### Cabs

**READY CAB COMPANY**

1850 Taylor Ave.

(502) 451-4114

www.readycab.com

Family-owned and serving the Louisville area since 1958, this company has the largest van fleet serving the Louisville airport and metro area. Group and convention rates are available, and special discounts are offered to military personnel traveling between Louisville and Fort Knox.

**YELLOW CAB**

1601 South Preston St.

(502) 636-5511

www.yellowcablouisville.com

Yellow Cab, Checker Cab, and Cardinal Cab are all part of Procarent, which was formerly the Lou-

isville Transportation Company. The enterprise started out as the Louisville Carriage Company, and they have provided continuous service to residents and visitors since 1893. Cabs are available 24/7 and all major credit cards are accepted. It costs $2.26 to get in the cab and then $2.05 for each mile. If the taxi has to wait, it's another 36 cents per minute. Most rides between downtown hotels and the airport come in at under $20.

> **i** Whether driving, biking, or walking downtown, you'll see way-finding signs that help you locate landmarks like the convention center, Slugger Field, Waterfront Park, Fourth Street Live!, and the Kentucky Center for the Arts. There are also nearly 30 informational kiosks with maps of downtown Louisville, directions, and lists of major attractions and monthly downtown events.

### Limos

**R&R LIMOUSINE**

(502) 458-1862

www.rrlimo.com

Apart from hired sedans, stretch limousines, vans, buses, and specialty vehicles, R&R Limousine offers auto detailing, concierge services, and even jet charters. All vehicles are late-model and professionally detailed and maintained, and each chauffeur must pass a series of driving and written tests, as well as undergo background checks and drug and alcohol screening before he or she can work for R & R. Chauffeured sedans for three people run about $74 per hour, and limos holding eight passengers go for $86 an hour; two-hour minimums are sometimes required.

**SANDOLLAR LIMOUSINE**
**(502) 561-4022**
**www.sandollarlimo.com**
Whether it's for sight-seeing, club hopping, bachelorette parties, dining events, weddings, or birthdays, Sandollar Limousine has what you're looking for. Luxury sedans, limousines, vans, charter buses, special-event vehicles, airport shuttles, and party buses are just some of the services offered. Visit their Web site for frequent special offers, including a black stretch limo with a four-hour minimum for $49 per hour.

# HISTORY

Louisville is situated at the Falls of the Ohio, an ancient limestone ledge that disrupts the course of the Ohio River. When European explorers and settlers began arriving in the mid-1700s, they discovered few signs of permanent Native American settlements in the region, which was used as hunting grounds by Cherokees from the south and Shawnees from the north. However, archaeological evidence suggests a continuous human presence did thrive in the area that became Louisville from at least 1000 BC until sometime around 1650. During this time the Adena culture and the subsequent Hopewell tradition thrived in the area, and hunting villages sprang up along Mill Creek and on the bluffs overlooking the Ohio River near today's Zorn Avenue. According to archaeologists, the very first humans to come to the area that is now Louisville were Paleo-Indian nomadic hunters, who followed herds of animals into Kentucky at the end of the Wisconsin glacial period, around 13,000 BC.

## EARLY HISTORY AND EXPLORATION

The identity of the first European to arrive in the area that would become Louisville is shrouded in mystery. Some historians believe that as early as 1170, three hundred years before Christopher Columbus sailed to the Americas, Prince Madoc of Wales and an entourage of nearly a dozen ships visited North America and the future site of Louisville. It has been suggested that a number of stone fortifications along rivers in Alabama and Kentucky might have been erected by these Welsh explorers, since no early native cultures were known to build structures of this kind. One fort across the river from Louisville in southern Indiana supposedly dated to this era, but it was removed in 1928 to make way for construction of a bridge. Native tribes told tales of white settlers in these areas—and later, of light-skinned Indians speaking something akin to Welsh—and members of the Lewis and Clark Expedition would hear these legends 600 years later.

Although it has been disputed, many claim that the first European to lay eyes on the area was René-Robert Cavelier, Sieur de La Salle, who in 1669 explored parts of the Mississippi and Ohio river valleys and claimed much of the land for France. Since the French were very well acquainted with the Ohio Valley, it is almost certain a Frenchman would have been the first European to come across the site of today's Louisville. According to historian George Yater, the first Anglo-Americans to pass over the rapids at the Falls of the Ohio were a party of five Virginians in 1742, who commented on "the great Rocks and large Whirlpools." It is also known that Christopher Gist of Baltimore explored areas along the Ohio River in 1751 and, following the French and Indian War in 1763, France relinquished control of the area of Kentucky to England. A party of British army engineers reconnoitering their country's newly acquired territory made the first detailed map of the Falls in 1766.

## SETTLEMENT

Since the rapids at the Falls of the Ohio created a natural barrier to river travel, settlements sprang up at the point where boats and canoes needed to be portaged across the rapids. According to Yater, the first individual to envision the Falls area as the site of a town was Pennsylvanian John Connelly, who most likely toured the area with his uncle in the 1760s. Impressed with the potential of the area, he tried, unsuccessfully, to enlist George Washington's aid in securing 2,000 acres of land in the vicinity in 1773 and was finally able to gain title to this land later in the same year thanks to the assistance of his friend Lord Dunmore, Virginia's royal governor. Connelly partnered up with another Pennsylvanian, John Campbell, to acquire a second track of land that doubled his holdings, and in April 1774 the two advertised half-acre lots for sale in the *Virginia Gazette*. Their plans to "lay out a Town" at the Falls of the Ohio suffered a setback, however, with the outbreak of Indian hostilities and the rumblings of the American Revolution. Connelly, who had sided with the Tories, was imprisoned by the Americans around 1779, and his land was seized in 1780. At about the same time, the Indians captured Campbell and turned him over to the British, effectively ending his and Connelly's involvement in the development of a town at the Falls.

This did not mean, however, that plans for settlement came to a halt in "the Burrough of Lewisville," the naming of which had been meant to honor French monarch Louis XVI. George Rogers Clark—sent to assert Virginia's claim over the Illinois country—had arrived with a company of militiamen and settlers in the spring of 1778, and their settlement on Corn Island would come to be regarded by most as the founding of modern-day Louisville. In the fall they moved to the mainland and built a fort in the vicinity of Twelfth Street, and in 1779 the first lots in the new settlement were sold. Fearful that they would lose claim to their land—the land that Connelly owned was seized by Virginia a year later—the settlers petitioned the Virginia General Assembly for a town charter that would confirm ownership. In May 1780 the Assembly granted the request and appointed trustees to govern the village and sell the remaining lots. In 1781, Fort Nelson, named for Virginia governor Thomas Nelson, was constructed in the area of today's Seventh and Main Streets, and for years it was considered the strongest fortification south of Pittsburgh.

## Did You Know?

Kentucky is one of the four Commonwealths in the nation. Four states in the U.S. have the official designation of Commonwealth: Kentucky, Massachusetts, Pennsylvania, and Virginia. An older term for "republic," *commonwealth* in this context refers to the common welfare of the public, and this description emphasizes a "government based on the common consent of the people" as opposed to one legitimized through an earlier Royal Colony status derived from the King of Great Britain. Kentucky is the only state outside of the first thirteen to use "Commonwealth" in its name.

## GRAVEYARD OF THE WEST

Early growth in Louisville was slow, and the federal census of 1800 reported only 359 residents, making it the fifth-largest community in Kentucky. Lexington, Frankfort, Paris, and Washington all had larger populations than Louisville. Although Indian raids (mostly for stealing horses) during its fledgling years discouraged many from settling in the area, much of the lag in development came as a direct result of the town's uneven topography. Instead of the flat surfaces that characterize today's downtown Louisville, the very first settlers encountered a hilly terrain that produced numerous mosquito-infested pools, causing malaria to be rampant. The fatalities caused by this and other diseases earned Louisville the unenviable nickname, "the Graveyard of the West."

Its relative isolation and inaccessibility was another factor in Louisville's slow growth. Although the Ohio River provided a water route to and from the town, flatboats proved to be the most effective and expedient in transporting goods like cured meats, tobacco, and farm produce downriver to points such as New Orleans in a matter of weeks. Using human muscle to power boats laden with luxury items upriver against the current was an entirely different matter and could take as long as four months.

## GROWTH

This all changed on the night of October 18, 1811, when inhabitants awoke to a loud hiss and roar coming from the river. Huddled together on the shore under bright moonlight, alarmed citizens watched in amazement as a strange craft plowed the muddy waves. It was the *New Orleans*—the first steamboat to navigate the Ohio—and it had made the trip from Pittsburgh in only eight days. Three and a half years later, the first steamboat from New Orleans, *The Enterprise,* made the trip upriver to Louisville in just 25 days, proof positive that the current could be tamed. Two-way traffic had arrived, and just as the river had made Louisville a town, the steam-powered riverboat would make her a city.

Thanks to the steamboat, the population of Louisville doubled in size between 1810 and

### A Taste for History

Offering authentic regional cooking and hospitality since the 1920s, historic **Doe Run Inn** (500 Doe Run Hotel Rd., Brandenburg; 270-422-2982) boasts what many consider the best fried chicken in the state. The famous Colonel Harland Sanders was even rumored on one occasion to confide that the fried chicken there was better than his own. Former owners Ken and Cherie Whitman claim that one secret to the juicy chicken's extra-crispy crust is the frying it gets in a cast-iron skillet that is 200 years old, which makes it almost as old as the original mill that started it all. Located on a peaceful stream discovered by Squire Boone in 1778, the working mill would eventually become a favorite retreat for those in search of a quiet getaway. Originally called Stevenson's Mill, construction on the main part of the structure began around 1780 and was finished around 1790; the smaller part was added on around 1800 and finally completed in 1821. Constructed primarily of native limestone and hand-hewn timbers, the rustic building has walls that are more than 2 feet thick. An old record book shows a payment made to Abraham Lincoln's father, Tom Lincoln, for his work as a stonemason on the newer part of the building.

About a half-hour's drive southwest from downtown Louisville, today's Doe Run Inn offers good Kentucky country fare that is served family style for parties of four or more. Apart from the fried chicken, favorites include braised beef brisket, hickory-smoked pork tenderloin, country ham with red-eye gravy, and shepherd's pie. The popular all-day, all-you-can-eat comfort-food buffet on Sundays features entree items such as pulled pork, smoked brisket, fried chicken livers, country ham balls, and sides like mashed potatoes, macaroni and cheese, spiced apples, and corn pudding.

To get there, take 31W south toward Fort Knox and turn right at the only traffic light onto KY 1638 in the town of Muldraugh. Then take KY 1638 and drive 9 miles; when the road ends, turn left on KY 448 and go another 1.2 miles. On the left-hand side of the road, you will see a DOE RUN INN sign; turn left and go straight for 0.3 mile.

1820, and 10 years later it became the largest urban area in Kentucky when the number of residents in the locale increased to more than 10,000. With its status as the first official city in the state in 1828, Louisville achieved a small degree of autonomy and an increased ability to levy taxes. A vigorous program to pave and level the streets began, and impressive buildings began rising, especially on Main Street, where bankers, merchants, importers, wholesalers, and hoteliers set up shop. Captain Basil Hall of the British Royal Navy visited in 1828 and reported finding "excellent accommodations at a hotel in Louisville, the best ordered up the whole, which we met with in all America," and characterized the city as "the most interesting station of all the backwoods." People kept arriving and the city teemed with visitors and residents alike, the riverfront becoming a busy commercial center during the day and a rowdy destination at night. One traveler, Henry Huffner, wrote in 1838: "I found on the bank . . . the greatest sight of steamboats I ever beheld. They lay as thickly as they could crowd, with their noses to the land, for the space of half a mile, many of them vessels of large burden, giving evidence at once that here was the greatest commercial port on the Ohio."

## SOLD DOWNRIVER

For years steamboats laden with valuable items would arrive in and depart from Louisville on a regular basis. Material goods, however, were not their only cargo. Despite early attempts at an egalitarian society—lots were originally limited to one half-acre per person and sold only to those who did not own a lot, a stipulation which was abolished when Virginia needed to raise more money—a distinct class system with would-be gentry at the top and menial laborers at the bottom had started to evolve by 1830 in Louisville. This would be compounded by the "peculiar institution" of slavery, a legacy from Kentucky's beginnings as a western extension of Virginia.

Although it was a border state between the North and the South, Kentucky was a slave state, and Louisville's significant black population and location on the Ohio River led to it becoming a stop on the Underground Railroad. Despite the distinct lack of a plantation culture in Kentucky that defined society in most of the southern states, Louisville reportedly had one of the largest slave trades in the United States before the Civil War, and the trade in human cargo contributed considerably to the city's initial growth. In 1850 it was reported that enslaved African Americans accounted for 32 percent of the population in the rural areas around Louisville, a figure that dropped to 25 percent by 1860. In that same year slaves made up 7.5 percent of the population in the city of Louisville, and although an increase in white immigration contributed to the relatively low percentage of enslaved blacks, much of the decline in slavery was attributed to Kentucky's role as a Union state in the War Between the States. Although the Emancipation Proclamation did not apply to Kentucky, the Union Army's decision in 1864 to recruit enslaved blacks—they automatically gained their freedom that way—and compensate their owners with $300 effectively ended slavery in the state.

## IMMIGRATION

Enslaved blacks and free men of color constituted just one segment of Louisville's ever-changing cultural makeup. Although Louisville's inception would arise as the product of primarily English and French endeavors, in the mid-1800s, large numbers of Irish and German immigrants would also leave their mark on the city.

The two major waves of Irish influence on Louisville were the Scots-Irish in the late 1700s, and those who fled the Irish Potato Famine of the 1830s. Although many of the Irish coming to Louisville successfully tried their hand as candle makers, grocers, and the proprietors of boardinghouses, many of them lived in Portland and performed the jobs that would normally be done by chattel slaves; this contributed to a major decrease in the number of slaves in Louisville prior to 1860. By the late 1860s, many Irish residents of Portland moved to today's Limerick district of Louisville, in order to be closer to their jobs with the nearby Louisville & Nashville Railroad. It remained the predominant Irish neighborhood in Louisville until the early 1900s.

The history of the Germans in Louisville reportedly began in 1787, when a man named Kaye built the first brick house in town. The Blankenbaker, Bruner, and Funk families came to the region following the American Revolutionary War, and in 1797 they founded today's suburb of Jeffersontown, originally known as Brunerstown. Subsequent German immigrants gradually followed the Ohio River after arriving on the continent at New Orleans, and would settle in various river towns, including not only Louisville, but also Cincinnati, Ohio, and St. Louis, Missouri.

Many Germans, well educated and liberal, arrived after the failed Revolution of 1848, and it's estimated that 35 percent of Louisville's population was German-speaking by 1850. Known as the "Forty-Eighters," they would introduce Louisville to two different concepts: kindergartens and bilingual education. Germans also founded some of the most significant churches and synagogues in the area and were instrumental in the development of banks, insurance companies, and newspapers in town. The Germantown and Butchertown neighborhoods grew up around the various meat-packing companies operated by Germans. The most prominent of these meat packers would be Henry Fischer, whose name still exists today as a popular local brand. Bakeries and confectioners run by Austrians and Germans sprang up throughout the city, and the Swiss ran many of the nearby dairy operations.

However, the influx of new residents resulted in tensions with the anti-immigrant Know-Nothing Party. These tensions grew as the arrival of the Irish increased the number of Catholics in the city, and because many Germans had ideas considered too progressive for their new neighbors. This culminated in the Bloody Monday riots of 1855, in which members of the Know-Nothing Party blocked access to polling stations for the Irish and Germans, and hired thugs started riots in the streets. Brutes targeted Irish Catholics and Germans, dragging them from their homes and attacking them on the streets and in their places of work. By the time it was over, more than a hundred businesses, homes, and tenements had been looted or burned. Conservative estimates placed the death toll at 22, while more-realistic estimates, including those of Bishop Martin Spalding, placed the death toll at over 100, with entire families consumed in the fires.

The riots had a profound impact on immigration to Louisville, and more than 10,000 citizens packed up and left for St. Louis, Chicago, and Milwaukee. This reverse immigration affected the arts, education, and commerce, and scores of businesses closed overnight. Empty storefronts became the norm in once-vibrant business districts, and many of the charred ruins lay untouched for years afterward, a silent reminder of that terrible day. Only the Civil War, with the increase in trade and commerce it represented, halted this trend.

## NORTH OR SOUTH?

In the years leading up to the Civil War, Germans in Louisville were vocal in their support of the North, but as would be expected, Kentucky was a state with divided loyalties. In the November 1860 presidential election, most Kentucky voters, including residents of Louisville, voted for John Bell of Tennessee, of the Constitutional Union Party. They gave native son and Republican candidate Abraham Lincoln less than 1 percent of the vote; but native Kentuckian John C. Breckinridge and his Southern Democratic Party didn't do well, either. In a state with 225,000 slaves, Kentuckians didn't care for Lincoln, because he stood for the eradication of slavery, and Breckenridge didn't win them over because his party was generally regarded as one of secessionists. The voters wanted to preserve the status quo—i.e., both to keep slavery and stay in the Union—and as a consequence, Kentucky was poised to weather the war as a neutral state.

After Confederate Brigadier General Pierre G. T. Beauregard ordered the April 12, 1861, firing on Fort Sumter, under the command of Union major Robert Anderson of Louisville, most Louisville residents were still divided as to which side they should support. Alliances were often determined

## Architectural Oddities

Standing in a median of the new four-lane section of Frankfort Avenue adjacent to the Sea Ray of Louisville boat dealership is a 70,000-pound historical structure that is 26 feet high and 35 feet wide; it is an old façade that serves as an entryway to the Butchertown neighborhood. Upon closer examination, you will see that this monument has a story to tell, its patriotic inscriptions and carvings of political figures such as George Washington and James Buchanan attesting to the dark days of Louisville's anti-foreigner sentiments of the mid 1900s. It is all that remains of the Heigold House, the former two-story residence of a German stonemason who witnessed this hostility for himself in the 1850s. As a demonstration of his patriotism, he painstakingly used his talents to adorn the façade of his brick house with chiseled declarations of his loyalty and support for the Union, and his house became a local icon after his death in 1865. His old house was eventually demolished in the 1950s, but preservation-minded individuals managed to have the façade saved, and it was eventually moved to its current location.

If you're interested in architectural oddities, you'll find a number of structures in the Derby City that have a story to tell. One of them is the largely overlooked Grotto and Garden of Our Lady of Lourdes near Eastern Parkway in the St. Joseph neighborhood. Read more about it in the Worship chapter on page 202. Another is the Wheelmen's Bench not too far from Churchill Downs, at the intersection of Third Street and Southern Parkway. Designed by famed sculptress Enid Yandell, the project was part of an 1890s civic event dedicating a new bicycle path from downtown Louisville to Iroquois Park. You can read more about Enid Yandell on page 152 in the chapter on parks and recreation.

by financial interests and existing family or business relationships. Prominent Louisville attorney James Speed, brother of Lincoln's close friend, Joshua Fry Speed, supported the Union, as did many blue-collar workers and professional men, such as lawyers. On the other hand, prominent newspaperman Walter Haldeman and Louisville's merchants, who had extensive trade with the South, largely supported the Confederacy. On April 20, two companies of Confederate volunteers left by steamboat for New Orleans, and five days later, three more companies departed for Nashville on the L & N Railroad. At the same time, Union recruiters rallied troops at Eighth and Main, and they left for Indiana to join other regiments in the North. On May 20, 1861, Kentucky officially declared its neutrality.

Although leaders in the North and the South pledged to respect Kentucky's neutrality at the onset of the war, it soon became apparent that actual neutrality would effectively be short-lived. Confederate supporters organized shipments of goods and arms to be sent downriver by steamboat, and in July the War Department authorized the establishment of Union training camps in Kentucky. In August 1861, Kentucky held elections for the State General Assembly, and Unionists won majorities in both houses.

On September 4, 1861, Confederate general Leonidas Polk, outraged by Union meddling in the state, invaded Columbus in the south. As a result of the Confederate invasion, Union general Ulysses S. Grant entered Paducah in the far west of the state. Jefferson Davis allowed Confederate troops to stay in Kentucky, and General Simon Bolivar Buckner invaded Bowling Green. The Kentucky State legislature, angered in turn by the Confederate invasions, ordered the Union flag to be raised over the state capitol in Frankfort on September 7 and declared allegiance. In addition, the legislature denied any member of the Confederacy the right to land, titles, or money held in Kentucky.

By early 1862, Louisville had 80,000 Union troops throughout the city, and with so many troops came a variety of saloons, gambling establishments, and brothels. With the threat of Confederate invasion at a minimum, Louisville became a staging area for Union supplies and troops heading south. In July 1862, however, Confederate generals Braxton Bragg and Edmund Kirby Smith planned a successful invasion of Kentucky and eventually captured all of General William "Bull" Nelson's troops. Bragg then decided to take Louisville, as one of the major objectives of the Confederate campaign in Kentucky was the seizure of the Louisville and Portland Canal and the severing of Union supply routes. The city was evacuated, but the invasion never occurred. In October of 1862 when the Confederacy's main forces were turned back at the Battle of Perryville in central Kentucky, any threat to Louisville effectively ceased. Assured of their safety, most Louisvillians became disenchanted with both sides of the war.

## JOINED THE CONFEDERACY AFTER THE WAR

Although men on both sides of the conflict settled down and worked side by side in Kentucky's largest city, a large number of former Confederates acquired positions of authority in Louisville after the end of the Civil War. The image of the gentleman farmer blossomed, and many Louisvillians seemed to attain renewed appreciation for the "lost cause" as their city cultivated its image as the "Gateway to the South." The *Courier*—its editor Walter Haldeman just having returned from Confederate territory—became the city's most prominent newspaper, and in 1868 it joined with the *Journal,* whose editor, Henry Watterson, would become a spokesman for the idea of the New South. In the postwar years, the *Courier-Journal* would report on a number of tributes to the Confederacy, including a grand procession in honor of Robert E. Lee's funeral in 1870, and an 1877 celebration to mark the removal of the last federal troops from Louisiana and South Carolina. By the late 1880s, Confederate veterans largely took political control of the city, leading to the jibe that Louisville joined the Confederacy after the war was over.

This growing fondness for the side Kentucky had defeated, however, was due in no small part to evolving racial politics. Since the Emancipation Proclamation freed only those slaves in Confederate states, Kentucky slaves had to wait until the passage of the 13th Amendment in December 1865 for their freedom; this arguably made Kentucky the last state to free its slaves. Many residents were so resistant to any action that assisted or protected former slaves that the federal government brought in the Freedmen's Bureau to work on behalf of the blacks. It is estimated that the number of blacks in Louisville more than doubled between 1860 and 1870, and this compounded the resentment felt by some city residents. Over the next half-century the rise in the number of lynchings and other forms of violence would bear witness to the troubled state of Kentucky's race relations.

## 100 DAYS THAT LOUISVILLE OPENED ITS DOORS TO THE WORLD

As its reputation as a manufacturing center grew, and looking to the success of previous industrial and mercantile exhibitions in the region, Louisville assumed a representative position for its neighbors further south. This culminated in a type of trade show that cemented Louisville's identification with the South and had as its theme the South's most famed crop. The Southern Exposition, starring "Cotton: From Seed to Loom," opened on August 1, 1883, with the inauguration of President Chester Arthur. At the time, the gathering was larger than any previous

# Close-up

## A Tale of Two Monuments

### The Confederate War Veterans Memorial

Located at the intersection of Second and Third Streets in Old Louisville, across from the Speed Art Museum, is the largest Civil War monument in Kentucky. Completed in 1895, the Louisville monument was built with funding from the Kentucky Women's Confederate Monument Association at a cost of $12,000. Louisville sculptor Enid Yandell was chosen to carry out the project, but the fact that Yandell was a woman caused a scandal, and the Muldoon Monument Company completed the monument instead. German sculptor Ferdinand von Miller designed the bronze Confederate soldiers—an artillerist, a cavalryman, and an infantryman—at its base. Its dedication on May 6, 1895, was hurried along in order to coincide with the 29th annual reunion of the Grand Army of the Republic and the northern pride it engendered. The monument, one of 61 different Civil War–related sites in Kentucky so honored on the same day, was placed on the National Register of Historic Places on July 17, 1997.

As might be expected of any monument memorializing the South, this obelisk has seen its share of controversy, and individuals have called for its removal on more than one occasion. However, a sort of compromise was reached in 2002 when plans were initiated to make it part of a "Freedom Park," with trees transplanted from Civil War battlefields and renowned Louisville sculptor Ed Hamilton selected to make a civil rights monument to counter the Confederate memorial. (Hamilton has already made an Abraham Lincoln memorial statue in Louisville.) On November 17, 2008, funding was approved for such a park, with the Kentucky state government using $1.6 million of federal funds and the university spending $403,000.

### The Lincoln Statue

A dramatic photograph that a reporter from Louisville's the *Courier-Journal* took during the infamous Ohio Valley Flood of 1937 shows a remarkable sight: a statue of Abraham Lincoln apparently defying the laws of physics on the grounds of the Louisville Free Public Library at Fourth and York Streets, a glassy sheet of slate gray seemingly supporting the figure, giving the eerie impression that he's walking on water. Less than 2 miles from the Confederate memorial near the University of Louisville, it is the Derby City's most cherished statue of America's 16th president.

This one is the third cast of a statue commissioned by Charles Taft, half brother of William Howard Taft, for the city of Cincinnati in 1910, and displayed in 1917. Two years later a second cast was sent to Manchester, England. Louisville businessman and philanthropist Isaac W. Bernheim approached sculptor George Grey Barnard about producing a Lincoln statue for Louisville in 1920, and Barnard decided to replicate his Cincinnati statue. Dedicated at high noon on October 26, 1922, during a ceremony in which Bernheim was accompanied by "an assembly comprised of gentile and Jew, of Southerners and Northerners, and of every shade of secular society," the statue was derided by some for its rough features and pathetic visage. It remains, nonetheless, one of the city's most recognized and beloved statues.

American exhibition, with the exception of the 1876 Centennial Exposition held in Philadelphia. Organizers had built a huge exhibit hall—then rumored to be the largest wooden structure in the world—on the southern outskirts of town, and advertised it at home and abroad as the "100 Days that Louisville Opened Its Doors to the World." Louisville—at that point not even 100 years old, and with a population of some 120,000 inhabitants—was thrilled when its invitation was accepted and throngs of visitors flooded the city. "This fact, of itself, speaks volumes for the energy and self-respect of the community, for the Exposition is the most ambitious that has been undertaken in this community, with the exception of the Centennial," commented a reporter from *Harper's Weekly* shortly after the fair opened. So successful was the three-month event that organizers repeated it for the next four years, and Louisville basked in the glow of its success.

Essential to this glow was an invention that was largely unknown up to that point: the incandescent lightbulb, the design of which had been significantly improved upon by a previous resident of Louisville. His name was Thomas Edison, and although most credit an Englishman, Joseph Swan, with the lightbulb's invention, Edison garnered much of the praise and facilitated its use in this country and abroad. The Louisville Board of Trade contracted with Edison for 5,000 incandescent lamps—4,600 bulbs for the exhibition hall, and 400 for an adjacent art gallery, reportedly more than all the electric lights installed in New York City at that time—and their use at the Southern Exposition would popularize this form of lighting across the nation. "The Exposition was the first large space lighted by incandescence, and many electrical pioneers felt that the Louisville success did more to stimulate the growth of interior electric lighting than any other Edison plant," wrote George H. Yater in his book, *Two Hundred Years at the Falls of the Ohio*. Another Edison development, an electric engine tugging a line of cars through the grounds of the adjacent DuPont estate, would foreshadow the arrival of the first electric streetcar in Louisville in 1889.

After the exposition was finally closed down—the massive exhibit hall, built as a temporary structure to last one year only, was showing signs of distress—the building was dismantled and the materials used in the construction of nearby mansions. The footprint of the old exposition structure would serve as the foundation for the rapidly growing city's first suburb.

> **i** A stone marker and plaque at the entrance to St. James Court in Old Louisville commemorate the Southern Exposition of 1883; you'll find them in the grassy circle in front of the Conrad-Caldwell House Museum at 1402 St. James Court.

## A NEW GOTHAM

Spurred on by the throngs of visitors who had flooded the city for the Southern Exposition and the influx of capital that had been generated, Louisville entered an unprecedented period of prosperity and growth. As the city grew, so did its sense of pride. The *Courier-Journal*, taking inventory of the new construction stimulated by the Southern Exposition, reported a total of $10 million spent on building materials in 1887 alone, and it proclaimed Louisville "A New Gotham." In the Southern Extension, the site of the exposition grounds at the outskirts of town, an affluent neighborhood with hundreds of mansions and townhomes sprang up, and Third Street, its major thoroughfare, became the city's choicest address. Subsequent streetcar lines stimulated the development of other neighborhoods and communities around Louisville, and the city continued to grow.

One of the city's first skyscrapers, the Columbia Building, opened on January 1, 1890, and heralded a period of modernization. Passenger train service received a boon at 7:30 a.m. on September 7, 1891, with the arrival of the first train at the newly completed Union Station, a majestic turreted stone structure touted as the largest train station in the South. About the same time, the renowned landscape architect Frederick Law Olmsted carried out the design of Louisville's system of parks—the most notable being Cherokee, Iroquois, and Shawnee Parks—which were connected by tree-lined parkways. Developers in the Highlands capitalized on the creation of Cherokee Park to attract home buyers, and the resultant Cherokee Triangle would emerge as another bastion of elegant residences in the prospering city.

## EARLY 1900s

With the incredible building boom in Louisville came a natural increase in the number of businesses, something that would change the makeup of the downtown area. Market Street saw a decline, and Fourth Street toward Broad-

# Close-up

## Louisville Time Line

| | |
|---|---|
| 1751 | Explorer Christopher Gist covers areas along the Ohio River. |
| 1769 | Daniel Boone and John Finley are first to see the distant bluegrass at Pilot Knob. |
| 1774 | James Harrod begins constructing the first permanent settlement in Kentucky at Fort Harrod. |
| 1775 | Daniel Boone builds the Wilderness Trail and establishes Fort Boonesboro. |
| 1778 | George Rogers Clark is recognized as the founder of Louisville after he travels with soldiers and settlers from Redstone, Pennsylvania, down the Ohio River to Corn Island. The settlers establish Fort Nelson, the first permanent settlement at the site of Louisville. |
| 1780 | The Virginia legislature and governor approve the town charter of Louisville. |
| 1780 | Louisville's first fire department is established. |
| 1792 | Kentucky becomes the 15th state, and Frankfort is named the capital. Isaac Shelby becomes Kentucky's first governor. |
| 1796 | The Wilderness Road opens to wagon traffic in eastern Kentucky. |
| 1798 | Kentucky legislature passes resolutions opposing United States Alien and Sedition Acts. |
| 1803 | Meriwether Lewis and William Clark use the Falls of the Ohio and the Louisville area as the meeting point to begin the Lewis and Clark Expedition. |
| 1811 | The *New Orleans* is the first steamboat to visit Louisville. |
| 1815 | *The Enterprise* is the first steamboat to travel from New Orleans to Louisville. |
| 1816 | Louisville's first library, the Louisville Library Company, opens to the public with subscription-based service. |
| 1828 | Louisville (pop. 7,000) becomes an incorporated city and elects John Bucklin as its first mayor. |
| 1830 | The Louisville and Portland Canal is completed, allowing boat traffic to travel from Pittsburgh to New Orleans, circumventing the Falls of the Ohio at Louisville. |
| 1830 | The *Louisville Journal* is launched by A. J. Buxton and George D. Prentice. |
| 1850 | Census names Louisville 10th-largest city and Kentucky 8th-most-populous state. |
| 1850 | Louisville & Nashville Railroad Company is founded. |
| 1850 | Louisvillian Zachary Taylor, 12th president of the United States, dies in office after serving only four months and is buried in Louisville. |
| 1855 | August 6th marks the "Bloody Monday" Election Day uprisings, where Germans, Irish, and Catholics are beaten and shot by members of the "Know-Nothings." |
| 1860 | The Louisville Water Company begins pumping water to customers. |
| 1861 | Kentucky declares its neutrality in the American Civil War; it is the birthplace of both Union president Abraham Lincoln and Confederate president Jefferson Davis. |
| 1867 | Thomas Edison, age 19, fired as a telegraph operator for spilling acid on boss's desk. |
| 1875 | Aristides wins the first Kentucky Derby on May 17 in front of 10,000 spectators at the Louisville Jockey Club, later named Churchill Downs. |
| 1876 | Professional baseball launches the National League with the Louisville Grays team as a charter member. |
| 1883 | John "Bud" Hillerich makes a baseball bat in his father's wood shop from white ash, later founding Hillerich & Bradsby, the manufacturer of the "Louisville Slugger." |
| 1884 | The *Courier-Journal* publisher Walter Haldeman launches the *Louisville Times* as an afternoon newspaper. |

| 1890 | Tornado hits Louisville on March 27; 78 people killed and 766 buildings destroyed. |
|------|------|
| 1891 | Union Station passenger train hub opens; largest train station in the South. |
| 1893 | Louisville sisters Patty Smith Hill and Mildred Jane Hill write the song "Happy Birthday to You" for their kindergarten class, originally titled "Good Morning to All." |
| 1902 | The Louisville Free Public Library opens. |
| 1916 | Woodrow Wilson appoints Louisville liberal Louis Brandeis to U.S. Supreme Court. |
| 1916 | The Ford Motor Company opens its first Louisville assembly factory. |
| 1919 | Abram H. Bowman leases a piece of land from the federal government to open the area's first airfield, later named Bowman Field. |
| 1922 | WHAS goes on air as Louisville's first radio station. |
| 1924 | F. Scott Fitzgerald writes *The Great Gatsby* during visits to Seelbach Hotel. |
| 1925 | The *Courier-Journal* creates and hosts the first National Spelling Bee. |
| 1928 | Stone fort dismantled to make way for the Big Four Railroad Bridge. |
| 1934 | Kaelin's Restaurant claims to be first to serve a hamburger with cheese. |
| 1936 | The U.S. Gold Depository is established at Fort Knox. |
| 1937 | In January, the Ohio River floods the city, cresting at 27.15 feet above flood stage. |
| 1937 | The Louisville Orchestra performs its first concert on November 2. |
| 1947 | Standiford Field opens to commercial passengers. |
| 1948 | Charles Farnsley becomes mayor of Louisville; brings Louisville into modern era, repaving a mile a day of roadways and creating the Louisville Fund for the Arts. |
| 1949 | City commissions Austrian typographer Victor Hammer to design official city seal. |
| 1950 | The first issue of *Louisville Magazine* is published by the Chamber of Commerce. |
| 1959 | Bill Samuels Sr.'s distillery in Loretto, Kentucky, releases Maker's Mark. |
| 1960 | Louisvillian Cassius Clay wins boxing gold medal for U.S. at 1960 Olympics in Rome. |
| 1964 | Cassius Clay defeats Sonny Liston to become the heavyweight boxing champion of the world, and changes his name the following day to Muhammad Ali, announcing himself to be a member of the Nation of Islam. |
| 1974 | On April 3, a tornado reaches 250 mph and stays on the ground for nearly 20 minutes, damaging 1,800 homes. |
| 1975 | Jefferson County Public Schools ordered to racially integrate classes by busing. |
| 1976 | Last passenger train leaves Louisville and Union Station terminal closes. |
| 1984 | William DeVries and Allan Lansing implant the Jarvik-7 artificial heart into Bill Schroeder. |
| 1984 | Louisville baseball legend Pee Wee Reese inducted into Baseball Hall of Fame. |
| 1985 | "Mayor for Life" Jerry Abramson elected for first of four consecutive terms. |
| 1987 | The last edition of *The Louisville Times* is published. |
| 1988 | Kentucky voters approve the creation of a state lottery. |
| 1999 | Doctors at Jewish Hospital perform the world's first successful human hand transplant. |
| 2000 | Voters approve merger of Louisville and Jefferson County governments. |
| 2001 | Miss America 2000, Heather French, and Kentucky Lt. Gov. Stephen Henry marry in Louisville. |
| 2003 | Louisville becomes the U.S.'s 16th-largest city; Glenn Hack to design new official seal. |

way would emerge as the city's central business corridor. During the first half of the 20th century it would also gain a reputation as Louisville's premier shopping and entertainment district. Restaurants, movie houses, and department stores provided a bit of bright light and glamour to a population that might have otherwise been overwhelmed by the gravitas of two world wars and the Great Depression.

Among notable events in early-20th-century Louisville was the outbreak of World War I, which would lead to Louisville becoming home to Camp Zachary Taylor. During his frequent visits to Fourth Street and other points of interest around the town, a soldier by the name of F. Scott Fitzgerald would become inspired to write his classic, *The Great Gatsby*. In 1917, the first foreign-bred horse, the English-bred colt "Omar Khayyam," won the Kentucky Derby, and two years later, Sir Barton was the first horse to win what would eventually become known as the Triple Crown.

The most significant event in the city's first decades of the 1900s occurred in early 1937, when after a month of heavy rain throughout the Ohio River Valley, Louisville was inundated during the "Great Flood of '37." At the crest on January 27, 1937, the waters reached 30 feet above flood level in Louisville, submerging some 70 percent of the city and forcing the evacuation of 175,000 residents. In Louisville, 90 people died. Photojournalist Margaret Bourke-White and others documented the flood and its aftermath in a series of famous photos. Later, flood walls were installed to prevent such disasters in the future.

# RECENT HISTORY

Flood walls notwithstanding, the Ohio River has managed to leave its banks in recent years, although with neither the deadliness nor ferocity of 1937. As the calendar turned from February to March in 1997, for example, large amounts of rain fell on central Kentucky and extreme southern Indiana; the subsequent deluge resulted in record flooding along smaller streams and, in some places, the worst flooding along the Ohio River since the Great Flood of 1937. But water hasn't been the only element to leave its mark in the last half of the 1900s. On April 3, 1974, an F4 tornado hit Louisville during the Super Outbreak of tornadoes that struck 13 states. Although it was only responsible for two deaths, the twister covered 21 miles and destroyed several hundred homes in the Louisville area, along with causing extensive damage in Cherokee Park.

Other weather events of historic significance include a freak "thunder-snow" storm on January 17, 1994, that dropped some 2 feet of snow on the city overnight, effectually shutting it down for a week. Most recently, Louisville was brought to a weeklong standstill after Hurricane Ike hit in September 2008, and then again in late January 2009, after an ice storm blanketed the state and left tens of thousands without power. In both instances, the city lost thousands of trees, which toppled under the forces of nature and blocked streets and major thoroughfares.

For a detailed historical time line of the city of Louisville, go to the informative Web site of the Unofficial Fan Site of Louisville, Kentucky, at http://www.louisville.cc. In the meantime, you will find some of its highlights in the Close-up above.

# ACCOMMODATIONS

Finding a place to lay your head in Louisville isn't hard. The majority of lodging establishments in the city are clustered in five convenient locations—downtown, the area around the airport, Bardstown Road, the East End, and southern Indiana—and rooms can be found in quaint bed-and-breakfast inns or high-rise buildings in the center of it all. In addition to budget motels and extended-stay accommodations, there are also grand hotels steeped in tradition and sleek contemporary hideaways focusing on art, showing that the area has something for every taste and budget.

## Price Code

Louisville is generally a bargain when it comes to the cost of lodging, but visitors will experience a tremendous increase in room rates during the spring when the Kentucky Derby attracts throngs of visitors to the city. Accommodations can run the gamut from inexpensive roadside motel rooms to luxurious suites in grand hotels, and this key will give you an idea of the starting rate for a night for two in a standard room. Room rates do fluctuate, so it's always best to confirm with the hotel, motel or bed-and-breakfast when making your reservations.

$....................$50 to $75
$$..................$76 to $125
$$$................$126 to $200
$$$$..............more than $200

## BED-AND-BREAKFASTS

The bed-and-breakfast industry really began to take off in this country during the 1980s, and they are thriving today largely due to the atmosphere of warmth and coziness that most hotels and motels simply can't match. In addition, when all is said and done, the price of a nice B&B is usually comparable to that of a good hotel. In and around Louisville you will find everything from restored Victorian mansions to quaint country cottages where you can lay your head, and each inn has a style of architecture and distinct personality that is sure to please. Antiques, beautiful gardens, gourmet breakfasts, personal attention, and much more make a comfortable bed-and-breakfast the way to go when you're staying in the Derby City.

## Old Louisville

Drive a few minutes and you're at the Kentucky Fair and Exposition Center, Churchill Downs, Downtown Louisville and the convention center, or the Louisville International Airport; walk a few minutes and you're at the Speed Art Museum, the University of Louisville, or Spalding University. Its central location is reason enough to choose Old Louisville for your bed-and-breakfast stay in the Derby City. However, it's the amazing assortment of architecture and the hundreds of beautiful Victorian homes that will really win you over. With its National Register status and blocks and blocks of stunning mansions and homes from the late 1880s and early 1900s, Old Louisville is the perfect backdrop for a quaint and inviting inn.

### ALEKSANDER HOUSE                $$
**1213 South First St.**
**(502) 637-4985**
**www.aleksanderhouse.com**
A graceful 1882 home centrally located in one of America's most significant historic preservation districts, the Aleksander House has 14-foot ceilings, original gleaming hardwood floors, period light fixtures, stained-glass windows, and fireplaces. Each guest room is uniquely deco-

parlor, game room, party room, and bar. A fountain and lush garden adorn the off-street gated parking. All beds have memory-foam pillow-top mattresses and fine linens.

**CAMPION HOUSE**     **$$$**
**1234 South Third St.**
**(502) 212-7500**
**www.campionhouse.com**
At the time of this writing, innkeepers Anne and Alan Bird hadn't yet completed the renovations on this 1880s mansion that will join the ranks of Old Louisville bed-and-breakfast inns, but rooms will be available in the near future. In the meantime, two suites are available in the Carriage House—both with living room and full kitchen at one end, and a bath with whirlpool tub and shower. Bedrooms feature queen-size beds and large closets with iron and ironing board for your convenience. Each suite includes individually controlled heat and air-conditioning, multiline phones, cable TV, and high-speed Internet access.

rated in eclectic or period furnishings with fine linens and down comforters. Rooms are spacious with queen- and king-size beds, writing desks, telephones, cable, wireless Internet, and private baths. Other amenities include terry-cloth robes, hair dryers, coffeemakers, irons and ironing boards, refrigerators, and overhead fans. Romantic "sweetheart" and spa packages available.

**AUSTIN'S INN PLACE**     **$$$**
**915 South First St.**
**(502) 585-8855**
**www.austinsinnplace.com**
Just blocks from the center of downtown Louisville and at the outskirts of Old Louisville, this moderately priced inn is housed in two beautifully refurbished 1888 Victorian homes. An ideal location for family reunions, Austin's Inn Place is also a popular choice for office parties, wedding receptions, business meetings, and training sessions. Elegantly decorated throughout, this B&B features eight guest rooms, three dining rooms, a

## CENTRAL PARK INN $$$
**1353 South Fourth St.**
**(502) 638-1505**
**www.centralparkbandb.com**

Listed on the National Historic Register, this magnificent three-story residence from 1884 displays an array of period furnishings and examples of exquisite handcraftsmanship. Once home to vinegar manufacturer Vernon Price, the stone residence sits directly across from Old Louisville's Central Park, one of 18 Olmsted-designed parks in the city, and is just blocks from I-65. Seven rooms, all with private bath, include four elegant queen and king guest rooms, a two-bedroom suite, and the Carriage House, which has its own kitchenette. Package deals are offered, as are regular specials such as "Stay Three Nights and Get the Third Night Free."

## THE COLUMBINE $$
**1707 South Third St.**
**(502) 635-5000**
**www.thecolumbine.com**

A stunning, white-columned Greek Revival facade greets overnighters at this former residence of one of Louisville's mahogany kings. Built in 1896, the Columbine is located only two blocks away from the University of Louisville, and it is a very short walk to campus where you can visit the Speed Art Museum, Rauch Planetarium, and a cast of Rodin's famous statue, *The Thinker*. With its abundance of gleaming millwork, glorious double staircase, and amber-hued stained-glass window on the landing, the Columbine is one of the most popular bed-and-breakfasts on Millionaires Row.

## DUPONT MANSION $$$
**1317 South Fourth St.**
**(502) 638-0045**
**www.dupontmansion.com**

Beautifully restored, the award-winning DuPont Mansion is a favorite venue for overnight, weekend, or extended stays in Old Louisville. All guest rooms in this rare 1879 decorative Italianate mansion—with ornate carved Italian marble fireplaces, hardwood floors, plaster moldings, 10-foot windows, and 14-foot ceilings—offer private in-suite baths and whirlpool tubs. Antique furnishings, a banquet-style dining room, crystal chandeliers, and formal gardens add to the ambience. Amenities include king- and queen-size beds, in-room color cable television, telephone, wake-up service, climate controls, fireplaces, fluffy towels, hair dryers, armoires, on-request laundry assistance, and turndown services. In 2003, the Louisville Historical League presented owners Herb and Gayle Warren an award in recognition of their efforts to restore the DuPont Mansion.

## 1888 ROCKING HORSE MANOR $$
**1022 South Third St.**
**(502) 583-0408**
**www.rockinghorse-bb.com**

Located close to downtown on Old Louisville's Millionaires Row in a beautifully restored Richardsonian Romanesque mansion from 1888, this popular inn combines Old World charm and modern amenities to ensure a memorable stay for its guests. Towering ceilings, hand-carved fireplace mantels, stained glass, and solid pocket doors abound, giving a glimpse of what it must have been like to enjoy a life of luxury at the height of Kentucky's Gilded Age. The mansion was once home to bourbon baron Max Selliger. Spanish and Portuguese spoken.

## GALLERY HOUSE $$
**1386 South Sixth St.**
**(502) 635-2550**
**www.thegalleryhouse.com**

Although this quaint Victorian near the corner of Sixth and Magnolia looks like it's been there for at least a hundred years, it is actually one of the newest additions to the neighborhood. Adhering to strict neighborhood guidelines for architectural continuity, the owners built a modern bed-and-breakfast with contemporary amenities and old-fashioned charm. Since a chef and an artist are the owners, you're sure to enjoy interesting interior decor and get a good morning meal to boot. While you're here, make sure to buy a souvenir box of Louisville Cookies, luscious house-made chocolate creations sporting a fleur-de-lis, the symbol of Louisville.

## INN AT THE PARK $$$
**1332 South Fourth St.**
**(502) 638-0045**
**www.innatpark.com**

Herb and Gayle Warren, the owners of the DuPont Mansion, operate this comfortable inn overlooking picturesque Central Park as well. Arguably one of the most beautiful of Old Louisville's bed-and-breakfasts, this redbrick mansion was built in the 1880s for Judge Russell Houston according to plans by renowned local architect, Mason Maury. Beautiful mahogany wainscoting, coffered ceilings, and a gently curving staircase greet guests upon their arrival. A fireplace with rare double-flue design and Rookwood-pottery surround keep watch as innkeeper Helga Vikre serves overnighters her famous gourmet breakfasts. Apart from five guest rooms in the main house, there are also three whirlpool suites in the carriage house.

## MAGNOLIA COTTAGE $$$$
**1386 South Sixth St.**
**(502) 635-2550**
**www.thegalleryhouse.com**

Part of the Gallery House property, the Magnolia Cottage offers long-term guests complete privacy in a cozy turn-of-the-century urban cottage just steps from Central Park and St. James Court. Ideal for business travelers who enjoy having a place to meet with clients or host meetings, the cottage features a classic floor plan with living room, bedroom, dining room, kitchen, and bath. At 750 square feet, the cottage sleeps four when the sleeper sofa is used. Extended stays only.

## THE MAYFLOWER $$$$
**425 West Ormsby Ave.**
**(502) 634-7804**
**www.mayflowerapts.com**

Looking for something different in Old Louisville? The historic Mayflower has furnished executive suites in a boutique setting, with a four-star restaurant—Buck's—on the ground floor. The Mayflower was designed by renowned architect

Valentine Peers Collins, and completed in 1926 at the height of the Roaring '20s. With its distinctive two-story, limestone facade and Beaux Arts design, it became one of Louisville's most distinguished residential addresses, and today it is a popular choice for extended stays.

## SAMUEL CULBERTSON MANSION $$$
**1432 South Third St.**
**(502) 634-3100**
**www.culbertsonmansion.us**

A beautiful example of Renaissance Revival architecture, this sprawling mansion at the heart of Old Louisville's Millionaires Row was built in 1897 for Samuel Culbertson, the Kentucky Derby president who started the "garland of roses" tradition in 1932. His sons would achieve fame as the "Little Knights of Kentucky" when local author Annie Fellows Johnston immortalized them in her best-selling *Little Colonel* series. Today, their spirit lives on in the lavish suite bearing their moniker, and guests can enjoy it for a reasonable rate.

# Other Parts of Town

## BASHFORD MANOR
## BED-AND-BREAKFAST $$
**2227 Bashford Manor Lane**
**(502) 295-9005**
**www.bashfordmanor.com**

Named for the famous nearby farm that produced three Derby winners—and was unfortunately razed in the 1970s—this recent addition to the roster of Louisville bed-and-breakfasts sits just off Bardstown Road at the outskirts of South Louisville. A significant horse farm in its own right, it was known as the old Bray Place for many years, producing Derby winner Lookout in 1893 and runner-up Proctor Knott in 1889. Additional services offered include dry cleaning and in-room massages.

## 1840 TUCKER HOUSE $$
**2406 Tucker Station Rd.**
**(502) 297-8007**
**www.tuckerhouse1840.com**

Nature, history, and tranquility seem to coexist at the Tucker House, a Federal farmhouse set on five

# Close-up

## Good Times to Stay at an Old Louisville Inn

In addition to the weeks of the Kentucky Derby Festival, overnight stays at the bed-and-breakfasts in Old Louisville are especially popular during the first weekend in October, when hundreds of thousands of art lovers flock to the neighborhood for the annual St. James Court Art Show. Rates can be expensive and rooms tend to book quickly, so you won't want to overlook two other popular, albeit less crowded, times to enjoy a night in Old Louisville, one of the country's most picturesque neighborhoods. The first one is the weekend before Halloween when the annual Spirit Ball takes place at the nearby Conrad-Caldwell House. After dancing the night away at this popular Victorian-inspired masquerade ball, guests appreciate having their accommodations just steps away. The other time is the first weekend in December when the neighborhood pulls together for the yearly Old Louisville Holiday House Tour. Private homeowners deck out their dwellings in holiday finery and invite the public inside for this very popular neighborhood event, and many choose to make one of the local B&Bs their base for exploration. In addition, there is a popular garden tour in July and a blues festival in October. Many inns offer special packages for weekends with neighborhood events, so call or visit their Web sites for more information.

wooded acres with gardens and a spring-fed lake. Enjoy the beautiful landscape from the comfort of the deck or brick patio, or put on a pair of hiking boots and explore the area more completely. On-premise sights include the original stone springhouse, dry-laid masonry wall, and the quarry that supplied the stone for the foundation of the main house over 160 years ago. Overnighters can choose to lay their heads on a comfortable queen-size bed or an authentic 1820s rope bed, and they can refresh themselves in the in-ground pool. Special last-minute deals could get you 10 percent off.

### INN AT WOODHAVEN $$
**401 South Hubbards Lane**
**(502) 895-1011**
**www.innatwoodhaven.com**
With the nearby parks and its many porches and gardens, this Gothic Revival mansion from 1853 is a popular destination for overnighters in search of a respite from the hustle and bustle of Louisville's East End business corridors. The main house features elaborately carved woodwork, winding staircases, and spacious rooms tastefully decorated with antiques and period fixtures; additional lodging is available in the Carriage House and the charming Rose Cottage.

### PINECREST COTTAGE $$
**2806 Newburg Rd.**
**(502) 454-3800**
**www.pinecrestcottageandgardens.com**
Surrounded by 100-year-old trees and carefully tended perennial beds, this well-appointed guest house strives to offer accommodations that feel like home the moment you walk in. Apart from a TV/VCR with cable hookup, you will also find a modern, fully stocked kitchen with every convenience, a sun porch, a living room with working fireplace, and a large bedroom with king-size bed, cedar closet, and full bath. A studio couch in the living room converts to a double bed. Located just minutes from Bellarmine University, the Pinecrest Cottage has an in-ground pool and is available for nightly or long-term rentals. Call for rates.

## Across the River

### ADMIRAL BICKNELL INN $$
**600 East Main St.**
**New Albany, IN**
**(812) 981-8000**
**www.admiralbicknell.com**
Just a few short blocks from the shopping and restaurants of downtown New Albany, the stately Admiral Bicknell Inn is located in the town's his-

toric district on Mansion Row, with the Ohio River flowing behind it. Rooms have private in-suite baths, top-of-the-line Jameson pillow-top mattresses, feather beds, down comforters, 400- to 800-thread-count sheets, Egyptian cotton towels, plush robes, plus Natura soaps and lotions, high-speed Internet access, phone, and television with DVD or VCR players.

### 1877 HOUSE COUNTRY INN    $$
2408 Utica-Sellersburg Rd.
Jeffersonville, IN
(812) 285-1877
www.bbonline.com/in/1877house

Less than 7 miles from downtown Louisville, this 1870s farmhouse and quaint cottage sit at the top of a hill on two and a half scenic acres near the interstate. Working fireplaces and year-round hot tub offer coziness in the fall and winter, and brick patios and gazebos ensure relaxation in the spring and summer. The front porch has rockers and a swing that make it an ideal place to watch the sun set over the Louisville skyline in the distance. Many package specials available.

### HONEYMOON MANSION    $$
1014 East Main St.
New Albany, IN
(812) 945-0312
www.honeymoonmansion.com

With its gazebo and wedding chapel, this cozy inn on New Albany's Mansion Row is a favorite with wedding parties and newlyweds; however, this doesn't mean they don't welcome everyone in search of a little peace and tranquility at this elegant Victorian retreat. Common areas include a dining room and breakfast room in addition to the front parlor, rear deck, and gardens. Complimentary snacks, sodas, and movies available nightly.

### MARKET STREET INN    $$–$$$
330 West Market St.
Jeffersonville, IN
(812) 285-1877
www.innonmarket.com

This stately Second Empire mansion from 1881 in downtown Jeffersonville was fully restored with every modern amenity in 2005. Near the river and just two blocks from restaurants and shopping, Market Street Inn has seven beautiful guest rooms, including three large suites. Highlights include plenty of parking and a large third-floor deck with fountain and outside fireplace. In addition, two dining rooms can accommodate up to 32 people, with food prepared by a professional chef.

### OLD BRIDGE INN    $$
131 West Chestnut St.
Jeffersonville, IN
(812) 284-3580
www.oldbridgeinn.com

Built by a prominent Jeffersonville family in 1836, this neoclassical residence turned bed-and-breakfast sits right across the river from downtown Louisville. The inn is named for the old Big Four Railroad Bridge, which spans the river and can be seen from the inn. The house has a cozy front parlor and features five bedrooms with private baths and fireplaces; 18 people can be accommodated in all. Among the many amenities you will enjoy are wireless Internet and complimentary beverages.

## For More Information

For more information about bed-and-breakfast inns in the Louisville area, visit the Louisville Bed and Breakfast Association at www.louisvillebedandbreakfast.org; for B&Bs throughout Kentucky, visit the Kentucky Bed and Breakfast Association online at www.kentuckybb.com.

## HOTELS AND MOTELS

With more than a hundred hotels and motels spread out across the Louisville metro area, you're sure to find the place that's right for you, be it a trendy high-rise near the airport, an elegant room in the heart of downtown, or a cozy getaway in the East End. Familiar names include Crowne Plaza, Hyatt, Hilton, Marriott, Sheraton, and Holiday Inn, and you'll find over 18,000 rooms with competitive rates and a variety of amenities to satisfy every taste and budget. For more information about lodging in the Louisville area, visit the Web site of the Louisville Convention and Visitors Bureau at www.gotolouisville.com/stay/index.aspx.

## Downtown

### COURTYARD BY MARRIOTT $$$
100 South Second St.
(502) 562-0200
www.marriott.com/hotels/travel/sdfdt-courtyard-louisville-downtown/
Just one block from Kentucky International Convention Center and directly across from the new arena, the Courtyard by Marriott is within walking distance of the riverfront and Fourth Street Live!, as well as a number of other downtown nightspots. A full, hot breakfast is included, and inexpensive covered parking is available. The staff, courteous and well-informed, is known as one of the friendliest in the city.

### ECONO LODGE DOWNTOWN $$
401 South Second St.
(502) 583-2841
www.econolodge.com
With I-65, I-71, and I-64 all just two blocks away, this affordable hotel in downtown Louisville is popular among business and leisure travelers alike. Also nearby are the Kentucky International Convention Center and the restaurants and nightclubs of the Fourth Street Live! entertainment district. Free amenities include continental breakfast and hot coffee, high-speed Internet access, parking, and free local calls, and there is also an on-site exercise room.

### GALT HOUSE HOTEL & SUITES $$$
140 North Fourth St.
(502) 589-5200
www.galthouse.com

Although the current structure overlooking the Ohio River was started in the 1970s, the tradition of hospitality at Kentucky's largest hotel goes back to the early 1800s when the first Galt House opened. With 1,290 guest rooms to choose from, overnighters at the Galt House can opt for executive suites, river-view parlor suites, two-bedroom river-view suites, deluxe guest rooms, and extended-stay apartments. For a good view, check out the rooftop fitness center or Rivue, one of six restaurants and lounges on the property, located on the 25th floor of the Rivue Tower.

i Recent renovations at the Galt House have added a number of nice touches, including a space known as the Conservatory. Modeled after the Crystal Palace in London, this glass-domed space spans Fourth Street, linking the hotel's Suite and Rivue Towers. It's a place where you can check your e-mail with wireless Internet access, relax with a coffee from a casual deli, or have a drink at the watering hole known as Al J's. This is a popular stop for a drink in town because of the waterfront views and the unique aquarium-top bar that spans some 30 feet.

### HAMPTON INN $$$
101 East Jefferson St.
(502) 585-2200
www.hamptoninn.com
Also located near all the major interstates, this 173-room hotel in downtown Louisville offers free self-parking and complimentary breakfast to its guests. Other perks include a fitness room and the area's largest indoor pool, a business center, baggage storage, free shuttle, and an inviting lobby that features a martini bar, library, and soothing water wall.

### HYATT REGENCY $$$
320 West Jefferson St.
(502) 581-1234
louisville.hyatt.com

With 393 spacious guest rooms, direct connection to the convention center, and the bright lights of the Fourth Street Live! entertainment district right outside its front door, it's hardly surprising that this is a favorite among out-of-town visitors. Active guests especially enjoy the heated pool, 24-hour gym, and outdoor tennis court. Other pluses include a multilingual staff, express check-in kiosks, and lots of meeting space.

### LOUISVILLE MARRIOTT
### DOWNTOWN                          $$$$
**280 West Jefferson St.**
**(502) 627-5045**
**www.marriott.com**
One of Louisville's newest hotels, the glitzy 17-story downtown Marriott has 591 rooms and 25 suites. Aside from a Starbucks coffee bar, the hotel has a sports bar and a trendy Italian grill where hungry guests can take a break. More than a dozen other restaurants—many in the Fourth Street Live! entertainment district—are just a couple of blocks away. Complimentary services include toll-free calls and in-room coffee and tea; however, guests have to pay for parking.

### RESIDENCE INN                    $$$
**333 East Market St.**
**(502) 589-8998**
**www.marriott.com/hotels/travel/sdfgj-residence-inn-louisville-downtown**
Located in the heart of the medical district with University, Jewish, and Norton Hospitals all within walking distance, this Marriott property offers 140 suites, each with a fully equipped eat-in kitchen and separate living and sleeping areas. Complimentary features at this six-story smoke-free hotel include buffet breakfast and in-room tea and coffee; other services such as grocery shopping and restaurant deliveries are available as well.

### 21C MUSEUM HOTEL                 $$$$
**700 West Main St.**
**(502) 217-6300**
**www.21cmuseumhotel.com**

Louisville's 21c Museum Hotel is truly one of a kind: a 90-room boutique hotel in the heart of Museum Row that is an epicenter for art and activity. Dedicated to Southern-style hospitality and contemporary art from living artists, this hotel features a 9,000-square-foot contemporary museum with an eye-catching collection of cutting-edge art. But the art doesn't stop there; owners Steve Wilson and Laura Lee Brown want their guests to interact with art wherever they go. At check-in they will find themselves treading across a video installation of a couple dozing in bed, Abbas Kiarostami's *Sleepers,* and by the time they reach the elevator they have become part of Camille Utterback's and Romy Achituv's wall projection, *Text Rain, in* which letters fall out of the sky and sprinkle the viewers.

In their rooms, guests discover preprogrammed iPods with a variety of music, as well as award-winning design and decor, 42-inch HDTV flat-screen televisions, Wi-Fi, 500-thread-count Egyptian cotton sheets imported from Italy, silver mint julep cups, gourmet coffeemakers, minibar refrigerators, Malin + Goetz bath amenities, and nightly turndown services. The hotel also offers a full exercise facility with a steam room, sauna, and spa services. Most recently, the readers of *Condé Nast* chose 21c as the best hotel in the country. If you can't spend the night, make sure to pop in and enjoy an hour or two wandering around. (Also see the Close-up in the Attractions chapter.)

**i** The Brown Hotel is the birthplace of one of Louisville's most favorite dishes, the hot brown. Developed by chef Fred Schmidt in the 1920s to satisfy the appetites of late-night dancers, it's an open-faced sandwich with shaved turkey breast and toast points smothered in cheesy Mornay sauce before it is topped with tomato slices and bacon strips and popped under the broiler. Although many eateries throughout the region serve hot browns—or at least their versions of it—you can get the original at one of the Brown's restaurants.

# 🔍 Close-up

## Stay at One of These Grand Hotels

**The Brown Hotel   $$$$**

335 West Broadway

(502) 583-1234

www.brownhotel.com

The Brown, a lovely hotel built in Louisville's old theater district in 1923, has long been a magnet for prominent guests and celebrities. The stately Georgian Revival structure has 16 stories trimmed in stone and terra-cotta, and an interior with classic English Renaissance architecture that makes it one of the most treasured landmarks in the city. The opulent two-story lobby has ornate, hand-painted ceilings, Botticino marble flooring, finely carved mahogany furnishings, and Palladian-style windows. All guest rooms at this AAA Four Diamond hotel feature goose-down duvets, feather beds, 310-thread-count sheets, and three multiline phones. Bathrooms with Spanish marble and granite-top vanities are a feature of the 293 elegantly appointed guest rooms and suites. Apart from a complimentary airport shuttle, guests have access to 26,000 square feet of meeting space, a business center, and a 24-hour fitness center. The English Grill, one of two on-site restaurants, is consistently voted one of the city's best restaurants.

**Seelbach Hilton   $$$$**

500 South Fourth St.

(502) 585-3200

www.seelbachhilton.com

After a recent $12 million renovation, Louisville's most famous place to sleep has managed to maintain the elegance of a grand hotel, while offering its guests the most modern of amenities. Updates include new furniture, lighting, carpets, wall treatments, 37-inch HDTVs in the more than 300 guest rooms, and Precor machinery in the fitness center, which has nearly doubled in size. The lobby's original skylight, covered for the last 50 years, was recently restored to the appearance it had when the hotel opened in 1905, and a soft blue glow now washes over the gleaming marble and hand-painted murals that have made the Seelbach one of the most elegant stays in the city. Located directly adjacent to the Fourth Street Live! entertainment district in the heart of downtown Louisville, the Seelbach is just steps away from the convention center and many nightclubs and restaurants. Of course, with its own five-diamond restaurant, the Oakroom, and the Old Seelbach Bar, which was recently named one of the 50 best bars in the world, you won't ever have to leave if you don't want to.

### Near the Airport

**CANDLEWOOD SUITES
LOUISVILLE AIRPORT**      $$
1367 Gardiner Lane
(502) 357-3577
www.ichotelsgroup.com

Renovated in 2007, this all-suites hotel with 200 rooms spread out over three floors is especially popular with extended-stay employees of nearby companies, such as GE, Ford, UPS, Humana, Brown-Forman, and Jewish Hospital. International travelers especially like the foreign-language television options, and everyone loves the Candlewood Cupboard, where you can purchase sodas for 50 cents, and meals, snacks, and sundry items at value prices. With fully equipped kitchens, it's easy to stay in and cook for yourself. You can also do your laundry at no cost while you work out at the gym or relax in your suite. For an extra charge, you can even bring your pet along.

### CROWNE PLAZA
### LOUISVILLE AIRPORT                    $$$
**830 Phillips Lane**
**(502) 367-2251**
**www.cplouisville.com**
Stylish guest rooms and comfortable suites at this 588-room hotel feature amenities like free high-speed wired and wireless Internet, generously sized work desks, flat-screen televisions, in-room movies, and coffeemakers. Extensively renovated, the hotel also offers its guests complimentary shuttles and a terrace bar with live entertainment and happy hour on the weekends. With 28 meeting rooms and 55,000 square feet of flexible space, it's a popular place for conferences and conventions. An on-site business center, indoor/outdoor pool, and fitness center make this a favorite for guests wanting to stay near the airport. Pets can stay for an additional fee.

### ECONO LODGE AIRPORT                    $
**6109 Preston Hwy.**
**(502) 966-5445**
**www.econolodge.com/hotel/ky120**
Located less than 3 miles from the Expo Center, the airport, and Six Flags, this pet-friendly property has interior corridors and rooms with refrigerator, basic cable, and free Wi-Fi Internet. The University of Louisville, Freedom Hall Arena, and the Ford Motor Plant are also nearby.

### HILTON GARDEN INN
### LOUISVILLE AIRPORT                    $$
**2735 Crittenden Dr.**
**(502) 637-2424**
**www.hiltongardeninn.com**
With downtown Louisville only 7 miles north on I-65, this smoke-free facility puts all of the area's many corporate offices and attractions within comfortable reach. In addition, it's directly adjacent to the Kentucky Expo Center and Six Flags Kentucky Kingdom, and only 1.5 miles

from Churchill Downs. Besides 24-hour access to the free airport shuttle, overnighters enjoy landscaped outdoor patios, an indoor heated pool, and ergonomic Herman Miller Mirra chairs at the spacious in-room workstations.

### LOUISVILLE EXPO AIRPORT RED
### ROOF INN                    $$
**4704 Preston Hwy.**
**(502) 968-0151**
**www.redroof.com**
A newly renovated property with all rooms featuring contemporary furniture, new bathrooms with granite countertops, comfortable easy chairs, and more, this location offers "On Demand Video" with a selection of free TV channels, pay-to-view premium channels, movies, music, and games. Kids 17 and younger stay free when occupying the same room with an adult family member, and one "well-behaved" family pet per room is welcome, at no additional charge.

## East End

### EMBASSY SUITES LOUISVILLE                    $$$
**9940 Corporate Campus Drive**
**(502) 426-9191**
**http://embassysuites1.hilton.com**
About 15 minutes from downtown and the Louisville International Airport, Embassy Suites Louisville is located in the busy, business-filled Hurstbourne Corridor. Each spacious suite on the property features a nicely decorated living room and a private bedroom with a wide range of standard amenities. In addition to a 24-hour fitness center, guests are invited to enjoy a cooked-to-order complimentary breakfast and daily Manager's Reception with free beverages and appetizers.

## *Across the River*

### HOLIDAY INN LOUISVILLE-NORTH                    $
**505 Marriott Drive**
**Clarksville, IN**
**(812) 283-4411**
**www.holidayinn.com**
Less than two miles from downtown Louisville and just steps from the Atlantis Water Park and

Derby Dinner Playhouse, this nine-floor hotel has more than 350 guest rooms, 301 of them for non-smokers. The Falls of the Ohio Interpretive Center is less than a mile away and a 13-mile drive will get you to the nearest casino. Pets are allowed for a $35 nonrefundable fee and among the languages spoken by the hotel staff are Afrikaans, Arabic, Spanish, and Tagalog.

**SHERATON LOUISVILLE
RIVERSIDE HOTEL**                                $$
**700 West Riverside Drive
Jeffersonville, IN
(812) 284-6711
www.sheraton.com**
Although it's located across the river in Jeffersonville, it's still an easy five-minute drive from the Louisville International Airport. Nearly 200 posh guest rooms and suites—many with breathtaking views of Louisville's nighttime skyline—feature amenities such as flat-screen TVs, free high speed Internet, and sumptuous bedding. For those in search of an extra bit of comfort, the Club Level offers larger rooms and VIP access to a lounge with complimentary breakfast, beverages and hors d'oeuvres. The Bristol, a popular upscale restaurant chain, has an on-site location here with great views of Louisville.

**VALUE PLACE**                                $
**1811 Independence Court
Clarksville, IN
www.valueplace.com**
Situated right off of I-65 and less than 2 miles from downtown Louisville, this extended-stay establishment is perfect for people wanting to

---

# Campground

**Louisville Metro KOA**          $
900 Marriott Dr.
Clarksville, IN
(812) 282-4474
http://koa.com/where/ky/17138

If hotels and motels aren't your thing, you'll be happy to know there's an RV park less than five minutes from downtown Louisville. With quick and easy access from I-65, the Louisville Metro KOA makes an ideal base camp for enjoying the city's major events, conventions, and attractions. You'll find all the conveniences you need here, and each RV site includes full hookups and cable television. All campers have access to free wireless Internet as well. A pool and water park are located just half a block away, and in addition, there is RV service available next door.

---

spend a week or longer in the area. Suites sleeping one, two, or four people feature high-speed Internet access, daily housekeeping, and local and long-distance telephone service; kitchen dishes, utensils, and cookware are available upon request. In addition, there are laundry facilities and vending machines, as well as private entrance and security cameras in all public areas. A $100 refundable deposit is due at check-in.

# ATTRACTIONS

People know Louisville for several different things. It's home to the most exciting two minutes in sports—the famous Run for the Roses at the Kentucky Derby—and as the home of the legendary Louisville Slugger baseball bats. Hardly surprising, it's also where Kentucky Fried Chicken has its headquarters, and it's a town that produces one-third of the bourbon in the world.

But there are some things you might not know about Louisville. For example, the fact that 90 percent of the world's disco balls are produced here, or that it boasts one of the country's largest Victorian neighborhoods. It's also home to the nation's largest urban forest, and its collection of cast-iron facades can rival those of New York City's SoHo neighborhood. There are more than 120 parks, and heavyweight champion Muhammad Ali grew up here. These are just some of the reasons that Louisville is an interesting city to explore. Take the time to discover Louisville and you might be surprised at what you learn.

## VISITOR INFORMATION

For an up-to-date listing of "everything Louisville," check out the Web site at www.louisville.com. In addition to calendars of upcoming events in the Derby City, you'll find directories with guides to local attractions, restaurants, lodging, nightlife, shopping, and more. You will also find local news items and useful information about Louisville real estate. Another good source of information is the downtown visitor center.

### LOUISVILLE CONVENTION AND VISITORS BUREAU DOWNTOWN VISITOR CENTER
**301 South Fourth St.**
**(502) 379-6109**
**www.gotolouisville.com**
If you're looking for a place to start your exploration of the Derby City, pop in at the Louisville visitor center downtown at the corner of Fourth and Jefferson. Friendly volunteers are on hand to tell you about all of the local attractions, as well as to help you organize tours of the city. This is where you can get discounted tickets to the Derby Dinner Playhouse, Dinosaur World in Cave City, Falls of the Ohio interpretive center, Farmington Historic Plantation, Frazier International History Museum, Glassworks, Historic Locust Grove, Kentucky Derby Museum, Kentucky Museum of Art and Craft, the Louisville Science Center & IMAX Theatre, the Louisville Slugger Museum, Muhammad Ali Center, Riverside, the Farnsley-Moremen Landing, the Louisville Zoo, the Speed Art Museum, and more.

You can also get a $3 Transit Authority of River City (TARC) "Day Tripper" Pass, which allows unlimited trips during any one-day period on the city's bus system, and on the downtown trolley system. With the pass you'll receive a brochure featuring Louisville's main tourist attractions. There are also a number of items available in the gift shop, including bourbon-themed memorabilia, clothing, and books on the city's haunted past. There's also information about the Kentucky Bourbon Trail. In addition, an informative display brings to life Kentucky's most famous son, Colonel Harland Sanders himself.

The downtown visitor center offers free, one-hour guided walking tours of Louisville, "Possibility City," weather permitting. Reservations are preferred, but walk-ins will be taken based on availability. Call to schedule. You'll explore Fourth Street, Whiskey Row, Museum Row, and the civic district, with several stops along the way.

**i** Two historic neighborhoods also offer information centers to help you during your stay: Historic Main Street Visitor Center (627 West Main Street; 502-568-2220; www.mainstreetassociation.com) and Visitor Center in Historic Old Louisville (218 West Oak Street ; 502-637-2922; www.oldlouisville.org).

## Helpful Periodicals

*TRAVELHOST OF GREATER LOUISVILLE*
**7202 Highway 329**
**(502) 241-2643**
**www.travelhostlouisville.com**
Published bimonthly, *TravelHost* represents Greater Louisville and southern Indiana to visitors and guests from around the world. It is the oldest and best-known visitor services publication in the country. *TravelHost* features relocation tips and comfort services in addition to a wealth of information about tour guides, lists of the region's best restaurants, art galleries, day trips, historic places, performing arts, shopping, and museums. There are useful maps as well.

*WELCOME TO GREATER LOUISVILLE*
**812 South Third St.**
**(502) 584-2720**
**www.kytravel.com**
Updated every other Wednesday since 1951, *Welcome to Greater Louisville* has lots of helpful hints for Derby City tourists. In addition to useful information about local points of interest, restaurants, shopping, and lodging, readers learn about the tours, conventions, and special events that make Louisville an interesting place to live and play. Tips on vacation rentals, spas, theater, and sports are included as well. The publisher, Editorial Services Company, also distributes an annual *Kentucky Travel Guide* that makes it easy to discover the best the state has to offer.

# LOUISVILLE ATTRACTIONS

*BELLE OF LOUISVILLE*
**401 West River Rd.**
**(502) 574-2992**
**www.belleoflouisville.org**
Approaching a hundred years in existence, this historic steamer on Louisville's downtown waterfront is still going strong today. When the calliope plays, you're welcome to step on board and journey back in time when this, the oldest operating steamboat in the nation, carried passengers and goods to all major ports along the Ohio River. Tickets for regular sightseeing excursions start at $16 and can include lunch or dinner buffets. For the most up-to-date cruise calendar and listing of special events, call toll-free at (866) 832-0011. You can also get information about their smaller sister ship, the *Spirit of Jefferson*.

## Keeps on Ticking

When you're in downtown Louisville near the river and need to know what time it is, look across the water and find one of the world's largest timepieces. The clock—which has been atop the old Colgate building (a former prison) since 1924—measures almost 40 feet across and reportedly ranks as the second largest in the world. Bigger than London's famous Big Ben, Jeffersonville's Colgate clock has hands that are 16 and 20.5 feet long. Although the plant recently closed down, the clock is still working, and it's lit by red neon at night, when it can be seen more than a mile away.

## CATHEDRAL OF THE ASSUMPTION
433 South Fifth St.
(502) 582-2971
www.cathedraloftheassumption.org

Located on the site of the old St. Louis Church, Louisville's redbrick neo-Gothic cathedral was designed by William Keeley and Isaiah Rogers, two of the country's finest 19th-century architects. Constructed in 1852, it is one of the oldest public buildings in the city, as well as the third-oldest Catholic cathedral in the United States in continuous use. The steeple rises 287 feet and was counted as North America's tallest spire when it was completed. The coronation window is one of the oldest surviving examples of hand-painted stained glass in the country.

It is open most days for viewing, and on Sundays, the Archdiocese of Louisville History Center provides an opportunity to experience the Catholic heritage of the Archdiocese of Louisville through objects and artifacts from its earliest beginnings in 1775 to the present day.

## THE EMBROIDERERS' GUILD OF AMERICA
426 West Jefferson St.
(502) 589-6956
www.egausa.org

The Embroiderers' Guild of America is a national nonprofit educational organization offering study and preservation of the heritage and art of embroidery. Their Embroidery Resource Center displays historic and modern embroidery from around the world. The Margaret Parshall Gallery displays needlework on a rotating schedule, as well as from individuals and groups outside the EGA. The Leslie Durst Gallery displays pieces from the EGA Collection. The galleries are open to the public Monday through Friday from 9 a.m. to 4:30 p.m.

## FRAZIER INTERNATIONAL HISTORY MUSEUM
829 West Main St.
(502) 753-5663
www.fraziermuseum.org

Covering 1,000 years of history, the Frazier International History Museum houses a priceless col-

### Louisville's Museum Row

With its unique streetscape and local cultural institutions, West Main Street has evolved into a popular destination that is enjoyed by residents and visitors alike. Known as Museum Row, it is home to a number of interesting attractions and one-of-a-kind stops that include the Glassworks Gallery, the Frazier International History Museum, 21c Museum Hotel, the Louisville Slugger Museum & Factory, the Louisville Science & IMAX Theatre, the Kentucky Museum of Art and Craft, the Kentucky Show, and the Muhammad Ali Center. If you stop by the Main Street Visitor Center & Gift Shop between Sixth and Seventh Streets, you can pick up a free walking-tour brochure to help you navigate. Or you can simply download a copy at www.MainStreetAssociation.com. Since many museums offer reciprocal discounts, make sure to show your ticket stubs or visit www.museumrowonmain.com for details. You can also check out a video about West Main Street at www.downtowndevelopmentcorp.com/vid_westmain.aspx.

lection in a 100,000-square-foot, state-of-the-art facility on downtown Louisville's historic West Main Street. Exhibits with a heavy emphasis on historical arms and weapons bring the past to life with the help of live multimedia presentations, educational programming, costumed interpreters, and hands-on experiences. Visitors come face-to-face with people and stories that changed the world forever, and leave with a broader under-

# Close-up

## Talk of the Town

In case the infamous red penguins perched along the roof and the breathing chandelier over the sidewalk outside didn't tip you off, **21c Museum Hotel** (700 West Main St.; 502-217-6300; www.21cmuseumhotel.com) is not your run-of-the-mill hotel. The exterior installations, however, give just an inkling of the distinctive artistic works that await you inside, where galleries and public spaces house a colorful assortment of sculpture, photography, and video installations. The good news is that you don't need to be staying at this trendy 90-room hideaway to enjoy the sights. Just walk on in and wander from gallery to gallery, where you'll find the first museum on the continent dedicated solely to collecting and exhibiting contemporary art of the 21st century.

21c Museum Hotel is the brainchild of Louisville philanthropists and contemporary art collectors Steve Wilson and Laura Lee Brown, whose mission of combining art and hospitality has made the converted block of buildings at the corner of Seventh and Main one of the most talked-about undertakings in the region. The hotel features a 9,000-square-foot contemporary art museum that is funded and managed by the International Contemporary Art Foundation, and dynamic exhibitions showcase emerging talent alongside acclaimed international artists. Rotating displays include work by video artists such as Bill Viola and Tony Oursler, and the photography of Andres Serrano, Sam Taylor-Wood, and David Leventhal. Sculptors like Yinka Shonibare and Judy Fox and multimedia artists such as Chuck Close, Alfredo Jaar, and Kara Walker are featured as well. The gallery is open 24/7 and the video installations can be viewed from 7 a.m. to 1 a.m.

---

standing of history and an increased respect for the human spirit. Open seven days a week, a regular adult ticket costs $9—although the museum offers discounted tickets to children, seniors, and members of the military.

**GLASSWORKS**
**815 West Market St.**
**(502) 584-4510**
**www.louisvilleglassworks.com**
Located in the historic Snead Manufacturing Building in the heart of downtown Louisville, this multiuse facility with its working glass studios, galleries, and walk-in workshop showcases the wondrous art of glassblowing seven days a week. Monday through Friday from 10 a.m. to 4 p.m., you can take a self-guided tour ($4.50) that will reveal the versatile, magical nature of glass; on Saturday you can take a guided tour ($6.50) at 11 a.m., 1 p.m., and 3 p.m.

**KENTUCKY MUSEUM OF ART AND CRAFT**
**715 West Main St.**
**(502) 589-0102**
**www.kentuckyarts.org**
Open Monday through Saturday, the Kentucky Museum of Art and Craft is a nonprofit organization founded in 1981 to promote and support art and craft excellence in the Bluegrass State. In addition to supporting creative types, this museum also provides educational programs to schoolchildren and adults, with partial support by the Fund for the Arts and the Kentucky Arts Council. The Gallery Shop features the work of approximately 200 artists at any one time, and offers work in all media, from folk art to furniture. The Gallery Shop works with artists and clients on commission and ships to all corners of the globe. A regular adult admission costs $5, but members get in for free. Their Web site is www .kentuckyarts.org.

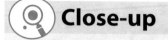 **Close-up**

## Gallopalooza Horses

If you're driving or strolling around town and come across a brightly painted horse in front of a business, you're most likely seeing part of the Gallopalooza herd. Started in 2003, this public art project raises money for a number of local charities and organizations including Brightside, the community beautification program. In addition to beautifying the streets and generating civic pride, Gallopalooza, Inc. encourages tourism and showcases local artists as well.

The idea of adorning animal statues and placing them on the city streets comes from the Swiss, who started decorating cows and placing them on the streets of Zurich in 1998. Chicago retailers were the first to bring the concept to this country, and by the year 2000, approximately two dozen cities had adopted similar public art endeavors. The last herd raised more than $700,000. For more information about Gallopalooza, Inc., go online at www.gallopalooza.com.

**KENTUCKY SHOW**
**501 West Main St.**
**(502) 562-7800**
**www.kentuckyshow.com**
Native Kentuckian Ashley Judd narrates this exciting, large-screen multimedia experience that captures the visual essence of the Bluegrass State. From its people and culture, to the history, music, and geography that define the Commonwealth, viewers get an eyeful of all things Kentucky. General admission is only $7, and the Kentucky Center is the location. Showings daily at 1 p.m. and 3 p.m. except Monday; Tuesday through Saturday, there's an 11 a.m. show as well.

**LOUISVILLE FREE PUBLIC LIBRARY**
**301 York St.**
**(502) 574-1611**
**www.lfpl.org**
Just a block's walk from the Brown Hotel, the Louisville Free Public Library is a favorite stop for lovers of neoclassical architecture. The 1906 structure—one of a number of Carnegie libraries from the turn of the last century—was designed by architects Pilcher & Tachau of New York City and offers an assortment of eye-catching details on the interior. The contemporary North Building, designed by architects Lewis & Henry of Louisville, was built in 1969. In the small garden to the west you'll find one of only two public statues of

### Less Is More

When you're in downtown Louisville, you'll probably pass an austere-looking modern building off West Main Street without even realizing its architectural significance. The squat, boxy, five-story structure at 425 West Main was actually the last building designed by famed architect Ludwig Mies van der Rohe, who died in 1969. The American Life Building, his final design, was executed by his descendant firm in the early 1970s, and it is the only one of his buildings to have a Cor-Ten steel facade, earning it the nickname "the Rusty Building." Widely known for his use of the aphorism "less is more," Mies van der Rohe designed his American Life Building as part of the downtown revitalization project. The address is 3 Riverfront Plaza and the telephone number is (502) 582-9212.

Abraham Lincoln in the city. Open every day but Sunday, this, the main branch of the Louisville library system, also hosts regular exhibits, talks, and discussions that are open to the public.

> ℹ The National Spelling Bee originated in Louisville. The *Courier-Journal* started the contest in 1925 with just nine contestants. The Scripps publishing house took it over in 1941, and they still run the annual spelling competition today.

## THE LOUISVILLE PALACE
**625 South Fourth St.**
**(502) 583-4555**
**www.louisvillepalace.com**
The Louisville Palace might be listed on the National Register of Historic Places, but there's nothing old-fashioned about the presentations there. Touring Broadway shows, nationally acclaimed musical acts, and the latest in stand-up comedy are just some of the headliners that perform at this 1920s movie house jewel located near the heart of the Fourth Street Live! entertainment complex. You don't have to buy tickets to enjoy the stunning details of architect John Eberson's neo–Spanish Baroque masterpiece, however, because free tours of this, the Loew's United Artists Theater, are available. The 2,700-seat theater itself is a sight to behold, with a deep-blue *trompe l'oeil* ceiling that re-creates an early summer evening over a Spanish village. The awe-inspiring lobby has a curved, vaulted ceiling graced with the sculptured faces of 139 historic figures, such as Dante, Socrates, Beethoven, and even the architect himself. To arrange your tour, call (502) 583-4555 x224.

## LOUISVILLE SLUGGER MUSEUM
**800 West Main St.**
**(502) 588-7228**
**www.sluggermuseum.org**
Since 1884, Louisville Slugger has been the name associated with the great American pastime of baseball, and craftsmen at the Louisville Slugger factory along downtown's Museum Row have been putting prime lumber in the hands of the

game's most famous players ever since. A visit to the museum shows that the sport has changed in the meantime, but visitors leave convinced that the crack of the bat remains one of the sporting world's most thrilling moments. Lasting approximately 25 minutes, guided factory tours begin at 9 a.m., with the last factory tour of the day departing one hour before closing. The museum is open seven days a week and admission runs $10 a person, with discounts available for seniors and kids.

### Bats and Balls

When you're in downtown Louisville and looking for a photo op, go to 800 West Main Street. At the Louisville Slugger Museum you'll find the world's largest baseball bat. Erected in 1995 and made of painted hollow carbon steel, the bat is 120 feet tall and weighs 34 tons. Farther down the block, a three-dimensional baseball appears to smash a giant window in a sign for Kentucky Mirror and Plate Glass at 822 West Main. And a few blocks past that, another huge bat—the vampire kind—hangs upside down and clings to the brick wall of Caufield's Novelty, a costume and decoration store at 1006 West Main.

## LOUISVILLE STONEWARE
**731 Brent St.**
**(502) 582-1900**
**www.louisvillestoneware.com**
Since their beginnings in 1815, Louisville Stoneware has been dedicated to the craft of transforming clay into enduring and functional works of art. Utilizing the basic elements of earth, water, air, and fire, skilled artisans create timeless pieces of dinnerware, bakeware, serving pieces, and col-

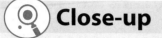 # Close-up

## This Won't Cost a Dime

There are a number of free attractions and activities in the area, so if you want to give your wallet a break for the day, consider one of these no-charge alternatives:

- Enjoy the art gallery at 21c Museum Hotel.

- Have your picture taken with Colonel Harland Sanders—well, at least with his wax replica—at the mini museum that honors him at the downtown Louisville visitor center.

- Tour the city's most elegant hotel, the Seelbach Hilton.

- Discover the history of America's native spirit at Jim Beam's American Outpost.

- Join the locals at the Jeffersontown Historical Museum.

- Take in the exhibits at the Louisville Nature Center.

- Stroll the streets of Old Louisville, America's grandest Victorian neighborhood.

- Visit the museum at the American Printing House for the Blind.

- Enjoy the dioramas and multimedia exhibits at New Albany's Carnegie Center for Art and History.

- Amble along the scenic pathways of historic Cave Hill Cemetery.

- Stop in for a visit to the Kentucky Museum of Art and Craft.

- View the 12,000 pieces in the permanent collection of the Speed Art Museum.

- Peek inside the lovely 851 Mansion tucked away behind the facade of Spalding University's main administration building.

- Heighten your awareness for history at the stunning Ferguson Mansion, the site of today's Filson Historical Society.

- Explore for fossils at the Falls of the Ohio State Park in Clarksville, Indiana.

lectibles that can be enjoyed and cherished for years to come. At Studio One, Louisville Stoneware's downtown location, visitors can witness artistry in the making with a tour ($7 for children and adults) of one of the nation's oldest stoneware manufacturing firms. Aside from a visit to the "History of Stoneware" museum, the Louisville Stoneware factory tour includes a stop at the factory retail store for browsing or shopping, and a behind-the-scenes look at the factory where you can watch talented artists at work. Tours can be arranged Monday through Friday from 10:30 a.m. to 1:30 p.m.

**MINT JULEP TOURS**
**140 North Fourth St., Suite 326**
**(502) 583-1433**
**www.mintjuleptours.com**
Located in the Galt House Hotel, Mint Julep Tours offers a variety of informative and entertaining guided tours of Louisville and nearby bourbon country that allow you to sit back and enjoy the

sights. The bourbon country and horse country tours are among the most popular, but there are also tours for those interested in Derby City history and its haunted past.

## MUHAMMAD ALI CENTER
**144 North Sixth St.**
**(502) 992-5329**
**www.alicenter.org**

If you're driving into Louisville from the west on I-64 or crossing the river on I-65, you'll probably spot a distinctive building near the water. Up close, it appears to be covered in random-colored tiles, but the farther away you get, the easier it is to see the images of Muhammad Ali. Inspired by the ideals and vision of Muhammad Ali, its founder and Louisville's native son, this downtown stop counts as both a cultural attraction and an international education center. Two and half levels of engrossing multimedia presentations and interactive exhibits immerse participants in a hands-on look at the Champ's life and the core values he still strives to observe today: respect, confidence, conviction, dedication, giving, and spirituality. Open till 5 p.m. every day except Monday, the Muhammad Ali Center charges $9 for general admission.

## ST. MARTIN OF TOURS CHURCH
**639 South Shelby St.**
**(502) 582-282**
**www.louisville-catholic.net**

St. Martin of Tours is the only church in the Louisville metro area that keeps its doors open to the public 24 hours a day, seven days a week. Although this is specifically "for the adoration of Jesus in the Blessed Sacrament," guards welcome respectful tourists who wish to enter and enjoy the craftsmanship of the German immigrants who constructed it in 1853, and then later enlarged it in 1861. Apart from the impressive pipe organ, Stations of the Cross, and windows of stained glass—all made in Germany—the interior is home to the full skeletal relics of two early Christian martyrs, Magnus and Bonosa, who are housed in glass reliquaries under the two side altars.

## SEELBACH HILTON
**500 South Fourth St.**
**(502) 585-3200**
**www.seelbachhilton.com**

No trip to Louisville would be complete without an obligatory stop at the fabled Seelbach Hotel. Built in 1905 by Bavarian brothers Otto and Louis Seelbach, this hotel has always been the overnight place for Kentucky's movers and shakers. And even if you're not staying here, there are other ways to enjoy it, such as stopping by for a drink in the Old Seelbach Bar or enjoying an elegant dinner in the Oakroom. Or, just come in off the street and enjoy the view in the majestic lobby, with its restored skylight and original murals depicting early Kentucky history. Then, take the stairs down to the basement and view the Rathskeller, the only room in the world made from Rookwood pottery. With its painted arches and vaulted ceiling, it was meant to replicate the beer-hall cellars of the Seelbachs' native Germany. Finish with a peek inside the Blackjack Room on the mezzanine level, the enclosed alcove in the Oakroom frequented by Al Capone on his many trips to the Derby City during the hotel's heyday in the 1920s. Secret panels in the wall allowed for a quick getaway to tunnels below the hotel when the police raided. If you want to learn more about the Seelbach, hotel historian Larry Johnson arranges informative guided tours on request. Call (502) 585-3200 x1091 for more information.

## THOMAS EDISON HOUSE
**729 East Washington St.**
**(502) 585-5247**
**www.edisonhouse.org**

Thomas Edison came to Louisville in 1866, at the young age of 19, to work as a telegraph key operator. He landed a job with the Western Union office on Second and West Main Streets. During his year as a telegrapher in Louisville, Edison became fascinated with improving the telegraph, and today, the small shotgun structure he occupied in the Butchertown neighborhood has a display that commemorates his time in Kentucky. Some of the interesting artifacts found

## Thomas Merton

On March 18, 1958, Thomas Merton, Kentucky's most well-known Trappist monk, was standing in downtown Louisville across from the Seelbach Hotel when he suddenly had an epiphany. As described in his book, *Conjectures of a Guilty Bystander:* "In Louisville, at the corner of Fourth and Walnut, in the center of the shopping district, I was suddenly overwhelmed with the realization that I loved all those people, that they were mine and I theirs, that we could not be alien to one another even though we were total strangers." Today, a historical marker commemorates the location of this revelation.

cotta, glazed brick, tile, marble, and stone. Look closely, and gargoyles, chameleons, serpents, and swans will jump from the facades of the old mansions and townhomes that typify the Old Louisville neighborhood. In short, Old Louisville is a feast for the eyes.

The wonderful examples of Richardsonian Romanesque, Victorian Gothic, Queen Anne, Italianate, Chateauesque, and Beaux Arts architecture make Old Louisville a virtual open-air museum. And those are just some of the styles on display. As a National Historic Preservation District, it ranks among the largest and most significant in the country; its picturesque boulevards, streets, and alleys boast hundreds of grand mansions and comfortable dwellings. They are embellished with architectural styles and elements of centuries past and from all corners of the globe.

Old Louisville has a very colorful history that really took off in the 1880s. First developed between the 1870s and the early 1900s, many considered the Southern Extension, as residents called it, Louisville's first suburb. A major catalyst to its growth came in 1883 when Louisville hosted the extremely successful Southern Exposition and received international attention when former resident Thomas Edison showcased his incandescent lightbulb. When it finally closed its doors in 1887, savvy developers started to sell off the land on the newly dubbed St. James and Belgravia Courts, realizing that image-conscious Victorians would snatch up anything reminiscent of London aristocracy. The rich and elite poured into the posh "new" neighborhood, and residents applied the name "Old Louisville" to the district in the 1950s.

While "urban renewal" caused the destruction of similar neighborhoods all around the country, most of Old Louisville somehow managed to escape the wrecking ball. After a blighted period in the 1940s, '50s, and '60s, residents of Kentucky's largest city started to realize that they had a diamond in the rough. Instead of giving in to the planned destruction of priceless examples of architecture, locals banded together and had the entire area placed on the National Register of Historic Places. The Old Louisville Preservation

at the museum include both cylinder and disc phonographs, as well as Edison business phonographs, and an Edison kinetoscope, the first home movie projector. Tickets for adults cost $5, and the hours of operation are Tuesday through Saturday from 10 a.m to 2 p.m.

## OLD LOUISVILLE

Less than a mile from downtown Louisville sits a Victorian gem, a neighborhood unlike most in this country. Most people wouldn't think it, but Kentucky can boast one of the most splendid residential neighborhoods in the entire nation. A leisurely stroll along the tree-lined streets of this charming historic district can transport a visitor back in time to an era when a man's home truly was his castle.

Take a stroll and you'll spy turrets, towers, bays and gables, wrought-iron fences, hand-carved doors, and stained-glass windows. There are also hidden balconies, secluded courtyards, and secret passageways—and details like terra-

# Close-up

## Get the Big Picture

Don't be surprised if you see someone looking down at you from lofty heights in downtown Louisville, or as you're speeding along one of the interstates. They're most likely part of the "Hometown Heroes" project, sponsored by the Mayor's Public Art Committee and the Greater Louisville Pride Foundation. The project, which includes vast murals of famous Louisvillians, enhances the sides of buildings and features celebrities such as Muhammad Ali and Diane Sawyer. Other personalities include radio host Bob Edwards and jockey Pat Day, immortalized in a five-story, digitally printed mural on the eastern wall of the Jefferson Educational Center at Second Street and Broadway. Sculptor Ed Hamilton and baseball great Pee Wee Reese are just some of the other larger-than-life celebs you'll spot throughout the city.

For a good way to discover Louisville, take a day and see if you can find them all:

**Muhammad Ali, boxer**—at Third Street and River Road, facing the Ohio River

**Judge Louis Brandeis, U.S. Supreme Court justice**—on the Chase Bank Building, best seen headed east on Liberty Street between Fifth and Fourth

**Pat Day, jockey**—at Second and Broadway, visible from I-65 North/South

**Bob Edwards, public radio personality**—624 Baxter Avenue, seen headed north

**Darryl Griffith, basketball player**—on the Watterson City Building, along I-264 East at Newburg Road

**Ed Hamilton, artist**—Glassworks Building at Ninth and Market Streets, facing Ninth Street

**Bud Hillerich, baseball bat maker**—Heyburn Building at Fourth and Broadway, seen headed west on Broadway

**Paul Hornung, football player**—Watterson City Building, along I-264 West at Newburg Road

**Patrick Henry Hughes, musician**—OK Storage building at Broadway and Barret Avenue

**Mary T. Meagher, Olympic swimmer**—Norton Suburban Hospital Building in St. Matthews, visible from I-64 East

**Tori Murden, transatlantic solo rower**—Kentucky Exposition Center, facing I-65 South past the Crittenden Drive exit

**Pee Wee Reese, baseball player**—on the Fetzer Building at 209 East Main Street, headed west from Slugger Field

**Colonel Harland Sanders, Kentucky Fried Chicken founder**—BP Apartment Building at Third and Guthrie Streets, viewable from I-65

**Diane Sawyer, TV news personality**—on the Starks Building on Muhammad Ali between Third and Fourth Streets, viewable from I-65

District today includes approximately 48 blocks of the residential core bounded by Kentucky and Bloom Street to the north, and between Sixth Street and I-65 to the east and west.

Old Louisville puts on its finery and southern charm in the springtime, just before the Kentucky Derby in May when crystal-blue skies provide the perfect backdrop for a colorful explosion of azalea, dogwood, and redbud blossoms. It shines in the crisp fall air of October as well, when hundreds of thousands flock to its quaint streets for the St. James Court Art Show to stroll beneath a canopy of spectacular fall colors. Since the 1970s, Old Louisville has undergone an impressive renaissance, but it is still one of the best-kept secrets around. About 20,000 people,

## Your Base for Exploring Old Louisville

### Visitor Center in Historic Old Louisville
218 West Oak St.
(502) 637-2922
www.oldlouisville.org

Near the intersection of Third and Oak Streets you'll find the visitor center in Historic Old Louisville. Staffed by friendly volunteers, the small office provides information about area attractions, annual events, restaurants, and bed-and-breakfasts. This is also where you can arrange for a guided tour to help you discover the neighborhood's colorful past. There are walking history and architecture tours during the day, and at night guided bus tours explore the haunted heyday of the district. In addition, for a suggested $2 donation, you can pick up self-guided walking-tour brochures that outline five different routes to help you traverse the neighborhood.

representing a wide spectrum of ages, incomes, races, and lifestyles, make Old Louisville their home today. This diversity, as well as the beautiful, turn-of-the-20th-century homes and friendly residents, makes Old Louisville an exciting place to live, work, and play. Whether you're coming to this part of town for a romantic stroll or a guided history tour, or if you're here for one of the many neighborhood events, you're likely to leave impressed with Old Louisville. Who knows? Maybe you'll come back for good.

**CONRAD-CALDWELL HOUSE MUSEUM**
**1402 St. James Court**
**(502) 636-5023**
**www.conradcaldwell.org**

Located at the northwest corner of scenic St. James Court, the Conrad-Caldwell House is a must for old home aficionados and lovers of Victoriana. An opulent masterpiece in stone, the Richardsonian Romanesque structure was built between 1892 and 1895 according to plans by renowned Louisville architect Arthur Loomis. The house was built for Theophilus Conrad, an Alsatian immigrant who made his fortune in the leather tanning business, and the original construction price was $75,000. After he died, the residence was occupied by the Caldwells, the family who would figure prominently in the home's current interior decor. Walk around its three floors today and enjoy gargoyles, swags, massive arches, and fleurs-de-lis, just to name a few of the details. Open Wednesday through Sunday till 4 p.m., the mansion charges $7 a person for tours.

### CRANE HOUSE
**1244 South Third St.**
**(502) 635-2240**
**www.cranehouse.org**

The Crane House opened in 1987 in Old Louisville in an attempt to provide a focal point for those interested in the history, culture, food, and language of China; however, it soon expanded to include all of East Asia. Today it has a library with thousands of holdings, and regular exhibits feature Asian art and historical artifacts. Educational programs include topics such as Chinese cooking, tai chi, origami, and language classes in Mandarin and Japanese. The facility is staffed from 9 a.m. until 5 p.m. Monday through Friday, and they are open to the public for programs and for the Asia Experience, which involves a tour of the Crane House, including the Asia Gallery; a brief history of the Crane House; and an introduction to the ritual of Chinese tea and tea drinking. The Asia Experience is free, but reservations are required.

**i** Locals, especially those who reside in the suburbs, will often refer to Old Louisville as "downtown" although it is its own separate neighborhood and is situated directly south of Louisville's city center.

# (◉) Close-up

## Discover Old Louisville on Your Own

In addition to walking-tour brochures that will get you around the neighborhood, the Visitor Center in Historic Old Louisville at 218 West Oak Street has useful information about regular year-round guided walking and driving tours of the neighborhood. If, however, you find yourself in Old Louisville when the visitor center is closed, don't worry; you can still explore the neighborhood on your own. Park your car at the visitor center or else around the corner on the 1200 block of South Third Street and start walking south. In a block or two, you'll enter the residential core of the neighborhood.

This stretch of Third Street was known as Millionaires Row back in the day, and you'll pass blocks and blocks of stone and brick homes and mansions that just can't be found in most parts of the country today. The architecture includes wonderful examples of Richardsonian Romanesque, Victorian Gothic, Chateauesque, Italianate and neoclassical structures, just to name a few of the styles. After several blocks of walking, turn right on Hill Street and proceed a block to Fourth Street, where you'll cross the street and turn right again. On the left-hand side of the street, just past the fifth house, you'll spy the gate to Belgravia Court, one of Old Louisville's famed, gas-lit walking courts. Turn left and enter this charming pedestrian area lined with shade trees and quaint townhomes; enjoy the two-block stroll to the center of St. James Court, where you'll find the aptly named Pink Palace. This is the heart of the neighborhood, the site of the famous Southern Exposition of the 1880s, and during its heyday in the 1920s and '30s, this was the place where many of the city's movers and shakers, artists and intellectuals made their home.

Continue your exploration of the neighborhood by walking north, with the Pink Palace at your back, to the opposite end of St. James Court. Central Park will be in front of you, and to the left you'll spy the crown jewel of Old Louisville architecture, the opulent Conrad-Caldwell House, which was completed around 1895. If the house is open, ring the bell and take a tour; it's worth the $7. If not, enter the park and stroll to the northwest corner, the corner of Sixth and Park. At Park, turn left and go down half a block, where you'll see an entrance to an alley on the right. Enter this alley and walk half a block to its center; on the left you'll see one of the hidden gems of Old Louisville, another walking court known as Floral Terrace. Built on the former site of the Dumesnil Botanical Gardens, the residents who built their homes here in the early 1900s have kept the floral motif going, and during the early spring, it's alive with dogwood blossoms and vibrant azalea bushes. To exit, turn right and follow the walkway to the main entrance on Sixth Street.

On Sixth Street, turn left and proceed to the corner with Ormsby Avenue; turn right and walk to the east. Along the way you'll pass some of the oldest and largest homes in the neighborhood. If you're looking for a bite to eat, pop in at Amici, a nice Italian restaurant on the right side of the street between Fourth and Third. They have a brick patio that's pleasant in the summer. Turn left at Second Street and go north for one block; at the corner with Oak Street, turn right, and in half a block you'll be back where you started. The walk takes about an hour, and it's a good way to see many of the neighborhood highlights.

For a different route that includes the same sights, check out the map for the Old Louisville Walking Tour on page xii.

## ILSON HISTORICAL SOCIETY
**1310 South Third St.**
**(502) 635-5083**
**www.filsonhistorical.org**
Founded on May 15, 1884, the Filson arose as the brainchild of 10 Louisvillians' common love of history. It was named in honor of John Filson, Kentucky's first historian, whose book, *The Discovery, Settlement, and Present State of Kentucke*, was published in 1784. The first president and primary founder was Reuben T. Durrett, and to honor Filson and the centennial of his historical publication, the organization was christened The Filson Club. From that small gathering of amateur historians in Durrett's home, the institution evolved into the state's premier privately supported historical society. Thousands visit annually to conduct research, attend programs, and tour the headquarters building, the Ferguson Mansion. Completed in 1905 at a cost of $100,000, the former residence of Edwin Hite Ferguson counts as a stunning example of Beaux Arts architecture. Open Monday through Friday from 9 a.m. to 5 p.m., the Filson welcomes visitors to stop by and learn about membership opportunities or to tour the breathtaking interiors of the first floor.

## FILSON MUSEUM
**1310 South Third St.**
**(502) 635-5083**
**www.filsonhistorical.org**
Located in the ornate carriage house behind the Ferguson Mansion, the Filson's small museum offers a self-guided tour through the rich and varied history of the Bluegrass State. Currently on display are artifacts from the pioneer, antebellum, Civil War, and postbellum periods of Kentucky's history, and they include "Kentucky Giant" Jim Porter's 7-foot-9-inch smoothbore musket, a genuine Kentucky moonshine still, Daniel Boone's legendary "Kill a Bar" tree carving, handmade quilts, a mid-19th-century firefighting hand-pumper, and Civil War uniforms, weapons, and accoutrements. The Filson also has an art collection, which is displayed throughout the Ferguson Mansion and in the museum; it contains one of the most extensive collections of antebellum portraiture in Kentucky. The museum is free and open to the public Monday to Friday, 10 a.m. to 4 p.m.

## NATIONAL SOCIETY OF THE SONS OF THE AMERICAN REVOLUTION MUSEUM
**1000 South Fourth St.**
**(502) 589-1776**
**www.sar.org/About/Museum**
The leading male lineage society in this country, the Sons of the American Revolution is an organization that perpetuates the ideals of the war for independence. Each member has traced his family tree back to a point where an ancestor supported the cause of American Independence during the period from 1774 to 1783. It is a nonprofit historical, educational, and patriotic corporation that strives to maintain and expand the values of patriotism and American citizenship, as well as increase respect for national symbols. The Society is headquartered on Fourth Street in Old Louisville, and their offices feature several galleries with original art and reproductions that commemorate important individuals and events associated with the Revolutionary War. Artifacts such as uniforms, flags, and documents are on display as well. Visitation is free.

## RAUCH PLANETARIUM
**108 West Brandeis Ave.**
**(502) 852-6664**
**www.louisville.edu/planetarium**
Located on the University of Louisville's main Belknap campus, the Rauch Planetarium allows you to tour the universe without ever leaving Louisville. Schoolchildren and adults alike enjoy informative shows on the planets, stellar constellations, and other astronomical wonders. A popular demonstration involves the "Skies over Louisville" and reflects the seasonal changes to show what stars and planets are currently floating in the night skies above the Derby City. A hit with amateur astronomers, these sessions permit audience members to ask questions and participate. Apart from standard astronomical fare, the Rauch Planetarium also presents a spectacular nighttime laser light show with a monthly

audiovisual experience that pairs pop songs in surround sound with lovely patterns and colors on the dome. Public hours are Friday from 8 p.m. to midnight, and Saturday from 11 a.m. to 2 p.m. General admission for planetarium programs and laser concerts is $7 for adults ages 13 to 60, and $5 for seniors and children under 13.

### SPALDING MANSION
**851 South Fourth St.**
**(502) 585-9911**
**www.spalding.edu**

When Spalding University opened in 1920, its sole structure was a beautiful mansion from 1871 known as the Tompkins-Buchanan-Rankin House. Prominent architect Henry Whitestone designed the Italianate building for the family of Joseph T. Tompkins, a wealthy dry-goods merchant and importer. Later, the Buchanans and Rankins lived here; George C. Buchanan, a distiller, had it redecorated in 1880 in hopes of making the mansion one of the most elegant in all of Louisville. Today, details such as a radiant stained-glass skylight, hand-tooled leather ceilings from Florence, ebony mantels, Viennese etched-glass doors, and brass chandeliers make the former residence a veritable museum.

Although the mansion is open to the public for free self-guided tours when the University of Louisville is in session, it can be tricky to find. That's because when the school completed their administration building in the 1940s, they erected it across the façade of the beautiful old mansion. The façade of this structure has disappeared, but the north and south sides of the original building are still visible; on the north are three deeply projecting bay windows, and on the south, a two-story loggia. The elegant drawing rooms of the mansion are gathering places for students and are used for official receptions; however, the mansion is very often empty and waiting for explorers. Use the side entrance to the north.

### SPEED ART MUSEUM
**2035 South Third St.**
**(502) 634-2700**
**www.speedmuseum.org**

## Old Louisville in Literature

A number of famous authors have called Old Louisville home and have immortalized this lovely Victorian neighborhood in their pages. One of the most famous was Alice Hegan Rice, who lived at 1444 St. James Court with her successful poet husband, Cale Young Rice. Her bestselling novel from 1901, *Mrs. Wiggs of the Cabbage Patch,* provided insightful social commentary on residents of the "Cabbage Patch" area located several blocks to the west. It was made into a play which opened in 1903 at the Macauley Theater, and a movie version was released in 1934, starring Pauline Lord and W. C. Fields.

Another famous writer was Annie Fellows Johnston, an Indiana native who spent a long time in the Louisville area. Her *Little Colonel* series, the first of which came out in the 1890s, was a highly influential and widely read series of books for young readers. Millions of copies were sold and translated into 40 languages. Much of the action centered around the Pewee Valley area to the east of Louisville; however, she used real people and actual places, such as today's Old Louisville, in the weaving of her tales. Two of her most noted characters were the *Two Little Knights of Kentucky,* who lived at 1432 South Third Street. The first book in the series, *The Little Colonel,* was made into a movie in 1935, starring Shirley Temple and Lionel Barrymore. For more information about other writers from Old Louisville, visit the informative Web site at www .oldlouisville.com/Literature.

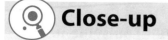 # Close-up

## Haunted Hometown

Abandoned tuberculosis hospitals, spooky Victorian mansions, scary mortuaries and morgues—Louisville provides a number of spine-tingling opportunities to explore its haunted past year-round. There are haunted tours of Old Louisville, "America's Spookiest Neighborhood," and attractions in other parts of town as well.

For updates about the ghosts, mysterious creatures, UFOs, odd characters, and other things that make Kentucky such an unusual state, check out the Unusual Kentucky blog at http://unusualkentucky.blogspot.com. Jason Scott Holland, local artist and author, gives regular informative and entertaining reports about the state's dark and wacky side.

### GHOSTS OF OLD LOUISVILLE TOUR

This guided bus tour explores the history, haunts, and heyday of Old Louisville, what many are calling "America's Grandest Neighborhood." Regular tours depart year-round at 7:30 on Friday nights from the Visitor Center in Historic Old Louisville at 218 West Oak Street. Private tours can be arranged as well. Reservations are required for the 90-minute jaunt, which includes a sweet treat and entrance into at least one Old Louisville mansion. Oh, and don't be surprised if a local ghost pops in to tell you a story. The price is $25 per person, and your spot can be reserved by calling (502) 637-2922. Go to www.louisvillehistorictours.com to find out more about this tour, which received a GEMmy Award from the Midwestern Travel Writers' Association for being a "gem" of regional tourist attractions.

### LOUISVILLE GHOST WALKS

Robert Parker, aka Mr. Ghost Walker, leads 90-minute walking tours of downtown Louisville that normally leave at 7:30 p.m. from the first-floor lobby of the Brown Hotel at the corner of Fourth and Broadway. Stories and stops include haunted sites like the Brown Hotel, the Brennan House, the Louisville Palace, the Seelbach Hilton, and more. The cost of the tour is $15 for adults and $5 for children. Reservations are required for all tours. Special private tours may also be arranged by reservation. Call Mr. Ghost Walker today at (502) 689-5117, or e-mail him at LouGhstWalks@aol.com for the current schedule. Parker, the author of *Haunted Louisville*, also offers haunted pub walks.

### MOONSHINE AND MADNESS TOUR

This popular bus tour departs the visitor center in Historic Old Louisville Saturday nights at 7:30 p.m. Sit back as a knowledgeable guide shares ghostly tales from Old Louisville's glory days in the early 1900s, when bootleggers and moonshiners roamed the neighborhood and gangsters hid out from the police. It was a "spirited" time, to say the least, and a phantom or two has been known to haunts the streets of Old Louisville in search of a friendly ear. Go to www.louisvillehistorictours.com to find out more about this tour, which includes a sneak peek inside a reportedly haunted house and a sampling of Happy Balls, the local bourbon candy. Your spot can be reserved by calling (502) 637-2922; the price is $25 per person.

Established in 1927 by Hattie Bishop Speed as a memorial to her late husband, the Speed Art Museum is Kentucky's oldest and largest art museum. Located next to the University of Louisville's Belknap Campus, the museum serves more than 180,000 visitors annually. More than 13,000 pieces make up its permanent collection, an extensive compilation that spans 6,000 years and ranges from ancient Egyptian to contemporary art. On display are a variety of paintings, sculpture, furniture, and decorative arts created for Kentuckians by Kentucky artists. The museum

## BAXTER AVENUE MORGUE

Housed in the basement of an eerie, 19th-century building at 451 Baxter Avenue, the Baxter Avenue Morgue has been rated as one of the best haunted houses in the nation by fans of *Haunted House*. Just blocks away from the city's main cemetery, the building was once home to the Vanderdark Morgue, a business that has a disturbing history in and of itself, and today its creepy past lends to the eeriness of the attraction. This haunted house is very graphic in nature, and parental discretion is advised, as it may be inappropriate for young guests. For prices and tour times at the Baxter Avenue Morgue, you can visit their Web site at www .baxtermorgue.com, or call (502) 589-0959.

## LOUISVILLE GHOST TOURS

Join a lantern-bearing guide in historic period attire for a leisurely stroll through the streets of the Derby City as you uncover dark mysteries and supernatural experiences at some of its most haunted landmarks. The 90-minute trek leaves nightly from the corner of Fourth and Liberty, and stops include the Seelbach Hilton, the Brown Hotel, and the Louisville Palace. In addition to hearing tales from the dark side, participants also learn a lot about the city's fascinating history. Reservations are required, and tickets cost $15 per adult. Call (502) 339-5445 for reservations or more information, or send an e-mail to contact@louisvilleghosttours.com.

## WAVERLY HILLS

Long considered the holy grail of American haunted sites, this tuberculosis hospital from the 1920s has achieved cult status around the world. At the zenith of the disease's sway in this country, thousands died at this state-of-the-art facility perched atop a windy hill in Louisville's Shively neighborhood. Today, many of the former patients are rumored to haunt the halls, even though they officially vacated the premises many years ago. Private half-night and full-night ghost hunts and paranormal investigations can be arranged, and historical tours are offered as well. For the Halloween season, there's also a haunted house. For more information, call (502) 933-2142, or go online at www.therealwaverlyhills.com. The office is open Monday through Friday from 9 a.m. to 5 p.m. but closes daily from noon to 1 p.m. Since Waverly Hills is such a popular destination, it is very difficult to make reservations at the last minute. Tours and investigations are often arranged months—if not years—in advance.

## HILLCREST AVENUE

The residents of Hillcrest Avenue on the blocks between Brownsboro Road and Frankfort Avenue take Halloween very seriously. Every year in October, boxes and crates full of ghostly decorations start emerging from cellars, and garages are emptied of life-size ghouls and goblins as the neighborhood pulls out all the stops in anticipation of their favorite day of the year. By the time October 31 rolls around, practically all of the houses have gone over the top with infamously elaborate Halloween displays that attract thousands of trick-or-treaters and curious onlookers from around the city. The neighborhood has embraced the tradition to such an extent that the Halloween decorations are often included in the selling price when houses on Hillcrest Avenue are bought and sold.

also has distinguished collections of 17th-century Dutch and Flemish works; Renaissance and Baroque tapestries;18th-century French art; and significant holdings of contemporary American paintings and sculpture. Native American and African-American pieces constitute a grow- ing segment of the museum's collection. In keeping with its ambitious mission of bringing great art and people together, the museum has brought major exhibitions of painting, design, photography, and sculpture to the region since undergoing a major $12 million renovation and expansion in 1997. Open daily except Monday, the Speed doesn't charge admission to view its permanent collection. Free tours of the "Best of the Collection" are available every weekend and when the museum is open late on Thursdays.

## OTHER PARTS OF TOWN

### CAVE HILL CEMETERY
**701 Baxter Ave.**
**(502) 451-5630**
**www.cavehillcemetery.com**
Established in 1848, Louisville's Cave Hill Cemetery has emerged as one of the premier historical cemeteries in the nation—not to mention as one of its most beautiful. Nestled behind brick walls near the scenic Cherokee Triangle neighborhood, some 300 acres of rolling, manicured grounds with ponds and pathways are home to beautiful mausoleums and funerary sculptures that memorialize 120,000 Louisvillians resting there. It's also an arboretum with hundreds of types of trees and shrubs that make for a beautiful and peaceful stroll. In addition to a list of the famous people buried there, the useful Web site has information about guided walking tours and special weekend events. If you're on your own and want to pay your respects to the Cave Hill's most famous resident, go the newer part of the cemetery and find the yellow line; it will lead you to the grave of Colonel Harlan Sanders.

### FARMINGTON HISTORIC PLANTATION
**3033 Bardstown Rd.**
**(502) 452-9920**
**www.historichomes.org/farmington**
Built between 1815 and 1816 for John and Lucy Fry Speed, both of whom came from wealthy Virginia families that moved to Kentucky in the late 1700s, Farmington is one of three historic home museums operated by Louisville's Historic Homes Foundation. The primary cash crop at Farmington, hemp, was used to make rope and rough bagging for the cotton trade, and the museum strives to show visitors a slice of life as it would have been lived by a gentleman farmer in early Kentucky. Abraham Lincoln, a close friend

of Joshua Speed, spent time here in 1841. Open for tours ($9) Tuesday through Saturday from 10 a.m. to 4 p.m.

### JEFFERSONTOWN HISTORICAL MUSEUM
**10635 Watterson Trail**
**(502) 261-8290**
**www.jeffersontownky.com**
Open Monday through Friday from 10 a.m. to 5 p.m., the Jeffersontown Historical Museum is located at the rear of the Jeffersontown branch of the Louisville Free Public Library. A modest space features exhibits and artifacts shedding light on the town's past, and on display is one of the largest doll collections in the Midwest. The Dolls of the World collection has 1,250 costumed dolls representing the dress and culture of peoples from across the globe.

### JOSEPH A. CALLAWAY ARCHAEOLOGICAL MUSEUM
**2825 Lexington Rd.**
**(800) 626-5525**
On the campus of the Southern Baptist Theological Seminary near Seneca Park, you'll find the Joseph A. Callaway Archaeological Museum. This small museum houses the Nicol Collection of Biblical Archaeology and the Eisenberg Collection of Egyptian and Near Eastern Antiquities. There is also an art gallery with rotating exhibits of a religious nature. Visitation is free, but the museum is closed on Sunday.

### LITTLE LOOM HOUSE
**328 Kenwood Hill Rd.**
**(502) 367-4792**
**www.littleloomhouse.org**
Staffed completely by volunteers, the Little Loom House is open for tours (at a cost of $3.50) on Tuesday, Wednesday, and the third Saturday of each month from 10 a.m. to 3 p.m., or by appointment. Three historic board and batten cabins from the 1800s, set on wooded grounds that were once home to renowned textile artist Lou Tate, serve as a cultural destination and education center for the preservation of the folk art of weaving. In addition to a coverlet collection,

weaving center, and exhibition, looms and spinning wheels are also on display.

## LOUISVILLE NATURE CENTER
**3745 Illinois Ave.**
**(502) 458-1328**
**www.louisvillenaturecenter.org**
Located right in the heart of the city, the Louisville Nature Center offers wonderful opportunities for nature study and recreation. Among the unique features are a pond and native wildflower garden, hiking trails through the Beargrass Creek State Nature Preserve, butterfly gardens, and wildlife exhibits. In addition to a watershed exhibit, there is a one-of-a-kind bird blind. You'll also find a library that provides a great place to do research and spend some time indoors when the weather is uncooperative.

## MUSEUM OF THE AMERICAN PRINTING HOUSE FOR THE BLIND
**1839 Frankfort Ave.**
**(502) 895-2405**
**www.aph.org**
The American Printing House for the Blind offers free tours of its factory Monday through Thursday from 10 a.m. to 2 p.m. Visitors witness the production of Braille publications, the recording of talking books, and a demonstration of special educational aids for visually impaired students. In addition, there is no admission charge to enter the museum, which is open Monday through Saturday. Full of hands-on discovery, the Marie and Eugene Callahan Gallery explores the history of education for the blind in a fun and accessible setting. Visitors are encouraged to touch objects and increase their understanding of how people with visual impairments experience the world. In addition to wrapping your arms around a floor-model tactile globe, you can also write your name using a mechanical Braille writer, and test your comprehension skills on computers equipped with talking software.

## PORTLAND MUSEUM
**2308 Portland Ave.**
**(502) 776-7678**
**www.goportland.org**

Louisville's river heritage is explored at the Portland Museum through vivid dioramas, life-size character mannequins, automated soundtracks, documentaries, and more. Housed in an 1852 Italianate mansion with a modern addition, the museum also uses long-term and temporary exhibits to tell the story of Portland, a historically rich neighborhood in Louisville that began as its own riverfront town. A popular draw is Captain Mary Millicent Miller, who tells how she became "a lady steamboat man," the first woman licensed as a steamboat master in America. Open Tuesday through Friday from 10 a.m. to 4:30 p.m., the Portland Museum charges $7 for general admission.

## RIVERSIDE, FARNSLEY MOREMEN LANDING
**7410 Moorman Rd.**
**(502) 935-6809**
**www.riverside-landing.org**
Perched atop a gentle rise overlooking the Ohio River just 13 miles from downtown Louisville, the Farnsley-Moremen House is the centerpiece of a 300-acre historic site called Riverside, the Farnsley-Moremen Landing. Aside from touring the impressive two-story brick "I" house with its full-height Greek Revival portico that was built in the 1830s, visitors can stroll the grounds. There they'll find the reconstructed 19th-century detached kitchen, seasonal ongoing archaeological excavations, and a kitchen garden where volunteers grow many of the same vegetables and herbs that would have been consumed during the period. Farnsley-Moremen is open every day but Monday for tours, and general admission is $6.

## WHITEHALL HOUSE AND GARDENS
**3110 Lexington Rd.**
**(502) 897-2944**
**www.historichomes.org/whitehall**
Part of Louisville's Historic Homes Foundation, Whitehall is a southern-style Greek Revival mansion that was built around 1855. A major drawing point, the grounds of the estate feature a lush variety of gardens, including the Entrance Garden, the Ralph Archer Woodland Garden, Annie's Garden, and the Formal Garden. The memory of those who lived at Whitehall and had

# Fort Knox Area

Distinguished for its notable past and less than an hour's drive from downtown Louisville, the Fort Knox area is home to many points of interest, including the world-famous Gold Vault, which stores 100 billion dollars worth of bullion. Although that particular sight is not open to the public, you should have no trouble getting into places like Armor Unit Memorial Park and Saunders Springs Nature Preserve. In the historic town of West Point you will find Tioga Falls, Bridges to the Past, Music Ranch USA, and Fort Duffield, the best-preserved earthen Civil War Fort in the country. The Schmidt Museum of Coca-Cola Memorabilia, the Hardin County History Museum and Swope's Cars of Yesteryear Museum can be found in nearby Elizabethtown, the namesake for the 2005 movie starring Kirsten Dunst, Orlando Bloom, and Susan Sarandon. Most of the attractions in the Fort Knox area are free, but go on-line at www.radcliff tourism.org for details or www.westpointky.org/tourism for more information.

Two of the most popular stops for visitors to the Fort Knox area are:

## Patton Museum
Fort Knox
(502) 624-3812
www.knox.army.mil/PattonMuseum

Located just 35 miles from Louisville, Fort Knox is home to the Army Armor Center and the U.S. Army Recruiting Command. The base encompasses 109,000 acres spread out over three Kentucky counties, and it has a population of over 23,000 soldiers, family members, and civilians. The main attraction at Fort Knox is the Patton Museum of Armor and Cavalry, which was established in 1949 to preserve historical artifacts and archival materials relating to mechanized cavalry and armor. On display are Patton's trademark ivory-gripped Colt pistol and the Cadillac staff car in which he was fatally injured. There is no fee for entrance, but donations are accepted. Fort Knox also has an unusually high number of German restaurants catering to the tastes of American military personnel who have spent time in Germany.

## Star Cafe
401 South Street
West Point
(502) 922-4414
www.wpstarcafe.com

In the sleepy hamlet of West Point, sample the whistle stop fare at one of the few remaining railroad hotels in the country. The decline in rail travel caused the eventual demise of the town's lodging business, but the dining room at the old West Point Hotel is alive and well today. Although guests can choose from a selection of salads and sandwich standards, most opt for the old-fashioned daily plate special ($7.50), which consists of an entrée item with two sides, and a homemade yeast roll or cornbread. Everyday entrées include roast beef, pork tenderloin, meat loaf, and fish on Fridays and chicken on Sundays. There are sides such as stewed tomatoes, pickled beets, green beans, mashed potatoes and pinto beans, and for dessert patrons can select almond pound cake with strawberries, German chocolate cake, buttermilk pie and banana cake with caramel icing, just to name a few. The Star Cafe is open Thursday, Friday, Saturday and Sunday.

a special affection for its grounds is kept alive in the well-tended gardens. Open Monday through Friday, the antebellum house welcomes visitors for guided tours from 10 a.m. to 2 p.m. General admission is $5.

# ACROSS THE RIVER

### CARNEGIE CENTER FOR ART AND HISTORY
**201 East Spring St.**
**New Albany, IN**
**(812) 944-7336**
**www.carnegiecenter.org**
Housed in an attractive turn-of-the-20th-century Carnegie library, the Carnegie Center for Art and History showcases local history and contemporary art today. Visitors are offered the opportunity to enjoy artworks in a variety of media and to learn more about the process of creative expression through a range of changing exhibitions and programs. The Carnegie Center is home to permanent history exhibits as well, and a favorite among visitors of all ages is *Grandpa Makes a Scene: The Yenawine Dioramas*. This collection of mechanized, hand-carved dioramas is based on creator Merle Yenawine's childhood memories from the rural community of Georgetown, Indiana, at the turn of the last century. Viewers enjoy the intricately detailed and often humorous scenes of the one-room schoolhouse, town carnival, and more. The Carnegie Center also hosts an annual fiber exhibition, *Form Not Function: Quilt Art at the Carnegie*, a juried event that explores the world of contemporary art quilts and features the work of fiber artists from across the United States. Hours are Tuesday through Saturday from 10 a.m. to 5:30 p.m. and admission is always free.

### CULBERTSON MANSION
**914 East Main St.**
**New Albany, IN**
**(812) 944-9600**
**www.indianamuseum.org/sites/culb.html**
With its carved rosewood staircase, marble fireplaces, hand-painted ceilings, and ornate crystal chandeliers, the Culbertson Mansion reflects the affluence of its namesake, William Stewart Culbertson, a man once considered Indiana's wealthiest. He spent about $120,000 to build the grand three-story French Second Empire mansion, which encompasses more than 20,000 square feet and contains 25 rooms. Aside from depicting the lifestyles of the upper-crust Victorians who lived there, the Culbertson Mansion shows how servants lived as well. Visitors may view the grand parlors, dining rooms, bedrooms, kitchen, and laundry room from April through December. Hours are Tuesday to Saturday, 9 a.m. to 5 p.m. and Sunday from 1 p.m. to 5 p.m. Admission for adults is $3.50 and $2 for children 4 to 11. Children under 3 are free.

### FALLS OF THE OHIO STATE PARK
**201 West Riverside Dr.**
**Clarksville, IN**
**(812) 280-9970**
**www.fallsoftheohio.org**
Right across the river from downtown Louisville are some of the largest naturally exposed Devonian fossil beds in the world. A park—located on the banks of the Ohio in Clarksville, Indiana, at exit 0, the very first exit as you cross the bridge off I-65—lets visitors explore the 386-million-year-old fossil beds, and an impressive interpretive center overlooking the fossil beds contains an exhibit gallery and informative video presentation. The interpretive center is open year-round, and the hours are Monday through Saturday, 9 a.m. to 5 p.m., and Sunday from 1 p.m. to 5 p.m. Admission is $5 on Friday, Saturday, and Sunday, and $4 for the other days. The state park is open seven days a week, 7 a.m. to 11 p.m.

### HORSESHOE SOUTHERN INDIANA
**11999 Casino Center Dr.**
**Elizabeth, IN**
**(866) 676-SHOE**
**www.horseshoe-indiana.com**
In addition to four floors of nonstop gaming, the Horseshoe Casino and Hotel in southern Indiana has a stage featuring top-of-the-line musical and comedy acts, as well as shopping and golf. There's also fine dining and casual fare available.

# Close-up

## Kidstuff

### HENRY'S ARK

You'll find Henry's Ark on a 600-acre farm in Prospect (7801 Rose Island Rd., Prospect; 502-228-0746). It's a private zoo that is home to more than 100 animals, and it is not unusual to find the animals roaming freely among the visitors. Henry Wallace, a former correspondent for *Time* magazine and several major newspapers, opened the family's private farm to the public some 15 years ago, and since then it's become a favorite with kids of all ages (adults, too). Henry's Ark is a not-for-profit 501(c)3 corporation and charges no admission fees, although they do accept donations. Visitors are also encouraged to bring food (carrots) to feed the animals. Open daily.

### HOLIDAY WORLD & SPLASHIN' SAFARI

Less than an hour west of Louisville, just off of I-64 in southern Indiana, is Holiday World (452 East Christmas Blvd.; Santa Claus, IN; 812-937-4401; www.holidayworld.com), one of the cleanest amusement parks in the nation. Celebrating Christmas, Halloween, Thanksgiving, and the Fourth of July, it has a variety of thrill rides, live entertainment, games, and attractions. Known for its wooden roller coasters—the Raven, the Legend, and the Voyage are especially popular with coaster enthusiasts—Holiday World opened in August of 1946, nine years before Disneyland. Today it is still a family-owned and -operated business. A popular attraction in the summer months is the Wildebeest, the world's longest water coaster. It's 0.3 mile of wild and watery uphills, drops, twists, and turns that begins with a ride up a conveyor lift and down a four-story drop at a 45-degree angle. Free soft drinks are a big hit with kids. General admission for one day is $41.95; children under two are free. The operating season runs from May to October.

### LOUISVILLE EXTREME PARK

Owned by Louisville Metro Government and operated by Metro Parks, the Louisville Extreme Park (East Witherspoon & North Clay St.; 502-456-8100; www.louisvilleextremepark.org) is considered one of the best skate parks in the nation. The space offers a great balance of street style and transition, and impressive features include a 24-foot full-pipe. In addition to 40,000 square feet of outdoor concrete skating surfaces and a wooden vert ramp, there are restrooms and lots of opportunities for bikers and in-line skaters of all ages. Centrally located downtown near Waterfront Park and Slugger Field, the skate park is accessible from all parts of the community—by bus, car, or by self-powered means via the RiverWalk and connecting multiuse paths. Free of charge, the park is open 6 a.m. to 11 p.m., seven days a week.

### LOUISVILLE SCIENCE CENTER

The region's leading resource for informal science education, the Louisville Science Center (727 West Main St.; 502-561-6100; www.louisvillescience.org) has come a long way since its founding as a "cabinet of curiosities in the Public Library System of Kentucky" in 1871. Now it's the largest hands-on science center in the state, an informative place with a four-story IMAX Theatre, 150 interactive exhibits and activity stations, teaching laboratories, a variety of educational programs, and distance-learning capabilities. A popular draw is the World We Create, a 12,500-square-foot permanent exhibit that lets visitors make use of their creative and problem-solving skills. There are more than 40 activity stations dealing with telecommunications, chemistry, physics, engineering, and manufacturing that encourage visitors to discover how technology, math, and the sciences affect our everyday lives. Another favorite is KidZone, the special hands-on space for children younger than age seven. Six activity areas allow children to explore the world brought down to their size. Entrance to the exhibition is every half-hour, starting at 9:30 a.m. daily, with the last admission one hour before closing.

## LOUISVILLE ZOO

The Louisville Zoo (1100 Trevilian Way; 502-459-2181; www.louisvillezoo.org) features exhibits with over 1,300 animals in naturalistic and mixed animal settings that represent both geographical areas and habitats. Included are the Asian Plains, the Islands, the African Veldt, North and South American Panorama, Aquatics, and the Australian Outback. The new four-acre Gorilla Forest Exhibit displays pygmy hippos and western lowland gorillas, and at the HerpAquarium, visitors can view 100 species of fish, reptiles, and amphibians exhibited amid ecologically balanced habitats from around the world. Admission rates are generally $11.95 for adults (12 and older) and $8.95 for children, but a Louisville Zoo membership gives you a full year of excitement and adventure that includes unlimited free admission to the Zoo during regular hours. Membership is $45 for individuals or $75 for families. The zoo is open daily year-round.

## RAY'S MONKEY HOUSE

In the Highlands children are always welcome at Ray's Monkey House and Kid Cafe (1578 Bardstown Rd.; 502-459-4373; www.raysmonkeyhouse.com). In addition to top-quality coffee and organic food and beverage items, there are also special kids' drinks like hot chocolate and milk steamers. The funky hangout in the Deer Park neighborhood is also a community gathering place with a focus on progressive issues such as sustainability, environmental responsibility, and social justice. Pictures of Cindy Sheehan, Hugo Chavez, and the Dalai Lama are some of the images you'll see hanging on the walls in this retro-hippy hotspot. In addition to outdoor seating, there are children's play areas and performance space for artists.

## SCHIMPFF'S CONFECTIONERY

Kids of all ages love to visit this region's oldest family-owned candy business, which has been delighting generations at its present downtown Jeffersonville location since 1891 (347 Spring St.; Jeffersonville; 812-283-8367; www.schimpffs.com). Live candy-making demonstrations are given, and the free Candy Museum offers a glimpse into the world of historic candy making, packaging, and advertising. Aside from its caramel and marshmallow modjeskas, Schimpff's is famous for its cinnamon red hots and hard candy fish; it's always a popular stop for kids and the young at heart. Open Monday through Saturday, Schimpff's also serves lunch at an old-fashioned soda fountain.

## STAGE ONE

Now in its seventh decade of existence, Louisville's nationally acclaimed professional theater for young audiences is dedicated to bringing the finest-quality theater to young people, teachers, and families. With a highly respected reputation among its contemporaries, the 501(c)3 nonprofit theater company has received numerous awards and commendations, including those from the American Alliance for Theatre & Education. Stage One also offers pre- and post-show discussions with the cast and crew, giving viewers a firsthand look into the life of a play as it is transformed from script to stage. (Located at 501 West Main St.; 502-625-0660; www.stageone.org.)

## WALDEN THEATRE

Started in an old log cabin in eastern Jefferson County in 1976 as a way to provide young people with the opportunity to grow and develop through the comprehensive study of theater, the Walden Theatre (1123 Payne St.; 502-589-0084; www.waldentheatre.org) has since taken up headquarters in the former St. Aloysius School in the Irish Hill neighborhood. The theater also operates a conservatory program, and those young actors regularly appear in the season productions. Adult tickets for evening performances generally cost $15. In addition to works by Shakespeare, productions during a typical season will include plays such as *The Crucible* and *Of Mice and Men*.

## HOWARD STEAMBOAT MUSEUM
**1101 East Market St.**
**Jeffersonville, IN**
**(812) 283-3728**
**www.steamboatmuseum.org**
A tour of the beautiful 1894 Howard mansion lets visitors step back in time and get a taste of the era of the great steamboat. Built by renowned steamboat builders, the Howards of Jeffersonville, the redbrick mansion features a grand staircase, original furnishings, brass chandeliers, stained-glass windows, and intricate carvings and details throughout. Master craftsmen from the shipyard fashioned much of the decor in the lavish residence, which is open year-round. Howard-built steamboats included the *City of Louisville* and the *Indiana,* in addition to the luxurious *J. M. White,* and models, photographs, paintings, and other artifacts from the period abound at this unique regional museum. Personal, informative tours are offered Tuesday through Saturday from 10 a.m. to 4 p.m. and Sunday from 1 p.m. to 4 p.m. Admission is $5 for adults; $4 for seniors and $3 for students. Accompanied children under 6 are free.

## SCHIMPFF'S CONFECTIONERY
**347 Spring St.**
**Jeffersonville, IN**
**(812) 283-8367**
**www.schimpffs.com**
One of the oldest continuously operated, family-owned candy businesses in the United States, Schimpff's Confectionery opened at its present downtown Jeffersonville location in 1891. Schimpff's is famous for its cinnamon red hots, hard candy fish, and modjeskas, and it's a popular stop for kids (and kids at heart) in search of a bit of nostalgia. Live candy-making demonstrations are given at the free Candy Museum, offering a glimpse into the world of historic candy making, packaging, and advertising. Open Monday through Saturday. Schimpff's also serves lunch at an old-fashioned soda fountain.

## SCRIBNER HOUSE
**East Main Street & Main**
**New Albany, IN**
**(812) 949-1776**
**www.countyhistory.com/scribnerhouse**
The oldest surviving structure in the town of New Albany, this early frame house was built in 1814 by New Yorker Joel Scribner, one of the city founders. He and his brothers, Abner and Nathaniel, named the settlement they established in honor of the capital of their home state. Although the house is not open on a regular basis—it opens for a Christmas tour in December and a National Preservation Week tour in May—tours can be arranged for small groups ($2 for adults; $1 for students).

# RESTAURANTS

Louisville has steadily gained notice as one of the country's most vital restaurant scenes. With several thousand restaurants, visitors from around the world are astounded by the variety and quality of fine dining offered in the area by chefs who have taken regional cuisine to a nationally recognized level. There are quiet cafes, coffeehouses, ethnic restaurants, bourbon lounges, casual eateries, and popular national chains, in addition to elegant five-diamond dining rooms and independently owned favorites. If you go hungry in Louisville, it's your own fault.

## INTRODUCTION TO THE LOCAL FLAVORS

Mainers have their Moxie, Texans have their Dr Pepper, and folks in the Bluegrass State have their Ale-8-One. Bottled in Winchester since 1926, the formula for this unique Kentucky soft drink developed by G. L. Wainscott is still a closely guarded family secret that traces its origins to northern Europe. Wainscott supposedly liked the ginger-based soft drinks he sampled during his many travels there and brought the inspiration back for a new soft drink. In need of a name for the new beverage, he sponsored one of the country's first "name-the-product" contests, and "A Late One" was chosen. The drink's logo, Ale-8-One, was adopted as a sort of pun for "the latest thing" in soft drinks. Most just refer to it as "Ale 8" (Pronounced "Ale-Eight") today.

Beer cheese, a central Kentucky specialty, is a tangy blend of sharp cheddar, beer, and spices that is most often served with crackers, celery ribs, and carrot sticks. Its prominence is owed to John Allman, the larger-than-life restaurateur who in the 1930s popularized the spicy snack at his legendary restaurant on the Kentucky River near Winchester. Different brands can be found at most supermarkets and specialty shops, but two of the most popular come from Kentucky Beer Cheese (www.kentuckybeercheese.com) and the restaurant that started it all, Hall's (www.hallsontheriver.com).

Benedictine is a cucumber and cream cheese spread invented by Louisville caterer and restaurateur Jennie Benedict in the late 1800s. A must at any holiday get-together in the Derby City, it most likely derived its inspiration from the delicate cucumber sandwiches served at English teas. Spread it on crackers, use it for dipping vegetables, make sandwiches out of it—Benedictine is a staple in many Louisville households.

The Blue Monday bar came about in 1921, when Kentucky native Ruth Hunt began selling the confections her friends and family had raved so much about from a small candy shop in her home. The business took off, and in 1930 she moved the store to its current location in Mt. Sterling. Her most famous product would be the Blue Monday bar, a sophisticated treat with a pulled cream candy center and dark chocolate coating. It has been produced for more than 60 years, ever since a traveling minister remarked that he needed a little sweet to get him through his "blue Mondays." Although it's more prevalent in eastern parts of the state, Blue Monday bars are common in specialty stores in the Derby City. Learn more about Ruth Hunt Candies at www.ruthhuntcandy.com.

Bourbon balls could be considered the unofficial state candy of the Bluegrass State. Although recipes and methods of preparation can vary, the standard bourbon ball consists of a chocolate coating around a butter cream center flavored with bourbon and chopped pecans. Often a whole pecan is placed on top to provide a bit of decoration. Most confectioners in the region make their own brand of bourbon balls, as do many of the major distilleries, but a Louisville favorite is the Happy Ball. Featuring the tastes of Guitard chocolate and nine-year-old Knob Creek bourbon, they're made by the Old Louisville Candy Company. You'll find more information at www.gethappyballs.com.

Burgoo is a thick, somewhat spicy soup that most likely has its roots in Irish or mulligan stew. Similar to the Brunswick stew of Georgia, burgoo arose from the need to make a hearty, filling soup using whatever meats and vegetables were available and in good supply. Early on, that meant venison, squirrel, opossum, and game birds—really anything the hunter managed to bring back—but nowadays most versions incorporate less-exotic meats such as chicken, mutton, or pork. Burgoo recipes in Kentucky are somewhat like chili recipes, in that there are many variations on the original, each calling for different sets of ingredients. Corn bread or muffins are served on the side, and burgoo is a fixture at many barbecues and Derby parties.

Something akin to a chocolate nut tart, the Derby Pie was invented in 1950 at the Melrose Inn in Prospect and is a registered trademark of Kern's Kitchen today. Kern's Kitchen diligently guards the trademark and secret recipe, which uses walnuts instead of pecans and is known only to a small group of people; the company has even filed several lawsuits over the years to protect its commercial rights. Because of this, others who make similar pies have had to alter their recipes slightly or come up with different names, such as May Day Pie, a reference to the First Saturday in May, the day of the Kentucky Derby. The original can be found in groceries and specialty shops year-round, but the most popular time of year is during—you guessed it—the Kentucky Derby. More information can be found at www.derbypie.com.

Henry Bain Sauce is a tangy, sweet-sour condiment invented by Henry Bain, the head waiter at the Pendennis Club in the 1880s, to complement the wild game brought in by customers.

In actuality nothing more than a tomato-based steak sauce, it was flavored with pickled walnuts and peaches, among other ingredients. Today, it's a mainstay of the traditional Derby lunch or dinner when it's served alongside slices of roasted beef tenderloin.

The hot brown is the brainchild of Louisville chef Fred K. Schmidt. When he used a holiday standard to construct an elegant sandwich to satisfy the appetites of late-night dancers in Louisville's elegant Brown Hotel in 1926, he probably never imagined that the comforting flavors of turkey, bacon, and cheese would one day evolve into the city's signature dish. Today, the open-faced sandwich can be found at restaurants throughout the region, but the most popular version is the original, still served at the Brown in downtown Louisville. If the original's not your thing, don't worry: one of the many variations that have sprung up is sure to please your palate. Vegetarian hot browns, seafood hot browns, Italian hot browns—you decide.

A mint julep is the quintessential beverage that can bring out a good southern drawl like no other. Long a symbol of Bluegrass gentility, it's been part of the local culture since the 1700s, and it is the only drink that comes to mind when talking about the Kentucky Derby. Concocted of bourbon, mint, sugar, and water, it's a potent libation that catches most first-timers off guard. Since fresh mint is an important ingredient, it's most often consumed in the spring and summer months; however, a number of brands, such as Early Times and Maker's Mark, have their own, premixed versions of the drink.

The modjeska got its start in 1883, when the eyes of the world were turned to Louisville, Kentucky, for the opening of the Great Southern Exposition. Helena Modjeska, the famed Polish actress who performed the lead role in Ibsen's *A Doll's House* at McCauley's Theater, inspired local confectioner Anton Busath to rename a delicious marshmallow specialty known as the caramel biscuit in her honor. Since then, modjeskas have delighted many a sweet tooth across the Bluegrass State with their billowy marshmallow centers draped in creamy caramel.

Rolled oysters were created in 1884 at Mazzoni's, when someone hand-rolled several raw oysters in an Italian batter known as *pastinga* and deep-fried them. Today, they're a staple at local bars and pubs. With a cold mug of the local microbrew, they can make a meal by themselves.

Smoked paddlefish is a new arrival on the Louisville food scene and came about when local tobacco farmers began turning to aquaculture as a way of making a living. One of the tastiest by-products has been the spoonfish, also known as the paddlefish or spoonbill catfish, and its firm, white flesh has become a favorite with seafood aficionados across the country. Lewis Shuckman of Louisville, a third-generation meat monger who operates the family business at his Main Street smokery in Louisville's West End, produces a wide variety of delicacies that embody the best Kentucky flavors. His smoked paddlefish has gained national recognition for its exceptional quality. Find out more at www.kysmokedfish.com.

Another of the delicacies that has resulted from the agricultural trend to diversify into aquaculture is spoonfish caviar, or paddlefish roe. A favorite with some of America's best chefs, spoonfish caviar has really taken off because of its uncommonly mild flavor and bright luscious berries. Caviar aficionados from Russia and Iran have even ranked it up there among the likes of the more-famous Sevruga varieties. Get more information at www.kysmokedfish.com.

### Price Code

This code represents the average price for two dinner entrees, exclusive of 6 percent tax, gratuity, or alcoholic beverages, appetizers, or dessert.

$....................$15 and under
$$..................$16 to $25
$$$................$26 to $50
$$$$..............More than $50

## DOWNTOWN / EAST MARKET

**BEARNO'S BY THE BRIDGE** $$
**131 West Main St.**
**(502) 584-7437**
**www.bearnospizza.net**

Although you'll find more than a dozen Bearno's pizza restaurants around town, this one, right next to the Second Street Bridge in the basement of the old L&N Railroad Building, seems to be a perennial favorite. It's been around since the 1970s, and readers of *Louisville Magazine* and the *Louisville Eccentric Observer (LEO)* frequently vote it the best pizzeria in town. A popular order is the Mama Bearno's Pizza for $24.99. It's a huge pie topped with lots of mozzarella cheese and then loaded with sausage, pepperoni, mushrooms, onions, green peppers, and olives.

**i** Every year in the middle of October, the Louisville Downtown Management District hosts Fleur De Licious, a week-long celebration of Louisville's downtown restaurants where diners can enjoy three-course meals at participating restaurants for $25 to $35 per person. This event provides a great opportunity for diners to sample the fare at some of Louisville's most upscale restaurants at very affordable prices. Participating can include local favorites such as Bistro 301, Blu, Morton's, Proof on Main, Vincenzo's, and White Oak Restaurant, among others. There are no passes or tickets to buy, so it's easy to participate; just show up at the restaurant of your choice and make your selection from the special prix fixe menu. Menus and lists of participating restaurants can be found online at www.fleurdelicious.info.

**BLU ITALIAN GRILLE** $$$
**280 West Jefferson St.**
**(502) 671-4285**
**www.blugrille.com**
Regional Italian classics with contemporary flair—otherwise known as "authentic Lou-Italian"—are on offer at this sleek and colorfully elegant restaurant in the Louisville Marriott Downtown. Popular lunch choices include items such as grilled panini and tomato and mozzarella salad; for dinner there are appetizers like mussels in sambuca broth and calamari fritti with red pepper aioli, and entrees including osso bucco and lamb chops with truffled

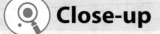 **Close-up**

## Bristol Bar & Grille

For more than 30 years, the Bristol Bar & Grille has been a Louisville culinary institution, with two generations of diners craving popular appetizers like the green chili wontons and arti- choke fritters with remoulade. Although some of the items, like the California club salad or the New York strip steak, are very American, the menu is slightly eclectic and reveals influences from Asia and the Southwest. Two standards from the main course section are the sweet chili linguine with Thai chili sauce and the Southwest chicken, a breast that is grilled and served with rice, black beans, and cilantro relish. Other entree favorites include the grilled pork loin with Dijon mustard sauce and skillet-fried potatoes and the Bristol burger, a grilled patty of fresh ground beef on an English muffin with lettuce, tomato, pickle, and onion. The Bristol is also the place to get a tasty version of the hot brown, as well as a taste of bison steak from the Kentucky Bison Company in nearby Goshen. For more information or to view menus from each of the locations, go online at www.bristolbarandgrille.com or see below.

cauliflower puree. For dessert you'll find standards like tiramisu, as well as new twists on old favorites. Think banana ravioli with caramel sauce.

**THE BRISTOL DOWNTOWN**          **$$**
**614 West Main St.**
**(502) 582-1995**
Situated in the historic downtown business dis- trict, this location is convenient to hotels, the- aters, museums, and more. Banquet rooms for up to 120 guests make it a popular choice for meetings and family get-togethers. Open Sun- day through Wednesday from 11 a.m. to 9 p.m.; Thursday, Friday, and Saturday from 11 a.m. to 10 p.m.; and Sunday from 11 a.m. to 2 p.m. for brunch, and for dinner from 2 p.m. to 9 p.m.

**THE BRISTOL EAST**          **$$**
**300 North Hurstbourne Pkwy.**
**(502) 426-0627**
Located in eastern Louisville along an oftentimes congested business corridor, the Bristol East is convenient to shopping malls. In addition to an attractive covered terrace, there is plentiful free parking. Brunch is offered Sunday from 10 a.m. to 2 p.m. and dinner from 2 p.m. to 10 p.m. Monday through Thursday they're open from 11 a.m. to 10 p.m. and on Friday and Saturday, they serve from 11 a.m. to 11 p.m.

**THE BRISTOL HIGHLANDS**          **$$**
**1321 Bardstown Rd.**
**(502) 456-1702**
Established in 1977, this is the original Bristol Bar & Grille. Located in the heart of the Highlands, this restaurant has private banquet rooms and a popular Sunday brunch. Hours of operation are Monday through Thursday from 11 a.m. to mid- night; Friday through Saturday from 11 a.m. to 2 a.m.; Sunday from 10 a.m. to 2:30 p.m. for brunch, and for dinner from 2:30 p.m. to midnight.

**THE BRISTOL JEFFERSONVILLE**          **$$**
**700 West Riverside Dr.**
**Jeffersonville, IN**
**(812) 218-1995**
This, the newest of the Bristol Bar & Grilles, offers some of the best views of the Louisville skyline. Serving breakfast, lunch, and dinner daily, the restaurant has banquet rooms seating up to 300 guests available through the Sheraton Hotel. Monday through Friday the hours of operation are 6:30 a.m. to midnight, with breakfast from 6:30 a.m. to 11 a.m. and the bar open until 1 a.m. Saturday the restaurant opens a half-hour later, but the rest of the day has the same hours. Sun- day hours are from 7 a.m. to 11 p.m., with break- fast from 7 a.m. to 10 a.m. and brunch from 10 a.m. to 2 p.m.; the bar stays open until midnight.

## THE BRISTOL PROSPECT $$
**6051 Timber Ridge Dr.**
**(502) 292-2585**
Located in the heart of Prospect, off Brownsboro Road (US 42), this location caters to the East End crowd. The atmosphere is light and airy, and there is a banquet room that seats up to 40 guests. Hours of operation are Sunday through Wednesday from 11 a.m. to 9 p.m., and Thursday, Friday, and Saturday from 11 a.m. to 10 p.m. Sunday brunch goes from 10 a.m. to 2 p.m.; dinner from 2 p.m. to 9 p.m.

## BROWNING'S BREWERY $$
**401 East Main St.**
**(502) 515-0174**
**http://browningsbrewery.com**
The legacy of Louisvillian and famed baseball player, Pete Browning, lives on at the restaurant bearing his name at Slugger Field in downtown Louisville. An on-site brewery sets this eatery apart from your run-of-the-mill ballpark eatery, however, and brewmasters concoct an ever-changing variety of beers and ales running the gamut from light to dark. Famed restaurateur Anoosh Shariat has designed a menu that brings Bluegrass flair to a classic pub setting, paying homage to America's pastime with an assortment of salads, sandwiches, appetizers, and hearty entrees that make this menu a home run. Fried green tomatoes, mussels steamed in light beer with smoked bacon and bleu cheese crumbles, bison short ribs, and beer-battered fish and chips are just some of the comfort-food finds in the lineup.

## CAFÉ BRISTOL $$
**2035 South Third St.**
**(502) 634-2723**
Located in the Speed Art Museum, the Café Bristol serves lunch only, Tuesday through Saturday. It's a popular destination after a morning in the museum or before an afternoon there.

## CAVIAR JAPANESE RESTAURANT $$$
**416 West Muhammad Ali Blvd.**
**(502) 625-3090**
**www.caviarsushibar.com**
The newest and most upscale Japanese restaurant and sushi bar in downtown Louisville, Caviar is located right around the corner from the Fourth Street Live! entertainment district in the heart of the city. The newly renovated facilities are on the first floor of the former Walnut Street Theater, a building listed on the National Register of Historic Places. Contemporary and traditional Japanese cuisine is offered in an eye-catching, modern setting, and there is an excellent selection of award-winning wines, beers from around the world, top-shelf spirits, and one of the most extensive sake lists in the region. Open for lunch and dinner six days a week, Caviar is closed on Sunday.

## THE ENGLISH GRILL $$$$
**335 West Broadway**
**(502) 583-1234**
**www.brownhotel.com**
Although it may set you back a few dollars, a meal at the English Grill is often a highlight of a visit to the Derby City. Located at the end of the sumptuous lobby in the legendary Brown Hotel, this equestrian-themed escape soothes the eye with glowing woodwork and rich tapestries. The menu—the seasonal brainchild of lauded chef Laurent Geroli—features a selection of continentally inspired dishes drawing on influences from local farmers and producers. Starter selections can include anything from Johnny corn cake salad with limestone lettuce and duck bacon to gratinée onion soup, and for entrees you might find spiced bourbon pork medallion with country ham and kale risotto, or the hotel's legendary sandwich creation, the hot brown. A popular dining option at the English Grill is the chef's table, a behind-the-scenes seven-course extravaganza with wine pairings for $150. ForbesTraveler.com named the English Grill "one of the finest restaurants in the nation." Closed Sunday.

## JEFF RUBY'S $$$$
**325 West Main St.**
**(502) 584-0102**
**www.jeffruby.com**
Styled after the great New York City steakhouses of the 1940s and '50s, Jeff Ruby's Steakhouse has

a distinct energy and feel that make it stand out from the rest. One of the most popular restaurants in downtown Louisville—it's at the corner of Fourth and Main at the Galt House—Jeff Ruby's is known for its eye-poppingly extravagant interior and impeccable service. The dark, rich interior is designed to be as visually exciting as the food, and the menu features dry-aged USDA prime beef, as well as seafood favorites and a sushi bar. Jeff Ruby's is one of three regional chain restaurants; the other two are in the Cincinnati area. Open for dinner at 5 p.m. every day except Sunday, Jeff Ruby's made national headlines during the weekend of Derby 2007 when the Cincinnati restaurateur himself refused service to O. J. Simpson and asked him to leave the restaurant.

## J. GRAHAM'S CAFE $$
**335 West Broadway**
**(502) 583-1234**
**www.brownhotel.com**
The place to get the most authentic version of the legendary hot brown sandwich, J. Graham's features the freshest local produce and offers its guests a bistro-style option for casual dining in the hotel. Open daily for breakfast and lunch from 7 a.m. to 2 p.m., the cafe offers a contemporary a la carte menu or full buffet with gourmet soups, salads, and entrees, as well as a tantalizing dessert display. This restaurant is named after J. Graham Brown, the wealthy Louisville businessman who had the swanky hotel built in 1923.

## MAKER'S MARK BOURBON HOUSE & LOUNGE $$$
**446 South Fourth St.**
**(502) 568-9009**
**www.makerslounge.com**
When the Fourth Street Live! entertainment district had its grand opening in October 2004, the Maker's Mark Bourbon House & Lounge was one of the first businesses to participate in the revitalization of downtown Louisville. An impressive 57-foot-long wooden bar outlined in marble, chic furnishings, and customized art-glass fixtures hinted at good things to come. Today, this upscale eatery is going strong, attracting a faithful clientele of locals and out-of-towners alike. It's also a popular stop along the Urban Bourbon Trail, a collection of Louisville establishments that promotes the state's rich distilling heritage while serving Kentucky bourbon and bourbon-based products. In addition to numerous bourbon cocktails and more than 60 bourbons available at the bar, guests can sample a wide variety of dishes from seasonal menus that make the most of local products. Appetizer selections might include items such as the canapé Lucile with homemade lamb sausage, muenster cheese, micro greens, and Dijon bourbon mustard, or the rock shrimp popcorn, shrimp that is marinated in bourbon buttermilk, deep-fried, and served with bourbon mustard aioli and sweet chili sauce.

## MAYAN CAFÉ $$$
**813 East Market St.**
**(502) 566-0651**
**www.themayancafe.com**
While many Mexican restaurants—many of them purporting to be authentic—can be found throughout the country, there aren't that many that specialize in the cuisine of the Yucatan Peninsula. Chef Bruce Ucán, a Mexican of Mayan descent, delights guests with creative dinner specials and seasonal desserts that enhance the consistent quality of his food, which combines the flavors of his native land with an approach to cooking that is upbeat and innovative. Roasted lima beans, seafood bisque, and the tasty handheld tortillas with different toppings known as *salbutes* are just some of the items that have gained him a loyal following in the Derby City. Sustainability is at the core of his business, and whenever possible, local produce, fish, and meat are featured on the menu; in addition, only compostable take-out containers and nontoxic cleaning supplies are used in the restaurant.

## MORTON'S, THE STEAKHOUSE $$$$
**626 West Main St.**
**(502) 584-0421**
Open every night for dinner, Morton's is part of a chain, with dozens of high-end steak-

houses across the country. Morton's Restaurant Group, the world's largest owner and operator of company-owned upscale restaurants, also has locations in Canada, Mexico, Puerto Rico, Hong Kong, Macau, and Singapore. The company operates Bertolini's Authentic Trattoria and Trevi in addition to the Morton's Steakhouse concepts. The Louisville location is downtown in the heart of Museum Row, and it's a popular destination because of its clubby atmosphere and inviting bar.

Among other things, Morton's is known for serving prime beef, sourced from a meat packer in Chicago, the birthplace of Morton's. The beef is aged on location for several weeks and then cooked to order in an 800-degree broiler for service. Cuts offered include porterhouse, filet mignon, New York strips, bone-in rib eyes, and prime ribs. Besides the printed menu, Morton's offers a visually presented menu whereby the server rolls a cart to the table and presents each item with a detailed description of how it's prepared. This is also when the server asks diners if they would like to order one of the signature desserts, like the soufflés that require advance notice for preparation.

## THE OAKROOM                               $$$$
**500 South Fourth St.**
**(502) 585-3200**
**www.seelbachhilton.com**
If you're up for a splurge in Louisville, definitely put the Oakroom at the top of your list. Wonderful Kentucky fine dining with polished service and elegant, paneled club surroundings make it worth every penny. Ever since chefs Jim Gerhardt and Michael Cunha, with the assistance of director of restaurants Adam Segar, upped the level of service and cuisine in the 1990s, this five-diamond gem has been the recipient of regular accolades from the national press. The menu, which changes seasonally, incorporates fresh local produce and regional ingredients as much as possible, and at $29, the Sunday brunch is one of the best gourmet bargains in town. Waffles

and omelets made to order, in addition to a variety of regional breakfast and lunch favorites, make it a great way to start a Sunday morning. When making your reservations, ask for Jamal, part of the old guard from the restaurant's early days, as your server.

**i** Today's Oakroom is located in the original gentlemen's billiards room; if you look on the walls to the west, you can still see ornately carved cue racks. Before you leave, make sure to poke your head inside the Oakroom's private dining alcove, known as the Black Jack Room, which is located behind the hostess stand. The Seelbach's most infamous visitor, Al Capone, used to play cards there during his frequent visits to Louisville in the 1920s. Secret panels in the walls (still visible, but nailed shut) mark the location where the mobster would make his getaway during police raids.

## OLD SPAGHETTI FACTORY                      $$
**235 West Market St.**
**(502) 581-1070**
**www.osf.com**
Named one of the 10 best family restaurant chains by *Parents* magazine, the Old Spaghetti Factory has some 50 locations in this country and abroad, in addition to the one in Louisville at the corner of Third and Market. Located in the historic Levy Building, the restaurant has decor consistent with that of every other Old Spaghetti Factory in the chain: eclectic antiques, chandeliers, and brass headboards and footboards as bench backs for the booths. As with the others in the chain, this one has as its most prominent feature a streetcar in the middle of the restaurant, with seating inside. The Old Spaghetti Factory is known for serving its famous "complete meals" that always include soup or salad, fresh-baked bread, milk, coffee, hot or iced tea, and vanilla or spumoni ice cream in addition to the entree item, which is often pasta and sauce.

# 🔍 Close-up

## Pizza in Louisville

The Derby City can boast an exceptionally large number of good pizza restaurants, something that is hardly surprising given the fact that Papa John's, one of the country's largest chains, is headquartered here. It is also the base for Snappy Tomato and Pizza Hut, which forms part of Yum Brands. If they don't satisfy your pizza cravings while you're in the 'Ville, try one of these popular pie parlors:

**BEARNO'S**      **$$**

131 West Main St.

(502) 584-7437

www.bearnospizza.net

Tossing pizzas since 1977, the Bearno's chain has always been a neighborhood favorite in Derby City. The flagship restaurant is downtown right next to the Second Street Bridge in the basement of the old L&N Railroad Building, but you'll find more than a dozen Bearno's pizza restaurants around town. Frequently voted by readers of *Louisville Magazine* and *LEO* as the best pizzeria in town, Bearno's offers a wide selection of appetizers, salads, Italian sandwiches, and specialty pizzas. Popular orders are the Mama Bearno's Pizza for $24.99—a huge pie topped with the lots of mozzarella cheese and then loaded with sausage, pepperoni, mushrooms, onions, green peppers, and olives—and the Super Bearno's Special for $37.99. It's a monster piled high with sausage, pepperoni, hamburger, ham, bacon, Italian sausage, onions, green olives, black olives, mushrooms, green peppers, banana peppers, and extra cheese. Other popular locations include the Bearno's Highlands (502-456-4556) at 1318 Bardstown Road; the Bearno's Bowman Field (502-458-8605) at 2900 Taylorsville Road; and the Bearno's Jeffersonville (812-282-3125) at 700 West Riverside Drive in Jeffersonville, Indiana.

**BOOMBOZZ PIZZA AND TAP HOUSE**    **$$**

1448 Bardstown Rd.

(502) 458-8889

www.tonyboombozz.com

According to owner Tony Palombino, the Boombozz name came from an Italian-American slang word meaning "wild and crazy." But there's nothing wild and crazy going on at his four Louisville-area pizzerias—it's just good, gourmet pizza that most fans agree is a cut above his major competitors. To back it up, Boombozz has won national awards for the best vegetarian pizza, best gourmet pizza, and best international pizza. Palombino's father opened the original wood-fired pizza restaurant in 1987, and today the restaurants offer a variety of traditional and newer creations including "pollotate," an old family recipe that features marinated chicken, roasted potatoes, and red onions on a garlic-and-olive-oil-glazed crust with Asiago and mozzarella cheeses.

Other popular choices are the pizza with garlic sauce, grilled chicken, portobello mushrooms, sweet red onions, tomatoes, and three cheeses, and the D'Sienna with fresh spinach and tomato cream sauce. For those not in the mood for pizza, there are lots of other choices, including oven-baked panini and salads. The Highlands location at the intersection of Bardstown Road and Eastern Parkway has a full bar and serves dinner until late. For information about the other stores, call the Springhurst location (2813 North Hurstbourne Pkwy.) at (502) 394-0000; the Clifton location (3334 Frankfort Ave.) at (502) 896-9090; and the J-town location (12613 Taylorsville Rd.) at (502) 261-0222.

**CLIFTON'S PIZZA COMPANY**    **$$**

2230 Frankfort Ave.

(502) 893-3730

www.cliftonspizza.com

Clifton's Pizza opened for business in March of 1990 in a 100-year-old building that originally housed a family-owned hardware store. As the clientele grew, so did the business, and live music soon became a nightly feature at Clifton's. On any given night you'll find anything from jazz to blues to bluegrass, and songwriters from all over the country are showcased every Tuesday evening by country singer and songwriter, Heidi Howe. The eclectic decor includes a wall of some 100 clocks in an upstairs dining room in addition to an antique bar and Italian bric-a-brac. The extensive menu includes close to two dozen house sandwiches, pastas, salads, and appetizers, in addition to an impressive array of specialty pizzas and build-your-own possibilities. Try the best-selling Clifton's Special with pepperoni, onions, mushrooms, sausage, and green pepper.

## IMPELLIZZERI'S PIZZA $$
1381 Bardstown Rd.

(502) 454-2711

http://impellizzeris.com

With the photos on the walls and the various Impellizzeris running the place, you know this is a family-owned pizzeria. Today, Baldassare Impellizzeri keeps alive the tradition his parents and grandparents started when they sold fresh fruits and vegetables to the families of Louisville. The friendly staff is always very accommodating and willing to help you decide what's best for you. The Sicilian-style deep-dish pizza—at least 2 inches high and smothered with a thick, peppery sauce made in-house—is popular, but there are also original and thin-crust varieties. Whichever crust you order, the pies are loaded and very filling. If you're up to it, order the Impellizzeri Super Pizza, loaded with pepperoni, ham, homemade Italian sausage and meatballs, mushrooms, banana and green peppers, onions, and black and green olives. It weighs 12 pounds and takes at least an hour to bake. Price: $49.99. There is a second Impellizzeri's at 4933 Brownsboro Road. Call (502) 425-9080 for more information.

## WICK'S PIZZA $$
975 Baxter Ave.

502) 458-1828

www.wickspizza.com

Students on a budget, couples on a special date, families with kids, sports fans—you'll find all these and more among the lively crowd at Wick's Pizza in the Highlands. Started by the Wickliffe family in 1991, Wick's Pizza has expanded to include four locations around town. The Dixie Wick's (502-995-4333) is at 10966 Dixie Highway; the Goose Creek Wick's (502-327-9425) is at 2927 Goose Creek Road; and the Middletown Wick's (502-213-9425) is at 12717 Shelbyville Road. It's a popular destination because there's a choice of over 60 foreign and domestic beers and 75 blends of liquor, but the pizza is the big draw here. Consistently rated one of the best in town, the pizza at Wick's isn't skimpy on toppings. Coming in at over 10 pounds with loads of pepperoni, Italian sausage, beef, tomatoes, onions, green and black olives, fresh mushrooms, and green peppers, the 18-inch Big Wick ($32.50) is a favorite.

## ZA'S PIZZA PUB $$
1573 Bardstown Rd.

(502) 454-4544

www.zaspizza.com

Open daily until 11 p.m. this quiet bar has been serving up some of the Highlands' favorite pizzas since 1996. Happy Hour is every day from 4 p.m. to 7 p.m., when it's only $1.50 for Bud Light on draft. The subs are a favorite, but most come in for the "Works" pizza, a 16-inch pie with ham, pepperoni, sausage, bacon, mushrooms, onions, green peppers, black olives, and extra cheese that goes for $24. There is also a good assortment of non-meat pizzas for vegetarians, including the "garden ZA" with spinach, garlic, and tomato; the "blanca ZA" with artichoke hearts, olive oil, tomatoes, and black olives; and a six-cheese creation with mozzarella, ricotta, Romano, parmesan, provolone, and cheddar.

**i** Designed by renowned Louisville architect Arthur Loomis in the Richardsonian Romanesque style, the Levy. Building (where the Old Spaghetti Factory is located) was one of the first electrified buildings in town. In 1984 the first floor and mezzanine were renovated for the restaurant, and trendy condos and apartments were added to the top floors. Today, strings of lights decorate the exterior of the building year-round, and when one has been drinking too much, locals often say that the boozer is "lit up like Levy's."

## OTTO'S CAFÉ $$
### 500 Fourth St.
### (502) 585-3200
### www.seelbachhilton.com/03_b_dining.php

Decorated in tones of sepia and black, this 1920s-style cafe on the ground floor of the Seelbach Hilton offers southern-inspired breakfast and lunch buffets seven days a week, with Kentucky-grown ingredients used to create new taste combinations whenever possible. A la carte menu choices include hearty soups, fresh salads, and a selection of delicious sandwiches, in addition to heart-healthy items that are available for both breakfast and lunch. A house specialty is the Kentucky Benedict, which is made with country ham and red-eye hollandaise sauce.

**i** A Louisvillian created the very first flavored chewing gum in the late 1870s. That's something to chew on. Although he never patented it, pharmacist John Colgan created "Taffy Tolu," using balsam of tolu, a fragrant medicinal herb used to flavor cough syrups, as a sweetener. So successful was his invention that he sold his pharmacy and began producing it full time, and by the end of the 19th century it was the most widely recognized product from Louisville. When it was sold at the 1893 World's Columbian Exposition in Chicago, Taffy Tolu Chewing Gum became an international sensation.

## PESTO'S ITALIAN AND PERSIAN CUISINE $$
### 566 South Fifth St.
### (502) 584-0567
### www.pestositalian.com

A popular downtown lunch spot known for its speedy service, Pesto's serves up classic, tasty Italian fare in an eclectic atmosphere; but on the weekends, when things slow down, it offers Persian food as well. Italian food is served Monday through Friday from 11 a.m. to 3 p.m., and Friday from 5:30 p.m. to 9 p.m. and Saturday from noon to 9 p.m. Persian as well as Italian fare can be had, including popular Iranian dishes like *ghormeh sabzi*, a savory medley of beef, chopped fresh herbs, kidney beans, lime, and Persian spices served with basmati rice, and *fesenjan*, Cornish hen simmered with pomegranate puree and crushed walnuts.

## PROOF ON MAIN $$$$
### 702 West Main St.
### (502) 217-6360
### www.proofonmain.com

Even the most jaded of critics can't help but be impressed by the exciting blend of Kentucky artisanal foods, boutique American spirits, and cutting-edge decor that have come to characterize one of the most talked-about restaurants on the national dining scene. Part trendy bistro, part snazzy lounge, part contemporary art gallery, Proof on Main is the brainchild of restaurateur Drew Nieporent and local philanthropists Laura Lee Brown and Steve Wilson. Open since March 2006, it is part of the 21c Museum Hotel on Louisville's old Distiller's Row and is a must-see for anyone who enjoys good food and provocative art.

Chef Michael Paley wows his patrons with his own brand of culinary artistry, showing off modern American fare imbued with flavors of the South and peasant Italy. A passion for small family farms and locally grown produce is evident in the ever-changing menu, which in the past has included Tuscan-inspired dishes such as Heritage Farms pork shank buckwheat pappardelle with braised rabbit, bone-in bison tenderloin, and pork cheek Milanese. Ever-changing offerings like the Kentucky bison carpaccio with pickled wild ramps, the Weisenberger grits (stone-ground) with Parmesan, and the chickpea and country ham fritters highlight the flavors of the Bluegrass State. Proof on Main is open for breakfast, lunch, and dinner seven days a week.

**i** For up-to-date information about the Derby City food scene and current and past reviews of the city's most popular eateries, check out the Web site of food critic Robin Garr at www.louisvillehotbytes.com.

## THE PUB LOUISVILLE $$
412 South Fourth St.
(502) 569-7782
www.luvthepub.com

Located next to the Hard Rock Café in the Fourth Street Live! entertainment complex, the Pub Louisville opened in late 2004. Touting itself as a high-energy, authentic British tavern featuring outdoor dining and live music, the Pub attracts crowds for its wide assortment of draft beers and a menu that boasts good gastro-pub fare. The menu combines the finest aspects of traditional pub grub with the nuances of internationally inspired dishes. Aside from fish and chips as good as any you'd get in London, diners enjoy the shepherd's pie and Scottish eggs, as well as the flash-fried calamari and London broil. The Pub opens daily at 11 a.m.

## RED STAR TAVERN $$$
450 South Fourth St.
(502) 568-5656
www.redstartavern.net

Upscale comfort foods highlight the menu at this contemporary American tavern that features flagstone walls, wood paneling, oversize leather booths, eclectic artwork, and an open kitchen for an intimate and inviting atmosphere. Aside from Kentucky, the chain has locations in Virginia, Florida, and Illinois. This one, a flagship eatery in the Fourth Street Live! entertainment district, offers an impressive selection of specialty cocktails, beers, and wines. The menu is known for its signature salads, appetizers, and mouthwatering steaks, pastas, burgers, and seafood. Red

Star opens daily at 11 a.m. for lunch and dinner; Sunday through Thursday, they're open till 11 p.m., and service goes until midnight on Friday and Saturday.

## RIVUE RESTAURANT & LOUNGE $$$
140 North Fourth St.
(502) 568-4239
www.rivue.com

In addition to contemporary cuisine and chic, ultramodern decor, amazing views await diners high atop the Galt House, at Rivue Restaurant & Lounge on the 25th floor. And the view never gets boring because it's always changing. The only restaurant in the world with a twin revolving floor, the Rivue offers its diners panoramic vistas that alternate between the sparkling waterfront and the gleaming lights of downtown Louisville. The menu at Rivue has starter items such as imperial crab croquant and Bull Island oyster stew, while main-course selections include dishes like lamb osso bucco or shrimp linguine. For dessert, you'll find tasty sweets like divinity pillars. Food can also be ordered in the lounge, but it's served tapas-style, and the assortment includes fondue, white bean hummus, and bison burgers. A long list of specialty drinks and cocktails has been created for guests looking for a nightcap as they enjoy the slowly turning view. Rivue opens for dinner at 5:30 p.m. every day except Sunday and Monday.

## SAFFRON'S PERSIAN RESTAURANT $$
131 West Market St.
(502) 584-7800
www.saffronsrestaurant.com

Located between the West Main performing arts corridor and the up-and-coming gallery/restaurant scene of East Market, Saffron's is easy to overlook. Fans of good Iranian food manage to find it nonetheless. Majid Ghavami, the proprietor of Saffron's Persian Restaurant, has been named the best restaurant host in Louisville on more than one occasion, and his food has won rave reviews for its straightforward and tasty preparation. Walk into the understated restaurant and the owner himself is usually there to greet you with a handshake or a kiss on the cheek. Among the house specialties are the rack of lamb, grilled salmon barberry, and pistachio soup with crushed pistachios blended with vegetable broth and seasoned with whispers of angelica seed and cinnamon.

## TENGO SED CANTINA $$
**432 South Fourth St.**
**(502) 540-1461**
**www.tengosed-ky.com**

Described as a Mexican-style party bar where Cancun meets Kansas City, Tengo Sed Cantina is an eclectic hangout with Tex-Mex-inspired food and a lively atmosphere. The margaritas are good as well. Featuring an outdoor deck that takes advantage of its prime location in the center of the Fourth Street Live! entertainment district, Tengo Sed Cantina opens for lunch Monday through Friday from 11 a.m. to 2 p.m.; they're open for dinner most weeknights as well. Popular bites include the chicken tacos and the mini Cuban sandwiches.

## VINCENZO'S $$$$
**150 South Fifth St.**
**(502) 580-1350**
**www.vincenzositalianrestaurant.com**

When it opened in 1986 in an old bank building attached to the rear of Louisville's Humana Building, Vincenzo's quickly became one of the best restaurants in the city. Today, the high-ceilinged, square-pillared dining room is a frequent destination for diners in search of elegant Italian cuisine. Amid the discreet colors of muted charcoal and copper, guests in comfortable wood and leather side chairs enjoy favorites such as the *filetto ripieno*—beef tenderloin stuffed with Stilton cheese and wild mushrooms in a dry vermouth peppercorn sauce—at large tables draped in fine damask. Vincenzo's is open Monday through Friday from 11:30 a.m. to 2 p.m. for lunch and from 5 p.m. to 10 p.m. for dinner; Saturday they are open from 5 p.m. to 11 p.m.

## WOLFGANG PUCK EXPRESS $$
**221 South Fourth St.**
**(502) 562-0983**
**www.wolfgangpuck.com**

Wolfgang Puck, a native of Austria renowned for his Los Angeles–area eateries, has opened more than 80 fast-casual restaurants across the country; his Louisville location became the first in the state. "Opening the first Wolfgang Puck Express in Kentucky was a great way to offer authentic recipes and signature dishes at affordable prices to guests who want to enjoy fresh, quality food," he said. "We look forward to offering Louisville locals a selection of the finest ingredients prepared to order." The menu at Wolfgang Puck Express features artisan pizzas, as well as assorted handmade sandwiches, pastas, soups, and fresh salads, such as the signature Chinois chicken salad. Other well-known dishes include rosemary rotisserie chicken, butternut squash soup, four-cheese macaroni al forno, and rigatoni with chicken bolognese.

## Z'S FUSION $$$$
**115 South Fourth St.**
**(502) 855-8000**
**www.zsfusion.com**

Creative and elegant, Z's Fusion—one of the most recent appearances on the Derby City food scene—is the brainchild of Mehrzad Sharbaiani, the founder of Z's Oyster Bar and Steakhouse, which has locations in Louisville and Indianapolis. To house the sleek new eatery, the old Kunz's restaurant at the corner of Fourth and Jefferson underwent a massive redesign, and today a swanky curved bar provides a focal point for the space that can seat nearly 400. Nonetheless, there's a cozy feel to it, and exquisite finishes of metal, granite, and bamboo, as well as eye-catching glass accents fabricated at the nearby Glassworks, make it a glittering showcase. The menu at Z's, a fusion of American, Asian, and European influences, changes often, but you'll find things like Korean barbecued pork tenderloin and flat-iron steak with Asian pesto in the meat section, and salmon glazed with bourbon, soy, and apricot in the fish section. For starters, you'll find dishes such as lemongrass mussels, curry fried green tomatoes, and crawfish mango crunch sushi rolls.

## Rollin' on the River

If you're looking for something close to the river in downtown Louisville, try one of these two restaurants.

**Joe's Crab Shack**                    **$$**
131 River Rd.
(502) 568-1171
www.joescrabshack.com
Started in the 1990s by two guys from Texas, the Joe's Crab Shack chain has grown to include some 120 beach-themed casual dining restaurants that serve seafood and American cuisine. The restaurants are known for the laid-back servers who dance, joke around, and embarrass diners on their birthdays. Like many of the locations across the country, the Louisville Joe's is on waterfront property and has large outdoor patio seating areas to enjoy the river views. Near the Kennedy Bridge, Joe's Crab Shack opens daily at 11 a.m.

**Tumbleweed Southwest Grill**         **$$**
1201 River Rd.
(502) 585-4107
tumbleweedrestaurants.com
Founded across the river in New Albany in 1975, Tumbleweed Southwest Grill is headquartered in Louisville, and the recent restaurant they built along the river in Waterfront Park not too long ago is the flagship of the chain. Tumbleweed serves American-Mexican food combining Tex-Mex and Southwestern influences. They specialize in things like chili con queso, fajitas, burritos, chimichangas, and a variety of salads, in addition to sandwiches, steak, and chicken. Parking is plentiful, but to get there you'll need to drive about a mile east of downtown on River Road. Nearby is the Silver parking lot and a large outdoor area for picnicking.

# OLD LOUISVILLE

**AMICI ITALIAN CAFÉ**                    **$$**
316 West Ormsby Ave.
(502) 637-3167
www.amicicafelouisville.com
Located just steps from the opulent mansions of Millionaires Row, Amici Italian Café offers outdoor seating in a romantic fern-laden brick courtyard where tinkling fountains and chimes put diners at ease. In the warm months it's a place to enjoy the signature drink, the Amici Bellini. Year-round you may choose from a wide variety of dishes that reveal the influence of northern Italy. Along with your cocktail, try the *prosciutto e melone* appetizer—thinly sliced prosciutto wrapped around melon wedges for $6.50—or the antipasto platter with an assortment of cured meats, cheeses, and pepperoncini. For a nice main course, try the grilled shrimp and scallop risotto, or the cheese tortellini with asparagus pesto and grilled chicken. Also available is a wide selection of salads, panini, pizzas, and soups.

**BUCK'S RESTAURANT AND BAR**          **$$$**
425 West Ormsby Ave.
(502) 637-5284
www.bucksrestaurantandbar.com
Buck's, the latest incarnation in a long line of restaurants that have graced the lower floor of the Mayflower Apartments on Ormsby Avenue, offers outdoor seating under a canopy of shade trees across from some of the largest Victorian mansions in the city. During the winter and fall, its main dining room is a popular gathering place for locals in search of a quiet lunch or dinner in 1920s elegance. From the abundant vases of white blossoms that adorn the bar to the trademark mismatched antiques-shop assortment of china and silverware that set the tables, Buck's Restaurant and Bar is an Old Louisville original. Definitely one of the pricier eateries in the neighborhood, Buck's has a diverse dinner menu that includes retro favorites like oysters Rockefeller, Kentucky trout dijonaise, and medallions of beef "Henry the Fifth," but fusion-inspired dishes appear as well. Crispy fish with hot sweet chili, spicy noodles

"Cantonese," and pork and rice pot stickers demonstrate the chef's adventurous side.

## COTTAGE INN RESTAURANT $$
**570 Eastern Pkwy.**
**(502) 637-4325**
The Cottage Inn Restaurant started off as a little house along Louisville's tree-lined Eastern Parkway in the 1920s, and the decor remains simple and unassuming today, with wainscoted beige walls, sturdy wooden tables and chairs, and an oversize picture window offering pleasant views of the garden outside. The menu—unpretentious as well—features a litany of sandwiches and entrees that would have been standards at most eateries across the nation in the 1950s and '60s:

burgers, BLTs and clubs, country-fried steak, liver and onions, pork chops, spaghetti and meatballs, and Salisbury steak. Popular daily lunch specials go for $6.99, and on Wednesday and Saturday evenings, the special is "All U Care to Eat Fried Chicken" with bread and two sides for just $9.99.

## D. NALLY'S $
**970 South Third St.**
**(502) 583-8015**
Offering no-nonsense home cooking at rock-bottom prices since 1960, D. Nally's is a tiny diner located on Third Street, midway between downtown and the main residential areas of Old Louisville. Aside from a wide assortment of breakfast options, diners will find lots of greasy-

## Close-up

## Another Hidden Treasure

In a neighborhood that's known as a hidden treasure, it's nice to find smaller gems tucked away here and there. One of them is **610 Magnolia,** one of the city's best restaurants ($$$$; 610 West Magnolia Ave.; 502-636-0783; www.610magnolia.com).

Located in a simple carriage house in the heart of historic Old Louisville, 610 Magnolia offers its guests an exceptional combination of southern hospitality and urban sophistication that earns it regular accolades from state and national press. The approach to food at 610 Magnolia is a simple one based on the farm-to-table agricultural movement, and there is an emphasis on ever-changing seasonal menus incorporating straightforward yet stylish preparations. With its rustic brick floors, wooden ceiling beams, mullioned windows, and French doors opening onto an inviting garden patio, the interior of the restaurant is an uncomplicated statement in elegance. This sets the stage for a unique dining experience where guests sit at polished mahogany tables set with Frette linens and Riedel crystal while enjoying a New American cuisine with global influences and a preference for local organic products.

This is the vision of Edward Lee, a New York City native who began working in restaurants at the age of 14. In addition to cooking in several establishments in the newly built Trump Tower on Fifth Avenue, Lee also graduated magna cum laude with a degree in literature from New York University, returning to the culinary world after a brief stint in publishing. During a visit to Louisville for the Derby, Lee was so impressed with the local restaurant scene and Kentucky's rich array of growers that he ultimately decided 610 Magnolia would be the perfect place to continue his culinary mission. Today, diners enjoy innovative creations like Kentucky fried duck with sweet potato polenta, and grilled sorghum quail with pumpkin seeds and roasted grapes for starters, and main courses such as wild boar chop with bourbon mustard and braised bacon Carolina rice, and Chesapeake striped bass with mussel risotto and broccoli rabe.

610 Magnolia is open to the public for dinner only on Thursday, Friday, and Saturday, when a six-course prix fixe menu is served nightly; during the rest of the week 610 Magnolia is available for private events. Lee also allows guests the opportunity to choose between specially selected wine pairings.

# 🔍 Close-up

## A Tale of Two Burgers

Some of the city's best-known burger joints are located in Old Louisville. The Granville Inn at 1601 South Third Street (502-635-6475) serves a burger that's popular with the U of L crowd, and the Tavern at 1532 South Fourth Street (502-637-4200) is known for their famous knockerburger, served 22 hours a day. And, of course, there's always the infamous never-closes Juanita's Burger Boy at 1450 South Brook Street (502-635-7410) and its super double-decker burger boy with two quarter-pound patties, sauce, and cheese. Two of the most popular burger stops are just minutes from downtown Louisville, however. Try one of these for a quick lunch or afternoon snack:

**DIZZY WHIZZ DRIVE-IN**      $

217 West St. Catherine St.

(502) 583-3828

At any given time of day, you'll likely find an interesting cast of characters patronizing this place, an old drive-in-style neighborhood hamburger joint that opened in 1947. Since there's usually a good-size crowd most times of day, you can reasonably assume: 1) the burgers are decent; and 2) the prices are fair. The Dizzy Whizz offers a wide variety of menu options including breakfast anytime, but the main draw is the "Whizzburger." A regular whizzer—a half-pound version is also available—features two smallish flat-grilled patties sandwiched on a toasted double-decker bun with American cheese, lots of shredded lettuce, and a zesty dill tartar-style sauce. It's the perfect match to a side of fries or onion rings and a freshly blended chocolate malt.

**OLLIE'S TROLLEY**      $

978 South Third St.

(502) 583-5214

www.ollieburgers.com

In Old Louisville, at the corner of Third and Kentucky, stands something of a fast-food relic: It's Ollie's Trolley, a vestige of the days when the Ollie's Trolley chain had outlets across the country—not to mention a dozen scattered throughout Louisville, its city of inception. In addition to walk-in buildings shaped like bright red-and-yellow streetcars, the chain's gimmick featured a secret blend of 23 herbs and spices—more than twice as many as the Colonel used in his fried chicken—and a legendary owner, a fastidious coot by the name of Ollie, who insisted that his burgers be served rare and only with his special secret sauce.

Today, the burgers are usually well-done, but the Ollie Burger with everything still has a thick, flavorful third-pound patty on a bun, topped with a slice of melted mozzarella cheese and dressed with a thick slice of fresh tomato, crisp lettuce, sliced raw white onion, and a slathering of the "secret" Ollie Sauce. (The sauce is a slightly spicy mayonnaise-based concoction with herbs, somewhat akin to Thousand Island dressing.) Like the Ollie's Trolleys of the good ol' days, this one is take-out only, but if you can't wait until you get home, there are a couple of metal tables in a corner of the tiny parking lot that surrounds Ollie's. And, they only accept cash.

---

spoon favorites such as fried chicken, patty melts, and steak sandwiches. Closed Sunday, D. Nally's serves Monday through Friday from 6 a.m. to 8 p.m. and Saturdays from 6 a.m. to 2 p.m.

**ERMIN'S BAKERY AND CAFE**      $$
1201 South First St.
(502) 635-6960
www.erminsbakery.com

This well-known neighborhood restaurant was started in 1993 after two cousins by the name of Ermin arrived in this country as refugees from war-torn Bosnia. With them they brought a family tradition of baking that helped make their small store popular throughout the city. Since then, Ermin's has grown to include five different locations—three in the downtown Louisville area; one in New Albany, Indiana; and one in Prospect. All food at Ermin's is prepared in-house at the location in Old Louisville, and all produce and meats are delivered daily to ensure the freshest products possible. Healthy food—no preservatives are used—and hearty portions make Ermin's a good spot for breakfast, lunch, and dinner. Ermin's opens at 7 a.m. Monday through Friday, at 8 a.m. on Saturday, and at 9 a.m. on Sunday.

## GRANVILLE INN                                    $$
**1601 South Third St.**
**(502) 635-6475**
The place where locals mingle with students, Granville Inn has been popular with the University of Louisville crowd since it opened its doors in 1939. Reputed to serve some of the best burgers in the city, the Granville is also known for its sandwiches, beer, and pizza. Extremely cheap—it's hard to find anything over $10—and laid back, it's the quintessential neighborhood watering hole. The best part? It's open seven days a week to 4 a.m.

## MASTERSON'S                                      $$
**1830 South Third St.**
**(502) 636-2511**
**www.mastersons.com**
Nicholas Mastoras, a Greek immigrant from the small island of Othoni, started this Old Louisville culinary landmark in 1939. Directly adjacent to the campus of the University of Louisville, Masterson's started off as a small drive-in restaurant known as the "Little Mansion." It was expanded and renamed several times, and in 1972 it became known as "Masterson's Food & Drink." It has grown from that small diner to a full-service restaurant with 42,000 square feet of space, with room for 1,500. Aside from a wide variety of typical American restaurant selections, Masterson's is popular for the $15 Sunday brunch, which goes from 11 a.m. to 4 p.m. In addition to a salad bar and made-to-order omelet station, patrons will find carved roast beef, fried chicken, fish, and an assortment of breads, sides, and vegetables.

## THE RUDYARD KIPLING                              $$
**422 West Oak St.**
**(502) 636-1311**
**www.therudyardkipling.com**
Catering to the bohemian in all of us, the Rudyard Kipling opens its doors Friday and Saturday nights for whole-grain pizzas and other bar snacks, including unique soups like their famous burgoo, or soup beans and corn bread. In addition to good Bloody Marys and sangria, there's a selection of wine and imported beers. The biggest draw, however, is the regular live music, poetry readings, and avant garde theater events that have made the Rudyard Kipling a mainstay among the city's literati. Located in a historic house that has been converted into a neighborhood watering hole, the Rud—as the locals call it—often opens during the week for special productions and concerts.

**i** One of the local companies to use the space at the Rudyard Kipling is Finnigan's Productions, a theater troupe that strives to showcase alternative theater that is socially relevant. Showcasing cutting-edge and thought-provoking dramatic works, Finnigan's Productions puts together the Festival of Funky Fresh Fun every spring to celebrate local talent with an evening of 10-minute plays by local writers and directors. The most recent festival included works by Jeffrey Scott Holland, Carridder Jones, Carlos Manuel, Tad Chitwood, Nancy Gall-Clayton, Doug Schutte, Todd Zeigler, Andy Epstein, Christa Kreimendahl, Sherry Deatrick, and Nathan Green. To contact Finnigan's Productions, call (502) 876-0532 or go online at www .finniganbeginagain.com.

## THIRD AVENUE CAFÉ                          $$
**1164 South Third St.**
**(502) 585-2233**
**www.thirdavecafe.com**

This popular hangout at the intersection of Third and Oak is easy to find—just look for Elvis. If his mannequin look-alike isn't at one of the sidewalk tables or on the corner bench outside the front door, he'll probably be perched on a stool at the bar inside. The crowd around him will most likely consist of a lively mix of students from nearby universities and regulars from the neighborhood who drop in for popular appetizers such as the shrimp cakes, or fried strips of portobello mushroom with horseradish sauce. The eclectic menu features a good array of vegan and vegetarian dishes, such as a black bean and tofu burrito, the vegetarian Reuben, and curry roasted vegetables. Closed Sunday.

# BARDSTOWN ROAD

Bardstown Road has reigned as Louisville's "Restaurant Row" since the 1980s, and is home to some of the city's most eclectic eateries. Many culinary delights can be found in the stretch of Bardstown Road that extends from Baxter Avenue toward the Watterson, through neighborhoods often referred to by the locals as Phoenix Hill, Irish Hill, the Highlands, and Douglass Loop. If you're driving here on Friday or Saturday night, don't be surprised to find yourself in bumper-to-bumper traffic during peak hours.

## AMAZING GRACE                               $
**1133 Bardstown Rd.**
**(502) 485-1122**
**www.amazinggracewholefoods.com**

Located near the busy intersection of Grinstead and Bardstown Road, Amazing Grace prides itself on having a wonderful selection of organic, vegetarian, and natural foods, with only organic produce. Primarily a grocery and health food store, they also have a small, excellent deli with mostly vegan and some vegetarian items. There's not much room to sit down, so hungry patrons like

## Be Original

When deciding where to go for that hot brown or that slice of Derby Pie, consider one of the Louisville Originals. It's a coalition of local restaurants that have banded together in the last few years with the goal of supporting, marketing, and promoting independent restaurants in the city. Aside from frequenting local farmers' markets and buying grocery-store produce with the Kentucky Proud logo, eating at one of the Louisville Originals is a great way to promote sustainable eating habits in the area. For a list of the participating restaurants, go online at: www.louisvilleoriginals.com.

Here you will also find information about the Louisville Originals reward program, where you accumulate points for each dollar you spend at any participating restaurant. Spend $150 and earn 150 points, which is good for a $10 gift certificate for use at any Louisville Originals restaurant. Cards are free at any of the member establishments, where you can also get the Louisville Originals gift card—a single gift card accepted at all of the Louisville Originals restaurants. The gift cards can be purchased online, over the phone (877-229-7299), or at any Louisville Original establishment, and the amount can be as low as $25 or as high as $1,000.

to pop in and grab a sandwich or a wrap before heading off to enjoy it in nearby Cherokee Park. Soups and a salad bar are available as well.

# 'Cue in the 'Ville

**BOOTLEG BAR-B-Q**                                 $

9704 Bardstown Rd.

(502) 239-2778

www.bootlegbbq.net

Open every day at 11 a.m., Bootleg Bar-B-Q consistently ranks up there with the best barbecue in the city. Although it really only dates to 1991, the little tin-roof trailer out alongside Bardstown Road just south of the Gene Snyder Freeway looks like it's been there forever. And the flavors and mellow, middle-of-the-road aromas produced there bespeak a pitmaster with years of experience. The lineup of hickory-smoked meats includes mutton—a Kentucky specialty—as well as chicken, turkey, beef brisket, and, of course, pulled pork, spare ribs, and baby back ribs. Moist and flavorful, the meats stand up to a nice variety of sauces that run the gamut from mild and slightly sweet with a tomato base to a Carolina-style mustard sauce with a potent kick, or from a spicy red sauce reminiscent of Texas and Louisiana to a tart, pitch-black dip straight out of the western reaches of the state. Bootleg also has a newer location in Okolona at 7508 Preston Highway; call (502) 968-5657 for details.

**FRANKFORT AVENUE BEER DEPOT**     $$

3204 Frankfort Ave.

(502) 895-3223

Considering its position in the middle of a relatively affluent neighborhood, in the shadows of the regal-looking buildings of the old reservoir, the Frankfort Avenue Beer Depot comes across as decidedly downscale. The spartan environment with its pool hall feel and aromas of stale beer and cigarette smoke doesn't do much to help that image, either. But most will tell you the barbecue here makes it worth the stop, as is evidenced by a parking lot that is usually full of cars. Ribs and chicken are the specialties, but locals have been known to make the trip for the tasty sides alone. The green beans are peppery and studded with bits of pulled pork, the potato salad and baked beans are savory and flavorful, and the onion rings are thick-cut and fried golden brown.

**MARK'S FEED STORE**                           $$

1514 Bardstown Rd.

(502) 458-1570

www.marksfeedstore.com

Mark's Feed Store on Bardstown Road has been a Louisville tradition since 1988. The motto there is "Friendly Folks Servin' Famous Food," and most locals agree that the 'cue isn't bad and the service is good. Although they're sure to ruffle feathers in some food circles, the people at Mark's believe the best barbecue comes from Kentucky, and they've cultivated a style of cooking handed down from a third-generation pitmaster from the eastern part of the state. Only the finest-quality pork, beef, and chicken end up in real hickory wood smokers, and then they're lightly topped with one of Mark's signature sauces. Several of the menu items at Mark's Feed Store have evolved as one-of-a-kind dishes, and are carefully guarded secrets. They include award-winning barbecue, ribs, onion straws, sweet fried corn, and homemade buttermilk pie, in addition to trademarked specialties such as the Bird-in-a-Nest™, which includes seven Honeywings™ resting on a nest of onion straws. The Bardstown Road location and the three other locations (11422 Shelbyville Rd., 502-244-0140; 10316 Dixie Hwy., 502-933-7707; 3827 Charlestown Rd., New Albany, IN, 812-949-7427) are open Sunday through Thursday from 11 a.m. to 10 p.m., and Friday and Saturday from 11 a.m. to 11 p.m.

## OLE HICKORY PIT BBQ  $$

6106 Shepherdsville Rd.

(502) 968-0585

www.myspace.com/olehickorypit

There's a truck-size pink pig perched on the roof of the Ole Hickory Pit barn, but don't let it fool you, because this Louisville culinary landmark has been doing more than pork since it opened in 1932. Aside from the more-familiar pork dishes like ribs, pulled pork sandwiches, and smoked ham, there's also mutton—the specialty from the western part of the state. And over the years, Ole Hickory Pit's signature mutton sandwich, piled high with slices of sweet, gamey, smoky meat, has attracted a faithful following. The extensive menu also includes some 20 barbecue sandwiches and platters, plus burgers, chili dogs, fried fish, chicken, and even a veggie plate. In addition, there are lots of from-scratch sides, including fried corn bread, new potatoes, country-style beans, silver dollar–size corn cakes, white beans with ham hock, macaroni and cheese, potato salad, coleslaw, and baked beans.

## RITE-WAY BAR-B-CUE  $

1548 West Catherine St.

(502) 584-9385

If the old neon sign looks like a collector's item from the 1940s, that's because Rite-Way Bar-B-Cue has been a neighborhood landmark in the West End since the Johnson family opened it just after World War II. The eatery occupies a small storefront in a pale-blue, two-story frame house on a shady block of St. Catherine Street, across from Young's Chapel AME Church and around the corner from the California Community Center. In the austere interior, an ancient butcher's scale and glass display cases hint at the joint's early days, and since most people stop by to take their orders to go, there's only a couple of tables

to provide community seating for a handful of diners. Many say the ribs—a rack of about eight is meaty and lean, with gently smoked meat tender enough to slide from the bone, and a good textural combination of tenderness and crispness from the crunchy, caramelized edges—are as good as any they ever ate. The sauce—thin compared to the thick, sweet, tomato-based versions common in so many barbecue places across the country—is tangy and spicy, with the distinct sharpness of vinegar that so many barbecue aficionados say is the hallmark of true southern 'cue. Kalvin Brown, the hospitable proprietor who married one of the Johnson daughters, tends to the well-used smokers today. Rite-Way Bar-B-Cue is open most days from noon to midnight.

## SMOKETOWN USA  $$

1153 Logan St.

(502) 409-9180

Attractively renovated with exposed brick walls and eclectic decor featuring '40s-era movie posters, Smoketown USA makes good use of an old storefront at the corner of Oak and Logan, midway between Germantown and Old Louisville. Built in 1862, the building originally housed a grocery, feed and seed store, and a livery. The menu combination— it offers both "Louisville-style barbecue" and Tex-Mex favorites—is just as unusual as the setting, which has a thrift-store sort of feel because everything you see is for sale. The aromatic scents of hickory smoke and pork wafting up from the black smoker out back let diners know this is old-school barbecue, with ribs so tender that you hardly need to chew. Sides are popular, too, and options include Mexican rice with a marked cumin-chili flavor, slow-cooked mixed greens with a ration of small black-eyed peas, garlic, and onions, and spicy Texas pintos that aren't too fiery.

## ASIATIQUE                                    $$$
**1767 Bardstown Rd.**
**(502) 451-2749**
**www.asiatiquerestaurant.com**

Fans of fusion cuisine love the Pacific Rim flavors that award-winning chef Peng Looi serves up at his relaxed and trendy Bardstown eatery. Looi combines Asian influences with traditional Western techniques to create a delicious dining experience based on the use of fresh ingredients, tastes, and textures. Main-course selections can include items such as roasted quail with noodle galette, crisp spinach and warm shiitake-shallot sauce, or bacon-wrapped pork loin stuffed with goat cheese, spinach, and red pepper. A signature item is the wok-seared Pacific salmon with roasted shallot, tomato concasse, and Sichuan hot oil. Reservations are accepted for groups of any number seven days a week, and they're recommended for the weekends. For special events like Derby week and New Year's Eve, reservations are accepted three months in advance (although a credit card is required to hold a table for such events).

## AVALON                                       $$$
**1314 Bardstown Rd.**
**(502) 454-5336**
**www.avalonfresh.com**

Sleek and stylish, Avalon has treated diners in the Derby City to a lively blend of trendy decor and fresh American cuisine with hints of Southern style since 2002. Today, it is a space with three levels of dining areas that envelop guests in a cocoon of autumnally hued walls, adorned with a dazzling array of art that—at first glance—might make visitors think they had stumbled into a gallery by mistake. The elegantly eclectic menu highlights the chef's internationally inspired creations that redefine many classic American dishes. The result is a colorful assortment of appetizers and entrees that blend country-inspired favorites with continental sophistication—best described as down-home chic. There is outdoor seating with heating and cooling to ensure your comfort at any time of the year.

## BAXTER AVENUE STATION                        $$
**1201 Payne St.**
**(502) 584-1635**
**www.baxterstation.com**

Chug chug. Chew chew. That's the motto at Baxter Avenue Station, an eclectic American eatery with 24 beers on tap and 30 wines for under $30. Over the years, the 100-year-old neighborhood tavern has evolved into a comfortable, casual bistro that the *Courier-Journal* has recognized as one of Louisville's 20 most popular. Diners enjoy appetizers like black bean cakes or shrimp and grits, and main courses such as salmon croquettes, smoked pork chops, and bourbon fried chicken, in a comfortable atmosphere by the fireplace or on the heated enclosed deck. Not too far from Bardstown Road and just a few minutes from downtown in the Irish Hill neighborhood, Baxter Avenue Station is closed Sunday and Monday.

## DE LA TORRE'S                                 $$$
**1606 Bardstown Rd.**
**(502) 456-4955**
**www.delatorres.com**

Open Tuesday through Saturday for dinner at 5:30 p.m., Louisville's lone Spanish restaurant showcases the flavors of Madrid and other parts of the Iberian Peninsula in a fine dining setting. Entrees include standards such as tenderloin of beef with Madeira sauce and Castilian-style roast lamb, in addition to prepared-to-order paella, the national dish of Spain. Tapas are big at De La Torre's, and an adjacent bar—La Bodega—specializes in the appetizer-like morsels, with several dozen different kinds. Spanish omelet, spicy mussels, chicken croquettes, and house-made chorizo are some of the more-popular choices.

## DRAGON KING'S DAUGHTER                        $$
**1126 Bardstown Rd.**
**(502) 632-2444**
**www.dragonkingsdaughter.com**

Restaurateur Toki Masabuchi puts a new twist on sushi at this recent addition to the Bardstown Road restaurant scene. In addition to fusion-

# (Q) Close-up

## Louisville a la Mode

**HOMEMADE ICE CREAM & PIE KITCHEN**    $$
1041 Bardstown Rd.
(502) 618-3380
www.piekitchen.com

The Homemade Ice Cream & Pie Kitchen has been a Louisville institution for more than 25 years. What started off as a small lunch counter in the Highlands neighborhood really took off when fresh-baked pies and homemade ice cream joined the roster and eventually defined the restaurant. Nowadays it has grown into a city-wide chain, with three on Bardstown Road alone. Although they're known for their pies, cakes, cookies, and home-churned ice cream, desserts aren't the only thing on the menu at five of the nine Homemade Ice Cream & Pie Kitchens scattered throughout the Louisville area. Among other items served seven days a week, you'll find fresh-made sandwiches, homemade pastas, mixed green salads, freshly baked breads, and premium sliced meats, in addition to a daily choice of soups. Besides the Lower Highlands location at 1041 Bardstown Road, you'll find a deli at these stores:

- Upper Highlands at 2525 Bardstown Rd., one block from the corner of Bardstown Rd. and Taylorsville Rd. (502) 459-8184

- Middletown at 12531 Shelbyville Rd. in the Kroger Shopping Center (502) 245-7031

- St. Matthews at 3737 Lexington Rd. in the historic Vogue Plaza (502) 893-3303

- Shelbyville at 1732 Midland Trail (502) 633-6330

These locations serve desserts only:

- Jeffersontown at 12613 Taylorsville Rd. (502) 267-6280

- Springhurst at 3598 Springhurst Blvd. (502) 326-8990

- Fern Creek at 5606 Bardstown Rd. (502) 239-3880

- Clarksville in Indiana at 1370 Veterans Pkwy. (812) 288-6000

inspired sushi rolls, diners will find colorful salads and appetizers, as well as a large assortment of tacos and pizzas that whimsically blends flavors from the Orient with popular Western presentations. Popular taco selections include tempura shrimp, and ground beef with spicy kimchi; for something different, try the sashimi pizza—organic spring lettuces, raw ahi tuna, salmon, white tuna, red onions and sliced avocado on flat bread with tamari-sesame sauce and fried garlic chips. The decor at the Dragon King's Daughter is as colorful and inviting as the dishes served there.

Open seven days a week, the DKD has a popular happy hour from 3 p.m. to 5 p.m. daily.

**EL CAPORAL**    $$
**2209 Meadow Dr.**
**(502) 473-7840**
**www.mycaporal.com**
One of the first Mexican restaurants in the Derby City, El Caporal has grown to include a number of locations throughout the area. This one, just off of Bardstown Road and past the Watterson on the southern end, and the one across the

river in Clarksville, Indiana, are the two most popular in the chain. Among the usual Tex-Mex suspects in the culinary lineup, you'll find fajitas, tacos, burritos, carnitas, and carne asada.

## JACK FRY'S                              $$$
**1007 Bardstown Rd.**
**(502) 452-9244**
**www.jackfrys.com**

Housed in a simple wooden building painted white, Jack Fry's is a Louisville icon. Originally established in 1933 by Jack Fry and his wife, Flossie, the restaurant became a place frequented by Jack's kind of people: gamblers, amateur boxers, and fans of the racetrack. As a result, it became a sportsmen's hangout, and Jack was often found conducting his bookmaking and bootlegging affairs from the back room. Numerous black-and-white photographs fill the walls of the current Jack Fry's, which reopened in 1987 after a stint as a Mexican restaurant. Today the crowd has become somewhat more refined, but the boisterous din of conversation still reminds patrons of its early days. Among the most popular items you'll find at Jack Fry's are the shrimp and grits with red-eye gravy and shitaki mushrooms and the warm brie salad. Open for dinner daily at 5:30, Jack Fry's also serves lunch Monday through Friday. Most nights there's live jazz.

## KASHMIR INDIAN RESTAURANT         $$
**1285 Bardstown Rd.**
**(502) 473-8765**
**www.kashmirlouisville.com**

Open daily, Kashmir has offered casual Indian dining in a small cottage at the heart of Louisville's Highlands neighborhood since 1999. Known for its friendly service, the restaurant specializes in the cuisine of northern India, featuring an extensive vegetarian menu in addition to many non-vegetarian items. Appetizers include samosas, pakoras, and tikkas, and they also offer savory lentil soup and lightly sweetened coconut soup. In addition, there's a variety of soft and flavorful breads—16 in all—to accompany your meal.

Tandoori specials, made in charcoal-fired clay ovens, are popular, and they also have a number of kormas, curries, rices, vindaloo, and *masala* dishes at reasonable prices. Entrees can be prepared mild to very hot to suit your taste.

Unusual traditional beverages such as a creamy mango *lassi* or sweet and spicy *masala* tea are available, as are Indian brews such as Taj Mahal, Kingfisher, and Flying Horse. On the weekend a variety of dishes can be sampled at the lunch buffet.

## LA BAMBA MEXICAN RESTAURANT        $
**1237 Bardstown Rd.**
**(502) 451-1418**
**www.labambaburritos.com**

"Burritos as big as your head" are what you find at this chain establishment offering large portions made in front of you as you wait. Serving both college towns and big cities, primarily in the Midwest, La Bamba has good, cheap food and the atmosphere is very casual. Open late, it's a popular stop after late-night adventures on Bardstown Road.

## LÁ QUÊ                              $$
**1019 Bardstown Rd.**
**(502) 238-3981**

No, it's not another Mexican food joint, or even a French bistro that you're speeding by on Bardstown Road. It's actually another Asian restaurant. Lá Quê, pronounced something like "la whey," is the Vietnamese name for basil (or cinnamon, depending on who you talk to), the fragrant herb that features so predominantly in the cuisine of Southeast Asia. The small restaurant has tile floors, yellow walls, and some Oriental bric-a-brac that make for a somewhat sparse atmosphere, but the Chinese, Thai, and Vietnamese dishes on offer are very reasonably priced. Popular is the flavorful and filling onion-studded fried rice with basil and shrimp, and the spring rolls—translucent rolls of rice paper stuffed with fresh herbs and slices of fresh avocado.

## The Cookie Lady

If you see a smiling woman in busy African prints on Bardstown Road, it's most likely the Cookie Lady. You'll know for sure by what she's got on top of her head. A familiar fixture at Louisville festivals, baseball games, and other events, the Cookie Lady often sells her sweet wares from a basket carried on her head, a skill learned in her native Uganda. Her real name is Elizabeth Kizito, and she got the idea for her well-known cookie business some 20 years ago, after baking up a batch of goodies at home to raise money for a birthday present for her son.

In 1989, she opened a bakery on Bardstown Road without the benefit of savings or a bank loan, and since then she's become a fixture on the Louisville food scene. Her Kizito Cookies are sold in restaurants, coffee shops, and other places throughout the city. Apart from a variety of cookies pulled out of the oven daily at her little bakery on Bardstown Road—chocolate chip, sugar, snickerdoodle, deluxe oatmeal, ginger snap, and peanut butter are just some of the flavors— there are assorted muffins, brownies, and biscotti as well. All her goodies are made with real butter and no trans fats. **Kizito Cookies** is located at 1398 Bardstown Rd.; (502) 456-2891; www.kizito.com.

**LILLY'S**　　　$$$
1147 Bardstown Rd.
(502) 451-0447
www.lillyslapeche.com

Another icon on the Louisville is a restaurant that—altho influenced—showcases a cuisine inspired. The menu changes frequently, based on availability as well as the growing season for fresh produce, and meats and dairy items come from regional farmers. Some of the vegetables even come from the restaurant's organic garden, which produces several varieties of radishes, beets, lettuces, tomatoes, and herbs. Friendly servers are able to tell you which items on your plate were actually picked just an hour before serving. The menu is constantly changing, but, depending on the time of year, you'll find things like Maker's Mark bourbon–smoked pork chops with celery root mashed potatoes, or chicken thighs stuffed with garlic, lemon, and parsley as main-course items, and starters such as lake trout stuffed with feta, jalapeño, red pepper, and mint, or fried oysters and Weisenberger grits.

**MOLLY MALONE'S IRISH PUB**　　　$$
**933 Baxter Ave.**
**(502) 473-1222**
**www.mollymalonesirishpub.com**
Open seven days a week for lunch and dinner, Molly Malone's is a place to enjoy hearty pub fare and lots of libations from the Emerald Isle. Although American bar standards such as queso and hot wings—and local favorites like fried green tomatoes—have found their way onto the menu, a good assortment of dishes re-creates the flavors of Ireland. The mussels are steamed in Harp Lager, and the smoked salmon is served with red onion, horseradish cream, and soda bread. In addition, there are Scotch eggs, bangers and mash, fish and chips, shepherd's pie, and traditional lamb stew. There's a popular weekday happy hour from 4 to 7 p.m. with $1 off premium drafts.

**PALERMO VIEJO**　　　$$$
**1359 Bardstown Rd.**
**(502) 456-6461**
Louisville, Kentucky, might be one of the last places on earth you'd expect to find an authentic Argentinean restaurant, but those in the know

# Out of Africa

There is a wide variety of ethnic restaurants to choose from in Louisville, so it's not difficult to get a taste of world cuisine during your stay here. If you're looking for a rare taste of Africa, try the two restaurants below; one specializes in Senegalese cooking, the other in Ethiopian.

### Chez Seneba    $$
4218 Bishop Lane
(502) 473-8959
www.chezseneba.omnicron.us

In Louisville, there's reportedly a community of nearly 1,000 Senegalese immigrants, and they seem to form the core clientele for Chez Seneba; but that doesn't mean the rest of us aren't invited to stop by and sample one of the spicy, aromatic dishes that constitutes West African cuisine. The menu offers dinners in huge portions for $10 or less, with enticing daily specials and appetizers such as *neems,* the eggroll-like fried cylinders stuffed with spicy beef, shrimp, green onion, rice noodles, and cilantro, and *fataya,* a choice of beef or fish with diced onions and tomatoes wrapped in a bread shell and deep-fried to a golden brown. A popular entree is the African-style chicken, grilled dark brown, with an exotic blend of garlic and herbs pushed deep into slits in the meat, which comes with a tangy, peppery mound of cooked onions on the side. With a glass of *bissap,* the minty, syrupy sweet hibiscus infusion that is the national drink of Senegal, a meal at Chez Seneba is an exotic and flavorful experience.

### Queen of Sheba    $$
2804 Taylorsville Rd.
(502) 459-6301
www.queenofshebalouisville.com

Louisville's first—and by most accounts, most authentic—Ethiopian restaurant is located in the old Mazzoni's near Bowman Field. It's not too far from Bardstown Road. The menu items at the Queen of Sheba include a variety of chicken, lamb, fish, beef, and vegetable dishes selected to represent the most popular flavors in Ethiopia; most of these are slowly cooked in a stew, with imported spices that add to the depth of flavors. In Ethiopian fashion, entrees are served together on a large round tray to make it easier to share, but don't expect to get silverware unless you ask for it. In Ethiopia food is normally eaten with your fingers—simply tear off a piece of the Ethiopian flatbread known as *injera* that comes with the meal and scoop up your food with it.

say Palermo Viejo is just as good as anything you'd find in its namesake neighborhood in the heart of Buenos Aires. Flaky empanadas with a variety of savory fillings and grilled steak served up on their own little *parrilla* are just some of the house specialties. With its good, affordable selection of Argentine wines, it's easy to enjoy a bottle or two of wine with dinner without breaking the bank. It's a smaller restaurant, not to mention very popular, so it's good to make reservations in advance. Open for dinner at 5 p.m. every day except Sunday.

### PITA HUT    $$
### 1613 Bardstown Rd.
### (502) 409-8484

Not too long ago, Jordanian native Khaled Imam opened a small restaurant specializing in Mediterranean cuisine on bustling Bardstown Road. Given Jordan's proximity to Syria, Lebanon, Israel, and Saudi Arabia, Imam's take on Mediterranean cuisine shows definite influences from the Middle East, and the result is something that pleases falafel fans in the 'Ville. Most find the offerings to be fresh, flavorful, and reasonably priced, and with its hot pitas, hummus, baba ganoush, fresh raw veggies, rice, and meat dishes, the lunch buffet is popular with herbivore and carnivore alike. Although the decor leaves a little to be desired, the value definitely makes up for it.

## RAMSI'S CAFÉ ON THE WORLD  $$
**1293 Bardstown Rd.**
**(502) 451-0700**
**www.ramsiscafe.com**

A perennial darling on the Louisville dining scene, Ramsi's Café on the World serves up a dizzying assortment of dishes drawing on culinary influences from all corners of the globe. The interior decor is as eclectic as the menu, where you'll find much-loved standards such as pollo nuevo havana, tortellini *graciela,* empress chicken, and lamb *biryani.* Other favorites—many of which are vegan or vegetarian—include the cubean burrito and Greek salad. Open late, Ramsi's has moderate prices that often attract a bustling crowd as diverse as the Highlands neighborhood where it is located. Don't try to make a reservation, though, because they don't take them at Ramsi's. Instead, show up and put your name on the list; if there's a wait—and during busy nights, there often is—head next door and browse the selection at Carmichael's Books. Ramsi's opens at 11 a.m. Monday through Saturday and at 10 a.m. on Sunday.

## SAPPORO JAPANESE GRILL
## AND SUSHI  $$$
**1706 Bardstown Rd.**
**(502) 479-5550**
**www.sapporojapanese.com**

One of the hottest sushi places in town, this sleek and stylish Asian eatery is located in the Deer Park neighborhood in the Highlands. Open daily for dinner at 5:30, Sapporo has a menu that includes an assortment of cold and hot appetizers, chicken and beef teriyaki, and *udon* (in broth) and *yakisoba* (pan-fried) dishes, in addition to award-winning sushi and sashimi. There's also *teppanyaki* lobster, scallops, and steaks grilled on the hibachi for those wanting be entertained by skilled chefs.

## SEVICHE LATIN RESTAURANT  $$$
**1538 Bardstown Rd.**
**(502) 473-8560**
**www.sevicherestaurant.com**

The chef/owner of Seviche, Anthony Lamas, has been featured on the Food Network, and the James Beard House has invited him to cook there twice, recognizing him as "a rising star of American cuisine." The son of Mexican and Puerto Rican parents, Lamas grew up in California amid the influence of many flavors that now define his cooking at this popular Bardstown Road eatery. One of the specialties of the house is the namesake ceviche (or seviche), a citrus-marinated seafood dish that originated in South America, and Lamas offers an entire section of the menu devoted to it. In addition to selections that include tuna with wasabi, cucumber, and seaweed, and *hamachi* with *rocoto* chile and ginger, there is also crab and yellow tomato ceviche flavored with lemon and cilantro, or shrimp seviche with avocado and tomato to choose from. Appetizers include a variety of Latin-inspired specialties such as *arepas* and empanadas, and for main courses, you're sure to find another specialty, *feijoada*, the Brazilian black bean stew studded with pieces of meat and sausage.

## SITAR  $$
**1702 Bardstown Rd.**
**(502) 473-8889**
**www.louisvillesitar.com**

This unassuming Deer Park restaurant serves "fresh and flavorful authentic South Indian and Indo-Chinese food." It is a popular retreat for vegetarians because there are so many non-meat items to choose from; however, there are enough selections on the menu to keep meat lovers happy as well. Chicken *pulao, mysore dosa, hydarabadi dum ka* mutton, and *thanjai* chicken

# Close-up

## Worth Leaving Bardstown Road

Here are five popular restaurants that are near Bardstown Road. They're not far, but they're off the beaten track.

### AL WATAN $$

3713 Klondike Lane

(502) 454-4406

The savory smell of warm spices permeates the small dining room at Al Watan, known for its friendly waitstaff. Lamb and yogurt dishes figure prominently on the menu. Aside from several sandwiches, you'll find lots of salads and appetizers perfect for sharing, such as baba ganouj and tabouleh. Entree items include the slices of seasoned cooked meat known as *schawarma*, lamb shish kabob with rice, and *kifta* kabob, spiced ground meat broiled on a skewer. Once your meal is finished, step next door to the bakery for freshly baked pita and Middle Eastern pastries.

### BISTRO LE RELAIS $$$

2817 Taylorsville Rd.

(502) 451-9020

www.lerelaisrestaurant.com

Louisville's favorite stop for French cooking, Le Relais, is located in the terminal building of historic Bowman Field, one of the oldest airports in the nation. A popular rear deck allows patrons in search of less-formal surroundings to watch the takeoffs and landings of smaller craft in the warmer months, while the art deco–inspired interior provides the backdrop for a more intimate experience. The bill of fare includes Gallic classics such as mussels steamed with white wine and garlic, tomato tarte tatin, steak-frites, *truite* meunière, and a mean mousse au chocolat. Closed Monday.

### COACH LAMP RESTAURANT & PUB $$$

751 Vine St., Louisville

(502) 583-9165

Despite the devastation wrought by Hurricane Katrina in Louisiana, some good did come of the situation when cities like Louisville received an influx of creative transplants from the Big Easy. One of them was Richard Lowe, a New Orleans chef who now cooks at the Coach Lamp Restaurant & Pub in the Original Highlands area of Louisville. The restaurant is housed in an old structure from 1872 that reportedly served as a stagecoach stop and then became a general store; after that, it was turned into a pub by Dominick Maier, whose previous bar had been destroyed

---

are some of the house specialties. The vegetable *biriyani* is a favorite as well. The staff is friendly and accommodating, and on the weekend the $6.99 lunch buffet attracts crowds.

## FRANKFORT AVENUE / BROWNSBORO ROAD / CRESCENT HILL AREA

### AUGUST MOON CHINESE BISTRO $$$
2269 Lexington Rd.
(502) 456-6569
www.augustmoonbistro.com

Located midway between the Highlands and the neighborhood of Crescent Hill, August Moon serves lunch and dinner seven days a week. Nestled against a park-like swath of trees along Beargrass Creek, the restaurant is housed in a contemporary building with soaring, open dining spaces, and austere walls in muted shades of gray. Throughout the room and lounge, which are divided by matte black knee-high planters, there are undraped tables and chairs and large square windows that reveal pleasant views. Chef Peng Looi, a native of Malaysia, uses the understated surrounding to wow his guests with a

by the Great Flood of 1937. A signature item at Maier's Bar and Grill was the roast beef and mashed potato plate, and the Coach Lamp still offers it on its lunch menu today. Aside from a selection of soups, smaller entrees, and sandwiches, the lunch menu offers traditional daily specials in the blue plate vein, including fried chicken or meat loaf with two sides, such as green beans seasoned with onions and smoky ham and creamy mashed potatoes.

**COME BACK INN**                    **$$**

909 Swan St.

(502) 627-1777

www.comebackinn.biz

There's usually a lively crowd at the Come Back Inn, in search of Italian-American pub favorites. When this cozy Germantown restaurant opened in 1996, people predicted that sooner or later it would have to reduce its portion sizes or raise its prices, but to date it hasn't happened. Portion sizes are still good, and the prices, modest. Pizzas, sandwiches, antipasto, and pastas—with lots of red sauce—are what you'll find on the menu. There's also a new take on a local favorite: the Italian hot brown. Dinner service only is offered Tuesday through Saturday from 4:30 p.m. until 10 p.m.; however, a second location across the river at 415 Spring Street in Jeffersonville serves lunch

every day except Sunday, and dinner Tuesday through Saturday. Call (812) 285-1777 for more information.

**LYNN'S PARADISE CAFE**                    **$$**

984 Barret Ave.

(502) 583-3447

www.lynnsparadisecafe.com

Pan-fried pecan chicken in Woodford Reserve mustard maple cream sauce. Gingersnap-encrusted cod with homemade guava ketchup. Hoppin' Juan, a black bean chili piled high with organic jasmine rice, zesty tropical mango chile salsa, cheddar cheese, sour cream, and cumin-scented blue corn tortillas. The food at Lynn's Paradise Cafe is as colorful and eclectic as its owner, Lynn Winter. The former woodworker sold her tools and opened Lynn's Paradise Cafe in 1991, intent on creating a unique setting that would attract a diverse group of people from around the world. Today, her funky diner with its cultivated kitsch in Louisville's Highlands neighborhood has gained cult status among foodies across the Bluegrass State and beyond. Among the many accolades Winter has received, *Bon Appetit* named Lynn's Paradise Cafe one of the 100 best neighborhood restaurants in the United States, and *Esquire* proclaimed it one of the four most fun restaurants in America.

colorful hodgepodge of Asian-inspired dishes that include house favorites like Indonesian-style spicy calamari and wok-seared salmon with vegetables and spiced tomato concasse.

**i** Among his many accolades, Chef Peng Looi has been invited to cook at the James Beard House four times. He is the owner of another popular restaurant, Asiatique, at 1767 Bardstown Road (also in this chapter).

**BLUE DOG BAKERY & CAFE**                    **$$**

2868 Frankfort Ave.

(502) 899-9800

www.bluedogbread.com

When baker Bob Hancock brought his $50,000 Spanish wood-fired oven to town and opened the Blue Dog Bakery & Cafe—a venture partially inspired by the renowned Acme Bakery in Berkeley, California—the bar was set for an entirely new standard of bread in Louisville. His authentic, European-style artisan breads are as good as any you'll find in this country or abroad. The bakery is located in the left half of the space, and on the other side you'll find a small restaurant with a nice variety of salads, quiches, soups, and sandwiches that complement the wonderful baked goods. The lemon tart—a sugar cookie crust filled with tangy lemon curd—is a great end to your meal, or a perfect afternoon pick-me-up with a hot cappuccino.

## You Can't Top the Tap

When you're in the Derby City, save yourself some money and don't bother with bottled water. The tap water here is consistently rated among the purest and best-tasting in the country. Many say it tastes better than any other tap water in North America. In one of the most recent blind taste tests, the Louis-ville Water Company was awarded the top prize in the annual "Best of the Best" Water Taste Test put on by the American Water Works Association.

### BOURBONS BISTRO                    $$$
**2255 Frankfort Ave.**
**(502) 894-8838**
**www.bourbonsbistro.com**
Located in a hip, casually elegant, vintage brick structure on Frankfort Avenue's restaurant row, Bourbons Bistro combines comfortable, cozy surroundings and innovative Kentucky-themed cuisine. The result is an enjoyable dining experience where the chef has devised a thoughtful menu with selections that can just as easily be enjoyed with a slosh of Evan Williams on the rocks or a Woodford Reserve Manhattan as they can with a glass of sauvignon blanc or merlot. The bill of fare begins with a good selection of appetizers, offering items such as excellent fried green tomatoes and diver scallops with pickled green-bean salad; for main courses, chef Michael Crouch might offer grilled prosciutto-wrapped filet of beef, braised bison short ribs with cauli-

flower puree, or pecan-encrusted baked salmon with bourbon orange molasses. In addition, there are some 130 bourbons, with prices starting at $5 for many labels and going all the way to $45 for a shot of the choicest Kentucky dew. Dinner service starts daily at 5 p.m. Happy hour is from 4:30 p.m to 7 p.m.

### CAFFÉ CLASSICO                    $$
**2144 Frankfort Ave.**
**(502) 895-0076**
**www.caffe-classico.com**
Available at this European-style café are a number of panini and specialty sandwiches, including tuna salad with wasabi and ginger mayo, smoked turkey club, curried chicken salad, and the West Coast with cucumber, avocado, lettuce, and chipotle mayonnaise. Panini favorites are the Prosciutto with the namesake Italian ham grilled with fresh mozzarella, tomato, and spinach on ciabatta, and the Americano with smoked ham and Swiss cheese. Dinner guests at Caffé Classico can opt for appetizers such as salmon croquettes, Belgian fries with three dipping sauces, mussels steamed with white wine, shallots, and garlic, and empanadas with beef, chicken, or vegetarian fillings. Aside from pizzas and salads—including the most popular "Tortoni Buenos Aires" salad, a layered chef creation with tomato, hard-cooked egg, cucumber, avocado, mozzarella, and carrots—there are also entrees like grilled flank steak with rustic mashed potatoes. Caffé Classico serves lunch and dinner six days a week. Weekends often see the addition of live entertainment, including musical ensembles and dance performances.

### EL MUNDO                    $$
**117 S Keats Ave.**
**(502) 899-9930**
**www.502elmundo.com**
A perennial favorite on the local Mexican food scene, this unfancy Clifton eatery incorporates fresh, local ingredients for a variety of Mexican staples, but often with a different take. Favorites include the guacamole, fish tacos, tamales, beer-braised bison tacos, and the veggie chili relleno.

There's also an ever-changing selection of daily specials for something different. And if you like your food with a little kick, ask the server for one of their house-made hot sauces. The choice of beers is good, but don't leave without ordering a margarita or two—they make them the old-fashioned way, without mixes.

## GENNY'S DINER $$
**2223 Frankfort Ave.**
**(502) 893-0923**
An old-school neighborhood dive, Genny's has a no-nonsense menu that features a lot of fried food among a selection of mostly burgers, breakfast fare, and sandwiches. Fried chicken livers, grilled cheese sandwiches, fried green tomatoes—those are the kinds of things served here. Genny's is the birthplace of the frickled pickle chip, a crunchy dill-pickle slice lightly coated with egg batter and deep-fried, and the Sweet Daddy. Weighing in at 20 ounces—that's a pound and a quarter—of beef formed into a triple-deck hamburger, it easily qualifies as the largest in town. It's topped with lettuce, tomato, onion, pickles, and mayo. Cheese is extra. Genny's opens at 8:30 a.m. Monday through Saturday.

## GRAPE LEAF $$
**2217 Frankfort Ave.**
**(502) 897-1774**
**www.grapeleafonline.com**
Nestled in the heart of Clifton for more than 15 years, owner Nabil Al-Saba's Grape Leaf is one of the city's most popular Mediterranean restaurants. When it's not too cold outside, the adjacent grape arbor is a popular place to sit and enjoy the inviting smells of cinnamon, pepper, and cardamom. Inside or out, it's food like the gyro-style strips of beef and lamb wrapped in pita and fresh Greek salads with feta that keeps customers coming back for more. Open every day at 8 a.m., the Grape Leaf is also a popular breakfast spot. The large morning selection includes *fatoosh* salad with hard-boiled eggs or falafel and lamb sausage biscuits.

## IRISH ROVER $$
**2319 Frankfort Ave.**
**(502) 899-3544**
**www.theirishroverky.com**
Easily the best—and most authentic—place to eat Irish in the city, the Rover has made its home in a 150-year-old building that at one time served as a saloon. Beers and whiskey are still pushed across the counter today, although now it's most likely Irish whiskey and Guinness, which has been shipped directly from Dublin. The menu leans heavily to the comfort-food side, and salmon, lamb, and leeks make appearances on more than one occasion. Fish and chips are available in both adult- and child-size portions. A popular appetizer is the Scotch egg, a hard-cooked egg that is wrapped in sausage and batter-fried. A second location, the Irish Rover Too, is in La Grange at 117 East Main Street. Call (502) 222-2286 for more information. Both locations are closed on Sunday.

**i** La Grange is the old stomping grounds of famed film director D. W. Griffith and Tom Blankenship, bassist for the Louisville band My Morning Jacket.

## KT'S RESTAURANT & BAR $$
**2300 Lexington Rd.**
**(502) 458-8888**
**www.ktsrestaurant.com**
A Louisville tradition since 1985, KT's was built on the site of the old Kentucky Tavern, a popular neighborhood watering hole in the 1950s. Today, it's a popular, casual place for families, couples on dates, singles dining alone, or even large groups wanting to celebrate, and the extensive menu features standard appetizers like spinach queso and chips, coconut shrimp, and artichoke dip with chips. Huge entree salads are a draw, as are specialities like the Maker's Mark bourbon sirloin and charbroiled salmon with lemon dill sauce. Located at the edge of the Cherokee Triangle neighborhood and across from the golf course at Cherokee Park, KT's is open seven days a week.

## L & N WINE BAR & BISTRO $$$
**1765 Mellwood Ave.**
**(502) 897-0070**
**www.landnwinebarandbistro.com**

Open for dinner at 5:30 p.m. Monday through Saturday, L & N features one of the city's most diverse wine lists, offering a carefully chosen bottle list from wine-producing regions all over the world, in addition to nearly 80 wines by the glass. Wines are available in two-ounce tastes, six-ounce glasses, or by the bottle, and all of the wines are served in varietally correct Riedel crystal stemware. Design your own wine flight, or let the staff create one for you. If the little restaurant has a homey vibe, that's because the dining area is spread out in rooms inside of an old brick house in the Butchertown neighborhood. Exposed brick on the walls provides a nice backdrop as you peruse the extensive menu created by the chef, Rick Adams. The list of bistro/comfort-food fare includes items such as the house-smoked pork chop with Granny Smith apple and mission fig compote, and bison strip au poivre.

## MAIDO $$
**1758 Frankfort Ave.**
**(502) 894-8775**
**www.maidosakebar.com**

In addition to good beers and wines, this Kansai-style sake pub serves a variety of small dishes and sushi. The portions are smaller—and the prices lower—so guests can try more dishes and share with family and friends. Open every day except Sunday, Maido offers a "super happy bar menu" from 4 p.m. to 6 p.m. Monday through Thursday. Items like miso soup and Japanese pickles go for $1; sushi croquettes and California rolls go for $2; and red snapper tempura rolls and eggplant with miso sauce only cost $3.

## NORTH END CAFÉ $$
**1722 Frankfort Ave.**
**(502) 896-8770**
**www.northendcafe.com**

Offering breakfast, lunch, and dinner Tuesday through Sunday, North End Café opens daily at 8 a.m. The restaurant was started in 2003 in two renovated shotgun houses, with a decor that blends historic architectural elements from the original design with modern accents and a collection of artwork from Louisville's up-and-coming artists. The menu highlights a wide variety of items prepared with a health-conscious approach. Only the freshest seasonal ingredients available are used, and when they don't use the vegetables and fresh herbs grown in their multi-acre garden in Simpsonville, they buy from local growers. At breakfast, popular choices include the cornmeal buttermilk pancakes and the smoked trout hash; for lunch, the grilled salmon sandwich and the chicken and dumplings are a hit; at night, tapas like empanadas and calamari get their own section of the menu. There is also a number of vegetarian and organic menu choices.

## PAT'S STEAK HOUSE $$$
**2437 Brownsboro Rd.**
**(502) 893-2062**
**www.patssteakhouselouisville.com**

Consistently voted the best steakhouse by readers of local publications such as *Louisville Magazine*, *Kentucky Monthly*, and *LEO*, Pat's Steak House has a tradition of serving up grilled cuts of beef and thick pork chops and veal cutlets that goes back to 1958. A hundred years before that, it was an inn and stagecoach stop, so its roots as a place for hospitality run very deep. Inside, the restaurant's comfortable dining rooms provide the ideal, old-school atmosphere for guests to relax and enjoy, bathed in the warm amber glow of aged wood. In addition to hand-trimmed cuts of beef, you'll find thick-cut pork chops and veal cutlets. There are also items like pan-fried oysters, country ham, baked salmon, and fried chicken, in addition to meat loaf, chicken livers, and frog legs. They also have a good selection of salads, sandwiches, and desserts, too. Payment at this historic Louisville Irish landmark is by personal check or cash only, and an ATM is located at the front entrance. Open at 4:30 p.m. Monday through Saturday for dinner, Pat's Steak House is closed on Sunday.

## PORCINI $$$
**2730 Frankfort Ave.**
**(502) 894-8686**
**www.porcinilouisville.com**

Specializing in the cuisine of Italy's northern regions since 1992, Porcini is another one of those restaurants that receives regular accolades from readers of the area's top food publications. The menu changes frequently, but you can usually expect to find standards such as cheese-filled tortellloni with mushrooms and prosciutto, or calamari friti in the antipasto section. In the entrees you might find grilled rack of lamb with Madeira sauce, or grilled chicken breast stuffed with mascarpone and arugula, served with fava beans. Dishes like orecchiette with spicy sausage and penne alla carbonara make up the pasta selections. Porcini opens for dinner every day except Sunday at 5:30 p.m.

## SARI SARI $$
**2339 Frankfort Ave.**
**(502) 894-0585**
**www.gosari.com**

This tiny Filipino place where chef Lourdes Fronteras re-creates the distinctive cuisine of her native country adds a distinctive element to Louisville's ethnic dining scene. Part Spanish, part Asian, part Pacific Rim, the cooking of the Philippines usually has something to offer most palates. The menu has entree selections divided into categories, such as chicken, beef, pork, fish, rice, and noodles, and specialties, and the unique blend of Eastern and Western influences becomes evident at first glance. Oriental standards such as fried rice, noodles, and stir-fries share the stage with Hispanic-inspired favorites like tamales, *escabeches,* and adobos, but distinct names like *pancit, sinigang,* and *lumpia* hint at the uniquely Filipino flavors in store.

Appetizers at Sari Sari include favorites such as the Philippine vegetable egg rolls known as *lumpia,* and the Pinatubo pancake, an East Asian omelet with walnuts, spinach, and bean sprouts. *Tinolang isda* is a tasty soup with tuna and vegetables in a tamarind broth that Lourdes serves as a special every now and then. For main courses, diners can sample *pancit bihon,* a popular Filipino dish with cellophane noodles and stir-fried vegetables seasoned with fresh limes, and butterfish *inoong-onan,* a savory fish stew with ginger, lemongrass, tomatoes, and garlic. For a taste of Spanish-inspired dishes, diners should try the pork or chicken adobo, where vinegar, garlic, and soy form the flavorful backbone of the namesake marinade, or the thick, tomato-based stew flavored with vegetables and spices known as pork *menudo.*

## SHIRAZ MEDITERRANEAN GRILL $$
**2011 Frankfort Ave.**
**(502) 891-8854**
**www.shirazmg.com**

Kabobs and things like falafel, hummus, lentil rice, and bulgur wheat salad are served up at the no-frills Shiraz Mediterranean Grill. Aside from the Frankfort Avenue location, you can pick up your *koobideh* or shish kabobs at the following locations: 3501 Poplar Level Road (502-632-2232); 2210 Holiday Manor (502-426-9954); 2105 North Hurtbourne Parkway (502-426-3440); and 153 South English Station Road (502-244-1341). Most locations are open before noon six or seven days a week.

## VARANESE $$$
**2106 Frankfort Ave.**
**(502) 899-9904**
**www.varanese.com**

An eclectic Mediterranean-style restaurant that can comfortably seat about 150 guests, you can dine at the bar, in the dining room, or on the four-season patio, which has a dramatic 20-foot slate water wall. Enclosed by serpentine glass doors that retract to provide an outdoor dining experience, the space is ideal for enjoying John Varanese's eclectic menu. The array of options ranges from stuffed grape leaves and fried green tomato salad to new signature entrees such as the seared boneless pork chop and caramelized orange salmon. A popular dessert is the fried banana topped with homemade oatmeal cookie dough ice cream. Varanese opens daily at 5 p.m. for dinner.

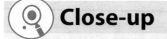

# Close-up

## Compassionate Cuisine

**Zen Garden Vegetarian Restaurant** ($$; 2240 Frankfort Ave.; 502-895-9114; www.zengarden restaurant.org), Louisville's first gourmet Asian vegetarian restaurant, is open every day except Sunday.

Not merely a place to feed the body, it is also a place where non-meat eaters (or those simply looking for a healthier alternative) come to restore heart and soul. Zen Garden founder Huong Tran, a refugee from the war in Vietnam, arrived in Louisville in 1975. She had owned a French restaurant in Saigon and calls her style of cooking "compassionate cuisine." She wants diners to realize that vegetarian cookery "not only delights but will also make your body and spirit stronger." Balance, delicacy, and subtlety are the hallmarks of the dining experience at her laid-back, simple restaurant.

Popular appetizers include Vietnamese crepes that are fried crispy and filled with mushrooms, bean sprouts, and tofu; soft spring rolls stuffed with rice noodles, lettuce, and tofu; pot stickers or steamed dumplings with soybean and vegetable filling; and crispy tofu, which is lightly battered, deep-fried, and served with bean sauce. For entrees, you'll find more than 20 different dishes to choose from, including fresh green beans and mock duck, eggplant in crispy soy, sweet and sour crispy tofu, and hot Singapore noodles with shredded tofu, cabbage, celery, bean sprouts, carrots, snow peas, and curry spice.

In addition to more details about what else is on the menu, the Zen Garden Web site has additional information about the charities and humanitarian endeavors they support. Among them are the Compassionate Service Society (CSS), which helps tsunami victims rebuild their communities; CSS Project Nepal, which involves giving the people of Nepal material and emotional support; and the Lac Viet Academy of Louisville, a nonprofit instructional program and resource center serving immigrant children and their families in the South End of Louisville.

## ST. MATTHEWS

### BLUEGRASS BREWING COMPANY $$
3929 Shelbyville Rd.
(502) 899-7070
www.bbcbrew.com

The largest microbrewery in the state, the Bluegrass Brewing Company was founded in 1993. At this location in East St. Matthews, some of the region's best beers are crafted under the supervision of head brewer Jerry Gnagy. Pull up a chair at the spacious and inviting bar, or watch the brewing operation through large windows in the dining room as you enjoy your meal or dine alfresco in the beer garden. Aside from an assortment of burgers, sandwiches, and brick oven pizzas, you'll find entree items such as the New York strip with mashed potatoes and asparagus, and a fish platter with fries and coleslaw. Open seven days a week at 11 a.m., BBC has a second location downtown (closed Sunday) on Theater Square at 660 South Fourth Street. Call (502) 568-2224 for more information.

### CAFÉ LOU LOU $$
106 Sears Ave.
(502) 893-7776
www.cafeloulou.com/main

When chef-owner Clay Wallace came back home to Louisville after working in New Orleans, he decided to combine the influences of the two cities to produce an Italian-Mediterranean-Cajun menu in a setting known for its bright colors and penchant for eye-catching art; hence, Café Lou Lou was born. Among the offerings, you'll spy Louisiana-inspired dishes such as shrimp and grits with Cajun spices and a jambalaya-style pasta dish with crawfish, shrimp, and smoked sausage, in addition to a good version of the muffaletta. There are plenty of Mediterranean dishes, too, including gyros and a flatbread appetizer made of crisp lavash topped with spinach, tomatoes, cheese, and smoked salt. The huge menu includes a wide variety of pizzas and pastas as well. There's also a Café Lou Lou in the Highlands at 2216 Dundee Road. Call (502) 459-9566 for more information.

## DEL FRISCO'S                    $$$
**4107 Oechsli Ave.**
**(502) 897-7077**
**www.delfriscoslouisville.com**
One of Louisville's hidden fine-dining treasures, Del Frisco's is tucked away in a small nondescript row of businesses behind the Old Sears Building off Sears Avenue. Once through the front door, you enter a warm atmosphere with deep wood tones and thick carpets. USDA Prime corn-fed, aged steak occupies a prominent position on the menu, and aside from rib eye, sirloin, filet mignon, and prime rib, you'll find a popular chateaubriand for two. There's also a good selection of seafood and poultry dishes at this old-school steakhouse, along with classic starters such as shrimp cocktail, escargots, lobster bisque, and spinach salad with hot bacon dressing. Sides, including potatoes au gratin and sautéed mushrooms, are very popular here as well.

## EQUUS                           $$$
**122 Sears Ave.**
**(502) 897-9721**
**www.equusrestaurant.com**
Founded by John S. "Jack" Corbett Jr. and son Dean in 1985, Equus is a fine-dining establishment serving American regional cuisine that has received rave reviews around the country. Corbett utilizes classical cooking techniques with an emphasis on traditional flavors and seasonal ingredients to create a sophisticated menu of what he describes as modern American fare. His culinary team supports local farmers and producers, and they take pride in knowing the growers who supply the food they serve. Popular entrees include Shrimp Jenkins, a dish of fried Carolina shrimp flavored with brown sugar, rosemary, Worcestershire, Tabasco,

and bourbon, and slow-baked beef brisket with mashers and a fried onion ring. Equus (Latin for "horse," by the way) is open Monday through Saturday from 6 p.m. to 11 p.m. Next door is Jack's Lounge, named in honor of Dean's father, which opened in 2000 and serves a variety of comfortfood items (pot roast with truffled mashed potatoes, hot browns, shrimp and crawfish etouffeé, etc.) in a less-formal setting.

## HAVANA RUMBA                    $$
**4115 Oechsli Ave.**
**(502) 897-1959**
**www.myhavanarumba.com**
Until the government in this country lifts the silly ban on travel to Cuba, most of us can only dream of enjoying a bite to eat in an authentic Havana restaurant. In the meantime, however, diners in Louisville have found a couple of good Cuban places where they can imagine. One of them is Havana Rumba, which shares the same business strip as Del Frisco's, and is not too far away from Equus. The interior successfully creates a sunny tropical feel with cool tile and walls painted hues of deep red and bright yellow; bright paintings of Cuban life and assorted bric-a-brac adorn the walls. Custom-made tables featuring wooden tops laminated with Cuban cigar-box covers and seating on imported leather-and-wood *taburetes* round out the authentic feel. By the time the menu arrives, you're all set to enjoy a real taste of Havana. The selection is extensive, and popular main courses are the roast pork known as *lechon asado,* the shredded skirt steak dish known as *ropa vieja,* and the deep-fried chunks of marinated pork known as *masas de puerco.*

## LOTSA PASTA INTERNATIONAL
## FOOD SHOP                       $$
**3717 Lexington Rd.**
**(502) 896-6361**
**www.lotsapastalouisville.com**
Known for delicious handmade deli sandwiches and tantalizing gourmet items, Lotsa Pasta has a secluded cafe with free Wi-Fi service where you can enjoy a bite to eat before filling up your shopping basket. Large windows open onto a garden patio,

and there are specialty coffees, teas, and pastries offered as well. St. Matthews' favorite gourmet stop started off as a pasta shop in 1982, and quickly grew to include a bakery, deli, and cheese counter. Italian delicacies and house-made pastas are still a mainstay at Lotsa Pasta, but hard-to-find international items and local goodies line the shelves as well. Lotsa Pasta is open daily.

## HURSTBOURNE LANE / EAST END

### CORBETT'S $$$$
**5050 Norton Healthcare Blvd.**
**(502) 327-5058**
**www.corbettsrestaurant.com**
When famed Louisville restaurateur Dean Corbett converted a historic Louisville home known as the Von Allmen mansion into his latest eatery, he pulled out all the stops in anticipation of bringing five-star elegance to the Bluegrass State dining scene. "I really believe this restaurant will challenge the definition of fine dining in Louisville, and we hope to show our guests a new level of elegance and flavor with cutting-edge technology and creative cuisine," says Corbett, who assembled an all-star team of managers to join him in overseeing the operation. Meticulous planning has addressed every detail, from the in-house water purification system down to the ironing board and iron in the spacious employee dressing room. Corbett's menu showcases the abundance of local purveyors as well as the best ingredients from around the world. Guests may select from an a la carte menu or choose five-course tastings for $65 and nine-course tastings for $100 for the ultimate in Kentucky fine dining.

### LIMESTONE $$$
**10001 Forest Green Blvd.**
**(502) 426-7477**
**www.limestonerestaurant.com**
In addition to dining areas designed for easy relaxation, this swanky East End restaurant has a bar that's ideal for meeting friends after work. There's also a patio perfect for seasonal dining, and the restaurant has wheelchair access

and plenty of parking just steps from the front door. The menu features fare that incorporates the best of "new Southern cooking with old Southern charm," and chef-owner Jim Gerhardt has received numerous accolades for creating an ever-evolving selection that celebrates the use of Kentucky products. His sophisticated yet unpretentious interpretation of regional classics includes favorites such as fried green tomatoes with sautéed calamari, filet of salmon roasted on bourbon barrel staves, and hot and sweet jumbo shrimp on a Kentucky grit cake with red-eye gravy and country ham crisp.

### MITCHELL'S FISH MARKET $$$
**4031 Summit Plaza Dr.**
**(502) 412-1818**
**www.mitchellsfishmarket.com**
An ever-changing menu printed twice daily at Mitchell's Fish Market restaurants allows diners to sample the finest and freshest seafood from around the world. From the waters of the Great Lakes to the Gulf of Mexico, from Cape Cod to the coasts of Chile, from the Bering Strait to Chesapeake Bay—there are more than 80 selections for fish lovers. The Louisville link in the chain is a sleek and stylish eatery just off the Gene Snyder at the Summit. The Louisville Mitchell's Fish Market serves lunch and dinner seven days a week.

### MOJITO TAPAS RESTAURANT $$
**2231 Holiday Manor Center**
**(502) 425-0949**
**www.mojitorestaurant.com**
Open seven days a week for lunch and dinner, this restaurant in the Holiday Manor shopping center has become one of the city's most popular restaurants in recent years. The draw is the innovative cooking of chef-owner Fernando Martinez, who specializes in small-plate Spanish tapas with a Cuban vibe. What was already a good place for tapas was kicked up a notch or two in early 2007 after Martinez spent a couple of months in Europe, taking a six-week intensive culinary program at Le Cordon Bleu in Paris and traveling to Spain for culinary influence. With more than 30 tapas plus salads, flatbread dishes,

# Close-up

## Go Deutsch

There are a number of German dining options in the region, and many of them can be found in the Fort Knox area, where there are no fewer than five German restaurants.

Two of them are the **Schnitzel Barn** (270-828-8300) at 5580 Flaherty Drive in Vine Grove, and **Uncle Frank's German Food** (270-352-4444) in Radcliff at 821 North Dixie Boulevard. If you don't want to leave the 'Ville in search of your German food fix, try these two local favorites:

**ERIKA'S GERMAN RESTAURANT** $$

9301 Hurstbourne Park Blvd.

(502) 499-8822

Located in a former Chinese fast food restaurant, Erika Masden's German restaurant does a good job of re-creating the flavors of her native Nuremberg. For starters, you'll find things like potato pancakes, Franconian wedding soup, and goulash soup; for main courses, the bratwurst plate is popular, and there's a wide assortment of schnitzel (cutlets of pork, chicken, or veal that are fried crisp) as well. The restaurant is located on a short street just off Hurstbourne Lane, which can be a bit challenging to get to if you don't know your way around. If you're driving east on I-64 from downtown, make sure to split off on the "Local Access" ramp, not the main ramp for southbound Hurstbourne. Turn right at the foot of this ramp, and watch for the turn into Erika's before the traffic light at the main ramp.

**GASTHAUS** $$$

4812 Brownsboro Center

(502) 899-7177

www.gasthausdining.com

Started in 1993, the Gasthaus offers one of the region's most authentic German dining experiences. The ambience at this family-run establishment in the East End, conveniently located off I-71, is enhanced as much by the authentic cuisine as it is by the authentic surroundings. While waltzes and march music play softly in the background, waitresses wearing colorful dirndls, the traditional folk dress of Germany, serve guests hearty and filling fare as good as any found in the Old Country. The restaurant is run by the Greipels—Michael, Annemarie, and their children—who, in addition to German beers and wines, also offer a warm and welcoming atmosphere in which to enjoy their home-cooked Teutonic staples. Since the Gasthaus opened, the menu has grown to include a large selection of starters, salads, and main courses; the dishes are authentic, and everything is made from scratch, using only the finest and freshest ingredients. In addition to favorites like wiener schnitzel and sauerbraten, you'll find a wonderful assortment of cakes and pastries freshly baked by Frau Greipel herself.

sandwiches, and paella—all reasonably priced and portioned—it's a place for an affordable feast with a group of friends who like to sit around and share their food.

**SELENA'S AT WILLOW LAKE** $$
**10609 Lagrange Rd.**
**(502) 245-9004**
**www.selenasrestaurant.com**
Located in Anchorage, Selena's is housed at the

old Willow Lake Tavern, a quaint brick building that dates back to the 1920s. Outside, there's an inviting wraparound patio perfect for alfresco dining well into the fall, thanks to the presence of outdoor heaters; inside, it is broken up into warmly lit chambers furnished with comfortable booths and tables. Alan Salmon, the owner of Selena's at the Willow Lake Tavern, named the restaurant in honor of his culinary mentor of sorts, a second-generation Sicilian woman named Selena D'Avanza, who was a childhood neighbor when he lived in Florida. Today, the menu features an eclectic collection of appetizers and entrees based on her Italian and Creole recipes.

### Z'S OYSTER BAR & STEAKHOUSE $$$$
**101 Whittington Pkwy.**
**(502) 429-8000**
**www.zsoyster.com**

Listed as one of Tom Horan's "Top 10 Seafood Restaurants" in the United States, Z's Oyster Bar & Steakhouse features select cuts of prime Midwestern aged beef that is hand-cut to order and cooked just the way you like it. In addition, oyster lovers can select from the best shellfish available—from the West Coast, East Coast, or the Gulf—thanks to the day-boat fishermen who supply the bulk of the fresh seafood that is simply and expertly prepared. With a *Wine Spectator* award-winning wine list of over 600 different selections, it's easy to find something to go along with signature cuts of meat such as the porterhouse or pork rib chop. This pricey, classy restaurant also houses a private dining room that seats 20 to 60 for company functions or family get-togethers.

**i** Fresh seafood in Louisville? Yes. Believe it or not, visitors always comment on the quality of the fish and fruits of the sea available here. Louisville is the main UPS hub in the country, so fresh fish is flown in daily. Many Derby City chefs are able to put items like oysters, salmon, tuna, lobster, and clams on their guests' tables less than 24 hours after they were plucked from the waters of the Atlantic, Pacific, or Gulf of Mexico.

# ACROSS THE RIVER

### EL CAPORAL $$
**515 East State St.**
**Clarksville, IN**
**(812) 282-7174**
**www.mycaporal.com**

This restaurant—part of a local chain that started off in Louisville as the area's first well-known Mexican restaurant—is one of the more-popular Mexican joints in southern Indiana. The interior is bright and cheerful, and it's especially popular with families who have small children. Aside from the usual Tex-Mex selections like tacos, burritos, and enchiladas, you'll also find fajitas, carnitas, carne asada, and a good chili relleno. The homemade flan is a favorite dessert.

### JOE HUBER FAMILY FARM
### AND RESTAURANT $$
**2421 Scottsville Rd.**
**Borden, IN**
**(812) 923-5255**
**www.joehubers.com**

Now in its seventh generation of descendants who are included in operations, the Joe Huber Family Farm and Restaurant in southern Indiana has become a local institution. Anytime of year, it's a popular destination for homemade jams and jellies and the wide variety of wines from its vineyard, but this is also where people go to pick strawberries in the summer. In the fall the Farm is known for its pumpkins and harvest-time activities. The restaurant, where everything is made from scratch and served family-style, is a big draw, too. A spacious dining room overlooks the lake, and there are flower gardens and a mini farm and playground that are especially nice for children. The menu includes country-fried chicken, Huber honey ham, their famous fried biscuits with apple butter, chicken and dumplings, a variety of fresh vegetables, and homemade pies, cobblers, and more. Since it's often crowded—especially in the fall and during the holidays—it's always good to plan ahead for a visit to Huber's.

### LA ROSITA MEXICAN GRILL $$
**1515 East Market St.**
**New Albany, IN**
**(812) 944-3620**
**www.larositagrill.com**

Tucked away in a hidden residential area of New Albany, La Rosita Mexican Grill features vibrant fare typical of many eateries in Mexico City, the

# A Meal with a View

Looking for a place with something good to eat, and something good to look at? Try one of these three places across the river in Jeffersonville. They're all down by the Ohio and have great views of the Louisville skyline during the day and at night.

**The Bristol Jeffersonville**  $$
700 West Riverside Dr.
Jeffersonville, IN
(812) 218-1995
www.bristolbarandgrille.com

This, the newest of the six Bristol locations, offers one of the best views of the Louisville skyline. They serve breakfast, lunch, and dinner daily. The bison quesadilla—flank steak with jack cheese, cheddar, fresh salsa, and ancho chili sauce in a flour tortilla—is a popular lunch option. (Also see text listing.)

**KingFish**  $$
601 West Riverside Dr.
Jeffersonville, IN
(812) 284-3474
www.kingfishrestaurants.com

KingFish restaurants have been serving up seafood in Kentuckiana since 1948. Aside from spectacular views of Louisville's skyline, the Jeffersonville King-Fish has a great sampler with coconut shrimp, pan-fried oysters, clam strips, sea scallops, and crab cakes. There are also two other high-volume KingFish locations in the Louisville area: 3021 Upper River Road (502-895-0544) and 1610 Kentucky Mills Drive (502-240-0700).

**Rocky's Sub Pub**  $$
715 West Riverside Dr.
Jeffersonville, IN
(812) 282-3844
www.eatatrockys.com

On the day Elvis died—no joke!—Bronx native John Fondrisi opened the doors to his 40-seat Italian-American eatery in what was Duffy's hamburger stand on Market Street in Jeffersonville. More than 30 years later, he's expanded to the current, larger location, which includes impressive riverfront seating and vistas of the Derby City.

chef's old stomping grounds. Aside from the usual suspects like carne asada, burritos, and quesadillas, the menu also showcases authentic Mexican specialties such as tortas, huaraches, pambazos, and other items not normally found in most local Tex-Mex establishments. For something different, try the tamal, which is draped in sauces the color of the Mexican flag and sprinkled with cheese, or the shrimp cocktail. A second La Rosita location off of Grant Line Road at 113 Grant Line Plaza specializes in tacos and such. Call (812) 948-7967 for more information.

**THE WINDSOR RESTAURANT
AND GARDEN**  $$$
**148 East Market St.**
**New Albany, IN**
**(812) 944-9688**
**thewindsorrestaurant.com**

Housed in a 140-year-old building that was once a small hotel in downtown New Albany, the Windsor retains the high ceilings, rich millwork, and ornate ceiling fixtures of another era. In a statement of simple elegance, black cloths drape the tables, which are topped with sleek napkins and single roses in tall bud vases, and the dinner menu showcases the kitchen's innovative, slightly international take on down-home fare. A modest list of main courses allows the chef to concentrate on the execution of dishes such as pan-roasted beef tenderloin with morel reduction, and duck breast in sassafras brine, and sides include items like potato puree, sautéed summer squash, fettuccini, corn pudding, and the tasty house fries, which are seasoned with rosemary, thyme, sage, garlic, and Parmesan. The Windsor is open seven days a week; however, dinner is generally served only Tuesday through Saturday.

## OTHER PARTS OF TOWN

### CHECK'S CAFÉ
**1101 East Burnett Ave.**
**(502) 637-9515**
**www.checkscafe.com**
Established in 1944, Check's is a Germantown tradition that has been family operated for three generations. The atmosphere is that of a friendly neighborhood saloon, and it's the kind of place that seems to be dark even on a sunny day. That aside, Check's has been said to have some of the best home-cooked bar food in the 'Ville. In addition to burgers, bean soup, chili, chicken, fish, homemade soups, and hand rolled oysters, you'll find bratwurst and other German-American favorites. Check's Café is open seven days a week for lunch and dinner. The closing time varies depending on the crowd.

### DOE RUN INN $$$
**500 Doe Run Hotel Rd.**
**Brandenburg**
**(270) 422-2982**
**www.doeruninn.com**
This rustic old mill turned country inn, located about 40 miles outside of Louisville, is famous for its hearty country cooking, among other things. The cast-iron fried chicken is worth the drive alone, but there's a lot more by way of good food and rustic surroundings. The Greer family serves up generous helpings of standard restaurant fare with lots of Kentucky specialties such as trout with tomatoes and molases, champagne cider

chicken, country ham biscuits and smoked port loin. For more information on this historic Kentucky eatery, read the description on page 25 in the History chapter.

### RUTH'S CHRIS STEAK HOUSE $$$$
**6100 Dutchmans Lane**
**(502) 479-0026**
**www.ruthschris.com**
The world's largest fine-dining company, Ruth's Chris Steak House, has more than 100 franchises around the world; one of them is in Louisville, off the Watterson Expressway. Serving up pricey prime steaks and chops since 1965—when Ruth Ann Udstad bought a New Orleans steak restaurant that had opened in 1927 at the corner of Broad and Ursuline—this tony restaurant chain is known for appetizers such as its barbecued shrimp and crab-stuffed mushroom, in addition to sides like creamed spinach and Lyonnais potatoes.

> **i** The Louisville Ruth's Chris Steak House is located at the top of the Kaden Tower, a 15-story office building in east suburban Louisville. The earth-tone building has eye-catching grillwork over the outside windows and a distinctive cantilever design which provides open interior space. Originally named the Lincoln Tower, the building opened in 1966 as the headquarters for the Lincoln Income Life Insurance Company. The architect of the project, William Wesley Peters, based the unique design of the office tower on three separate projects started by his old boss, Frank Lloyd Wright. Wright was also his father-in-law. For more information about this unique structure, go to the Web site for the Unofficial Fan Site of the City of Louisville, Kentucky, at www.louisville.cc.

### TOAST ON MARKET
**736 East Market Street**
**(502) 569-4099**
**www.toastonmarket.com**
Closed on Monday, Toast on Market opens at 7 a.m. six days a week for breakfast, lunch, and

# 🔍 Close-up

## Two Good Catches

If you're looking for a riverside eatery where the locals go, try one of these off-the-beaten-path restaurants on opposite sides of Louisville.

**CAPTAIN'S QUARTERS**

**RIVERSIDE GRILL** $$

5700 Captain's Quarters Rd.

(502) 228-1651

www.cqriverside.com

Once an early tavern catering to river travelers in the Harrods Creek area, the Captain's Quarters has been heavily rebuilt into the iconic East End hangout it is today. With lots of patio and deck seating, it's especially popular for people wanting to sit outside and enjoy the views with a glass of wine or a bite to eat. The menu has a fairly standard mix of sandwiches, salads, and burgers, but there are some additions—such as stuffed grape leaves and tuna tataki—that give it an eclectic flair. Although fish and seafood don't figure as prominently as you'd expect on the menu of a riverside restaurant, there is a hand-breaded Atlantic cod sandwich many think is the best in the city, in addition to creamy clam chowder in a bread bowl and fish tacos. Open seven days a week, Captain's Quarters also has a relaxing Sunday brunch featuring omelet and carving stations, waffles, fried chicken, steamed shrimp, seafood entrees, sides, desserts, pastries, and much more. It is served year-round on Sunday from 10:30 a.m. to 2:30 p.m., and costs $17.95. Captain's Quarters has been selected by readers of *Louisville Magazine* as the "Best of Louisville" for outdoor dining.

**MIKE LINNIG'S** $$

9308 Cane Run Rd.

(502) 937-9888

www.mikelinnigsrestaurant.com

Some nights it bustles with activity and lively conversation, others—especially on sultry summer evenings—flickering lanterns cast a mellow mood over the picnic area under a canopy of towering oak trees. Nearby, the Ohio River drifts lazily along behind a flood embankment. Fish lovers have been flocking to this southwest Louisville restaurant since 1925, and whatever the atmosphere, the seafood is always a hit with customers. The portions tend to be huge and affordable, and the fish sandwich is regularly voted best in town, giving the folks at the Captain's Quarters a run for their money. One bite of the gigantic fillets coated in tender, crunchy batter, and the reason becomes clear. There are also clams, crawfish, oyster stew, peel-and-eat shrimp, clam chowder, turtle soup, frog legs, pan-fried oysters, battered salmon, and crab cakes—and chicken, onion rings, burgers, pork cutlets, rib-eye sandwiches, steaks, and more for those looking for something different. Mike Linnig's is closed on Monday. In addition, they usually close every year after Thanksgiving and reopen in late January.

brunch. For lunch, they offer a wide variety of salads and sandwiches, including four versions of the grilled cheese; breakfast—served all day—includes different preparations of pancakes, french toast, omelets and other other egg dishes like the "drowned egg" in tomato cilantro sauce. During the week, Toast on Market closes at 2 p.m.; they stay open till 3 p.m. on the weekends.

A second location is at 141 East Market in New Albany. Call (812) 941-8582 for more information.

**WILD EGGS** $$

**3985 Dutchmans Lane**

**(502) 893-8005**

**www.crackinwildeggs.com**

In 2008 Louisville's breakfast and brunch crowd

was thrilled when Shane Hall and business partner J. D. Rothberg opened an eggs-themed morning and early-afternoon hangout on Dutchmans Lane. With a pleasantly cheerful, slightly quirky and hip decor, Wild Eggs has a menu that features a creative selection of breakfast and lunch items, including omelets, scrambles, frittatas, pancakes, waffles, French toast, sandwiches, and soups—all offered seven days a week. Choices include popular items like the fresh vegetable Farmers Market Skillet and Kalamity Katie's Border Benedict, with green chili cheddar corn cakes, topped with chorizo, two poached eggs, *queso fundido, pico de gallo,* sour cream, green onion, and fresh avocado. Wild Eggs also offers custom-blended coffee at an espresso bar, and mimosas made with fresh-squeezed orange juice at the cocktail bar. A second Wild Eggs location recently opened at 1311 Herr Lane in the Westport Village shopping center. Call (502) 618-2866 for details.

# COFFEE SHOPS, TEA HOUSES, ETC.

## Downtown

### BLUE MOUNTAIN COFFEE HOUSE
**400 East Main St.**
**(502) 582-3220**
**www.bluemountaincoffeehouse.com**
Closed on Sunday, the Blue Mountain Coffee House serves a variety of Jamaican imports as their standard brews. They also serve tapas and light fare in addition to a nice wine selection, but the main draw is their good coffee drinks. Trendy with somewhat of a beach theme, this newcomer arrived on the Louisville coffeehouse/wine-bar scene in 2007. The ambience is pleasing to the eye, and a portion of the wine bar is actually a large, curved tank full of beautiful exotic fish. Situated on Main Street, just across from Slugger Field, this is the place to stop before a game for a nice espresso, or during the afternoon when you're looking for a break. There's free Wi-Fi, but when ordering, you need to get a pass code to use it.

### DERBY CITY ESPRESSO
**331 East Market St.**
**(502) 442-0523**
**www.myspace.com/derbycityespresso**
A coffee shop that sells beer; no wonder this trendy gallery district cafe is popular with the afternoon and nighttime crowds. A laid-back coffeehouse/bar with interesting found art and even more interesting customers, Derby City Espresso features a variety of beans from Sumatra, Colombia, Yemen, Java, Ethiopia, and India. Every one of the single shots uses at least 14 grams of coffee in a double shot basket. And in addition to hot and iced espresso drinks, there are also many kinds of tea to choose from. Closed on Sunday, Derby City Espresso opens at 11 a.m. daily, Monday through Saturday.

### MRS. POTTER'S COFFEE
**718 West Main St.**
**(502) 581-1867**
**www.mrspotterscoffee.com**
Mrs. Potter's Coffee is a locally owned shop located in the heart of downtown Louisville on Museum Row. They offer espresso, loose-leaf teas, real-fruit smoothies, and shakes, in addition to breakfast and lunch, which is served all day long. Mrs. Potter's Coffee offers free Wi-Fi and indoor/outdoor seating, making it a popular place to take a break when you're in the downtown area. Artwork from local creative types hangs on the walls, and every month a new artist is showcased. You can view the artwork during regular store hours, or stop by the first Friday of every month for the First Friday Trolley Hop, when they are open until 10 p.m. Open daily, Mrs. Potter's closes at 5 p.m. Sunday through Thursday, and at 7 p.m. on Friday and Saturday.

### SEATTLE'S BEST COFFEE AT BORDERS BOOKS
**400 South Fourth St.**
**(502) 562-2100**
**www.borders.com**
There are a number of Borders Books in Louisville, but the shop located at the entrance to Fourth

Street Live!, Louisville's premier entertainment district, is one of the most popular. The attractive two-level store has a knowledgeable, friendly staff ready to help find the perfect book, CD, or movie, and there's also a Seattle's Best Coffee that offers lunch and desserts in addition to a good cup of joe. The children's department is very popular, and this centrally located bookstore also boasts the largest selection of African-American fiction in Kentuckiana.

---

## Starbucks

If you keep your eyes peeled you'll eventually find the Starbucks logo you've been looking for, as there are a number of them in Derby Town. Two of them are especially good for people-watching, however. The Starbuck's off the main lobby of the Seelbach Hilton (502-585-3200) at 500 South Fourth Street has been designed to reflect the elegance of the hotel, and always attracts an interesting mix of locals and out-of-towners; and the Starbucks at 972 Baxter Avenue, right in the middle of all the Bardstown Road action, usually attracts a lively cross section of Highlands residents and visitors. Call (502) 625-1815 for more information, or go online at www.starbucks.com for a store locator.

---

## Bardstown Road

**CITY CAFE**
**1250 Bardstown Rd.**
**(502) 459-5600**
**www.citycafelunch.com**
In addition to daily specials priced at only $6.85 that highlight cuisines from around the world, this popular lunch spot at the Mid-City Mall has a variety of coffee drinks and beverages. Open daily

at 11 a.m., the Highlands City Cafe is located next to the Baxter Avenue Cinemas. City Cafe also has locations at 505 West Broadway (502-589-1797), open Monday through Friday from 10:30 a.m. to 3 p.m.; and at 500 South Preston (502-852-5739), open Monday through Friday from 7:30 a.m. to 3 p.m.

**COCO'S CHOCOLATE CAFÉ**
**1759 Bardstown Rd.**
**(502) 454-9810**
**http://cocoschocolatecafe.com**
It's chocolate heaven at Coco's Chocolate Café, where you can stop by and indulge in a sweet treat at a reasonable price. In addition to coffees, drinking chocolate, and other beverages, there's an assortment of truffles, dipped chocolates, mousses, cakes, and more—all made from the finest and richest ingredients. Coco's is also the perfect place to pick up a special gift for your next holiday party or family event.

**DAY'S ESPRESSO & COFFEE**
**1420 Bardstown Rd.**
**(502) 456-1170**
**www.dayscoffee.com**
Open at 6:30 a.m. during the week and at 7 a.m. on weekends, Day's is one of the more-popular Bardstown Road coffeehouses. And although they've gained a faithful following since opening in 1994, they've resisted attempts to branch out, maintaining the single location in the middle of the Highlands. Paintings and prints for sale by local artists hang on the walls, and there's a nice selection of fair-trade items, hand-bagged beans, and loose-leaf teas in addition to good coffee and espresso.

**HIGHLAND COFFEE COMPANY**
**1140 Bardstown Rd.**
**(502) 451-4545**
**www.highlandcoffee.com**
Since 1999, Highland Coffee has offered shade-grown, fair-trade, organic coffees and espresso beverages in the rear portion of this small strip mall in the Highlands. (The Blockbuster store is the most visible part from Bardstown Road.) All

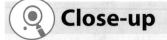 Close-up

**HEINE BROTHERS' COFFEE**

1295 Bardstown Rd.

(502) 456-5108

www.heinebroscoffee.com

For many, this small store behind Carmichael's Bookstore is *the* coffee shop in Louisville. The coffee, roasted in-house, is affordable and good, and the servers are known for being friendly and polite. In addition, the business approach is one that tries to be environmentally conscious, focusing on fair trade and organic coffees only. Founded in 1994, the original location at the busy and colorful corner of Longest and Bardstown Road has expanded to include a number of coffeehouses around town; there are four locations on Bardstown Road alone. The original Heine Brothers' is open Monday through Thursday from 6:30 a.m. to10 p.m., and Friday and Saturday from 6:30 a.m. to 11 p.m. Sunday they're open from 7 a.m. to 10 p.m.

**Other Heine Brothers' Coffee locations:**

*1449 Bardstown Rd.*

Mon–Thurs, 6:30 a.m.–11 p.m.
Fri and Sat, 6:30 a.m.–midnight
Sun, 7 a.m.–11 p.m.

*119 Chenoweth Lane*

Mon–Fri, 6 a.m.–10 p.m.
Sat, 6:30 a.m.–10 p.m.
Sun, 7 a.m.–9 p.m.

*2200 Bardstown Rd.*

Mon–Thurs, 6:30 a.m.–10 p.m.
Fri and Sat, 6:30 a.m.–11 p.m.
Sun, 7 a.m.–10 p.m.

*4123 Shelbyville Rd.*

Mon–Fri, 6 a.m.–10 p.m.
Sat, 6:30 a.m.–10 p.m.
Sun, 7 a.m.–10 p.m.

*3060 Bardstown Rd.*

Mon–Thurs, 5:30 a.m.–10 p.m.
Fri, 5:30 a.m.–11 p.m.
Sat, 6:30 a.m.–11 p.m.
Sun, 7 a.m.–10 p.m.

*2714 Frankfort Ave.*

Mon–Thurs, 6:30 a.m.–10 p.m.
Fri and Sat, 6:30 a.m.–11 p.m.
Sun, 7 a.m.–10 p.m.

of the coffees and teas at HCC are purchased from suppliers who share the same social and environmental concerns as the owners, Greg and Natalie Hofer. This guarantees that farmers are paid fairly and that natural habitats are preserved in coffee-growing regions. A portion of the proceeds from many HCC coffees supports various causes throughout the world, including the Dian Fossey Gorilla Fund. The Songbird coffees help support and preserve various bird habitats in their respective coffee-growing regions. Open till midnight on weekends and till 11 p.m. on weeknights, Highland Coffee Company has free Wi-Fi; however, you need to make a purchase and get the access code from someone at the counter first. Next door is the Knit Nook (502-452-1919), which hosts a popular "Stitch and Bitch" session every Thursday from 6 to 9 p.m.

**KRISPY KREME**
**3000 Bardstown Rd.**
**(502) 451-4880**
**www.krispykreme.com**

In 1937, Vernon Rudolph brought a secret recipe from a French chef to North Carolina and created a glazed donut that would start a craze. It quickly spread to neighboring Kentucky, and today, Krispy Kreme's offerings have evolved past the original recipe to include a variety of treats, from apple fritter to New York cheesecake donuts. The location on Bardstown Road still has that old-fashioned donut-shop feel to it, attracting hordes of fans in search of hot donuts straight from the fryer. The coffee is good, too.

## QUILLS COFFEE
**930 Baxter Ave.**
**(502) 742-6129**
**www.quillscoffee.com**
A trendy Highlands hangout with old hardwood floors, exposed brick, and hip artwork on the walls, Quills has dedicated and talented baristas who make a mean cup of coffee. The coffee shop is housed in a rehabbed old building, and with two rooms upstairs, it's not a problem to find a place to sit down and enjoy a latte or cappuccino. In addition to an assortment of baked goods to go along with your cup of coffee, you can also choose from a variety of Cellar Door chocolates. Try the red latte, a drink made from steamed milk and tea espresso that has 5 times more anti-oxidants than green tea, and 10 times more than most other teas.

**i** Cellar Door Chocolates, a local con-fectioner specializing in truffles and other gourmet sweets, is located at 101 West Main Street. Call (502) 561-2940, or go online at www.cellardoorchocolates.com for details.

## RAY'S MONKEY HOUSE AND KID CAFE
**1578 Bardstown Rd.**
**(502) 459-4373**
**www.raysmonkeyhouse.com**
Top-quality coffee and organic beverages and food items aren't the only thing on the menu at this funky, Deer Park neighborhood hang-out. It's also a kid-friendly community gathering place with a focus on progressive issues such as sustainability, environmental responsibility, and social justice. In addition to outdoor seating, they also have spaces for groups to meet and children to play. Ray's Monkey House also provides a place for artists to perform and do their thing.

## Frankfort Avenue Area
### BLUE DOG BAKERY & CAFE
**2868 Frankfort Ave.**
**(502) 899-9800**
**www.bluedogbread.com**
Apart from an assortment of cookies and pastries baked daily, the Blue Dog Bakery & Cafe has some wonderfully elegant desserts that make for a relaxing afternoon break or an early-morning shot in the arm. A popular choice is the individual lemon tart, a saucer-size treat with tangy lemon curd in a crumbly sugar cookie crust. In addition to hot coffee and espresso drinks, you'll also find a nice variety of soups, sandwiches, salads, and quiches meant to complement the tasty baked goods produced next door in a $50,000 Span-ish wood-fired oven. Authentic, European-style artisan breads—as good as any you'll find—are a draw at the Blue Dog Bakery & Cafe, so don't forget to take a loaf of bread along.

### CAFFÉ CLASSICO
**2144 Frankfort Ave.**
**(502) 895-0076**
**www.caffe-classico.com**
Several years ago, when Caffé Classico popped up on the Louisville coffeehouse scene, people assumed it would fall in the same category of self-service establishments that have become de rigueur in this country: You walk in and order your drink; if you stay, you take it to your table and perhaps grab a cookie or sandwich to go with it. But, enter Caffé Classico in the 'Ville and you'll notice it's a different cup of tea all together. Sit down and relax a bit, because this isn't an eat-and-run kind of place. Or a drink-and-run kind of place. A server will take your drink order, and bring you a menu if you want a bite to eat. The lunch menu includes several seasonal soup selections and salads, in addition to sandwiches and light entrees. Aside from Viennese coffee by Julius Meinl, you'll find the beverage selection includes an assortment of juices, draft beers and wines as well.

## JAVA BREWING COMPANY
2309 Frankfort Ave.
(502) 894-8060
www.javabrewingco.com

After Mike and Medora Safai began firing their roaster at the Java Brewing Company in the Crescent Hill neighborhood in 1999, their handcrafted micro-roast coffee became an instant success. Actively integrating the latest technologies of roasting and brewing techniques for gourmet specialty coffees, JBC offers a wide choice of gourmet beans at affordable prices. Employees are well trained to educate customers in the expertise of coffee, and they've been rewarded with a loyal—and growing—clientele. Java Brewing Company is involved with coffee-growing communities here and abroad, and they take a leading role in supporting charities and various community-based projects. Java Brewing Company also has locations at 462 South Fourth Street (502-561-2041); at 9561 US 42 in Prospect (502-292-2710); 135 South English Station Road (502-489-5677); and 516 West Main Street (502-568-6339).

## ZEN TEA HOUSE
2246 Frankfort Ave.
(502) 618-0878
www.zenteahouse.org

Located between the neighborhoods of Crescent Hill and Clifton is the Zen Tea House, an offshoot of the Zen Garden Restaurant. In addition to light fare and compassionate vegetarian cuisine, there is a vast assortment of fine loose-leaf teas from estates around the globe. In addition, the second floor of the tea house has been designed as a large relaxing space for tea meditations, which—under the instruction of the Compassionate Service Society—are offered regularly. Open to the public free of charge, the tea meditations help heal the body, mind, and spirit. Read more about the Zen Garden Vegetarian Restaurant, located next door at 2240 Frankfort Avenue, in the Close-up earlier in this chapter.

# Other Parts of Town

## EXPRESSIONS OF YOU
1800 West Muhammad Ali Blvd.
(502) 584-6886
www.myspace.com/expressionsofyouopenmic

Located in the Russell Community of West Louisville, Expressions of You is part cafe, part coffeehouse, part bookstore, art gallery, and open-mic venue. According to the mission statement on the back of its menu, its goal is "[t]o create a warm and relaxing environment, where people within the community can come together socially, spiritually, and intellectually to encourage unity, prosperity, and intellectual stimulation." In addition to a full-service cafe with sandwiches, salads, soups, desserts, and specialty coffee drinks, there are also breakfast, lunch, and dinner items. The bookstore and gallery feature local and national authors, and on Saturday nights the open mic draws a crowd. A unique aspect of this business is that it is also a ministry, which offers substance-abuse recovery assistance and advice to first-time buyers or those refinancing a home. Saturdays from 2:30 p.m. to 4:30 p.m. people gather to recite inspirational poetry and Christian-themed works.

## OLD LOUISVILLE COFFEEHOUSE
1489 South Fourth St.
(502) 635-6660
http://oldlouisville.info/Restaurants/Coffee/default.htm

Located across from a beautiful row of Chateauesque townhomes at the corner of Hill and Fourth in historic Old Louisville, this is a favorite hangout for both local residents and students at the nearby U of L. Co-owner Pamela Campbell says: "We like to stay involved with the local community and provide an outlet for musicians, clubs, and organizations here." As a result, you'll find a lot more than steaming milk and brewing coffee going on at the Old Louisville Coffeehouse. Among the several weekly events hosted in-house are free massages from massage therapist Dave Collins from noon to 4 p.m. on Sunday, and music from the University of Louisville Jazz

Ensemble from 2 p.m. to 4 p.m. on Saturday. The Old Louisville Coffee House sits diagonally across the street from one of two gateways to picturesque Belgravia Court and St. James Court.

**i** Free Wi-Fi. Hotspots for free wireless access are available at many private businesses and all public libraries throughout Louisville. In Old Louisville, St. James Court is a Wi-Fi hotspot, and in the Highlands, so are portions of Baxter Avenue, from East Breckinridge Street to Highland Avenue. Downtown you'll also find free Wi-Fi at Fourth Street Live! and on all 85 acres of Waterfront Park. In addition, Louisville International Airport, the University of Louisville, and Papa John's Cardinal Stadium are all wireless hotspots. The Louisville Wireless Hotspots campaign identifies all the wireless points in the metro area. You can find a listing of access points, including free access, at their Web site at www.louisvillehotspots.com.

**SUNERGOS COFFEE**
**2122 South Preston St.**
**(502) 634-1243**
**www.sunergoscoffee.com**
From the ratty sofa and beat-up '50s-era furniture to the eclectic assortment of lamps dangling from the ceiling, this gem in the St. Joseph neighborhood is your quintessential coffeehouse. Its comfortable, unpretentious vibe attracts a wide array of java drinkers, but it's the excellent on-site micro-brewed coffee that keeps them coming back from all parts of town. The name of the coffee shop is derived from the Greek word *sunergos*, which was used in the first century to refer to relational collaborative service. This theme is evident in the development and operation of this company today. Aside from a thorough appreciation of fine coffee, the folks at Sunergos want to encourage creative reflection in their patrons.

# SHOPPING

Being a river town, commerce has always played an important role in the economy of Louisville. Early explorers traded with Native Americans when they portaged their canoes around the Falls of the Ohio, and adventurers like Lewis and Clark loaded up on stores before heading into the unknown areas that lay ahead to the west. For most of the 1800s and early 1900s, steamboats laden with porcelain and furniture from New Orleans, the latest fashions from Philadelphia, and a multitude of sundries from Cincinnati and St. Louis docked at Louisville's waterfront and discharged their cargo before loading up and returning to their ports of origin. Among the items they took with them were massive hogsheads of tobacco, casks of bourbon, crates of stoneware, and sacks of grain. During the years of Prohibition, gangsters poured into town to snatch up truckloads of illicit whiskey, and in the years leading up to World War II, Depression-weary locals flocked to Fourth Street in downtown Louisville to avail themselves of the bargain bins in department stores such as Stewart's, Kaufman-Straus, and Levy Bros. In recent times shopping centers have sprung up on the outskirts of town to fulfill the needs of convenience-crazed Louisvillians with time and money on their hands.

Shopping in the Louisville area today runs the gamut from big-box chains and outlet centers to funky shops and specialty boutiques, but, like most cities in this country, retail stores and other venues for those in search of purchases have been slow in returning to the center of town. There are, nonetheless, a number of shops in the downtown area—the gallery district along East Market Street is especially popular among art lovers—that offer a wide variety of goods, and the number of stores and variety of merchandise increase every month. Mention shopping in Louisville, however, and most people think of the large malls such as St. Matthews or Oxmoor, or the newer Summit out in the East End, or else the eclectic storefronts along Bardstown Road or Frankfort Avenue come to mind. Aside from browsing for vintage clothing, consigned goods, and locally inspired crafts, these streets are great for people-watching while sipping a local brew or enjoying a morning coffee. Bardstown Road and Frankfort Avenue are also the places to go if you're interested in antiques and gift shops.

Stores dedicated to Kentucky-themed memorabilia and local souvenirs can be found throughout the city, but many visitors prefer to wait for one of the local art shows to buy their Louisville keepsakes. The Cherokee Triangle Art Show takes place every year the weekend before the Kentucky Derby, just steps from the hustle and bustle of Bardstown Road, and during the first weekend in October throngs of shoppers flock to the St. James Court Art Show in Old Louisville. Any time of year, however, is the right time to pick up a reminder of your visit to the Derby City. Whether it's a bottle of local small-batch bourbon, a customized bat from Louisville Slugger, a box of modjeskas from the candy store on the corner, or a Derby Pie from Kern's, you're sure to find what you're looking for in one of Louisville's many shops.

# BOOKSTORES

### A READER'S CORNER
**138 Breckenridge Lane**
**(502) 897-5578**
**www.areaderscorner.com**
Located in the heart of St. Matthews, A Reader's Corner opens Monday through Saturday at 10 a.m. Although new books are available, they specialize in used books and hard-to-find titles and have an inventory of more than 50,000 items. In addition to free wireless Internet, there's also a coffee corner where customers can purchase freshly brewed coffee while they wait. Soft drinks are also available, and at only 50 cents a can and $1.25 for large bottles, you can't beat the prices. You'll find Kizito cookies and the Kentucky ginger-based soda known as Ale-8-One as well.

### BARNES & NOBLE
**801 South Hurstbourne Pkwy.**
**(502) 426-0255**
**www.barnesandnobleinc.com**
The largest book retailer in the United States, Barnes & Noble has become famous for carrying all the titles you want, in addition to hosting lots of events such as author readings, fan circles, and children's readings. Among the Louisville outlets, the one on Hurstbourne Parkway in the East End is known for its great selection and friendly, knowledgeable staff. It's also popular among various book clubs that meet here, and for its weekly foreign language conversation groups.

### BORDERS BOOKS
**400 South Fourth St.**
**(502) 562-2100**
**www.borders.com**
Among other things, this centrally located bookstore boasts the largest selection of African-American fiction in Kentuckiana. The local interest section and the children's department are very popular as well. Located at the entrance to Fourth Street Live!, Louisville's premier entertainment district, the attractive two-level store has a knowledgeable, friendly staff ready to help find the perfect book, CD, or movie. Although there are several Borders Books in Louisville, this one, centrally located and just a block from the convention center, is the most popular among out-of-town visitors. They also have a Seattle's Best Coffee with lunch and dessert options, in addition to a good variety of specialty drinks.

> **i** When you leave the Carmichael's Bookstore on Bardstown Road, walk back and take a stroll through the neighborhood behind it; you'll be able to explore the old stomping ground of two of the Highlands' most famous writers. Sue Grafton, author of the Kinsey Millhone detective series, was born in 1940 and grew up in the Cherokee Triangle; she now resides most of the year in the Glenview part of Louisville. Born in 1937, Hunter S. Thompson—the father of gonzo journalism—attended the same grade school and high school as Grafton.

### DESTINATIONS BOOKSELLERS
**604 East Spring St.**
**New Albany, IN**
**(812) 944-5116**
**www.destinationsbooksellers.com**
Founded in 2004 by proprietor Randy Smith, Destinations Booksellers is Southeast Indiana's full-service independent bookstore. Located in New Albany's East Spring historic district, the cozy shop strives to be a place where ideas are exchanged and the public is encouraged to attend a variety of events. In the rear of the building, the Dueling Grounds Cafe offers a range of coffee drinks and teas, in addition to gourmet soups and sandwiches. Destinations is also a part of IndieBound, a community-oriented movement started by the American Booksellers Association that strives to highlight the benefits of shopping locally. As Smith points out, "When you shop locally, you are supporting local economies." For every $100 spent at a local business, $68 stays in the community; only $43 stays in the community when the same amount is spent at a big chain.

## (Q) Close-up

### National Bookseller of the Year

Say *books* in Louisville, and most people think of **Carmichael's,** a local bookstore that's been around since the 1970s. The original location opened at the corner of Longest and Bardstown Road in the Highlands; a second store followed on Frankfort Avenue in the Crescent Hill area, and although both stores are small, they offer a handpicked selection of titles. Both shops are on corners that normally buzz with activity, and the variety of books available reflects both the taste of the owners and the neighborhoods where they're located. From the start, Carmichael's has tried to be a neighborhood gathering place open seven days a week and in the evenings. The efforts have paid off handsomely; not only is Carmichael's a Louisville institution, but they're also considered one of the best independent bookstores in the nation.

In 2009, just a year after Carmichael's celebrated its 30th anniversary, *Publishers Weekly* magazine announced that the Louisville bookshop had been selected as the Bookseller of the Year. It is the single most prestigious award for independent bookstores, and every year a jury of professionals in the book industry chooses just one store in the United States for the honor. In addition to the level of community involvement and management-employee relations, booksellers are judged on their performance based on a broad set of criteria that includes excellence in buying, customer service, and marketing. A founding member of the Louisville Independent Business Alliance, Carmichael's has a mission to spread the word about the importance of buying from locally owned businesses and is an active part of the Keep Louisville Weird campaign. For more information, visit Carmichael's Bookstore online at www.carmichaelsbookstore.com. The original store (1295 Bardstown Rd.; 502-456-6950) is open Sunday through Thursday from 8 a.m. to 10 p.m.; Friday and Saturday from 8 a.m. to 11 p.m. The second store (2720 Frankfort Ave.; 502-896-6950) is open seven days a week from 9 a.m. to 9 p.m.

**i** The sales tax is 6 percent in Louisville (Jefferson County, Kentucky) and 7 percent in Southern Indiana (Clark, Floyd & Harrison counties).

## BOUTIQUES AND GIFT SHOPS

**EDENSIDE GALLERY**
1422 Bardstown Rd.
(502) 459-2787

Located next to Day's Coffee near the Bardstown Road intersection with Eastern Parkway, Edenside Gallery has a little something for everyone. Apart from home furnishings and glass art pieces, they carry work by award-winning local and national artists. They also have paintings, crafts, curios, and jewelry at average prices.

**LUNA BOUTIQUE**
1310 Bardstown Rd.
(502) 454-7620
www.lunaboutique.net

Luna Boutique was established in 2003 by Mary Beth O'Bryan to provide a cozy yet vibrant boutique atmosphere for shoppers on Louisville's Restaurant Row. Many customers pop in to browse after dining next door at the casual but upscale Avalon restaurant. On sale are a collection of fashionable pieces from around the world, including jewelry, casual wear, home accessories, baby items, and spa products, many of which promote creative designers who value fair trade.

**MELLWOOD ARTS AND ENTERTAINMENT CENTER**
1860 Mellwood Ave.
(502) 895-3650
www.mellwoodartcenter.com

Just minutes from downtown Louisville, this former meat-packing plant turned arts complex features almost 200 studios, galleries, and specialty shops embodying the potential for community-based art. Creative types come here for the opportunity to collaborate with others, shop the stores, or enjoy dining at one of the on-site restaurants. Open seven days a week.

### NITTY GRITTY
**996 Barret Ave.**
**(502) 583-3377**
**nittygrittyvintage.com**
Specializing in authentic attire for theme parties and events, Nitty Gritty is an eclectic vintage clothing and retro costume shop with two floors of men's and women's outfits ranging from the 1920s to the '80s. The Nitty Gritty also stocks new items such as wigs, fedoras, go-go boots, and more to complement your retro look. They sell housewares and items by local artists as well.

## Kentucky-Themed Gift Shops

### BOURBON BARREL FOODS
**1201 Story Ave.**
**(877) 307-6418**
**www.bourbonbarrelfoods.com**
Housed inside historic Butchertown Market, Bourbon Barrel Foods is a maker of gourmet food products that reflect the rich heritage of Kentucky's Bourbon Country, a picturesque area known as the "Napa Valley of the Bluegrass." Using the staves of spent oak bourbon barrels to impart flavor to a variety of sauces, spices, and condiments, owner Matt Jamie has come up with a line of products that embody the best of the Bluegrass State. Bourbon-smoked sea salt, paprika, and pepper, and Kentucky-brewed soy sauce and sorghum are just some of the innovative products available here and at other shops throughout the region.

### HADLEY POTTERY
**1570 Story Ave.**
**(502) 584-2171**
**www.hadleypottery.com**

All of the designs at this stoneware company were created or suggested by Mary Alice Hadley, a painter from Old Louisville who designed a set of dishes for the family's Ohio River cruiser in 1940. Her artistic endeavors met with such success that she soon began creating similar pieces for friends and acquaintances. Today, the company bearing her name produces ceramics that are sold the world over. Her original artwork and hand-painted murals are on display in the showrooms of an old building built in 1848.

### THE LOUISVILLE COMPANY
**712 South Barbee Way**
**(502) 777-0790**
**www.louisvillecompany.com**
Specializing in uniquely Louisville gifts about Louisville, from Louisville and by Louisvillians, this company offers products that benefit nonprofit, charitable, and educational organizations locally, regionally, and nationally. When you want to say "I love Luavul" with a gift, their Web site is the place to visit.

### LOUISVILLE SLUGGER MUSEUM & FACTORY
**800 West Main St.**
**(877) 775-8443**
**www.sluggermuseum.org/giftshop.aspx**
Aside from being the place to pick up personalized versions of America's favorite baseball bat, mini-bats, and Bionic Gloves, the gift shop at the Louisville Slugger Museum & Factory is home to hundreds of great gift ideas. From T-shirts and sweatshirts to caps and other sport apparel, you're sure to find that perfect something for the inner sports fan in all of us. The gift shop and personalized bat store is open seven days a week.

**i** You can also find an assortment of Louisville-themed apparel and merchandise at cafepress.com/oldlouisville.

### LOUISVILLE STONEWARE
**731 Brent St.**
**(502) 582-1900**
**www.louisvillestoneware.com**

## Need That Perfect Kentucky Souvenir?

If a personalized baseball bat from Louisville Slugger or a bottle of small-batch whiskey isn't what you're looking for, consider taking back a box of bourbon balls as a tasty reminder of your visit to the Derby City. Although recipes and the manner of preparation vary throughout the state, the standard bourbon ball consists of a chocolate-coated buttercream center flavored with aged whiskey and pecans. Most of the major distilleries have their own brand, as do regional confectioners, but a Louisville favorite is the variety produced by Ron and Jane Harris in their Third Street mansion just south of downtown. Named after Ron's Aunt Happy, the lady who passed down her cherished recipe, Happy Balls get their distinctive flavor from hand-selected pecans that are soaked in nine-year-old Knob Creek bourbon and covered in a layer of semisweet Guittard chocolate. You can find Happy Balls at local gifts shops and specialty stores such as Paul's Fruit Market, or if you're downtown, you can pick up a box at the Louisville Convention and Visitors Bureau at the corner of Fourth and Jefferson. For more information call (502) 637-2227, or go online at www.gethappyballs.com.

skilled artisans create an ever-changing line of dinnerware, bakeware, serving pieces, and collectibles that embody the style of the region. Some designs at this, one of the oldest stoneware companies in the nation, are understated, some are more exuberant, but they all demonstrate that everyday objects have an important place in the home.

**LOUISVILLE VISITOR INFORMATION CENTER**
**Fourth and Jefferson**
**(502) 584-2121**
**www.gotolouisvillestore.com**
Located adjacent to the Kentucky International Convention Center and the Hyatt Regency, the Louisville Visitor Information Center is the perfect place to purchase Louisville merchandise—and to have your picture taken with the life-size wax figure of Colonel Sanders. The visitor center is open seven days a week and offers a variety of items, including bourbon-themed T-shirts, books of local interest, and Happy Balls, Louisville's favorite bourbon ball.

**MINT JULEP TOURS**
**140 North Fourth St.**
**Suite 326**
**(502) 583-1433**
**www.mintjuleptours.com**
Located in the Galt House Hotel, the gift shop at the offices of Mint Julep Tours has a limited variety of local merchandise including sweets, souvenir books, and whiskey-themed memorabilia. Take one of their informative and entertaining tours of nearby bourbon country and you'll have plenty of time to browse the distillery gift shops. Right next door to Mint Julep is a small Regalo gift shop.

**PAUL'S FRUIT MARKET**
**4601 Jennings Lane**
**(502) 458-7641**
**www.paulsfruit.com**
Providing fruit baskets and food gifts since 1945, Paul's Fruit Market is a local favorite when it comes to fresh produce and regional delicacies. Apart from whiskey-based condiments and sauces, the selection features fruitcakes and

Since its beginnings in the early 1800s, Louisville Stoneware has had artists who have dedicated their time and talent to the craft of transforming clay into enduring forms of functional art. Utilizing the basic elements of earth, water, air, and fire,

fudge from the Trappist monastery at Gethsemani, Bauer's modjeskas, Happy Balls, Maker's Mark bourbon chocolates, and more. Open daily, Paul's Fruit Market carries a wide variety of goods with the Kentucky Proud label. There are additional shops on Shelbyville and Taylorsville Roads.

### REGALO
**980 Barret Ave.**
**(502) 583-1798**
**www.regaloart.com**
John Freels, J. D. Dotson and Laura Applegate operate this Louisville favorite. Voted the best place to buy a unique gift for six years in a row by readers of *LEO* magazine, Regalo features a lineup of contemporary, innovative items for the bar, home, or office. Featuring many products that are the work of local artists, Regalo opens seven days a week at 10 a.m. In addition to clocks, lamps, and frames, you'll find a number of paper items and fashion accessories, as well as soy candles, handcrafted jewelry, local sculpture, in-house designed and printed T-shirts, baby gifts, and presents with a Louisville edge. Regalo also operates two shops in the Galt House Hotel (502-561-4024).

### TASTE OF KENTUCKY
**11800 Shelbyville Rd.**
**(800) 444-0552**
**www.atasteofkentucky.com**
Traditional and contemporary Kentucky artisans are showcased in three Taste of Kentucky stores across Louisville; the others are located in the Mall St. Matthews and the AEGON Center downtown. Regional books and music are available for purchase, as are an assortment of Kentucky favorites like Kern's Derby Pie, sourmash bread mixes, local honey, calendars, sauces, and stoneware. Popular sweets include Mom Blakeman's pulled candy, Old Forester gourmet bourbon chocolates, and candies by Ruth Hunt.

### VISITOR CENTER IN HISTORIC OLD LOUISVILLE
**218 West Oak St.**
**(502) 637-2922**
**www.oldlouisville.org/businesses**

A small gift shop at the visitor center in Historic Old Louisville offers an assortment of Louisville-themed merchandise; however, their specialty is souvenirs and mementos touting the district's rich Victorian past and ghostly reputation as the country's most haunted neighborhood. Included are a selection of books, T-shirts, totes, postcards, craft items, and condiments from Bourbon Barrel Foods. Prints and cards from Paducah artist Tracey Buchanan are available, as are photographic designs from local artists Mark and Claudette Rego. This is also the place to stop for your two-packs, four-packs, or nine-packs of Happy Balls, the official candy of Old Louisville.

### WHY LOUISVILLE
**1538 Bardstown Rd.**
**(502) 456-5400**
**www.whylouisville.com**
Why Louisville (WHY = What-Have-You) opened in 2005 in the heart of the Highlands, Louisville's main thoroughfare of local, independent businesses, and their lineup features souvenirs and curiosities such as shirts designed by local and regional artists, jewelry, books, paper goods, knickknacks, and—what-have-you. Located right next door to the Doo Wop Shop, Why Louisville is open seven days a week.

## BUYING ANTIQUES AND SUCH

### ANTIQUE MARKET AT DISTILLERY COMMONS
**200 Distillery Commons, Suite 460**
**(502) 583-5510**
**www.antiquesatdistillery.com**
Located at the corner of Lexington and Payne Streets, the Antique Market at Distillery Commons has over 50 merchants offering upscale items in an air-conditioned showroom with over 10,000 square feet of ground-level shopping. The vendors include collectors, antiques dealers, and designers from the surrounding region with a selection of fine art, porcelain, furniture, silver, glass, lighting, antique rugs, and accessories for every room. Excellent lighting and wonderful vignettes allow easy viewing of the selections. Closed on Monday.

## ARCHITECTURAL SALVAGE
618 East Broadway
(502) 589-0670
www.architecturalsalvage.com

Offering "the fashionable, the fascinating and the just plain fun," Architectural Salvage has been a favorite stop for designers, collectors, and creative types in search of original and reproduction architectural antiques since the 1980s. Housed in an old building with 24,000 square feet and four architectural salvage yards in downtown Louisville, this collection of thousands of unusual and hard-to-find items attracts a steady stream of clientele from around the nation. Closed Sunday.

## CRAZY DAISY ANTIQUE MALL
1430 Mellwood Avenue
(502) 560-1335
crazydaisyantiquemall.com

Open Monday through Saturday from 9 a.m. to 5 p.m. and Sunday from noon to 5 p.m., the Crazy Daisy Antique Mall is conveniently located off of I-64 in the trendy East Main Street and Frankfort Avenue corridors of Louisville. Featured are over 100 vendors of quality furniture and collectibles ranging from early primitives to vintage items from the 1960s. In addition to an impressive display of majolica pottery, you'll also find books, eye popping art, and a large collection of jewelry. There are also Kentucky-made collectibles and Kentucky Derby memorabilia in abundance. With more than 20,000 square feet of space, the Crazy Daisy also has an outdoor courtyard and rough room for those in search of furniture in need of restoration. Parking is never a problem and the building is handicapped accessible.

## DAVID R. FRIEDLANDER ANTIQUES
129 St. Matthews Ave.
(502) 893-3311

Specializing in collectibles, toys, and dolls, rare and out-of-print books, estate jewelry and furniture, this inviting St. Matthews shop has been around for more than 40 years. Aside from offering appraisal services, they also buy silver and other items, and deal in artifacts and primitive art. Open Monday through Saturday and by appointment.

## DERBY CITY ANTIQUE MALL
3819 Bardstown Rd.
(502) 459-5151
www.derbycityantiquemall.com

This family-owned and -operated antiques mall on the south end of Bardstown Road has more than 30,000 square feet of booth space and lighted showcases. Some 170 dealers offer a variety of hard-to-find items from the new to the old. Items on display include silver, flatware, glassware, furniture, jewelry, and collectibles. The air-conditioned facility is wheelchair accessible and has plenty of parking space. Gift certificates and layaway are available. Open daily.

## DOVER HOUSE ANTIQUES & MERCANTILE
2000 Frankfort Ave.
(502) 899-1699

In addition to unusual and interesting gifts, shoppers will find quality home accessories and custom furnishings at this high-end location in the Crescent Hill neighborhood. Proprietors Kevin Wolfe and Clarence R. Smith are members of the Vermont Antique Dealers' Association and make frequent buying trips to New England to stock their shelves with early English and Chinese export porcelains, period American country and formal furniture, and an impressive assortment of tole, mirrors, prints, silhouettes and samplers. Open Monday through Saturday from 10 a.m. to 5 p.m., the shop also has a bridal registry with items from Simon Pearce.

## EUROPEAN ANTIQUE MARKET
933 Barret Ave.
(502) 585-3111
www.euroantiquemarket.com

European Antique Market LLC is a direct importer of French and European antiques, which includes an inventory of custom furniture, architectural elements, lighting and art form the 17th century through Brocante of the 20th century. Among others, Louis XV, Louis XVI, Louis Phillipe, Regency, and Gothic styles are represented. Painted and country French furniture is a big draw. Owner Shawn Stucker has an office in France and has been dealing in antiques for more than two decades. He regularly travels throughout France and England, buying entire estates and purchasing inventory at markets; since he does all his own buying, he can eliminate the cost of the middle man and pass the savings on to his customers. Open Tuesday through Saturday from 10 a.m. to 4 p.m., and by appointment, the European Antique Market is just steps from Lynn's Paradise Cafe, making it an ideal stop before or after lunch.

### GOSS AVENUE ANTIQUES & INTERIORS
946 Goss Ave.
(502) 637-4878
www.gossantiques.com

Long one of the Derby City's most-visited antiques malls, Goss Avenue Antiques is housed in a former textile mill from the 1880s. Scores of dealers offer a variety of fine antiques and interior accessories that include all types of furniture, lamps, mirrors, paintings, rugs, silver, glassware, collectibles, and more. Known for its well-trained and helpful staff, Goss Avenue Antiques is the largest antiques mall in the area. An on-site restaurant offers breakfast and lunch for those wanting a break from browsing. Open daily.

### ISAACS GALLERY
7807 Shelbyville Rd.
(502) 425-2825
www.carrollisaacsgallery.com

The collection at this family-run business in St. Matthews includes antique and estate jewelry, 18th- and 19th-century antique silver hollowware, Faberge, and other Russian objects. They also have an exceptional collection of European, American, and Oriental furniture and accessories, antique walking sticks, oriental rugs, and export porcelain. In addition, Isaacs Gallery offers appraisal service for antiques and estate jewelry. Open Tuesday to Saturday.

### JOE LEY ANTIQUES
615 East Market St.
(502) 583-4014
www.joeley.com

"Part carnival, part museum, part treasure hunt," Joe Ley's has been a destination for antiquers and curiosity seekers for over 35 years. Housed in a schoolhouse from 1890, this must-see shop has two acres of goodies spread out over three floors. Joe Ley Antiques attracts people from all over the world with its constantly changing and colorful inventory. The shop has become a popular place for the filming of music videos and commercials, and has been written up in magazines like *House Beautiful, Travel and Leisure,* and *Southern Living.* Open daily.

> **i** Across the street from Joe Ley's, you'll find Muth's Candy Store (630 E. Market St.; 502-585-2952; www.muthscandy.com), a Derby City favorite since 1921. Aside from handmade bourbon chocolates and old-fashioned favorites like peanut brittle, peppermint sticks, and hand-dipped caramels, you'll also find the local specialty, the modjeska. An irresistible combination of a soft marshmallow wrapped in light caramel, it was created by Edgar Busath, who shared the original recipe with his friend Rudy Muth. Open daily except Sunday and Monday.

### TRACE MAYER ANTIQUES
3700 Lexington Rd.
(502) 899-5335
www.tracemayer.com

Trace Mayer Antiques carries a variety of period English, Continental, and American decorative and fine arts. In addition to drawings, watercolors, and paintings, items for sale include candlesticks, chandeliers, prints, porcelain, pottery, and sculpture. The wide variety of boxes such as tea caddies, sewing kits, lap desks, card cases, miniatures, tobacco chests, and snuffboxes is a draw for many. Closed Sunday and Monday.

## CLOTHING

### CHERRY BOMB
1602 Bardstown Rd.
(502) 384-5114

With great music always playing in the background, the mood is eclectic and upbeat at the

Cherry Bomb. The fashionable, friendly staff and ever-growing collection of clothing and accessories make it one of the most popular shopping stops for young people on Bardstown Road. Almost all items in the shop are vintage or created by local artists. Furthermore, the shop buys and sells vintage clothing, shoes, and handbags. The selection is fairly priced and includes accessories like sunglasses, handbags, hair items, and tights.

### CLAY & COTTON
**1341 Bardstown Rd.**
**(502) 456-5536**
**www.clayandcotton.com**
Just a few blocks from scenic Cherokee Triangle, this trendy boutique has been featured in local press like *Louisville Magazine* and national publications such as *Southern Living*. The feature item is women's apparel by designers from around the world, with a mantra of "practical but elegant" and "comfortable and flattering." Like its counterpart at the Summit shopping center, the Highlands location also has a selection of bedding items, rugs, fabrics, pottery, bath products, kitchen accessories, and professional cookware.

### DOT FOX CLOTHING CULTURE
**1567 Bardstown Rd.**
**(502) 452-9191**
**www.dotfoxclothingculture.com**
A wide selection of "independent and progressive lines of men's and women's clothing, shoes and accessories—plus an abundance of ridiculously fantastic kitsch" has been on sale at this quirky boutique since 2004. Located between Bonnycastle and Alta Avenue, Dot Fox is regularly voted one of the best women's boutiques in the 'Ville. Open seven days a week.

### THE MAKERY
**1572 Bardstown Rd.**
**www.themakery.bigcartel.com**
Opened in October 2007, this cozy Highlands shop features works by independent artists, designers, crafters, and makers. In addition to a good assortment of local, handmade cloth-

---

## Need a Break?

If you want to take a pause from shopping along Bardstown Road, one of Louisville's most popular areas for shopping and people-watching, why not take a stroll through Cherokee Triangle? One of Louisville's three historic preservation districts, the picturesque Cherokee Triangle neighborhood is just steps away from the hustle and bustle of Bardstown Road. Century-old trees line the streets, providing shade and beauty, and historic homes that reflect an eclectic mix of architectural styles dot this scenic area. Part of the larger area of Louisville called the Highlands, Cherokee Triangle's boundaries are Bardstown Road to the southwest, Cherokee Park and Eastern Parkway to the southeast, and Cave Hill Cemetery to the north. Cherokee Road—just one block away—runs parallel to it, so if you're in the northern end of Bardstown Road and need a break, head over to this scenic neighborhood and enjoy the view.

---

ing, you'll find accessories, jewelry, housewares, affordable art, plush items, stationery, and more. Closed on Monday.

## CONSIGNMENT AND THRIFT SHOPS

### ANNIE'S ATTIC
**12695 Shelbyville Rd.**
**(502) 244-0303**

**12338 Shelbyville Rd.**
**(502) 244-2303**
**www.annies-attic.com**

This locally owned, family business specializes in new and consigned, upscale home furnishings, artwork, and home accessories. Located in the heart of Middletown in two separate shopping centers, the inventory changes daily. Items of interest include armoires, stained glass, greeting cards, and lamps. They are also a Trapp candle retailer and have a wide selection of aromas and sizes.

### MARGARET'S CONSIGNMENT
**2700 Frankfort Ave.**
**(502) 896-4706**
**www.margaretsconsignment.com**
A popular stop in the Crescent Hill area, Margaret's Consignment is known for its ever-changing and affordable selection of classy, designer clothing and other items, often arranged by color. Items include cocktail attire, evening gowns, pants, skirts, suits, purses, and some jewelry. Don't forget to look upstairs. Since there are so many items on display in close quarters, this is reportedly not the best place for women to shop if they have young children with them or need to push around a stroller.

### NEARLY NEW THRIFT SHOP
**1250 Bardstown Rd.**
**(502) 454-6633**
People in Louisville rave about the incredible bargains they have found at this thrift store in the lower level of the Mid-City Mall. Staffed by friendly and courteous clerks, the Nearly New Thrift Shop features secondhand clothing in great condition and at rock-bottom prices. Aside from a wide variety of attire for men, women, and children, an assortment of accessories and knick-knacks can also be found.

### PLATO'S CLOSET
**2727 South Hurstbourne Pkwy.**
**(502) 493-1044**

**4414 Outer Loop**
**(502) 961-5992**
**www.platoscloset.com**
Two of more than 900 franchise-owned and -operated businesses throughout North America, the Plato's Closets in Louisville are recycling retail stores that specialize in clothes for teens and twenty-somethings. They buy and sell the latest looks in gently used clothing and accessories from brand-name designers for both girls and guys.

### RELLEK FINE CONSIGNMENT
**817 East Market St.**
**(502) 365-4222**
Rellek is a popular place to discover hard-to-find home furnishings or something out of the ordinary to hang on the wall, but at first glance you might not believe you're in a consignment store. The elegant, SoHo-like space has easy-to-maneuver pathways, and it's been arranged in merchandised tableaus, with clear sightlines and eye-catching displays. The layout is not surprising when you learn that owner Greg Keller (Rellek is his last name spelled backward) has worked as a visual merchandiser for Nordstrom, Tommy Hilfiger, and Nautica. Items are consigned at very reasonable prices, so they tend to not stay too long.

## FLEA MARKETS

### SHELBY COUNTY FLEA MARKET
**820 Buck Creek Rd., Simpsonville**
**(502) 722-8883**
**www.shelbycountyfleamarket.com**
One of the largest and oldest flea markets in the area, the Shelby County Flea Market is open to the general public year-round on Saturday and Sunday from 9 a.m. to 5 p.m. Spread out over six buildings and in outdoor spaces, some 500 vendors sell everything from antiques and collectibles to new and used merchandise. Also for sale are CDs and records, clothing, jewelry, books, crafts, and even fresh produce. The spacious lounge area and the game room with arcade and pool tables make it a popular destination for families on the weekend. Located about 20 miles east of Louisville.

## FOOD

One of the disadvantages to shopping in downtown Louisville is the obvious lack of good gro-

## Look for These Labels

When shopping in the Louisville area at grocery stores, specialty shops, farmers' markets, or roadside stands, make sure to keep an eye out for items with the Kentucky Proud or the Kentucky Crafted labels. "Kentucky Proud" is the official trademark of the state department of agriculture, and it strives to support sustainable farming habits and keep food dollars at home by promoting the best local food products. By the same token, the "Kentucky Crafted" label strives to develop the state's industry in arts and crafts by supporting local artisans. To learn more about the Kentucky Proud program, go online at www.kyagr.com/kyproud/index.htm. To learn more about the Kentucky Crafted program, go online at www.kycraft.ky.gov.

cery stores and food marts. The city has been in negotiations with a large chain to come downtown, but as of yet there have been no takers. Many people in the city center shop for food just south of Broadway at the Kroger—the region's most visible chain—at 924 South Second Street, but the selection is somewhat limited and the location is not very nice. Others go to ValuMarket in the lower Highlands at 1502 Bardstown Road (or the store will actually deliver to you if you want). Some prefer to use the Kroger at 2200 Brownsboro Road, or else make the five-minute drive across the river to Clarksville and use the Walmart at 951 Lewis and Clark Parkway. Despite the lack of downtown food stores, there are plenty of opportunities throughout the Derby City to fulfill your grocery needs.

**AMAZING GRACE**
**1133 Bardstown Rd.**
**(502) 485-1122**
**www.amazinggracewholefoods.com**
A small local store, Amazing Grace offers a large selection of organic, vegetarian, and natural foods. In addition to fresh organic produce, there is a vegetarian and mostly vegan deli with salads, soups, sandwiches, and wraps to go. In addition, natural herbs and remedies are available, as are organic pet food, environmentally friendly cleaning supplies, incense, candles, and fair-trade gifts.

## Farmers' Markets

When you're out and about in Louisville's shopping districts, don't forget about the many farmers' markets in the region. Neighborhood markets offer a great way to mingle with the natives while experiencing the bounty of local growers and producers. One of the most popular takes place Saturday mornings when shoppers visit the parking lot of the Presbyterian Church at 1722 Bardstown Road to stock up on farm-fresh eggs, herbs, flowers, baked goods, honey, cheeses, potted plants, meats, and a wide variety of locally grown fruits and vegetables. Another favorite is the Heart of St. Matthews Farmers' Market at 4100 Shelbyville Road. The largest market in the city, over 70 vendors gather here to bring a variety of locally grown foods and products from the region into the Louisville community. For more information about farmers' markets in the area, go online at www.kyagr.com/marketing/farmmarket/directory.htm.

## BURGER'S MARKET
**1105 Ray Ave.**
**(502) 454-0461**

This neighborhood shop in the Cherokee Tri-angle district is popular with students at nearby Collegiate School, so you might want to avoid the times right before classes begin and after they let out. Apart from regular grocery items, the shelves are also lined with gourmet and specialty treats. Homemade soups, sandwiches, and ready-to-eat items are available as well. Open every day but Sunday.

## DOLL'S MARKET
**2843 Brownsboro Rd.**
**(502) 896-4753**

This upscale neighborhood grocery offers traditional and gourmet items without all the glitz of the larger chain stores. In addition to an excellent selection of dressings, condiments, sauces, and spices, the store also features a bakery, deli, hot bar, and salad bar where you can pick up items such as garlic-stuffed olives or fresh mozzarella by the pound. Prices can be on the high side, but lots of specials are offered on the take-out food, which is a popular alternative to stopping at the fast-food restaurant. Service at this homey market is usually fast, and the staff friendly. Open seven days a week.

## LOTSA PASTA INTERNATIONAL FOOD SHOP
**3717 Lexington Rd.**
**(502) 896-6361**
**www.lotsapastalouisville.com**

Undeniably Louisville's favorite stop for gourmet items and delicious handmade sandwiches, Lotsa Pasta is open daily. Although it started off as a pasta shop in 1982, it quickly grew to include a bakery, deli, and cheese counter. While Italian delicacies and products are still a mainstay at Lotsa Pasta, hard-to-find international items and local goodies line the shelves as well. In a secluded corner of the store with large windows opening onto a garden patio, a cafe with free Wi-Fi service offers a quiet spot to enjoy one of the many specialty coffees, teas, and pastries that are offered daily.

# Ethnic Food in Louisville

Although a number of small ethnic food stores—many of them catering to the Hispanic community—can be found throughout the greater Louisville area, many shoppers go to Preston Highway for their ethnic food needs. Stores such as La Tropicana carry a variety of import items from Latin America and sell fresh items from an on-site bakery and butcher shop. Other areas with concentrations of ethnic food shops can be found along Dixie Highway and the southern end of Bardstown Road. The neighborhood around the Iroqois Manor shopping center at South Third Street—an area with a sizable immigrant population from the Caribbean, Asia, and Eastern Europe—has a number of specialty stores catering to the Asian community. The ValuMarket also has an assortment of hard-to-get items from around the world, including fresh produce.

If you're looking for out-of-the-way restaurants for good ethnic food, consider Vietnam Kitchen (502-363-5154) at 5339 Mitscher Avenue or Luna's Rotisserie (502-962-8898), a hole in the wall specializing in roast chicken and central Mexican favorites, at 5213 Preston Highway. Popular taco trucks include Las Gorditas (502-492-0112) at 4756 Bardstown Road, and Tacos Toreados (502-468-3524), a trailer that parks in front of Choi's Asian Food Market in Lyndon every day but Monday. See the restaurants section for more ethnic dining options.

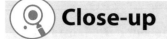 **Close-up**

## Two Local Favorites

### RAINBOW BLOSSOM NATURAL FOOD MARKET

In business in the Louisville area for more than 30 years, Rainbow Blossom Natural Food Markets have five locations specializing in items free of synthetic preservatives, artificial colors, or flavors. Convinced that the more customers know about a product, the easier it is for them to make informed choices, they provide experienced health advisors to answer questions and a large selection of free information pamphlets.

All shops are open for business seven days a week. For more information, go online at www.rainbowblossom.com.

East End/Springhurst Market
3608 Springhurst Blvd.
(502) 339-5090

Highlands Market
3046 Bardstown Rd.
(502) 498-2470

Middletown Market
12401 Shelbyville Rd.
(502) 244-2022

New Albany Market
3003 Charlestown Crossing Way
New Albany, IN
(812) 941-0080

St. Matthews Market
3738 Lexington Rd.
(502) 896-0189

### VALUMARKET

Touting itself as "Louisville's family-owned grocery" for more than 30 years, ValuMarket prides itself on being an active member in the community. Each store is tailored to the community it serves, so the selection may vary from location to location; however, there is a preference for local products and those with the Kentucky Proud label. The ValuMarket at Iroqois Manor (5301 Mitscher Avenue) in South Louisville is popular because of its large selection of items catering to the nearby Cuban and Vietnamese populations. Go online at www.valumarket.com for more details. Open seven days a week.

315 Whitington Pkwy., (502) 423-7110

7519 Outer Loop, (502) 239-7375

5301 Mitscher Ave., (502) 361-9285

1250 Bardstown Rd., (502) 459-2221

205 Oakbrooke Dr., (502) 955-9563

**PAUL'S FRUIT MARKET**
4601 Jennings Lane
(502) 458-7641
www.paulsfruit.com
Specializing in gourmet and local food and fresh produce, several Paul's Fruit Markets are located throughout the city. For more information, read about Paul's Fruit Market in the Kentucky-Themed Gift Shops section of this chapter.

**WHOLE FOODS MARKET**
4944 Shelbyville Rd.
(502) 899-5545
www.wholefoodsmarket.com
The chain that started in 1980 with one store in Austin, Texas, is now the world's leader in natural and organic foods, with more than 270 stores in North America and the United Kingdom. One of them is in the St. Matthews neighborhood, near

Louisville's two most popular malls. The selection of natural and organic foods runs the gamut from canned and dried goods to fresh produce and hand-cut meats. The dizzying selection of cheeses and gourmet items is enough to make the most jaded of foodies swoon.

## MALLS AND OUTLETS

### EDINBURGH PREMIUM OUTLETS
**11622 North East Executive Dr.**
**Edinburgh, IN**
**(812) 526-9764**
**www.premiumoutlets.com**
Located 35 minutes south of Indianapolis on I-65, Edinburgh Premium Outlets has 85 stores offering discounts of up to 65 percent off. Brands include Adidas, Anne Klein, Banana Republic, Calvin Klein, Coach, Gap Outlet, Gymboree, J.Crew, Liz Claiborne, Nautica, Nike, Polo Ralph Lauren, and Tommy Hilfiger. From Louisville the trip is about 70 miles. Take Interstate 65N to exit 76B. Open daily.

### GREEN TREE MALL
**757 East Lewis and Clark Pkwy.**
**Clarksville, IN**
**(812) 283-5678**
**www.greentreemall.com**
After the River Falls Mall closed several years ago and converted into a huge Outdoor World, Green Tree Mall on the Lewis and Clark Parkway became the only mall left across the river. Although many businesses have gravitated to the newer Veterans Parkway down the road, the Green Tree Mall remains the biggest shopping attraction in Clarksville. More than 70 stores and restaurants can be found on one floor, including a Dillard's, Sears, JCPenney, and Burlington Coat Factory. Open daily, but store and restaurant hours vary.

### JEFFERSON MALL
**4801 Outer Loop**
**(502) 968-4101**
**www.shopjefferson-mall.com**
Located on Outer Loop just down from Preston Highway in Okolona, Jefferson Mall is easily accessible from I-65, I-265, and I-264. With almost a million square feet of leasing space, Jefferson Mall is the shopping center of choice for most residents of the South End. Jefferson Mall is the home to more than 120 popular stores and restaurants that include JCPenney, Dillard's, Macy's, and Old Navy. Open daily, but hours for individual stores and restaurants vary.

### MALL ST. MATTHEWS
**5000 Shelbyville Rd.**
**(502) 893-0311**
**www.mallstmatthews.com**
Located on Shelbyville Road just off of the Watterson Expressway in St. Matthews, this mall was the first true indoor mall in Louisville; today, it is still one of the most popular shopping centers in the Louisville area, although traffic in that part of town can get frustrating (by Louisville standards, at least) during peak hours. At over a million square feet, the Mall St. Matthews has more than 130 stores, including Aeropostale, Ann Taylor Loft, Arhaus, Aveda, Brooks Brothers, Brookstone, Harold's, Pottery Barn, and Williams-Sonoma. Open every day of the week; hours vary for individual stores and restaurants.

### OXMOOR CENTER
**7900 Shelbyville Rd.**
**(502) 426-3000**
**www.oxmoorcenter.com**
Considered by many to be the most prestigious of the local malls, Oxmoor Center is located in St. Matthews, just down Shelbyville Road from the Mall St. Matthews. The drive from downtown Louisville takes about 10 minutes. Oxmoor Center is home to more than 100 specialty shops and eateries, including American Eagle Outfitters, Dick's Sporting Goods, Gymboree, Banana Republic, California Pizza Kitchen, Old Navy, and Pottery Barn Kids. Open daily, but store and restaurant hours vary.

### THE SUMMIT LOUISVILLE
**4300 Summit Plaza Dr.**
**(502) 425-3441**
**www.thesummitonline.com**

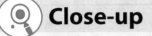

# Close-up

## Trolley Hops

Trolley hops are a wonderful way to experience the variety of two of Louisville's favorite gallery/shopping districts while mingling with the locals. Stoll, Keenon & Ogden and AT&T sponsor a monthly hop to the hotspots along Main and Market Streets, and Maker's Mark and Stella Artois sponsor the one that hits the favorites in the Frankfort Avenue area. Participating galleries along the route will be identified with an Art Zone sign, and all you need to do is board or exit at any TARC stop along they way. The ride is free.

### FIRST FRIDAY TROLLEY HOP

### www.firstfridaytrolleyhop.com

On an average trolley hop evening, several thousand people will turn out for this celebration in the downtown gallery district. According to the Web site: "It's an art show. It's a tourist attraction. It's a street party." This popular trolley hop has been bringing new visitors and new life to the Main and Market corridor since 2001, when a group of artists and art gallery owners suggested using the Transit Authority of River City's (TARC's) historic trolleys to connect the increasing number of galleries in the downtown district. The First Friday Trolley Hop takes place on the first Friday of each month, with trolleys running from 5 to 11 p.m., rain or shine. Although many of the galleries close around 9 p.m., restaurants, clubs, and shops stay open later.

### FRANKFORT AVENUE TROLLEY HOP

### www.fatfridayhop.org

On the last Friday of every month, the Transit Authority of River City (TARC) teams up with the businesses along the Frankfort Avenue corridor to showcase the best the neighborhood has to offer. From 6 p.m. to 10:30 p.m. trolleys run every 12 minutes, and shops extend their hours for those wanting to take advantage of the variety of boutiques, studios, and galleries that feature handcrafted furniture and gifts, regional art, fine antiques, apparel, and more in the district. Once you've worked up an appetite, check out one of the locally owned bistros, pubs, or cafes in the area for a bite to eat, and top it all off with a nightcap at one of the local nightspots.

The Summit is Louisville's newest shopping mall. It is located off of Brownsboro Road in the East End, about a 20-minute drive from the city center. With nearly 400,000 square feet of retail space, it is home to more than 50 stores and restaurants, including Pier 1, Gap, Express, Barnes & Noble, and Bath and Body Works. A manicured plaza area offers lovely plantings, unique sculptures, architectural details, and conversational seating areas. Open from 10 a.m to 9 p.m. Monday through Saturday, and from noon to 6 p.m. on Sunday.

## MUSIC STORES

### BOOK & MUSIC EXCHANGE
### 1616 Bardstown Rd.
### (502) 454-3328

Centrally located in the Highlands, this eclectic shop is the place for avid readers who don't want to spend a fortune on new books. Simply take in your old paperback—you can buy them there for $1—and trade it in for a different one when you've finished it. It works the same way for CDs and video games. On-street parking is scarce on that stretch of Bardstown Road, so you may need to drive around for a bit.

## DOO WOP SHOP
**1587 Bardstown Rd.**
**(502) 456-5250**
**www.doowop.com**
For more than 35 years, the Doo Wop Shop has been the store where "we rent everything musical." Included in the inventory are a wide variety of musical instruments and the latest in karaoke needs. Apart from the Bardstown Road stores, the Doo Wop Shop has locations on South Hurstbourne Parkway in Louisville, as well as in Frankfort and Lexington.

## EAR X-TACY
**1534 Bardstown Rd.**
**(502) 452-1799**
**www.earx-tacy.com**
"Louisville's Neighborhood Record Store since 1985" has two stories and 10,000 square feet of floor space filled with almost every music genre imaginable in CD, cassette, and vinyl formats. They also carry a large stock of VHS tapes and DVDs, including many hard-to-find items, as well

as T-shirts and toys. You'll also find a stage for live performances and a selection of stickers promoting Louisville. In 1995, the ear X-tacy label was formed.

## UNDERGROUND SOUNDS
**2003 Highland Ave.**
**(502) 485-0174**
**www.myspace.com/undergroundsounds**
A favorite among those in search of used vinyl, Underground Sounds is located near the busy intersection of Bardstown Road and Highland Avenue. According to their MySpace page, they've got music "From Dylan to the Stones to the Dead to Prince to the Roots to D'Angelo to 13th Floor Elevators to obscure funk stuff the bands don't even remember to local greats like Vampire Squid, Slint, Ayin, Crappy Nightmareville, Teneia Sanders, Cabin, AM Sunday, to Coltrane to Miles to Donny Hathaway to Quicksilver Messenger Service to Modest Mouse to TV on the Radio to Tom Waits to Frank Zappa to Floyd to countless others."

# THE ARTS

W hat I found was a city reshaping itself around the arts," wrote Rita Lombardi for Boston's *Big, Red & Shiny* magazine after a 2008 visit to Louisville. After expressing enthusiasm for the variety and quality of art in this Ohio River Valley city, she concluded that Louisvillians were "closer to art and its world than they dreamed they would ever be." As a final warning, she advised major art centers like Boston and New York "to watch out" because "[t]he world isn't your oyster anymore . . . the oyster is up for grabs." Among the reasons for her optimism, she cited, among others, the 21c Museum Hotel, the number of up-and-coming art galleries and gatherings such as regular trolley hops designed to get people out and about in the city's different arts districts. Fortunately, many in Louisville share her optimism, bolstered by the reputation archieved by artistic performance venues like Actors Theatre of Louisville and the Kentucky Ballet. There will always be those who view this city as a cultural backwater, however, when it comes to the arts. Those people, generally, haven't been to Louisville. You'll be pleased by what the arts hold in store for you in Kentucky's largest city. From regional crafts and inter-national art exbits to classical concerts and original theatrical productions, there's something here for you.

## GALLERIES

### CHAPMAN FRIEDMAN GALLERY
624 West Main St.
(502) 584-7954
www.chapmanfriedmangallery.com
Housed in a spacious venue in the heart of the historic Main Street business district, this popular gallery hosts exhibits that change every four to six weeks. Regional artists, as well as national and international ones, showcase works of con-temporary fine art, and clients come in search of commissioned pieces as well. The large inventory includes furniture pieces, photography, painting, sculpture, and ceramics.

### CRESSMAN CENTER GALLERY
100 East Main St.
(502) 852-0288
http://louisville.edu/a-s/finearts/cressman_center.html
Located at the corner of First and Main on the ground floor of a parking garage, the Cressman Center serves as a downtown showcase for the University of Louisville's Hite Institute of Art.

Contemporary art with a strong glass component is on display, and visitors are meant to acquire an understanding of the process behind the products they're contemplating. Walk in the door and look one way, and you see students at work in the hot shop; look in the other direction and you'll find the gallery with their finished pieces on display. The building is part of the new wave of green buildings to go up in downtown Louisville, and heat from the glass workshop is recycled to warm the building.

### GALERIE HERTZ
1253 South Preston St.
(502) 635-3727
Open Thursday, Friday, and Saturday, Galerie Hertz provides a unique setting for a wealth of realist and surreal paintings, drawings, sculpture, and much more. Approximately half of the works are by local and regional artists, and owner Billy Hertz displays his work as well. Even though they're only open three days a week, Hertz says, "If you drive by and the gates are open, come on in!"

## Bike Stands

Louisville is one of those cities across the USA where bicycle racks that combine security with the aesthetics of art are popping up all over the place. In the downtown area, there are some 30 sculptures, ranging from abstract designs to whimsical sea creatures, and there are plans for more on the way. The Louisville Downtown Management District paid artists only $2,000 per piece, and the racks became the property of the city once they were installed, but in return, they got public exhibition space guaranteeing that thousands of people will see their work. So, if you're walking downtown and spot a group of Stone Age figures or a fanciful flourish of burnished metal, take a closer look and see if a bike is attached. For more information and a list of the sculptures and their locations, visit www.ldmd.org.

## GLASSWORKS
**815 West Market St.**
**(502) 584-4510**
**www.louisvilleglassworks.com**
This multiuse facility located in the heart of downtown Louisville glorifies glass as art, showing it as a magical, mysterious, beautiful medium. Located in the historic Snead Manufacturing Building, there are three working glass studios, two glass galleries, a walk-in workshop, daily tours, and more. Open seven days a week.

## THE GREEN BUILDING GALLERY
**732 East Market St., 3rd Floor**
**(502) 561-1162**
**www.thegreenbuilding.net**

A variety of thought-provoking artists exhibit their work at the gallery in the award-winning Green Building, which opened in the fall of 2008 in the East Market District, the heart of NuLu, Louisville's arts district. Renovation of the 110-year-old masonry structure began in 2007 when owners Augusta and Gill Holland decided to make theirs the first commercial building in Louisville to go for LEED platinum certification (the U.S. Green Building Council's designation of a sustainable building). Aside from the gallery, the mixed-use facility houses 732 Social—a street-facing cafe—from James Beard–nominated Ton Brothers, event spaces, and an indoor-outdoor courtyard at the rear, complete with a green wall vertical garden.

## HIGGINS MAXWELL GALLERY
**1200 Payne St.**
**(502) 584-700**
**www.higginsmaxwell.com**
European fine art is on display in this gallery, started in 1996 near the Highlands neighborhood, but they specialize in vintage American artists and paintings sold on consignment. Local artists are represented as well. A popular stop for collectors looking for works from artists of the Ohio Valley School and the Wonderland Way, the gallery is also available to rent for cocktail parties and other events.

## KAVIAR FORGE & GALLERY
**1718 Frankfort Ave.**
**(502) 561-0377**
**www.craigkaviar.com**
Award-winning bronze and iron furniture, architectural gates, rails, liturgical work, and more can be viewed at this workshop, which specializes in a wide range of forged-metal pieces. Antique machines, tools, and metal lend the space an air of cluttered artistry, and a window in the gallery looks out over the forging area, affording visitors a glimpse of artist Craig Kaviar in action. An attractive outdoor sculpture garden surrounds the studio and gallery.

# Art off the Beaten Path

## Mellwood Arts and Entertainment Center

1860 Mellwood Ave.
(502) 895-3650
www.mellwoodartcenter.com

Creative types come to this former meat-packing plant turned arts complex for the opportunity to collaborate, shop, browse, and dine at one of the on-site restaurants. Just minutes from downtown Louisville, it houses almost 200 studios, galleries, and specialty shops that display the potential for community-based art. Open seven days a week.

## OBJECTS OF DESIRE GALLERY

**1503 Bardstown Rd.**

**(502) 458-4164**

**www.objectsofdesiregallery.com**

Established in 1990, this gallery near the bustling intersection of Bardstown Road and Eastern Parkway has emerged as one of the region's premier shops for showcasing contemporary, wearable art. A smartly designed space provides a dramatic backdrop for the works of established and newly emerging artists, whose art challenges conventional notions of wearability and ownership, and nationally and internationally recognized metalsmiths and fiber artists are showcased on a regular basis through permanent displays and group or solo exhibitions.

**i** Located at the historic Water Tower off of Zorn Avenue at 3005 River Road, the Louisville Visual Arts Association provides a wide array of programs for art education and community outreach, in addition to hosting regular exhibits by emerging and established artists from the community. Find out more about their schedule by calling (502) 896-2146, or by going online at www.louisvillevisualart.org.

## ZEPHYR GALLERY

**610 East Market St.**

**(502) 585-5646**

**www.zephyrgallery.org**

Zephyr Gallery is a contemporary fine arts gallery that has advocated regional talent while contributing to Derby City culture for some 20 years. The oldest cooperative gallery in the region, Zephyr Gallery boasts a member base composed of 24 local artists who own the gallery, and allow visitors direct personal access. Regular shows display the work of member artists in a broad range of media and styles, and additional viewing allows for exploration of the extensive inventory housed in a private storage facility. Gallery hours are 11 a.m. to 6 p.m. Wednesday through Saturday, or by appointment.

# Fund for the Arts

The oldest united arts fund in the nation, Louisville's Fund for the Arts has raised nearly $160 million since it was established in 1949. It has continually progressed from the very first campaign in 1949, which raised $99,000, now bringing in millions of dollars each year. In addition to annually awarding more than 200 community access grants to schools and community organizations throughout Kentucky and Southern Indiana, the Fund provides facilities and administrative support, as well as generous financing for more than two dozen area arts programs and groups. Another important feature of this program is ArtSpace, a mixed-use development run by a sister organization at 323 West Broadway that includes the Brown Theatre, as well as arts administration offices, classrooms, meeting spaces, a rehearsal hall, and a costume shop. Get more information about the Fund for the Arts at www.fundforthearts.com.

# PERFORMING ARTS

As in other cities, funding for the arts has been dwindling in recent years, and this has had an impact on the region's stages. Nonetheless, the performing arts have remained a vital part of Louisville's cultural landscape, and on any given night, visitors and residents alike will have a variety of live concerts, musicals, and stage productions to choose from.

## Kentucky Center for the Performing Arts

Dedicated in 1983, the Kentucky Center for the Performing Arts (501 West Main St.; 502-562-0100; www.kentuckycenter.org) is one of the city's main venues for live stage productions and theatrical events. It also serves as the base for the PNC Broadway Series, a program that brings popular musicals and touring stage productions to the Derby City. In addition, it hosts a number of artworks by Alexander Calder, Joan Miró, John Chamberlain, and Jean Dubuffet, among others. The Center has three performance spaces: Robert S. Whitney Hall, the largest with 2,406 seats, and named for the founding conductor of the Louisville Orchestra; Moritz von Bomhard Theater, with 619 seats, named for the founder of the Kentucky Opera; and the 619-seat Boyd Martin Theater, also known as "the MeX," which was named for the well-known Louisville *Courier-Journal* film and theater critic. In addition, the Center also administers the Brown Theatre, eight blocks away on Broadway, next to the Brown Hotel. Completed in 1925, this 1,400-seat space was modeled on the Music Box Theater in New York City.

ⓘ Arts Rush is a program in which the area's largest performing arts organizations offer day-of-show tickets for select performances for only $10. Tickets are available two hours before curtain on a first-come, first-served basis, and the number of tickets and location of available seats within the house varies by venue, presenting organization, and show. All ticket sales must be made in person at the box office. Check out the list of eligible performances at www.kentuckycenter.org/artsrush.

## Dance and Music

**KENTUCKY OPERA**
**323 West Broadway**
**(502) 584-4500**
**www.kyopera.org**
Designated the State Opera of Kentucky in 1982, the Kentucky Opera was founded by Moritz von Bomhard in 1952, and counts as one of the first regional opera companies in this country. Under Bomhard's direction, the opera grew from a small organization to become a thriving, innovative company respected by appreciative audiences for the quality of its productions. In the 1950s alone, five world-premiere works were presented at the Kentucky Opera—quite a feat for a small regional company—and the spirit of artistic innovation lives on today. Although the warhorses by Mozart, Puccini, and Verdi make regular appearances on the Kentucky Opera stage, contemporary works are featured as well. Tickets range in price from $30 to $105 for a single show, and from $78 to $253 for a season subscription of three performances.

**LOUISVILLE BALLET**
**315 East Main St.**
**(502) 583-3150**
**www.louisvilleballet.org**
Louisville Ballet, the State Ballet of Kentucky, was founded in March 1952 as a civic ballet company. Today, it reaches an audience of nearly 50,000 people each year, and has earned a national reputation as one of the country's leading regional

ballet companies. It has over 65 world-premiere ballets to its credit, and a repertoire of over 150 works by noted choreographers such as Sir Frederick Ashton, Erik Bruhn, George Balanchine, Antony Tudor, Jack Carter, Choo-San Goh, Jose Limon, and Paul Taylor.

## LOUISVILLE ORCHESTRA
**323 West Broadway**
**(502) 587-8681**
**www.louisvilleorchestra.org**
Founded in 1937 by then mayor of Louisville, Charles Farnsley, and conductor Robert Whitney, the Louisville Orchestra is regarded by many as the cornerstone of the Louisville arts community. Today the programs it offers are as diverse as the audiences it attracts. A full-time, 71-member ensemble offers a wide variety of concerts that include traditional fare with world-renowned guest artists, in addition to lighter classical and pops performances. Also the resident performing group for the Louisville Ballet and the Kentucky Opera, the Louisville Orchestra holds performances at the Kentucky Center for the Performing Arts and other venues throughout the city; ticket costs vary.

## Musical Theater

### DERBY DINNER PLAYHOUSE
**525 Marriott Dr.**
**Clarksville, IN**
**(812) 288-8281**
**www.derbydinner.com**
Located across the river from downtown Louisville, the Derby Dinner Playhouse is one of the country's oldest and largest, continually operating dinner theaters. Since opening in 1974 under the general management of Carolyn Thomas, attendance at the Derby Dinner Playhouse has grown to over 200,000 patrons per year, with 8,000 season subscribers, and more than 3 million visitors have been attracted in all. Guests enjoy a variety of musical entertainment productions after helping themselves to a lavish buffet that features classic American cuisine. In addition to a

variety of vegetables, fish, beef, and turkey, selections include a full salad bar, hot rolls, desserts, and beverage. A full bar is available as well. Single tickets average $35 per person, depending on the time of day and time of the show.

**i** Dedicated to strengthening the local arts community, Music Theatre Louisville is a nonprofit community-based theater that produces diverse and affordable entertainment while training and mentoring youth in the arts. Go online at www.musictheatrelouisville.com for more information.

### IROQUOIS AMPHITHEATER
**1080 Amphitheater Rd.**
**(502) 368-5865**
**www.louisvilleky.gov**
With seating for more than 2,407 and a stage that hosts a variety of performing arts and cultural programs, the Iroquois Amphitheater is the official amphitheater for the Commonwealth of Kentucky. For many, especially in the city's South End, it has become a summer tradition to take in at least one summer performance at the historic theater. Originally built in 1938 by employees from the Works Progress Administration, this outdoor theater in Iroquois Park recently underwent an $8.9 million renovation that carefully preserved portions of the original structure while adding much-needed updates.

**i** In 1893, two Louisville schoolteachers, sisters Patty and Mildred Hill, wrote the song "Good Morning to All" for their kindergarten class. The song did not become popular, however, until the lyrics were changed to the more recognizable "Happy Birthday to You." Downtown, at the corner of Ninth and West Main, under the entrance ramp to I-64, you'll find a plaque on a small concrete pedestal that remembers the writers of this song.

# 🔍 Close-up

## The Kentucky Derby of Theater

Actors Theatre of Louisville also hosts the annual **Humana Festival of New American Plays,** an event considered an essential part of the theatrical year in this country. Started by Jon Jory, this internationally renowned festival celebrates contemporary American playwrights and showcases new theatrical works. The Festival has been drawing producers, critics, playwrights, and theater lovers from around the world since 1976. Every February and March, theater people converge in Kentucky's largest city to get a glimpse of the future of American theater, while others come to see what their favorite playwright has been up to. Produced by the Actors Theatre of Louisville, the festival is made possible by the generosity of the Humana Foundation, the philanthropic arm of Humana Inc. that supports charitable activities and promotes healthy lives and communities. Some of the well-known works to come out of the Humana Festival of American Plays include *Agnes of God, Extremities, The Gin Game,* and *Crimes of the Heart.* Learn more at www.actorstheatre.org.

## Theater

**ACTORS THEATRE OF LOUISVILLE**
316 West Main St.
(502) 584-1205
www.actorstheatre.org

Housed in downtown Louisville in a structure that started off as two old buildings—the Old Bank of Louisville, designed by James H. Dakin in 1837, and the Myers-Thompson Display Building—Actors Theatre of Louisville was founded in 1964. It took off when Jon Jory, the son of Victor Jory, who played the part of the overseer in *Gone with the* Wind, was appointed director in 1969, and in 1974 it was officially designated the "State Theater of Kentucky." Today, the complex contains three performance spaces: the Pamela Brown Theater, the Victor Jory Theater, and the Bingham Theater. Actors Theatre of Louisville shows national favorites and local plays, and has premiered a number of Pulitzer Prize–winning works. Seasonal ticket packages for five plays start for as little as $93, something that has earned ATL one of the highest per capita subscription rates of any American theater company.

**BROWN THEATRE**
501 West Main St.
(502) 562-0188
www.kentuckycenter.org

An elegant reminder of the glory days of Louisville's theater district in the 1920s, the Brown Theatre is a lovingly restored showplace that combines Old World splendor and state-of-the-art technology to create a performance space that is both comfortable and beautiful. With seating for some 1,400 patrons, the Brown counts as a grand dame of Derby City's artistic community today. It is one of the main venues for theatrical and musical productions sponsored by the Kentucky Center for the Performing Arts.

### Actors Honor Roll

Among the many actors who honed their skills at Actors Theatre of Louisville are:

| | |
|---|---|
| Armand Assante | Holly Hunter |
| Kevin Bacon | Ken Jenkins |
| Kathy Bates | Will Oldham |
| Ned Beatty | Pamela Reed |
| Leo Burmester | Mercedes Ruehl |
| Timothy Busfield | Lili Taylor |
| Barry Corbin | John Turturro |
| Karen Grassle | Dianne Wiest |
| Harry Groener | Max Wright |
| Michael Gross | |

## BUNBURY THEATRE
**604 South Third St.**
**(502) 585-5306**
**www.bunburytheatre.org**
Striving to "create enriching, diverse, live theatrical experiences for the community and its artists in an intimate and professional setting," the Bunbury Theatre is located on the third floor of the Henry Clay building at the corner of Third and Chestnut. *The Cemetery Club, The Cocktail Hour, The Gin Game,* and *Between Daylight and Booneville* are some of the productions that have been staged since the theater's inception in 1991. In addition, *The Butterfingers Angel, Mary, and Joseph, Herod the Nut, and the Slaughter of Twelve Hit Carols in a Pear Tree* has become a yearly tradition. Tickets generally fall in the $10 to $20 price range.

## FINNIGAN'S PRODUCTIONS
**3911 Elmwood Ave.**
**(502) 876-0532**
**www.finniganbeginagain.com**
Bringing cutting-edge and thought-provoking works of theater to the stages of Louisville, Finnigan's Productions tries to showcase alternative theater that is socially relevant. Every spring the troupe puts together the *Festival of Funky Fresh Fun* to celebrate local talent with an evening of 10-minute plays by local writers and directors. The 2009 festival included works by Tad Chitwood, Nancy Gall-Clayton, Doug Schutte, Todd Zeigler, Andy Epstein, Christa Kreimendahl, Sherry Deatrick, Jeffrey Scott Holland, Carlos Manuel, Carridder Jones, and Nathan Green. Finnigan's Productions stages many of its plays at the Rudyard Kipling at 422 West Oak Street in Old Louisville.

## PANDORA PRODUCTIONS
**604 South Third St.**
**www.pandoraprods.org**
Showing its productions at the Bunbury Theatre in the historic Henry Clay building on the corner of Third and Chestnut, Pandora Productions strives to entertain, engage, and inspire its audience. The repertoire includes bold, cutting-edge, and rarely seen works of theater of special interest to those in the gay, lesbian, bisexual, and transgender community—or simply to those in search of good theater. Past productions have included *Kiss of the Spider Woman, Looking for Normal, Rocky Horror Picture Show, The Laramie Project,* and *Southern Baptist Sissies.* Advance tickets for single shows generally cost $15.

## THE PLAYHOUSE
**1911 South Third St.**
**(502) 852-7926**
**www.louisville.edu/theatrearts**
The white Victorian structure on the traffic island between Second and Third at Cardinal Avenue was built in 1874 as a small, interdenominational chapel for a local orphanage. The University of Louisville acquired the chapel in 1923 and converted the structure for use as a temporary theater, until a permanent theater could be erected. In 1977, the university dismantled the playhouse to make room for the construction of the William F. Ekstrom Library and put it away in storage. Rebuilt in 1980 at its current location, the Playhouse was expanded to include a basement and fully working scene shop; today it is one of two spaces where the University of Louisville Department of Theatre Arts holds its productions. The other is at the Thrust Theatre at 2314 South Floyd Street.

## STAGE ONE
**501 West Main St.**
**(502) 625-0660**
**www.stageone.org**
Dedicated to bringing the finest-quality theater to young people, teachers, and families, Louisville's nationally acclaimed professional theater for young audiences is now in its seventh decade of existence. With a highly respected reputation among its contemporaries, the 501(c)3 nonprofit theater company has received numerous awards and commendations, including those from the American Alliance for Theatre & Education. Stage One also offers pre- and post-show discussions with the cast and crew, giving viewers a firsthand look at the life of a play as it is transformed from script to stage. A typical season will include

productions such as *You're a Good Man, Charlie Brown, The Best Christmas Pageant Ever, Antigone,* and *If You Give a Pig a Party.* Tickets for the general public are generally $15.75 for a single performance.

## WALDEN THEATRE
**1123 Payne St.**
**(502) 589-0084**
**www.waldentheatre.org**

Started in an old log cabin in eastern Jefferson County in 1976 as a way to provide young people with the opportunity to grow and develop through the comprehensive study of theater, the Walden Theatre has since taken up headquarters in the former St. Aloysius School in the Irish Hill neighborhood. The theater also operates a conservatory program, and those young actors regularly appear in the season's productions. Adult tickets for evening performances generally cost $15. In addition to works by Shakespeare, productions during a typical season will also include plays such as *The Crucible* and *Of Mice and Men.*

**i** Several major motion pictures have been filmed in or around Louisville. Apart from *The Insider* and *Elizabethtown,* they include *The Hustler, Stripes, Goldfinger, Nice Guys Sleep Alone, Keep Your Distance,* and *Lawn Dogs.*

# NIGHTLIFE

**K**nown for its blend of lively music scene, art-world coolness, and trendy places to see and be seen, Louisville offers something for every nightlife taste. Bars and clubs in the 'Ville stay open until 4 a.m., so the nightlife here is thriving, to say the least. And for a city its size, the Derby City boasts some of the most exciting and diverse entertainment niches around. True, it's much smaller than well-known late-night meccas like Miami, New York City, or Los Angeles, but it still provides a great number and variety of diversion options for adult crowds of all ages. One thing that these other places don't have, by the way, is the quirky combination of bourbon, old money, hip architecture, vibrant art scene, indie rock, and cultivated southern "weirdness" that defines nightlife in Kentucky's largest city.

Many fun-seekers experience the diversity of the city's entertainment scene at lively venues in the downtown area and along Bardstown Road; however, there is also a wealth of neighborhood bars and low-key locales where visitors and lifetime residents alike can enjoy a quiet night out. One thing is certain: With the slew of bars and nightclubs all competing for patrons and a late curfew that keeps many people out till the sun comes up, Louisville can rightfully claim a spot as one of the liveliest cities around.

## FOURTH STREET LIVE! DISTRICT

### HOTEL
**410 South Fourth St.**
**(502) 540-1116**
**www.hotel-ky.com**
Hip and high-energy, Hotel strives to provide an entertainment experience on par with the leading clubs across the country, featuring international DJ talent, premium club service, and unique cocktails. Many locals think a night downtown would be incomplete without popping in at Hotel sometime during the evening. Located right next door to the Angel's Rock Bar, this club's main entry off the second-level outdoor deck calls to mind the grand lobbies so characteristic of the world's most renowned hotels. Patrons entering the nightclub are greeted by vibrant colors and a huge dance floor with a luxurious bar at its center, fully stocked with a variety of beers and spirits. A large portion of the nightclub is also dedicated to VIP parties and exclusive get-togethers.

### HOWL AT THE MOON
**434 South Fourth St.**
**(502) 562-9400**
**www.howlatthemoon.com**
The atmosphere at Howl at the Moon is noisy, song-filled, and liable to get you clapping. Billing itself as the "World's Greatest Rock 'n' Roll Dueling Piano Show," Howl at the Moon has talented entertainers who can tickle your funny bone as well as the ivories. This lively hangout features excellent drink deals that come in well-proportioned buckets, and after a sip or two, it doesn't take much to get the crowd crooning along to the best songs from the '70s to today. If you're looking for a high-energy, interactive evening, this is the place for you.

### IMPROV COMEDY CLUB
**441 South Fourth St.**
**(502) 581-1332**
**www.improvlouisville.com**
Founded by Budd Friedman in the mid-'60s in New York City, the Improv has become known as the place to go to see tomorrow's superstars

# Close-up

## Fourth Street Live! Is Breathing Life into the Heart of the City

Just a short walk from most downtown hotels, Waterfront Park, Slugger Field, Main Street, and other major attractions is Fourth Street Live!, the city's one-stop destination for dining, shopping, nightlife, and more (420 West Liberty St.; 502-584-7170; www.4thstlive.com). Located at the heart of a recently revitalized entertainment district that was Louisville's main business corridor for many years, Fourth Street Live! is once again bringing people downtown for a good time at all hours of the day. In addition to an assortment of retail outlets, on Fourth Street between Liberty Street and Muhammad Ali Boulevard, you'll find a number of restaurant and entertainment venues, including Hard Rock Café, Red Star Tavern, the Pub, the Improv Comedy Club, Sully's, and the world's first Maker's Mark Bourbon House & Lounge. You will also find bars and nightclubs such as Hotel, Saddle Ridge, Tengo Sed Cantina, Angel's Rock Bar, and Howl at the Moon (the latter featuring live music every night).

of comedy in a unique venue where burgeoning comics perfect their craft. Today, the Improv continues to showcase up-and-coming talent alongside the hottest stand-up comedians in locations across the country. The roster has included such stars as Robin Williams, Tim Allen, Steve Martin, Jerry Seinfeld, Garry Shandling, Roseanne, Steven Wright, Dennis Miller, Rodney Dangerfield, Lily Tomlin, Ellen DeGeneres, Drew Carey, Jim Carrey, and more.

### MAKER'S MARK BOURBON HOUSE & LOUNGE
**446 South Fourth St.**
**(502) 568-9009**
**www.makerslounge.com**
A hip, trendy hotspot at the heart of Fourth Street Live!, this is the place to get a night on the town started with an exciting happy hour. Visitors can enjoy an unparalleled variety of bourbons from Kentucky's distilleries at the attractive bar. The interior glows with rich tones of wood and tile, and bourbon-brown furnishings and exquisite draperies make the lounge a lush place to sit back and enjoy a drink. Visitors can sample a wide variety of contemporary, innovative dishes from the lunch and dinner menus, in addition to a wide assortment of whiskey cocktails.

### THE SPORTS & SOCIAL CLUB
**427 South Fourth St.**
**(502) 568-1400**
**www.thesportsandsocialclub.com**
Serving lunch and dinner in a classic pub atmosphere, the Sports & Social Club also offers dynamic nightlife, with bowling, live entertainment, and a fully equipped private party room. State-of-the-art technology includes an ultimate sports viewing room equipped with two 100-inch high-definition projectors and digital surround sound. The S&SC opens seven days a week at 11 a.m. for lunch, dinner, and late-night fun. Closing hours vary, but they're always open late.

### TENGO SED CANTINA
**432 South Fourth St.**
**(502) 540-1461**
**www.tengosed-ky.com**
"All fiesta, no siesta" is the motto at this popular watering hole at the heart of downtown Louisville's Fourth Street Live! entertainment district. Open six days a week, most days till 4 a.m., Tengo Sed Cantina offers a variety of Tex-Mex-inspired food and drink. Popular bites include the chicken tacos and beer-battered shrimp with zesty chili sauce and cilantro, but if you're with a group, the El Guapo platter is usually a hit. The platter includes mini Cuban sandwiches, mex wings,

chicken flautas, mexy rolls, and quesadillas, all for just $25. The margaritas are rumored to be some of the best in town, and the late-night crowd makes this a popular destination for out-of-towners. The stripper poles let you know that this is a place for adults at night.

> **i** Looking for a place to park while you're at the Fourth Street Live! entertainment district? Free parking is available after 6 p.m. and on weekends at Galleria Garage (Fifth Street between Muhammad Ali Boulevard and Liberty Street). For a map of garages and surface lots, visit www.ldmd.org.

## DOWNTOWN

### JAZZY BLUE CAFE & LOUNGE
**815 West Market St.**
**(502) 992-3242**
**www.jazzyblu.com**
Located in the lower level of the historic Glass-works building, in the space previously occupied by the now-defunct Jazz Factory, Jazzyblu focuses on smooth tunes from local performers with music ranging from neo-soul to traditional jazz. In addition to occasional concerts from regional and national acts, the club also features live music Friday and Saturday nights. Jazzyblu also has one of the best happy hours in town to help get the weekend off to a good start. Stop by on Friday afternoons and enjoy $1 drafts, $2 mixed drinks, and $3 martinis.

### PROOF ON MAIN
**702 West Main St.**
**(502) 217-6360**
**www.proofonmain.com**
If you're in search of a downtown nightspot that combines equal parts trendy cocktail lounge with hip art museum and stylish, upscale eatery, then a trip to Proof on Main will provide you with all of that and more. Known for an assortment of colorful cocktails—the Moscow Mule and the Whiskey Smash are popular choices—and an extensive wine list that *Food & Wine* magazine voted one of

the "50 most amazing wine experiences" in 2006, this is the place where locals and guests staying at the chic 21c Museum Hotel mingle. Week-nights at Proof (as it's known among Louisvillians) are fun and usually less crowded, but you're more likely to mingle with the who's who of Derby City on the weekends.

### THE RUDYARD KIPLING
**422 West Oak St.**
**(502) 636-1311**
**www.therudyardkipling.com**
Located in a 19th-century Old Louisville brick house that was converted into a neighborhood watering hole, the Rudyard Kipling is an eclectic, eccentric place that opens during the week for special productions and concerts. On Friday and Saturday the doors open at 6:30 p.m. for whole-grain pizzas and other snacks, such as their famous Rudyardburger and Boonesborough snappy cheese. Apart from the burgoo, the soup beans and corn bread (a specialty from the eastern part of the state) are popular as well. In addition to a selection of wine and imported beers, the Rud—as the locals call it—also has good Bloody Marys and sangria. The biggest draw, however, remains the regular poetry readings and avant garde theater performances that have made the Rudyard Kipling a mainstay among the city's bohemian set.

> **i** Louisville's smoke-free law went into effect on July 1, 2007, and required more than 20,000 bars, restaurants, bingo halls, private clubs, retail stores, factories, offices, and public buildings to enact a no-smoking policy.

### STEVIE RAY'S BLUES BAR
**230 East Main St.**
**(502) 582-9945**
**www.stevieraysbluesbar.com**
The only venue in town featuring the nation's top touring blues acts such as Roomful of Blues and Anson Funderburgh and the Rockets, Stevie Ray's also showcases many of Louisville's best local blues bands. The crowd gets especially large and

# 🔍 Close-up

## The Urban Bourbon Trail

After a day in the picturesque countryside touring the distilleries on the celebrated Kentucky Bourbon Trail, whiskey fans can continue the fun in Louisville on something known as the "Urban Bourbon Trail." Created by the Louisville Convention and Visitors Bureau to complement the Kentucky Bourbon Trail, the Urban Bourbon Trail offers a taste of the rich distilling heritage in the state's largest city. Evan Williams began distilling in Louisville around 1780, and dozens of distillers were active along Main Street's "Whiskey Row" until the 1920s, so it's not surprising to find many sites of interest.

The Urban Bourbon Trail directs visitors to well-known Louisville establishments that feature Kentucky whiskey, and most of them can be found in the bustling Fourth Street Live! entertainment district. Guests can sample a variety of bourbons in drinks at some of the world's best bourbon bars and enjoy inventive cuisine with the flavors of bourbon.

The Urban Bourbon Trail can be toured over any period of time, and participants can pick up a free passport at the downtown visitor center at the corner of Fourth and Jefferson, or by calling (502) 379-6109. When you visit each location and make a purchase there, the passport will be stamped; the completed passport can then be exchanged for a T-shirt and a chance in a prize drawing. The stops include:

**Maker's Mark Bourbon House & Lounge** (446 South Fourth St.; 502-568-9009). Sleek and stylish, this trendy hotspot at the heart of Fourth Street Live! is the place for happy hour drinks or a nightcap. In addition to numerous whiskey cocktails and more than 60 bourbons available at the bar, guests can sample a wide variety of dishes from the lunch and dinner menus. Read more about Maker's Mark Bourbon House & Lounge earlier in this chapter.

**Old Seelbach Bar** (500 Fourth St.; 502-585-3200). Located on the ground floor of the grande dame of Louisville hotels, the Old Seelbach Bar was named one of the "50 Best Bars in the World" by the *Independent* in 1999. Read more about the Seelbach on page 43 in the Accommodations chapter.

**Jockey Silks Bourbon Bar & Lounge** (140 North Fourth St.; 502-589-5200). More than 100 bourbons can be sampled at this Derby-themed watering hole at the Galt House Hotel; if you can't decide on one particular brand, then try the bourbon-tasting tray. Read more about the Galt House in the Accommodations chapter on page 41.

**Proof on Main** (702 West Main St.; 502-217-6360; www.proofonmain.com). Part of the fascinating 21c Museum Hotel, Proof on Main was honored as one of the "Best New Restaurants of 2006" by *Esquire*. Known for its eclectic, contemporary art. Read more about 21c Museum Hotel on page 42 in the Accommodations chapter.

**Blu Italian Grille** (280 West Jefferson St.; 502-627-5045). Located in the Louisville Marriott Downtown, this contemporary spot offers scores of bourbons and contemporary flair. There are also bourbon flights and bourbon-infused appetizers. Read more about the Marriott on page 42 in the Accommodations chapter.

**The Brown Hotel** (335 West Broadway; 502-583-1234). Another of Derby City's landmark hotels, the 1920s Brown Hotel has a glitzy lobby bar that provides the perfect backdrop for a quick bite to eat and a sip of America's native spirit. Read more about the Brown Hotel on page 43 in the Accommodations chapter.

**Bourbons Bistro** (2255 Frankfort Ave.; 502-894-8838). Named an "American Icon of Whiskey" by *Whisky* magazine in 2006, Bourbons Bistro is the only stop outside the downtown area; however, more than 130 bourbons make it worth the 2-mile drive. Read more on page 96 in the Restaurants chapter.

rowdy on weekend nights, and the dance floor teems with a mixed crowd of couples and singles. Usually closed on Sunday, Stevie Ray's has open blues and jazz on Tuesday nights, with no cover. On Friday and Saturday nights, shows start at 7:30 p.m. and have a $5 cover.

**i** The legal age to buy alcohol in Kentucky is 21; the legal age to buy tobacco is 18.

## VERNON LANES
**1575 Story Ave.**
**(502) 584-8460**
The oldest lanes in the Derby City, and some of the oldest in the country, Vernon Lanes has been a favorite with local bowlers for generations. The building in Louisville's Butchertown neighborhood was built around 1886, and it became a club in the early 1900s. Today its eight lanes have become something of a local icon. By car, it's only a couple of minutes from the city center of Louisville. It's also a popular stop during the Lebowski Fest every year. Downstairs, there's a hopping club where patrons gather for dancing and live music. One of the reasons it's so popular is that when guests look up at the ceiling, they can see balls gliding along the track as they return to the bowlers.

# BARDSTOWN ROAD AREA

## AIR DEVILS INN
**2802 Taylorsville Rd.**
**(502) 454-4443**
**www.myspace.com/airdevilsinn**
To find this popular neighborhood hangout near Bowman Field, look for the red neon sign with the devil. It's rumored to be the oldest neon in Louisville. Air Devils Inn opened immediately after the repeal of Prohibition in 1934, and after more than 70 years of continuous operation in the same building, it's one of the oldest and most well-known bars in Louisville. Although it has changed ownership several times throughout its history, it still maintains a reputation for cheap drinks, lively conversation, great bands playing

original music, and engaging, friendly bartenders. Open till 4 a.m. seven days a week.

## BACK DOOR
**1250 Bardstown Rd.**
**(502) 451-0659**
**www.thebackdoor.us**
Known to many as one of Louisville's most welcoming bars, the Back Door is adjacent to the Mid-City Mall in the heart of the picturesque Highlands neighborhood. Open seven days a week from 4 p.m. until 4 a.m., it is strictly a "21 and over" bar, and identification is rigorously checked. Happy hour runs daily from 4 p.m. until 8 p.m., with well drinks for $2.25, domestic beers for $5 a pitcher or $1.75 a pint, and import beers for $3 a pint. As one reviewer in *LEO* noted, the Back Door is "one of Louisville's favorite after-work, meet-my-friends, meet-strangers, game-of-pool, bag-of-wings, one-more-stop-before-home watering holes."

**i** The Back Door also has a separate poolroom with high-quality pool tables that are carefully maintained and well lighted. They operate the Metro Pool League, and competition is held every Monday night starting at 7:15 p.m. In addition, a total of six tables are available for individual play, competition, or for special parties.

## COCONUT BEACH CLUB
**426 Baxter Ave.**
**(502) 618-3311**
**www.myspace.com/coconut_beach**
One of the few places in Louisville where you can dance to salsa, reggaeton, bachata, merengue, and hip-hop, the Coconut Beach Club attracts a regular crowd that is young and mostly Hispanic. Apart from hot dancing, there's a full bar with reasonably priced drinks. A dress code—casual chic—is strictly enforced, and any individuals wearing hats, gang colors, or tank tops won't be admitted. The Coconut Beach Club opens Friday and Saturday only from 11 p.m. to 4 a.m.

# Close-up

## Meet the Bands

Louisville's independently owned and operated music venue since 1998, **Headliners Music Hall** (1386 Lexington Rd.; 502-584-8088; www.headlinerslouisville.com) stands apart from other nightclubs in the Derby City for one reason: Music is all they do. Well-known national, regional, and local acts perform several nights a week for reasonable—and what many often consider downright cheap—cover charges, and a variety of bands from Everclear and the Del McCoury Band to Everlast and even Slayer have stopped by. Housed in a large old building with brick walls that feature original hand-painted murals inside, the 600-capacity club features a large stage and high-fidelity sound, and a good-size open dance floor. There are two bars as well, one spreading handsomely across the rear of the ground floor, and the other serving a spacious balcony. Next to the Palace, many consider this the best place to watch live acts in Louisville. It's also a popular destination because the bands are much more accessible than at other venues, and it's easy to get to meet them.

For information on opportunities for salsa dancing in the region, check out the Web site for the Louisville SALSA/MAMBO Meetup Group at www.meetup.com/salsa-239.

### COMEDY CARAVAN
**1250 Bardstown Rd.**
**(502) 459-0022**
**www.comedycaravan.com**
For more than 20 years, Louisville's Comedy Caravan has been celebrating laughter with "jokes, jazz, and magical evenings." Located in the Mid-City Mall in the Highlands, the Caravan presents live comedy five nights a week from Wednesday through Sunday. In addition, the club holds special events on select Monday and Tuesday nights, including jazz, magic, and more. Unless otherwise noted, you have to be at least 18 to enter all shows, with the exception of Sunday, when you have to be 16 or older. Save $2 by purchasing tickets online.

### HIDEAWAY SALOON
**1607 Bardstown Rd.**
**(502) 485-0114**
**www.hideawaysaloon.com**
Open daily till 4 a.m., the Hideaway is a Highlands venue popular for its live artists and intimate,

friendly setting. Cover charges during the week are usually $2 or $3 for a range of local bands, and, depending on who's playing on weekends, $5 will usually get you in. It's popular with the musician set because the bands always get to keep all of the door money. It's also somewhat of a shrine to high-quality brews, because on tap at the Hideaway is a great variety of good craft and imported beers, such as Blue Moon and Sierra Nevada ($3.50), and local favorites like BBC Bourbon Barrel Stout and Browning's She-Devil IPA ($5). There are also selections from Cumberland Brews, Bell's, Magic Hat, Smithwick's, Guinness, Newcastle, and Flying Dog ($4). Woodchuck hard apple cider is also on tap. Happy hour is from 5 p.m. to 8 p.m. Monday through Thursday, when all beers are $1 off. Pool is available upstairs.

### JIM PORTER'S GOOD TIME EMPORIUM
**2345 Lexington Rd.**
**(502) 452-9531**
**www.jimporters.com**
Always hopping with multiple live bands, this sprawling nightclub complex is really popular with the 30-and-older crowd. If it seems like it's been around forever, that's because there are more than 18,000 square feet of space that, over the years, has amassed a collection of thousands of antiques and curios including china plates and

# The Kentucky Giant

**Jim Porter's Good Time Emporium** is named for Jim Porter, a legendary tavern owner, Louisville politician, and larger-than-life personality. Born in the early 1800s, Jim Porter was a small and sickly child—so small, in fact, that at the age of 14 he became a jockey at nearby Elm Tree Garden racetrack. But at age 17 something began to happen, and he started growing; in three years he reached the height of 7 feet 8 inches. He grew so fast that locals would take bets on how much he would grow in a week, and every Saturday night he would allow himself to be weighed and measured. Later, when asked how tall he was, he would respond "6 feet 21 inches." Around 1830, "Big" was added to his name, and locals called him Big Jim Porter, the Kentucky Giant.

Among other jobs, Porter worked as a hackney driver carrying passengers and goods from Louisville to the Portland Wharf, and in 1836 Jim toured for one year with a band of midgets performing *Gulliver's Travels*. When he returned he opened a tavern on the Portland Canal and became a prosperous citizen. Charles Dickens, calling on him during a visit to Louisville in 1842, described him as "a lighthouse walking among lampposts." When P. T. Barnum asked him to join his famous circus, Porter politely declined.

James D. Porter died quietly in his sleep on April 24, 1859, most likely from heart problems related to gigantism. He was laid to rest in a nine-foot coffin in Cave Hill Cemetery, and his funeral procession was the largest in the city's history. A life-size statue of Big Jim Porter stands in the Good Time Emporium today.

dolls, Victorian furniture, window treatments, and antique light fixtures. Live music is usually presented with three acts performing simultaneously on different stages. The acts include jazz, oldies, rhythm and blues, rock, alternative, big band, blues, contemporary, country, disco, and rockabilly. There are eight unique rooms, all under one roof for one admission price: the Ballroom, the Good Time Room, the Melody Bar, the Balcony Bar, the Billiard Parlour, Memory Lane, the Cubbyhole, and the Courtyard. Jim Porter's is popular with ballroom dancers as well, and Wednesday nights there is always salsa music.

**MOLLY MALONE'S IRISH PUB**
933 Baxter Ave.
(502) 473-1222
www.mollymalonesirishpub.com

There's a popular weekday happy hour from 4 to 7 p.m. with $1 off premium drafts at this Irish Hill establishment that stays open late. Open seven days a week for lunch and dinner, Molly Malone's is also a place to stop in for hearty pub fare and a drink or two. Old World pub style defines Molly's interior, but there's a huge outdoor deck and patio that are always hopping and good places to meet the locals. Molly's seems to be busy all the time, serving up everything from live Irish music to bangers and mash and smoked salmon. In addition, there are televised international rugby and soccer matches.

**MONKEY WRENCH**
1025 Barret Ave.
(502) 582-2433
www.myspace.com/monkeywrench1

Great food, a cool neighborhood, and a stylish industrial vibe all contribute to the ultra-hip atmosphere at the Monkey Wrench, located just a couple blocks off of Bardstown Road at the busy corner of Winter and Barret. The works of local artists adorn the walls, and striking lamps fashioned by Louisville-area glassblowers hang from the ceilings. When the room goes dim at night, the lights twinkle through the dark and transform the spartan space into a cozy den. It's an ideal spot to bring a date, hang out with a group of friends, or just come on your own. The crowd, usually on the younger side, is an eclectic mix of locals, as witnessed by the Derby City Roller Girls, who often show up after their Saturday-evening bouts for a drink. There's often live entertainment, and on Tuesday night it's two-for-one cheeseburgers.

**PHOENIX HILL TAVERN**
**644 Baxter Ave.**
**(502) 589-4957**
**www.phoenixhill.com**
Louisville is known for its music scene, and the Phoenix Hill Tavern showcases many of the country's best up-and-coming acts before they hit the big time. Around since 1976, the Phoenix Hill Tavern is a Louisville institution that has won 18 "Best of Louisville" Awards from *Louisville Magazine*. Locally owned and operated, it has also earned a reputation for staying on the cutting edge and keeping live music alive in the Derby City. Housed in a two-story building at the corner of Broadway and Baxter in the Highlands, this nightclub—reportedly the oldest in town—offers a variety of entertainment choices. There are five different bars, each offering a different type of music or entertainment, and Americana and memorabilia from the club's decades-long run cover the walls on the inside. Three of the stages have live music on weekends, and in addition to karaoke in the all-new "living room," there's an outdoor dance party on their rooftop deck bar. The crowd tends to be a diverse mix, but one thing they all have in common is their desire to have a good time and friendliness. Needless to say, this is a good place to meet the natives.

**SHENANIGAN'S PUB**
**4519 Bardstown Rd.**
**(502) 491-9148**
A friendly little neighborhood bar that's popular with students from nearby Bellarmine University, this pub also attracts local families and Highlands hipsters for its good bar food. The chili, spiked with Woodford Reserve bourbon, is popular, and so are the Bellarmine burger and the grilled cheese sandwiches with freshly made Irish potato chips. There's a divide between the bar and the dining area, so during the day it's also a regular destination for lunch and dinner guests. Like all bars in Louisville, there's no smoking; however, an inviting outside area provides the opportunity to light up.

For information on opportunities for salsa dancing in the region, check out the Web site for the Louisville SALSA/MAMBO Meetup Group at www.meetup.com/salsa-239.

## ST. MATTHEWS / EAST END

**CLUB OASIS**
**1506 Lakeshore Court**
**(502) 412-2275**
**www.cluboasisky.com**
Popular with the Latino crowd, Club Oasis is the place in town where people come for regular themed parties and the chance to dance hip-hop, salsa, merengue, bachata, reggaeton, and more. Well-known regional DJs work their magic, and national acts such as Pitbull pop in to entertain the lively crowds.

If you've got a craving for late-night pizza, try Saints Pizza (502-891-8883) in St. Matthews at 131 Breckenridge Lane. The kitchen is open until 2 a.m. Sunday through Thursday, and on Friday and Saturday, they serve until 3 a.m.

**DUTCH'S TAVERN**
**3922 Shelbyville Rd.**
**(502) 895-9004**

# Close-up

## For the Hungry Night Owls

If you're looking for a bite to eat after the bars have closed down, it's not that difficult to find a 24-hour place in Louisville. For example, the **Steak and Shake** restaurants at 10721 Fischer Park Drive, 2717 South Hurstbourne Parkway, 4545 Outer Loop, 4913 Dixie Highway, and 3232 Bardstown Road are open anytime, and so are the **Waffle Houses** at 4320 Bishop Lane, 4029 Taylorsville Road, 4706 Preston Street, 3347 Fern Valley Road, and 505 Indiana Avenue in Jeffersonville. But, if you want to find a late-night hangout that could make your visit to the Derby City a more memorable one, try one of these local favorites:

**Cafe 360** (1582 Bardstown Rd.; 502-473-8694; www.cafe-360.com). "Where international culture meets urban style" is the mantra of this 24-hour cafe and hookah lounge in the middle of all the action on Bardstown Road. American food, touched up with a dash of eclectic Indian flavor, is on the menu, and colorful works by local artists adorn the walls. With the exotic-looking hookahs scattered throughout the restaurant, free Internet access, and diverse music choices, this is a popular place to come and wind down after a night on the town. The bill of fare includes an impressive selection of more than a dozen sandwiches—all fresh and made to order—in addition to appetizers, soups, salads, sides, and entrees such as lamb *biryani* and southern fried catfish. There's also a huge selection of egg dishes and breakfast specialties.

**Denny's** (434 Eastern Pkwy.; 502-636-2538; www.dennys.com). The Denny's 24-hour restaurant on Eastern Parkway is without a doubt the most colorful of all the Louisville-area franchises in the chain. Especially the later it gets. With the main campus of the University of Louisville just on the other side of the viaduct, there's a constant student presence day and night, in addition to the regulars from the neighborhoods along shaded Eastern Parkway. And when city bars close in the wee hours of the morning, this seems to be a magnet for hungry, boisterous crowds that aren't quite ready to hit the hay.

**Juanita's Burger Boy** (1450 South Brook St.; 502-635-7410; www.juanitasdiner.com). Despite its name, Juanita's Burger Boy, serves more than just burgers. There are hearty breakfasts with eggs, country-fried steak, and biscuits with gravy, in addition to pancakes, T-bone steaks, rib-eye sandwiches, grilled cheese, pork chops, fried fish, patty melts, and lots of different sides. And all at extremely affordable prices. Although they do serve breakfast, lunch, and dinner to a very diverse clientele, the real Burger Boy doesn't really get started until the early hours

Dutch's Tavern is one of the oldest venues for live music in the city. Going strong since 1929, Dutch's is the quintessential neighborhood bar where everyone will get to know your name if you come around often enough. Located one block east from St. Matthews Station at the corner of Breckenridge and Shelbyville, the tavern features live entertainment every night of the week. Dutch's is also the place for fans of the Green Bay Packers. Every Sunday during the football season, the Packers can be seen playing on the big screen.

**JOE'S OLDER THAN DIRT**
**8131 New La Grange Rd.**
**(502) 426-2074**

When you spy the beat-up old moose who's lost his horns out in front, you'll know you've found Joe's Older than Dirt. Serving up good times and good food since 1937, this Louisville classic is the self-proclaimed location for serious beer drinkers because there are some 50 beers on tap. And beer's the perfect accompaniment to one of their most famous menu items, the fried bologna sandwich. By the way, for anyone who drinks all 50 beers (not in one visit, mind you), there's a T-shirt to commemorate the occasion. Joe's also

of the morning, when the more-colorful characters start to emerge. With its location near the University of Louisville's campus, Juanita's has become a hotspot for students looking for a late-night snack; in addition, it is also located near two neighborhood bars, which ensures a steady stream of interesting characters during the wee hours.

**The Tavern** (1532 South Fourth St.; 502-637-4200). The window signs on the unassuming white brick building at the corner of Fourth and Gaulbert in Old Louisville tell you everything you need to know, their red neon letters in tiny horizontal slits cheerily flaunting the three main virtues of the Tavern: BEER. WHISKY. FOOD. Another sign over the door of the friendly neighborhood bar touts their famous "Knocker Burger" and the plate lunches they've been serving "since 1933." It also says they're "open 22 hours a day," so you know there's always a late-night crowd there. It's up to you to find out which two hours they close.

**Twig and Leaf Restaurant** (2122 Bardstown Rd.; 502-451-8944). A Bardstown Road landmark since the 1940s, this small diner is often crowded on the weekends, so if you don't feel like waiting for a table, belly up to the counter and take a look at the menu. Served anytime, breakfast is very popular, and favorites include French toast dusted with powdered sugar and a Denver scramble with green pepper, onion, and ham. At lunch, two signature items are especially popular: Montezuma's Revenge consists of mounds of steaming pasta smothered with hot chili, shredded cheese, diced onion, tomato, and sour cream, and the Womb to the Tomb has a pair of open-faced chili cheeseburgers topped with shredded lettuce, tomato, and onion. Diners in search of something a bit more mainstay, say fried chicken or country-fried steak, or roast beef Manhattans or club sandwiches, will be happy to find a large selection of entree and sandwich items, in addition to the variety of dessert choices. Open 24 hours on the weekends.

**White Castle** (105 East Market St.; 502-584-1529). A late-night crowd orders miniature burgers known as sliders by the sackful at this castle-shaped regional chain restaurant that is open 24/7. The menu is short and sweet with non-burger options like fried chicken or fish sandwiches and sides of fries, onion rings, and cheese sticks; however, the hamburgers, cheeseburgers, and double cheeseburgers are what made them famous decades ago. All-beef patties are steam-grilled on a pile of onions and then served on square white buns with pickles. Extras like bacon and jalapeño cheese are also available. The East Market location is popular with the after-hours throngs leaving downtown bars and nightclubs after closing time at 4 a.m.

has all-season outdoor seating with a very family-friendly atmosphere. With its rough-hewn wood and rustic feel, it almost reminds you of being in a lodge in northern Michigan or Wisconsin. In addition to live music on Wednesdays, there's karaoke on Tuesdays. For a friendly smile, ask for Big Bertha as your server.

> **i** Looking for breakfast after that late night out on the town? Two local restaurants that specialize in breakfast and brunch are Toast on Market and Wild Eggs. Read about them on pages 106–107 in the Restaurants chapter.

## GAY BARS

Depending on where you come from and what your expectations are, you'll either be impressed or underwhelmed by the gay scene in Louisville. There are a number of alternative bars in town—including the Connection, one of the largest in the region—however, people here tend to go out mostly on Saturday nights, so the crowds during the rest of the week are sometimes disappointing. That having been said, there is vibrant gay nightlife in the Derby City, and the locals are generally very friendly and accommodating when it comes to out-of-towners. If you plan on going out for a serious night of dancing and revelry, most don't hit the bars and clubs before 11 p.m.

## THE CONNECTION
**120 South Floyd St.**
**(502) 585-5752**
**www.theconnection.net**

One of the largest gay bars in the region, the Connection often surprises first-timers with its size. In addition to several bars (a video bar known as DOC, Boots for the leather crowd, and Privates, a shower bar), the sprawling complex also houses a large dance floor and an impressive drag show in a large theater. It doesn't cost anything to stay in the front of the complex, but cover is around $5 to get back to the main dance floor and the theater, which has three shows a night on the weekends. In true Louisville fashion, the Connection is open late (till 4 a.m.), and the last drag show starts at 2:30 a.m. If the dance floor looks empty when you get there, go on back to the theater, because that may be where everyone is. When the first show is over, the dance floor usually fills up and stays that way for the rest of the night. During the week, the crowd size can be hit or miss, but Friday nights are usually busy, and it's rare not to find the place packed on Saturday nights. That's when you'll find lots of people—straight couples next to towering drag queens, for example—out on the dance floor for what many consider the best club music in town.

## THE PINK DOOR
**2222 Dundee Rd.**
**(502) 413-5204**
**www.pinkdoorlouisville.com**

Thursday is gay night at the Pink Door, a popular Deer Park noodle house on Douglas Loop. Late into the night, a friendly, high-energy crowd dances along to DJs playing requests; at 10 p.m. there are drink specials like $4.50 martinis, hot sake for $2.50, and Coors Light on draft for $1.50.

## STARBASE Q
**921 West Main St.**
**www.starbaseq.com**

Open Tuesday through Saturday from 8 p.m. to 4 a.m., this "industrial video bar, lounge, and club" is an innovative nightclub for gays and lesbians with DJs, dancing, and karaoke. The Galaxy Girls perform on Saturdays, and the first Friday of every month is the Camptown Cabaret. Gay-owned and -operated, Starbase Q recently expanded to over 40,000 square feet of space on multiple levels. A popular happy hour takes place Tuesday through Friday from 4 p.m. to 9 p.m. Closed on Monday.

## TEDDY BEAR'S BAR AND GRILLE
**1148 Garvin Place**
**(502) 589-2619**

Teddy Bear's calls itself a bar and grille, but you won't find any food there other than snacks from the vending machine. A tiny bar—an old-fashioned hole in the wall, some would call it—on an Old Louisville side street, Teddy Bear's generally attracts a crowd of older gay men; however, all ages and orientations tend to pop in. The staff is friendly and the clientele unpretentious. Popular draws are Beer Bust Sunday and all-night happy hour on Wednesday. Open daily from 11 a.m. to 4 a.m., Teddy Bear's has karaoke until 3 a.m. on Thursday. No cover charge.

## TINK'S PUB
**2235 South Preston St.**
**(502) 634-8180**
**www.tinkspub.talkspot.com**

One of the oldest clubs in the city, Tink's knows how to treat a lady, because every night is ladies night. In addition to nightly specials, visitors to this friendly neighborhood bar will find video poker, darts, pool, and karaoke. Although the crowd is mostly lesbian, everyone is welcome. Open till 4 a.m. seven days a week, Tink's has a daily happy hour until 9 p.m., and an all-day happy hour on Tuesday. No cover charge.

## Gay Theater in Louisville

### Pandora Productions
604 South Third St.
www.pandoraprods.org

Pandora Productions has a repertoire that includes bold and rarely seen theatrical works of special interest to those in the gay, lesbian, bisexual, and transgender community. Shows from past seasons include *The Kathy and Mo Show, As Bees in Honey Drown, Most Fabulous Story Every Told, Kiss of the Spider Woman, Looking for Normal, Rocky Horror Picture Show, The Laramie Project,* and *Southern Baptist Sissies.* All of the productions are staged at the Bunbury Theatre in the historic Henry Clay building on the corner of Third and Chestnut. Advance tickets for single shows generally cost $15.

### TRYANGLES
**209 South Preston St.**
**(502) 583-6395**

This casual flannel-and-jeans bar caters mainly to gay men over 30, though you'll find younger patrons as well. On one side there are tables and a square bar with stools and a pool-table area. The other side is darker and has a second bar with a small dance floor and stage setup where male strippers perform on Friday and Saturday nights. Conveniently located near the bridges downtown, Tryangle's has its own parking lot in addition to plentiful on-street parking. It is a block's walk to the Connection, so many guys out for a night on the town like to start with a drink at Tryangles and then head over to the Connection. Or else they take a break from the Connection and head over to Tryangles in the middle of the evening. No cover charge.

ℹ️ Louisville is generally a very gay-friendly city, and it is not uncommon to see gay couples out at popular straight bars or having dinner with friends at local restaurants. Although you'll find gay and lesbian individuals and families throughout the city, you'll discover a higher concentration of them downtown, in Old Louiville and in the Highlands, where it's not unusual to see same-sex couples holding hands while they walk. It's probably not a good idea, however, to walk and hold your same-sex partner's hand in other parts of town.

## MOVIE THEATERS

Catching a movie is a great way to escape the heat of Louisville's sultry summer evenings, or it can be a perfect way to cozy up with a date during a chilly winter's eve.

With more than a dozen movie theaters in town, it's not hard to find a good cinema with the kind of film you're looking for. Most movie houses show first-run flicks, and the average price for an evening show is $8.50 for adults; matinees are normally $6.50. For a comprehensive listing of Louisville movie theaters, show times, and current reviews, check out the Web site at http://louisville.mrmovietimes.com.

ℹ️ D. W. Griffith, the son of Jacob Griffith, a former Confederate colonel, was born near Louisville in 1875. He would become a pioneer in the motion-picture industry, and is credited with developing many of the basic techniques of modern filmmaking. His films included *The Birth of a Nation* (1915), *Intolerance* (1916), *Broken Blossoms* (1919), *Way Down East* (1920), *Orphans of the Storm* (1921), and *The Struggle* (1931).

### BAXTER AVENUE FILMWORKS
**1250 Bardstown Rd.**
**(502) 459-2288**
**www.village8.com**

Located in the heart of the Highlands neighborhood, on the back side of the Mid-City Mall,

Baxter Avenue Filmworks is far from the typical multiplex. This is the place to come for first-run, foreign, and independent films shown in eight wall-to-wall-screen auditoriums featuring state-of-the-art projection equipment and Dolby Digital surround sound. One of Baxter's biggest draws is its sleek design. Among the aesthetic touches you'll find hand-painted murals by local artists on the concourse walls, and in each theater; a mural celebrates one of the directors that has made a valuable contribution to film. In addition to a multimedia video wall above the concession stand, there are also lighted moving sculptures and vintage posters.

### CINEMA DE LUX 20 STONYBROOK
### 2745 South Hurstbourne Pkwy.
### (502) 499-6656
### www.nationalamusements.com

This East End multiplex has some of the largest screens in town, and it's very popular with teenagers who like to hang around. In addition, most say the sound system is first-rate, and that the comfortable stadium seating makes moviegoing an enjoyable experience. There's also a variety of concessions, from standard movie fare like popcorn and candy to chicken wings and pizzas. They even do a special VIP service for those wanting a bit of extra attention.

### CINEMARK TINSEL TOWN USA
### 4400 Towne Center Dr.
### (502) 326-0088
### www.cinemark.com

Super-clean restrooms, easy parking, and comfortable chairs with movable armrests and reclining seat backs make this one of the most popular cinemas in town. In fact, Cinemark boasts that there's not a bad seat in the house; this is largely due to stadium-design seating, which means that even when a tall person sits in front of someone shorter, everyone can see the movie. Among other pluses, viewers with special needs will find designated auditoriums with improved wheelchair accessibility.

**i** Located between Audobon Park and Shively, Louisville's last drive-in theater, the Kenwood Drive-In, closed on January 2, 2009, after 59 years of outdoor movies.

### VILLAGE 8
### 4014 Dutchmans Lane
### (502) 897-1870
### www.village8.com

Located in Dupont Village, this St. Matthews landmark continues to be Louisville's only discount movie house. Operating at full schedule seven days a week, every single day of the year, the Village 8 theaters range in seating capacity from 77 to 189, and can accommodate special shows for large groups. Village 8 also hosts a number of regular events such as the Jewish Film Festival, the Asian Film Series, and the International 48 Hour Film Festival. Village 8 also hosts "Louisville Exclusive Films," a project that brings a new first-run independent, foreign, or art-house movie to Louisville every Friday. Admission for adult matinees is only $3; evening shows are normally $4 for adults.

**i** The International 48 Hour Film Festival got its start in May 2001, when D.C. filmmaker Mark Ruppert had a crazy idea: to produce a film in 48 hours. Enlisting the help of filmmaking partner Liz Langston and several others, Ruppert set out to discover "if films made in only 48 hours would even be watchable." The answer was a resounding yes, and since then more than 150 competitions have taken place around the world, including the one in Louisville, which has blossomed under the oversight of Sheila Berman. For more information, go online at www.48hourfilm.com/louisville.

# PARKS AND RECREATION

O ne thing visitors to the Derby City—at least those who've had some time to get out and explore a bit—always comment on is the wealth of green space and parks available to its residents. As far as the number and quality of its parks is concerned, Louisville is a city that can compete with any other in the nation. In addition to large urban parks with hiking paths and beautiful landscaping, there are also landscaped parkways designed to connect different parts of the city. Wherever you go in Louisville, it seems that a park is close by. One of the reasons for this is a city government that values the parks and recreation programs offered to its citizens. And in Louisville they know how to do it right: Make the rounds of the parks here and you'll discover breathtaking scenic vistas, historic homes, nature centers, sports leagues, swimming pools, golf courses, community centers, campgrounds, conference centers, and more. Louisville parks have something for every taste, so get off the beaten path and lose yourself in one of the city's green spaces; you'll experience a side of the city that's normally reserved for the locals.

## CITY OF PARKS

On February 22, 2005, Mayor Jerry Abramson announced a multimillion-dollar, multiyear initiative with Metro Parks to add thousands of acres of land and protected green space to Louisville Metro's greenprint. Building upon the groundwork laid over a century ago by famed landscape architect Frederick Law Olmsted, this effort will complete Louisville's makeover into a City of Parks. This means the Derby City will become a community with one of the nation's largest parks expansions under way, one that will add 4,000 new acres of parkland with the 100-mile Louisville Loop trail encircling the entire metro area. This initiative's goal is the completion of more than 100 miles of paved trails connecting the city's diverse parks and neighborhoods.

### Olmsted Parks

Louisville is proud to have one of only four city park systems designed by Frederick Law Olmsted, the renowned "Father of American Landscape Architecture." With 18 parks and 6 parkways, Olmsted's Louisville park system counts as one of the genius's best-preserved works. For Louisvillians, these parks have become part of the local iden-

tity. The Louisville Olmsted Parks Conservancy has been charged with restoring, enhancing, and preserving these historic parks and parkways to enrich the life of everyone in the community. Learn more about Louisville's Olmsted-designed parks at the Conservancy Web site, where an informative video explains the vision behind the man's work (www.olmstedparks.org). If you want to experience Olmsted at his best, visit one of Louisville's flagship parks described below. Other Louisville parks designed by Frederick Law Olmsted are Algonquin Park, Baxter Square, Bingham Park, Boone Square, Central Park, Chickasaw Park, Churchill Park, Elliott Square, Seneca Park, Shelby Park, William B. Stansbury Park, Tyler Park, Victory Park, Wayside Park, and Willow Park. To find out more, visit the Web site for city parks at www .louisvilleky.gov/MetroParks.

### CHEROKEE PARK

Arguably the most beautiful of Louisville's city parks, this is one of the area's first spaces designed by Frederick Law Olmsted. Visitors to Cherokee Park enjoy a pastoral setting amid rolling hills and the open meadows and woodlands surrounding Beargrass Creek. The main feature of Cherokee Park is the 2.4-mile Scenic Loop, which has separate lanes for vehicle traffic (one-way) and recreational users such as bikers, in-line skaters, joggers, and walkers. A tip for vehicles on the Scenic Loop: The secret to navigating the park is to remember to always turn left to stay in the park, or turn right to exit the park.

---

## Enid Yandell, Sculptor

If you stroll (or drive) the entire loop in Cherokee Park, you'll pass the whimsical Hogan's Fountain. The main feature of this Highlands park, the fountain boasts a sculpture of the Greek god Pan, flanked by several turtles spouting water into the basin below. It is the work of Enid Yandell, a Louisvillian who became the first woman to join the National Sculpture Society. Born on October 6, 1870, Yandell was the daughter of Dr. Lunsford Pitts Yandell Jr. and Louise Elliston Yandell. She eventually studied with greats such as Auguste Rodin and Frederick William MacMonnies. A prolific sculptor, Yandell created numerous portraits and garden pieces along with small works and public monuments. At the Speed Art Museum in Old Louisville, the sculpture collection includes a nice selection of her works in plaster. If you enter Cherokee Park via Eastern Parkway, you'll see another of her works: a nine-foot statue of Daniel Boone commissioned by the Filson Club of Louisville. Yandell died on June 13, 1934, and is buried in Cave Hill Cemetery.

---

### IROQUOIS PARK

Planned by Olmsted as a scenic reservation of breathtaking vistas and forested hillsides, Iroquois Park is the pride of Louisville's South End.

Aside from the many hiking trails and bike paths, the park features a 1930s WPA amphitheater that hosts regular concerts and summer musical theater. Wonderful views of Louisville and the environs are visible from a lookout at the top of the hill, and pedestrians and bikers can use the road to get there daily; it's only open to motorists from 10 a.m. to 8 p.m. on Wednesday, Saturday, and Sunday from April through October.

### SHAWNEE PARK

Olmsted designed Shawnee Park, the jewel of the West End, as the greatest public space of the city. He envisioned its grand expanses as the place for parades, picnics, sports, concerts, and large public gatherings. At 230 Southwestern Parkway you'll find a state-of-the-art outdoor athletic complex, and the park also boasts access to the RiverWalk. With nearly 300 acres of land, this is also home to one of the city's public golf greens, the Shawnee Golf Course, which includes the three-hole BellSouth Youth Golf Academy.

## Louisville Metro Parks

As spectacular as they are, Olmsted-designed parks only comprise a fraction of the green spaces that make up the Louisville Metro Parks system. In all, there are 124 of them, each with its own distinct feel and diverse recreation programs. Find more details at www.louisvilleky.gov/MetroParks/parks.

## Other Parks

### E. P. TOM SAWYER PARK

Louisville is fortunate to have one of 52 Kentucky State Parks in its city limits. E. P. "Tom" Sawyer State Park was named in honor of Erbon Powers "Tom" Sawyer, a World War II veteran, University of Louisville Law School graduate, and Jefferson County judge, who died in a tragic automobile accident in 1969. He is survived by his wife and two daughters, Linda and Diane, who is the anchor of ABC's *World News*. Once a farm developed by the former Central State Hospital, the land this park occupies still has remnants of its early days, including barns and cemeteries. Gov-

# Close-up

## A Memorial to Lincoln

At Louisville's Waterfront Park, you'll find the Lincoln Memorial, dedicated on June 4, 2009. The memorial was funded by the State of Kentucky, the family of Harry S. Frazier Jr., and the Kentucky Historical Society/Kentucky Abraham Lincoln Bicentennial Commission as part of the two-year national celebration of the bicentennial of our 16th president's birth. The opening was celebrated with a sunset dedication featuring a program of readings and orchestral music that culminated with a dramatic performance of Aaron Copland's "Lincoln Portrait." Louisville native and actor William Mapother (and cousin of Tom Cruise) narrated.

This memorial, just east of the Big Four Bridge, was designed to tell the story of how Lincoln began developing his abhorrence of slavery as a young man while watching slaves being loaded onto riverboats on the Ohio River in Louisville. The focal point of the site is a 12-foot statue of Lincoln seated on a rock and gazing out over the river. A series of bas-reliefs depicts four scenes that represent Lincoln's lifelong ties to Kentucky. Nationally renowned Louisville artist Ed Hamilton created both the Lincoln statue and the bas-reliefs, which are sculptures made by chipping stone away from a flat surface to produce a picture. Hamilton has also sculpted the Washington, D.C., memorial honoring African-American troops of the Civil War known as the *Spirit of Freedom*.

World-renowned landscape architects from Hargreaves Associates designed the memorial site, and the tree-canopied landscape has an amphitheater facing the river that provides a frame for the sculptural pieces. Famous Lincoln quotes adorn the face of the granite amphitheater, and the parklike setting is planted with a variety of trees, several of which were Lincoln favorites. Hargreaves created not only Waterfront Park, but also the public spaces for the Sydney Olympics in 2000 and the future site of the 2012 London Olympics.

Open year-round during park hours from 6 a.m. through 11 p.m. daily, the Lincoln Memorial is free to the public. Parking is available off of River Road in the Lincoln Memorial parking lot, and the Silver and Purple parking lots in the park. Enter from the Promenade along the river's edge. Go to www.louisvillewaterfront.com/projects/lincoln for more information.

ernor Louie B. Nunn dedicated the park in the fall of 1971, and since then the population in eastern Jefferson County has boomed, resulting in thousands of people who come to enjoy the beauty of nature every day. Find out more at http://parks.ky.gov/findparks/recparks/ep.

### WATERFRONT PARK

Administered by the Waterfront Development Corporation, Louisville's Waterfront Park is a showcase for the downtown area, the emerald heart, as some call it. Waterfront Park is the front door to Kentucky for those crossing the bridges from Indiana, but it's also a playground for folks of all ages, and a gathering place for individuals from all over the community. In addition to grand views of the river, this park offers space for concerts and festivals, picnic areas, quiet places to read, and lots of walkways for strolling. The park also hosts a crowd of 350,000 every year for Thunder Over Louisville. Get more information online at www.louisvillewaterfront.com/park.

### GOLF

The golf craze has swept over Louisville as it has in most parts of the country. It seems you can't drive more than a few miles without another golf course popping up. Louisville golf has really been on the upswing since this is home to the Valhalla Golf Club, the PGA-owned course where the United States dramatically retook the Ryder Cup from the European team in 2008. For a comprehensive list of golf clubs in Louisville, check out www.golflink.com. Some of the more well-known courses are listed below.

In addition, Louisville has nine public golf courses, each of which offers a quality golfing experience at some of the most affordable prices in the nation. Consistently ranking among the best and most challenging courses in the state, the courses have their own unique character. To find out more, go online at www.louisvilleky.gov/MetroParks/golf.

**CHEROKEE GOLF COURSE**
**2501 Alexander Rd.**
**(502) 458-9450**

**LAKE FOREST COUNTRY CLUB**
**14700 Landmark Dr.**
**(502) 245-6184**

**SENECA GOLF COURSE**
**2300 Pee Wee Reese Rd.**
**(502) 458-9298**

**VALHALLA GOLF CLUB**
**15503 Shelbyville Rd.**
**(502) 245-4475**

**WOODED VIEW GOLF COURSE**
**2404 Greentree North**
**Clarksville, IN**
**(812) 283-9274**

i Famous golf personalities from the Louisville area include Bobby Nichols, Ted Schulz, and New Albany's Fuzzy Zoeller. Find out more about Zoeller's Covered Bridge Golf Course at http://www.fuz.com.

# SPECTATOR SPORTS

Say *Louisville* (remember not to pronounce the "s"), and the first thing that comes to mind is the Kentucky Derby. Actually, you can drop the "Kentucky" because there is only one Derby as far as the country is concerned. As Earth revolves on its axis, so Louisville revolves around its annual

Run for the Roses. It defines the city not only in a sports capacity, but also in its traditions and culture. The social calendar starts and ends with the Derby. The city can compete with any in the country for its sports legacy. It is home to Muhammad Ali and the Louisville Slugger, and its athletic creds grow when you consider that stars like Darrell Griffith, Harold "Pee Wee" Reese, Paul Hornung, Wes Unseld, and Phil Simms all grew up in the Louisville area. It also has one of the most vibrant college sports scenes in the nation, in addition to championship golf and more.

## Auto Racing

For car racing enthusiasts in the Derby City, the nearest race track is the Kentucky Speedway, which sits halfway between Cincinnati and Louisville on 816 acres of land near Sparta. The 1.5 mile track was designed to host a NASCAR Sprint Cup Series race and has hosted NASCAR Nationwide Series and Camping World Truck Series races, as well as IRL IndyCar Series and Indy Lights races. There are 66,089 grandstand seats and 50 luxury suites, with season packages starting at $139 per person. Find out more by going online (www.kentuckyspeedway.com) or writing the Kentucky Speedway at 400 Buttermilk Pike, Suite 100, Ft. Mitchell, KY 41017.

## College Sports

Louisville is as crazy as any town when it comes to college sports. Or maybe it's a little worse. It occupies a significant portion of what is covered in the local media, and if you tell someone you could care less how the local team is doing, they're apt to give you a strange look. They might even turn hostile. College sports are part of life in Louisville, Kentucky, and there's no way around it.

Mention sports here, and college basketball comes to mind; quickly followed by college football. The obsession for these two sports and the local teams that represent them is only intensified by the fact that the city doesn't have a major league team to divert the pent-up energy inherent in spectator sports. Even if negotiations finally land Louisville their own major league team, it's still unlikely that the Derby City would ever lose its fervor for college sports.

Often the analogy is drawn between this area and the Durham-Raleigh-Chapel Hill rivalry in North Carolina when it comes to the intensity of interest in the road to the NCAA's Final Four. In Kentuckiana, which basketball team you root for—the University of Louisville, Indiana University, or the University of Kentucky—is a comment on your character (or lack thereof) to many folks, and it's a topic of conversation throughout the entire year. Nonetheless, the hometown favorite remains U of L, although there seem to be almost as many UK supporters nowadays. The IU fans are generally less visible, but there are still quite a number of them as well. And although basketball is usually the most talked-about college sport, the loyalty shown to one particular school seems to extend to all of its teams.

## The Baron of the Bluegrass

Under Coach Adolph Rupp, the University of Kentucky men's basketball team reigned supreme in the 1940s and '50s. In addition to winning four national championships, they also ranked at the top of most polls, and counted as one of the most respected teams of the era. When Rupp, "the Baron of the Bluegrass," retired in 1972, he was known as the winningest coach in college history, a distinction that still stands today.

### UNIVERSITY OF KENTUCKY
**Rupp Arena**
**430 West Vine St., Lexington**
**(859) 233-4567**
**www.rupparena.com**
This is a holy shrine to many in the Bluegrass State. Best known as the home court of the University

of Kentucky Men's Basketball team, Rupp Arena annually hosts over 350,000 fans who come to watch the greatest game in sports. It is situated in downtown Lexington and within five hours of major cities such as Chicago, St. Louis, Nashville, and Atlanta; it takes about an hour and a half to drive there from Louisville. In addition to the men's team, the University of Kentucky Women's Basketball team, the UK Hoops, plays many of their games there as well, and every season sees a larger audience. But basketball isn't the only sport played there; the Horsemen of Arena Football 2 have called Rupp Arena home since 2004, the year they won the National Championship. For box office information, call (859) 233-3535, or e-mail them at boxoffice@rupparena.com.

### UNIVERSITY OF LOUISVILLE
**2800 South Floyd St.**
**(502) 852-5151**
**www.uoflsports.com/tickets/lou-tickets.html**
University of Louisville basketball tradition is firmly rooted in the 1960s when the Cardinals were led by Louisville native Wesley Unseld and Breckinridge County's Butch Beard. (Unseld was the only player to be the NBA's rookie of the year and MVP in the same season.) Today, the Cards have garnered a faithful following at their Freedom Hall venue that makes them one of the most successful college teams in terms of percentage to capacity annually. Games are often sold out, and when the new waterfront arena is completed in 2010, it is expected that their crowds will be even larger.

Although most would say that basketball is the most-followed college sport in town, the Louisville Cardinals football team has a solid Derby City fan base as well, and its popularity seems to have risen to almost the same level. When they play in town, they play at the new Papa John's Cardinal Stadium out near Churchill Downs. The men's football team, which has produced players such as Johnny Unitas, Deion Branch, and Sam Madison, achieved national respect under Howard Schnellenberger in the 1990s, when they overwhelmingly defeated Alabama at the Fiesta Bowl. Their clout soared even further when the team joined the Eastern Conference and in 2007 won the FedEx Orange Bowl under Bobby Petrino. Although football and basketball seem to dominate the local fan base, there are many more sports at the University of Louisville, including men's and women's soccer, golf, tennis, and track and field, in addition to the popular baseball and softball teams. For information about all of the different teams, go to www .uoflsports.com.

## Louisville Team Stats

Derby City is home to the University of Louisville Cardinals who compete in the NCAA's Division I and belong to the Big East Conference. The U of L men's basketball team won the NCAA Division I basketball championship in 1980 and 1986 under head coach Denny Crum, and recently they reached the NCAA Final Four in 2005 with head coach Rick Pitino. Under Bobby Petrino, the U of L football team finished seventh in the nation for the season in 2006, 19th in the final Bowl Championship Series rankings of 2005, and tenth in 2004. The school won its first Bowl Championship Series game, the Orange Bowl, in January 2007, and Petrino left soon thereafter to become the head coach of the Atlanta Falcons. Less than two days later, Steve Kragthorpe was hired to replace Petrino. The U of L baseball team advanced to the 2007 College World Series in Omaha, where eight teams competed for the national championship. U of L is one of only two schools in the last five years to participate in a BCD bowl, the Final Four, and the College World Series in Omaha.

## Horse Racing

Before there was the Louisville Slugger, before college basketball, football, and baseball, before car races, there was horse racing. And in Louisville, horse racing is synonymous with Churchill Downs. But that's not where it all began.

In Kentucky, horse racing has a rich history that dates back to 1789, when the first race course was laid out in Lexington. Racing in Louisville, however, dates back to 1783, when local sources reported that races were held in the downtown area on Market Street. To alleviate the problems associated with running horses on a busy city thoroughfare, officials developed a course known as the Elm Tree Gardens, located at the now-abandoned Shippingport Island in 1805. Some twenty years later, a new track, the Hope Distillery Course, was laid out at the site of Main and 16th Streets. A number of private tracks located on farms throughout the area also hosted races, and one of the more prominent was Peter Funk's Beargrass Track, located in an area now bordered by Hurstbourne Lane and Taylorsville Road.

In 1833, the Oakland Race Course, complete with clubhouse, opened near today's Seventh and Magnolia Streets in Old Louisville. This was followed by the opening of the Woodlawn Course just outside of today's St. Matthews in 1858. Although the site closed in 1870, its trophy, the Woodlawn Vase, has been used in the winner's presentation at the Preakness Stakes at Pimlico since 1917. To fill the void left by the closing of Oakland and Woodlawn, Churchill Downs, the most venerated of all American racetracks, officially opened in 1875. It was named for John and Henry Churchill, who leased 80 acres of land to their nephew, Colonel Meriwether Lewis Clark Jr., the president of the Louisville Jockey Club. In the same year it opened, Churchill Downs held the first Kentucky Derby and the first Kentucky Oaks.

So many years later, the original track has undergone many changes and expansions, but the annual Kentucky Derby and the Kentucky Oaks combined are still the number-one sporting event in the state.

A popular place for lunch and breakfast with the regulars at the track is Wagner's Pharmacy at 3113 South Fourth Street, at the corner of Fourth and Central, across from the infield gate to Churchill Downs. Open since 1922, Wagner's offers a true lunch-counter experience that you don't find often these days. Aside from traditional American breakfast items, they've got great homemade soups, burgers, and sandwiches. And even a grumpy waitress or two. The best part is you never know who will be eating there. You might find yourself next to a stable hand who doesn't speak English or a legendary horseman like D. Wayne Lukas or Bob Baffert. Even a Middle Eastern sheikh has been known to walk in with his entourage. Call (502) 375-3800 for more information.

**CHURCHILL DOWNS**
**700 Central Ave.**
**(502) 636-4400**
**www.churchilldowns.com**
The spring and fall meets allow spectators to enjoy "the sport of kings" during the city's most spectacular seasons, so plan early for your visit to America's most legendary racetrack. Contact Churchill Downs above for information. Organized tours of the facility, barns, and backside area are offered through the Kentucky Derby Museum. To schedule a tour, call (502) 637-1111. Casual tours—they're shorter in duration and do not begin until after Race 2—can be arranged for your party during a race day through a guest services representative. Stop by a guest services booth near admission gates 10 or 17 for more information.

Style tip: The old-fashioned dictum that forbade the wearing of white before Memorial Day never applied in Louisville. In Louisville, it's "Never wear white before Derby." Memorial Day is the last Monday in May; Derby is always the first Saturday.

## Minor League Baseball

The Louisville Bats, the AAA minor league baseball affiliate of the Cincinnati Reds, play their home games in Derby City at Louisville Slugger Field. They got their start when the St. Louis Cardinals switched their AAA team of the American Association, the Redbirds, from Springfield, Illinois, to Louisville in 1982, and they quickly gained a loyal following. To illustrate, they broke the minor league attendance record by drawing over 800,000 during their very first season. In 1983, the Redbirds became the first minor league team in history to draw over a million fans in a single season. After the American Association folded in 1998, the Redbirds eventually became affiliated with the Milwaukee Brewers and took on the name the Louisville RiverBats; in 2002, after they became affiliated with the Cincinnati Reds and moved to Slugger Field from Cardinal Stadium, the team dropped the word "River" and became known as simply the Louisville Bats. Go to the Bats Web site at www.batsbaseball.com to learn about their current schedule and ticket prices.

## Wrestling

Louisville is also the home of Ohio Valley Wrestling, a professional wrestling promotion that served as developmental territory for World Wrestling Entertainment from 2000 until 2008. Notable WWE performers trained in OVW include John Cena, Batista, Jillian Hall, Randy Orton, CM Punk, and Spirit Squad. Call (502) 473-0660 for more information or go online at www.ovwrestling.com.

# ANNUAL EVENTS

The Derby City celebrates its rich history and diverse culture throughout the year with many festivals, performances, and special events; whatever your interest, there always seems to be something going on in Louisville—and your visit wouldn't be complete unless you included at least one of its yearly festivals into your plans. Kick back and take it easy in the winter, or lose yourself in a flurry of spring-time activity. Find yourself in the beautiful scenery during the fall or have a ball experiencing Louisville's exciting nightlife during the summer. There are so many things you can do in this city, you'll have a hard time deciding how to fit it all in. To help you decide, go to www.gotolouisville.com for a complete and up-to-date listing of events. Remember that times, dates, and locations are subject to change, so call ahead or visit the Web sites listed to verify the details.

## KENTUCKY DERBY FESTIVAL

What the Run for the Roses is to horse racing, Louisville's Kentucky Derby Festival is to community celebrations. This, the most cherished of all the state's annual events, is one of the premier events of its kind in the world and has won the International Festivals & Events Association award for Best Overall Festival five times now. The most amazing part is that it's pulled off entirely by a force of volunteers. How a two-minute race could have evolved into a major two-week celebration baffles many people, but come to Louisville during the end of April or the beginning of May, and you'll see why. It's an explosion of spring where 1.5 million people gather to celebrate the vitality of their community while focusing on whimsy, fun, and tradition. It is *the* event that puts Louisville on the map every year, and it mixes excitement, international recognition, and a spirit that is unmatched anywhere. It's also the time of year that southern drawls tend to be at their strongest.

What many people don't know about the Kentucky Derby is that its most famous race, the Run for the Roses, is actually the culmination of the celebration and not the beginning. The Kentucky Derby Festival begins with Thunder Over Louisville, one of the nation's most impressive air shows and fireworks displays, two weeks

prior to the Run for the Roses, which is always the first Saturday in May. In between, you'll find a slate of special events, parties, charity galas, and community festivities meant to complement the spring meet at Churchill Downs. Below, you'll find a listing of some of the most popular events, but check out the Web site at www.kdf.org to get a complete listing of what's going on during Kentucky's most famous annual party. There are more than 70 events ranging from one of the country's largest mini marathons to an old-fashioned steamboat race. You can contact the Kentucky Derby Festival at:

**KENTUCKY DERBY FESTIVAL**
**1001 South Third St.**
**(502) 584-6383**

### CHOW WAGON AT WATERFRONT PARK

Derby Festival time means getting together for good food and great music down by the river, and in the Derby City, no reservations are needed for the ultimate dining and socializing event. The Derby Festival Waterfront Chow Wagon features the best in cold beverages, the hottest live music daily, and carnival-style cuisine during the week leading up to the big races. Aside from funnel cakes, ice cream, fried candy bars, fresh lemonade, corn dogs, and sausages, there's also pulled pork, roast chicken, brisket with Derby sauce, turkey legs, rib-eye sandwiches, Papa John's pizza, strawberry shortcake, slushes, frozen daiquiris, and margaritas. Ethnic favorites like gyros, kebabs, Italian meatball subs, fajitas, and jerk chicken are also available. For entertainment, more than 30 live concerts—with local and regional performers and a wide variety of musical genres, including urban, Latino, country, and rock—are showcased on the Miller Lite Music Stage. The Chow Wagon is open nightly till 11 p.m., but on Derby Eve it stays open till 1 a.m.

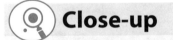 The Kentucky Derby Festival usually lasts for two weeks, but if Easter or Passover falls in between, the party is extended to three weeks.

### DERBY MARATHON AND MINI MARATHONS

These are the town's other big races, when months of training are put to the test. The mini has been run since the 1970s, and the full-length race completed its first decade of existence in 2009. Runners compete on the Saturday that falls between the Run for the Roses and the beginning of the Kentucky Derby Festival at Thunder Over Louisville. The races start simultaneously at 7:30 a.m. with runners in both races sharing the same start and finish lines. In 2009 the races attracted a record 12,000 registrants. A course map of both race routes and information about road closings and alternate driving routes to popular destinations can be found on the official race Web site at www.derbyfestivalmarathon.com.

### FILLIES DERBY BALL

One of the Derby Festival's oldest and most-anticipated events is the Fillies Derby Ball, which caps the opening day of the Derby Festival and is a prelude to two weeks of exciting activities. It normally takes place on the Friday before Thunder Over Louisville, and the highlight is the coronation of the Derby Festival Queen, selected by a traditional spin-of-the-wheel. The mayor attends with a cadre of the who's who of local businesses, and the Queen "knights" individuals to the Court of the Pegasus for their contributions to the community. The evening of pomp and circumstance begins at 6:30 p.m. with cocktails and is followed by dinner at 8:30 p.m. Individual tickets go for $150, and a corporate table of 10 runs $1,875. Call (502) 425-0406 or (502) 594-5971 for more information, or visit thefillies.org for more information.

## Close-up

### Cherokee Triangle Art Fair

Although it's not officially part of the Kentucky Derby Festival, the annual art fair held in the historic Cherokee Triangle neighborhood has become one of the most popular springtime events in Louisville. The fair, which started in the early 1970s as a neighborhood fund-raiser, attracts more than 200 juried artists to tree-lined Cherokee Parkway between Willow Avenue and Cherokee Road at the General John Breckinridge Castleman statue. Along with viewing and purchasing original arts and crafts, patrons also enjoy food, entertainment, and music. Family-friendly, the fair features a popular children's art activity tent, as well as a plant booth with a variety of herbs for sale, and the association booth with its offerings of clothing and other items with the Cherokee Triangle logo.

The Cherokee Triangle Art Fair is the major fund-raiser for Louisville's Cherokee Triangle Association, and its proceeds are returned to the local community in a variety of ways, including the funding of summer concerts, maintaining the landscaping, and making donations to various organizations and projects. Free and open to the public, the Cherokee Triangle Art Fair normally takes place on the weekend between Thunder Over Louisville and the Kentucky Derby. Visitors can attend from 10 a.m. to 6 p.m. Find out more at www.cherokeetriangle.org.

## GREAT BALLOONFEST

The weekend before the Kentucky Derby, U.S. Bank puts on five great balloon-related events that take place in the Kentucky Exposition Center and other locations throughout the city. Tens of thousands of spectators turn out as more than 50 hot-air balloons of all shapes, sizes, and colors congregate at dusk or float soundlessly above the city in various races. The "rush-hour" races early on Friday and Saturday morning provide a spectacular sight to passing interstate traffic as some 50 "hound" balloons take off from the Kentucky Exposition Center in chase of the "hare," who flies for about 30 minutes before crossing the Ohio River and landing in southern Indiana. The first competitors to drop their bag of Kentucky bluegrass seed within 200 feet of the target, a giant vinyl "X," take home the trophy. The Balloon Glow the night before the races provides enthusiasts the chance to chat up their favorite pilots as they fire up the burners on the stationary balloons and illuminate the night sky with radiant color. For details about all of the balloon events, check out the links on the Web site for the Kentucky Derby Festival at www.kdf.org.

## GREAT STEAMBOAT RACE

Since 1963 the *Belle of Louisville* has raced another historic steamboat on the Ohio on the Wednes-

---

### The Pegasus Pin

If you're in Louisville for the Kentucky Derby, make sure you get your Pegasus Pin, which you can pick up at local stores such as Walmart and Kroger. Pins cost $4 and get you free admission to most Derby events. Each year they unveil a pin with a new design that features that year's particular Derby Festival theme. Each pin envelope contains one of the pins in five different colors (red, orange, purple, green, and pink) and two coupons for products or discounted services. Some will contain a gold instant winner pin, which will make recipients eligible to win one of more than a dozen grand prizes, which will be awarded in May, following the conclusion of the festival. For details, check out the Web site for the Kentucky Derby Festival at www.kdf.org.

---

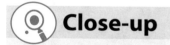 **Close-up**

## Dawn at the Downs

Are you an early riser? If so, check out Dawn at the Downs, a popular Derby tradition that gives visitors an opportunity to enjoy breakfast on Millionaires Row while watching contenders for the Kentucky Derby and Kentucky Oaks conduct their morning workouts.

While you sit back and feast Bluegrass-style, a host announces the horses on the track, discusses their past performances, and provides valuable insight into the big races. Morning workouts can also be followed on large television monitors, and the announcements are heard throughout the track.

This grand Kentucky breakfast buffet is served Monday through Thursday of Derby Week on Millionaires Row. Reservations are required and can be made by calling (502) 636-4400. Guests are also welcome to observe the morning workouts from the trackside rail as well; sections 116/117 of the first-floor clubhouse are available on a first-come, first-served basis, and a continental breakfast can be purchased at the Paddock Grill.

# Close-up

## The Mint Julep

A specially designed mint julep cup is presented to the Kentucky Derby winner each year. The mint julep, that most quintessential of southern drinks, has been the traditional beverage of Churchill Downs and the Kentucky Derby since the 1930s. Early juleps frequently contained wine or brandy, but people from the South prefer bourbon whiskey, still the ingredient of choice in the Bluegrass State. The mint julep arose from a taste for distilled spirits, and although the origin is unknown, one legend holds that a 19th-century Kentucky boatman on the Mississippi River who went ashore in search of springwater to mix with his bourbon added fresh mint growing on the banks as an afterthought.

To make your own mint julep, start with a jigger of good whiskey; traditionally, the whiskey used is straight aged Kentucky bourbon. The glass is also important. Often, the mint julep is served in a silver cup, about 4 inches tall and 3 inches in diameter, but in the absence of silver, a tall crystal glass is acceptable. The water must be ice cold and, if possible, from a limestone spring. The sugar should be super fine or powdered, and the ice is usually crushed but may be shaved. The only thing drinkers agree on is that the mint should be only the freshest available. Mull it with the sugar in the bottom of the glass, fill with ice and the bourbon, and then top off with water. Once the concoction is mixed, some prefer to sip it through a straw, while others drink it straight from the cup. Whatever you do, make sure to hold the cup by the rim with the thumb and forefinger so as not to disturb the frost on the silver.

## Mint Julep Glasses

Almost everyone who comes to Louisville for the Kentucky Derby leaves with a memento of the occasion. Souvenirs can range from toys to pins to artwork, but one of the oldest and most cherished Kentucky Derby collectibles is the official mint julep glass. Licensed by Churchill Downs, Inc., these glasses have been sold since the 1930s, and in their seven-decade history, they have varied in shape, size, color, and decoration. Some have been made of aluminum or bakelite, but most are glass, and there's a wide range in their values. Recent julep glasses might only cost a couple of dollars, but find one of the very first ones from 1939, and it'll most likely net you more than $5,000.

**i** Each year, almost 120,000 mint juleps are served over the two-day period of the Kentucky Oaks and Kentucky Derby. Required are more than 10,000 bottles of Early Times, 1,000 pounds of freshly harvested local mint and 60,000 pounds of ice.

day before the Run for the Roses. Because its most famous rival, the *Delta Queen*, is temporarily operating as a floating hotel at Chattanooga, the *Belle of Cincinnati* will replace the *Delta Queen* in future races as the opponent for the hometown favorite. In the past, the winner was determined by the first boat to cross the finish line at the Clark Memorial Bridge, but in upcoming competitions the victor will be the vessel that accumulates the most points from performing a series of tasks assigned throughout the race. One of the tasks will be a calliope contest between the two *Belles*; other tasks will be performed by the crews on board, as well as onshore. The race starts at 6 p.m. with departure at 5:45 p.m. The awards ceremony takes place immediately following the race at the Chow Wagon in Kroger's Fest-a-Ville on the Waterfront. Tickets for the *Belle of Louisville* cost $126; *Belle of Cincinnati* tickets cost $75. Both prices include dinner. For more information about this popular Derby event, visit the Web site for the *Belle of Louisville* at www.belleoflouisville .org.

 Every year the people at Woodford Reserve try to come up with an ultra-premium mint julep that only a millionaire could love. For $1,000 the first 50 people willing to put down the cash at the big race will get one of the state's finest (and most expensive) bourbons served in a 24-carat gold-plated cup with a silver straw. With ice from the Arctic Circle and cane sugar from the South Pacific, this mint julep is in a class all its own. To top it off, fresh mint is flown in from Morocco. The money raised goes to a charity for retired racehorses.

## PEGASUS PARADE

First held in 1956, the Pegasus Parade is the Derby Festival's oldest event. It began on a budget of $640 and now provides an impact in excess of $14 million to the Louisville economy. Even if the weather is cloudy and overcast, parade officials can expect to attract a crowd of at least 250,000 spectators along Broadway. With its colorful assortment of floats, inflatable character balloons, marching bands, equestrian units, and celebrity guests, it's not surprising that the parade—sponsored by Republic Bank—is consistently voted as one of Louisville's favorite events. The parade travels west on Broadway from Campbell to Ninth and starts at 5 p.m. on the Thursday before the Kentucky Derby. There is free viewing in most areas along the route; however, bleacher tickets can normally be purchased for $9, and chair seating goes for $11. Seating in the review stand costs $26.

## Close-up

## History of the Greatest Two Minutes in Sports

The **Kentucky Derby** is one of the oldest thoroughbred horse races in the country. From the time the Bluegrass State was settled in the 1700s, its fields were noted for producing superior horses, and racing became a popular pastime. In 1872, Colonel Meriwether Lewis Clark Jr., grandson of William Clark of the Lewis and Clark Expedition, visited the Epsom Derby on a trip to England. After that, he went on to Paris, where a group of racing enthusiasts had started the French Jockey Club and the Grand Prix de Paris, at the time the greatest race in France. After he returned home to Kentucky, Clark organized the Louisville Jockey Club and raised money for quality racing facilities in the area, including a track that became known as Churchill Downs. The racetrack was named for Clark's relatives and land donors, John and Henry Churchill.

The first race was run on May 17, 1875, in front of an estimated crowd of 10,000 people, with a field of 15 three-year-old horses. The winner was a colt named Aristides, under jockey Oliver Lewis, who would go on to ride the same horse to a second-place finish in the Belmont Stakes. The Kentucky Derby was first run at 1.5 miles (2.4 km), the same distance as the Epsom Derby and the Grand Prix de Paris, but in 1896, the distance was changed to its current 1.25 miles (2 km). Although the first meet proved successful, the track eventually fell upon financial difficulties, and in 1894 the New Louisville Jockey Club was incorporated to revive the undertaking. Nonetheless, the business floundered until 1902, when Louisville's Colonel Matt Winn convened a syndicate of local businessmen to acquire the facility. Under Winn, Churchill Downs prospered, and the Kentucky Derby has evolved into the preeminent thoroughbred race in the USA.

## RUN FOR THE ROSÉ

On the Tuesday before the famous Run for the Roses, hundreds of food service employees gather at the Kroger's Fest-a-Ville on the Waterfront for the annual Run for the Rosé. This event, sponsored by Kentucky Proud, sends waiters and waitresses out to run around an obstacle course in an effort to win bragging rights and great prizes—all while balancing a tray of six full wineglasses. It's lots of spills and thrills for participants and spectators alike at the Derby's most spirited event. The event usually starts at 11:30 a.m. and is free with your Pegasus Pin.

## Ken-Ducky Derby Festival

If horses don't float your boat, think ducks. They could make you a millionaire at the annual Ken-Ducky Derby. It's not affiliated with the Kentucky Derby Festival in any way, and it's held on the Festival Plaza at Waterfront Park in the fall, not the spring, when thousands of rubber ducks are dumped into the Ohio River. A rubber duck can be adopted for $5 at local banks and Kroger grocery stores, and the owner of the first duck to cross the finish line wins a new car. There's also a chance to win a fortune with the Million Dollar Duck. Proceeds from the event benefit the Harbor House of Louisville, a nonprofit training and development center for adults with physical and developmental disabilities and brain injuries. Get more information about this race at www.hhlou.org/events.php.

## THUNDER OVER LOUISVILLE

Two weeks before the Derby, the opening ceremonies for the festival kick off with the largest annual fireworks show in North America. Known as Thunder Over Louisville, this free massive pyrotechnics spectacular and air show on the Ohio River attracts 500,000 spectators to the Kentucky and Indiana shorelines, and can be seen for miles. The aerial maneuvers—with 100 planes, aerobatics teams, daring skydiving teams, and breathtaking stunts—start at 3 p.m., and the 28-minute fireworks display begins at 9:30 p.m. The show always features the latest in pyrotechnic power from Zambelli Internationale (America's "first family of fireworks"), with eight 400-foot barges assembled on both sides of the Second Street Bridge to form the stage. A highlight of the event occurs when the largest U.S. flag ever flown soars above the crowd via helicopter tow as the National Anthem plays in the background. For more information, visit their official Web site at www.thunderoverlouisville.org.

# OTHER EVENTS

## January

### LOUISVILLE BOAT, RV & SPORTSHOW

For more than half a decade this popular trade show and exhibition has chased away the winter blahs for many a sports enthusiast in the Derby City. Although the weather outside is cold and dreary, things always warm up at the Kentucky Exposition Center during the last part of January, when thousands flock to see the latest developments in outdoor sporting. A houseboat fest, kids' casting demonstrations, and boating and fishing seminars are just some of the highlights. In addition, the Kentucky Department of Fish and Wildlife is always on hand to dole out fishing and hunting licenses. A recent—and very popular—addition to the event is the DockDogs performance. Canine competitors run down a 40-foot dock and jump into a 40-foot-long swimming pool, making a big splash at the show. You'll find more at www.louisvilleboatshow.com.

## February

### HUMANA FESTIVAL OF NEW AMERICAN PLAYS

An internationally renowned festival that celebrates contemporary American playwrights, this prestigious event showcases new theatrical works and has been drawing producers, critics, playwrights, and theater lovers from around the world since 1976. Many converge in Kentucky's largest city in February and March to get a glimpse of the future of American theater, while others come to see what their favorite playwright has been up to. In any case, most agree it's a key event in the American theater scene. Produced by the Actors Theatre of Louisville, the festival is made possible by the generosity of the Humana Foundation, the philanthropic arm of Humana Inc. that supports charitable activities promoting healthy lives and communities. Learn more at www.actorstheatre.org.

## May

### ABBEY ROAD ON THE RIVER

Each year, tens of thousands of Beatles fans from all over the world flock to Louisville's waterfront for the largest Beatles festival in the United States. It takes place on Memorial Day weekend and lasts for five days. Although it had its start in 2002 in Cleveland, Ohio, the festival moved to its current location in 2005. Known as Abbey Road on the River, it gets bigger and better every year and attracts an average of at least 60 bands. Many types of tribute bands make an appearance, and while some bands look, sound, and act like the Beatles, others try to replicate the Beatles sound without dressing or acting like them. Still other bands celebrate the music of Lennon, McCartney, and Harrison without trying to reproduce the band's sound. In addition, there are speakers, collectors, and exhibits. For ticket prices or information about the sister event in Washington, D.C., over Labor Day weekend, go online at www.abbeyroadontheriver.com.

## June

### KENTUCKIANA PRIDE FESTIVAL

Generally held each year during the third weekend in June, the Kentuckiana Pride Festival attracts people of all ages to the Belvedere overlooking the Ohio River in downtown Louisville. Considered the largest celebration of diversity

and tolerance for the local LGBT community, the festival attracts nearly 10,000 annually. A live stage showcases regional and national talent and informational booths are set up to educate attendees about issues that affect the gay community. In addition, vendors offer arts and crafts, food and drink. There is no charge for admission; however, if you want to consume alcoholic beverages you will need to get a special identifying wristband. The festival usually kicks off at a Louisville bar with an official party two weeks prior to the gathering at the Belvedere and includes a parade and pagent. Visit www.kentuckianapride festival.com or call (502) 649-4851 for more information.

### KENTUCKY SHAKESPEARE FESTIVAL

The Kentucky Shakespeare Festival, most commonly referred to as "Shakespeare in the Park" in Old Louisville, is a cultural event that features free theater performances every summer in Central Park. What started as the Carriage House Players in 1949 is today the oldest free professional and independently operating Shakespeare festival in the United States, and each year, some 15,000 visitors enjoy the festival's Shakespeare performances. The shows are free because the festival stands by the firm belief that "art is for everyone—rich, poor, educated, illiterate, healthy, or disabled," and today, it is one of the most popular annual events in the Old Louisville neighborhood. Every year in June and July theatergoers can enjoy classics such as *Romeo and Juliet, Macbeth,* and *A Midsummer Night's Dream* amid the spectacular backdrop of America's grandest Victorian neighborhood. For information about upcoming performances, visit their Web site at www.kyshakes.org.

## July

### FORECASTLE FESTIVAL

Equal parts music, art, and activism, this summer festival on the *Belvedere* is a symposium for musicians, artists, and environmentalists that connects the progressive Midwest. The goal of Forecastle is to establish a cultural entertainment medium showcased in a scenic, outdoor environment, and since its inception in 2002, it has grown by leaps and bounds and counts as one of the most important events of its kind in the country. In fact, *SPIN Magazine* has named Forecastle as "One of the Top 101 things to do in America." It takes place normally the weekend after the Fourth of July. Tickets are available at ticketmaster.com or at independent record stores throughout the region. More information can be found at www .forecastlefest.com.

### LOUISVILLE BLUES-N-BARBECUE
Since 1998 the Louisville Blues-n-Barbecue Festival has been heating up midsummer in the Derby City with the intoxicating sounds of New Orleans and Memphis—and lots of great barbecue—at the Water Tower off of Zorn Avenue. Admission is $6 before 6 p.m. or $9 after, and kids 10 and under are free. Parking doesn't cost anything at this event that takes place on the Friday, Saturday, and Sunday after Independence Day. For more information, contact the sponsor, Bisig Impact Group, at www .bisigimpactgroup.com/blues.

### LEBOWSKI FEST
Lebowski Fest is a celebration of all things related to the 1998 Coen brothers' cult comedy, *The Big Lebowski*. For two days in the fall, fans of the film, also known as "achievers," come from far and wide to party with an array of Dudes and Walters and Maudes, not to mention a nihilist or two. It features unlimited bowling, white russians and oat sodas, costume and trivia contests, special guest performers, massive movie screenings, and more. The First Annual Lebowski Fest was held in 2002 in Louisville, but subsequent fests have been held in New York, Los Angeles, Chicago, Las Vegas, Austin, Seattle, London, and Edinburgh, and every year different cities join the list. For more information go online at www.lebowskifest.com.

## August

### STREET ROD NATIONALS
Each year during the beginning of August, street rod fanatics from around the country hit the road and head for Louisville, Kentucky, for four days of hot rod fun. Colorful street rods—vehicles traditionally built prior to 1949 that have been considerably souped up—flood the city and gather at the Kentucky Exposition Center, where a variety of activities take place. Spectacular vehicles are on display, and guests are encouraged to roam around and get to know the vehicles' owners, but there are other events the family will enjoy just as much. Aside from the commercial exhibitors, you'll find a swap meet and Women's World, with an assortment of arts and crafts, as well as children's games. For admission prices and yearly dates, visit the National Street Rod Association's Web site at www.nsra-usa.com.

### KENTUCKY STATE FAIR
Since 1904, the Kentucky State Fair has defined the Bluegrass State like no other event. Every year in August, this unique festival at the grounds around the Kentucky Exposition Center offers 11 consecutive, 16-hour days of non-stop excitement for the entire family. The Web site at www .kystatefair.org has the daily schedule and fare admission information, in addition to a useful map that is a great tool to help plan in advance for entering through the gates, parking, and catching a shuttle ride.

### LOUISVILLE ZOMBIE ATTACK
On the last Saturday in August, Bardstown Road—normally a lively place—becomes a hotspot for the dead. The *un*dead, that is. Dressed in their favorite and goriest zombie attire, thousands turn out for a walk at 8:29 p.m. from the corner of Bardstown Road and Eastern Parkway down to Bearno's Pizza, where the party begins at 9 p.m. Along the way, zombies "attack" passersby and other non-zombies, so if you're in the vicinity and not dressed the part, prepare to be ravished by a brain-famished mutant. Zombie movies are shown, and a DJ is there to liven things up. Prizes are awarded as well, for King, Queen, Hottest, and Grossest Zombies. The event is free and open to people of all ages. Find out more at www.louis villeisforlovers.com.

## September

### CORN ISLAND STORYTELLING FESTIVAL

The International Order of EARS (the acronym is a secret, known only to initiates) is a nonprofit, 100 percent volunteer-based organization dedicated to cultivating and perpetuating storytelling as both an art form and as a means of cultural preservation. The Corn Island Storytelling Festival, its largest annual event and one of the largest in the country, strives to achieve harmony between the popularity and marketability of ghost stories and the cultural, historical, and literary aspects of oral and musical presentation. Every year in the fall, storytellers from around the nation and the world gather to keep their craft alive at a number of private charitable events and public gatherings throughout the city. For details go to www.cornislandstorytellingfestival.org, or call (502) 245-0643.

### BLUEGRASS BALLOON FESTIVAL

On the last weekend in September, the Meijer grocery chain sponsors Kentucky's largest balloon event at the Bluegrass Balloon Festival. In addition to morning races and evening glows, the festival features afternoon races and tethered rides to give the crowds an idea of what it's like to float in one of the more than 70 balloons assembled. The fun continues with lively music, good food, and a fireworks spectacular that lights up the sky over historic Bowman Field on both Friday and Saturday nights. Admission is normally $10 per car or $3 per individual. Learn more at www.bluegrassballoons.com.

### IDEAFESTIVAL

Founded in 2000, this world-class event in Kentucky's largest city brings together the most diverse thinkers from across the nation and around the globe to explore and celebrate imagination and innovation. A cutting-edge nonlinear program designed to expand people's horizons and promote breakthrough thinking, the IdeaFestival utilizes a variety of venues to showcase and discuss key ideas in the arts, science, design, film, business, technology, and education. The lineup is designed to appeal to a broad cross section of people, and presenters are selected for their ability to communicate their ideas and achievements to a diverse audience. Past presenters have included personalities such as Anthony Bourdain and Will Shortz. An important aspect of the IF is accessibility, and considerable sponsor support allows for many free and affordable events that encourage participation by a large audience that includes students and young people. Visit their official Web site for more information at www.ideafestival.com.

## October

### BEAUX ARTS BALL

Louisville's premier black-tie gala for the gay and lesbian community, the Beaux Arts Ball is held yearly on the second Saturday in October, and most recently it's been held at the elegant Louisville Marriott Downtown. The evening starts with a host bar and is followed by a four-course meal with complimentary wine, and there's lots of music and entertainment. The night ends by dancing the night away to a mix of current hits and classic favorites, and a silent auction provides a chance to bid on an assortment of treasures. Tickets cost $150 per person and all proceeds go to VOICES of Kentuckiana, the area's only all-inclusive chorus, and the Care Coordinator Program of the Volunteers of America, an agency that assists local families living with HIV/AIDS. For more information, check out their Web site at www.beauxartsball.com.

### GARVIN GATE BLUES FESTIVAL

Every year during the second weekend in October, thousands of blues lovers flock to the area around Oak Street and Garvin Gate in Old Louisville for the Garvin Gate Blues Festival. The festival, which is the largest free neighborhood street music fest in town includes a live stage with fantastic blues, in addition to foods and drink vendors and artisan booths. Proceeds from sponsorships and vendor sales benefit the Garvin Gate Neighborhood Association, one of more than a dozen Old Louisville neighborhood orga-

## History on Tap

The **Water Tower** is a 19th-century historic landmark on the banks of the Ohio River, east of downtown Louisville. Home of Louisville's leading contemporary art center, the Louisville Visual Arts Association, the gleaming white structure in the Greek Revival style counts as the oldest ornamental water tower in the world. A towering standpipe column rises out of a Corinthian portico at its base, and this is topped by a wooden balustrade and pedestals supporting cast-zinc statues from J. W. Fiske & Company. The statues—10 in all—depict Greco-Roman deities, the four seasons, and an Indian hunter with his dog, and the reservoir's gatehouse on the riverfront was meant to invoke images of a castle along the Rhine. Constructed in 1856, the building began operations in October 1860 and was designated a National Historic Landmark in 1971.

nizations. For more information visit their official Web site (garvingatebluesfestival.com).

### HARVEST HOMECOMING

One of the region's favorite fall festivals, Harvest Homecoming has been drawing hundreds of thousands of visitors to the riverside town of New Albany during the second weekend in October for more than four decades. Conceived as a way of bringing together people to enjoy the talent, history, and natural beauty in southern Indiana, the event features a multitude of food and craft booths, farmers' market items, rides, and attractions. In addition, there are lots of contests and live music to make it a festival the entire family can enjoy. More details, including a calendar of events, can be found on the official Web site at www.harvesthomecoming.com.

### SPIRIT BALL

The Spirit Ball has become one of the social highlights of the Halloween season in the Derby City. Billed as a Victorian-inspired masquerade party, it takes place the Saturday before Halloween at the opulent Conrad-Caldwell House Museum on charming St. James Court. From 8 p.m. to midnight, revelers gather in historic Old Louisville to keep old traditions alive and celebrate the fall season. For $150 per person, the evening includes live music and dancing, expertly mixed cocktails, and gourmet fare, in addition to bourbon tastings, fortune-tellers, a silent auction, and more. All proceeds benefit the Conrad-Caldwell House Museum. Learn more about this adults-only costume gala by calling (502) 636-5023 or by going online at www.thespiritball.com.

## November

### LIGHT UP LOUISVILLE

The Derby City's kickoff to the holiday season begins with a dazzling display of twinkling lights, music, and free craft activities for children and families on the Friday after Thanksgiving each year at Jefferson Square Park in front of City Hall. The festivities usually begin at 3 p.m. with a variety of live entertainment and fun activities, and Santa Claus makes his appearance at 7 p.m. The evening culminates with a Zambelli fireworks display and the changing of the lights at the top of the AEGON Center, Louisville's tallest building; the white lights change to green and red for the remainder of the year. For more information about this popular event, visit the city's link at www.louisvilleky.gov/CommunityRelations/Light UpLouisville.

## December

### OLD LOUISVILLE HOLIDAY HOUSE TOUR

Every year during the first weekend in December, Victorian home enthusiasts flock to the Old Louisville neighborhood for a yuletide celebration

# Close-up

## St. James Court Art Show

Every year since 1957, art lovers have flocked to the streets of old Louisville during the first weekend in October for the St. James Court Art Show. What started off as a dozen local residents hanging their paintings from clotheslines on the green in the middle of St. James Court has grown into one of the top juried art shows in the nation today, attracting nearly 800 artists from North America and hundreds of thousand of visitors from the region and beyond. Artisans, artists, and craftspeople set up booths along stretches of Third Street, Fourth Street, Magnolia Avenue, St. James and Belgravia courts and offer an assortment of items such as jewelry, furniture, pottery, glassworks, photography and paintings. Higher-end displays tend to be situated on St. James Court, Belgravia Court and Magnolia Avenue, while booths on Fourth and Third streets often feature more consumer-oriented artistic items. During the fair, which begins at 10 a.m. on the first Friday, Saturday, and Sunday in October, the 19th-century Conrad-Caldwell House on St. James Court is open for tours, serving as a focal point for local politicians, charities, churches, media stations, and publishers who take the opportunity to promote themselves.

Although corporate sponsors are often recruited to defray the costs of the annual event, the St. James Court Art Show is put on by a group of neighborhood associations in Old Louisville and hundreds of volunteers. The show has been ranked #1 in the nation by *Sunshine Artist Magazine*. For more information, go on-line at www.stjamescourtartshow.com.

of the area's wonderful historic architecture. Private homeowners and local bed-and-breakfasts decorate for the season and invite the public inside for a glimpse of the past from noon to 6 p.m. on Saturday and Sunday. Tickets cost $20 in advance, $25 at the door, and all proceeds go to the Old Louisville Neighborhood Council, the local agency that safeguards the interests of the historic preservation district. The Conrad-Caldwell House Museum on St. James Court serves as the base for the event, and participants can pick up tickets there or browse the gift shop in the basement for holiday shopping needs. In addition, a Victorian tea is offered, as are caroling, holiday poetry recitations, and more. Get more information about this favorite Christmas event at holidayhousetour.com.

# DAY TRIPS AND
# WEEKEND GETAWAYS

Given its location, Louisville is the ideal base for exploring the rest of the state. In an hour you're in the heart of Bluegrass Country, where some of the most scenic landscapes and vistas in the state await you; drive a little over three hours and you'll be in the far reaches of the western part of the Commonwealth, where interesting destinations like Paducah, Henderson, and Owensboro require even less driving time. To the east, where the foothills of the Appalachians start to rise, three hours on the highway will get you to places like Pikeville and Ashland; drive two hours south and you'll be in the hilly, cave-ridden bottom part of the state, where Bowling Green is the largest urban center. And with southern Indiana right across the river, it's easy to make it to a wide variety of destinations in an hour or two. Wherever your day trip or weekend getaway takes you, you're sure to see that Louisville was a good starting point.

## BLUEGRASS COUNTRY

### Bardstown

One of the easiest day trips from Louisville is Bardstown, one of the oldest settlements in the Commonwealth and the self-proclaimed "Bourbon Capital of the World." Whiskey fans will want to check out nearby distilleries such as Four Roses Distillery, Heaven Hill, Tom Moore, Maker's Mark, and the Jim Beam American Outpost, but there's plenty to do if you're not into bourbon. The beautiful Abbey of Gethsemani and the Bernheim Arboretum and Research Forest are both nearby, as is the Kentucky Railway Museum. Diners looking for something different can also enjoy a movable feast on My Old Kentucky Dinner Train. You can learn more about these attractions by visiting the Bardstown-Nelson County Chamber of Commerce online at www.visitbardstown.com. Their telephone number is (502) 348-9545.

**ABBEY OF GETHSEMANI**
**3642 Monks Rd., Trappist**
**(502) 549-3117**
**www.monks.org**

Visitors have been welcomed at this, the country's oldest monastery still in use, from the first days of its foundation in 1848. Situated on more than 2,000 acres of farmland near Bardstown, the Abbey of Gethsemani is considered to be the "mother house" of all Trappist and Trappistine monasteries in the United States. Made famous when acclaimed author and poet Thomas Merton made it his home in the 1940s, today the abbey enjoys a brisk trade in homemade cheese, fruitcake, and fudge. The Welcome Center has films, archives, and a gift shop, and is open Monday through Saturday from 9 a.m. to 5 p.m.; no advance arrangements are needed to attend church services or walk the grounds.

**BERNHEIM ARBORETUM AND RESEARCH FOREST**
**P.O. Box 130, Clermont 40110**
**(502) 955-8512**
**www.bernheim.org**
Lakes, pavilions, quiet gardens, natural areas, and wildlife are just some of the draws at this wooded escape located just 30 minutes from Louisville. A popular attraction is the canopy treewalk that allows hikers to spend some time in the peaceful

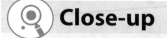

# Close-up

## A Taste for History

History fans and bourbon aficionados can explore the rich tradition and proud past of America's native spirit on the **Kentucky Bourbon Trail,** a collection of eight distilleries along a picture-perfect drive through the rolling hills of the Bluegrass State. Start off in the Frankfort area with Buffalo Trace, Woodford Reserve, Four Roses, and Wild Turkey, and then head over to Bardstown, the Bourbon Capital of the World, for a tour of the Getz Museum, Maker's Mark, Heaven Hill, Jim Beam, and Tom Moore. While experiencing the time-honored process of crafting fine bourbon whiskey, you can also learn the secrets of why Kentucky has the perfect combination of natural conditions that produce the best bourbon in the country. Get more information at www.kentuckybourbontrail.com.

**CENTRAL CORRIDOR (OFF I-64):**

**Buffalo Trace Distillery** (1001 Wilkinson Blvd., Frankfort; 502-223-7641; www.buffalotrace .com). In Franklin County, just a short distance from the state capital of Frankfort, millions of buffalo once found passage across the Kentucky River in their move toward the Great Plains. Today, their old trail—or trace—is only a reminder of a time when massive herds roamed the land. The spirit of this noble beast, however, lives on at the distillery that now bears its name. A working distillery has been on the site since 1787, and today it is the home to such brands as Pappy Van Winkle and Eagle Rare.

**Four Roses Distillery** (1224 Bonds Mill Rd., Lawrenceburg; 502-839-3436; www.fourroses.us). Situated about 15 miles from the state capital of Frankfort, this well-known distillery was constructed in 1911. It's easy enough to spot because the main building features distinctive Spanish Mission–style architecture that is rarely seen in Kentucky. The informative tour is entertaining as well; participants hear the legend about how a distiller smitten by a southern belle came up with the Four Roses brand.

**Wild Turkey Distillery** (1525 Tyrone Rd., Lawrenceburg; 502-839-4544; www.wildturkey bourbon.com). Visitors to the Wild Turkey Distillery follow the entire bourbon production process from grain delivery to bottling. Aside from viewing the towering column still, they also stroll through timber warehouses and observe the barreling of the whiskey. The no-frills facility, constructed by the Ripy brothers in 1905, occupies an impressive location on the crest of a hill overlooking the Kentucky River. The distillery name came about in 1940 when distillery executive Thomas McCarthy shared some bourbon samples with his friends on a wild turkey hunting trip. The next year, his friends requested more of "that wild turkey whiskey," and a brand was born.

**Woodford Reserve Distillery** (7855 McCracken Pike, Versailles; 859-879-1812; www.woodford reserve.com). Tucked away among the picturesque horse farms of the Bluegrass countryside, the Woodford Reserve Distillery has a rich heritage that can be rivaled by few other distilling locations in this country. The site traces the origins of its whiskey production back to 1812,

treetops overlooking a scenic valley. In addition, a visitor center offers an introduction to the history and the natural features of this forest, which distiller Isaac Bernheim established in 1929 as a gift to the people of Kentucky. After you plan your visit to Bernheim at the visitor center, you can check out upcoming programs and grab a

bite to eat at their small restaurant. The best part is that it's free.

**MY OLD KENTUCKY DINNER TRAIN**
**602 North Third St., Bardstown**
**(502) 348-7300**
**www.kydinnertrain.com**

and bourbon-distilling pioneers like Elijah Pepper, Oscar Pepper, and James Crow perfected their craft here. The only place where you can find two of the state's most famous exports—bourbon and thoroughbred horses—maturing side by side, this is also the smallest and oldest operating distillery in Kentucky today. A national landmark, the distillery consists of a collection of rustic limestone buildings on the banks of Glenn's Creek and is the only one in the state to use copper pot stills.

**WESTERN CORRIDOR (OFF I-65):**

**Heaven Hill Distilleries Bourbon Heritage Center** (Highway 49 and Gilkey Run Rd., Bardstown; 502-337-1000; www.bourbonheritagecenter.com). Visitors are invited to explore the birth of bourbon and the role of whiskey-making pioneers such as Evan Williams and Elijah Craig at the elegant white oak and limestone Bourbon Heritage Center for America's largest independent family-owned producer of distilled spirits. Interactive exhibits and tours of old-fashioned rickhouses bring to life the process by which award-winning bourbons are produced. Aside from Elijah Craig and Evan Williams, Heaven Hill has produced bourbons such as Henry McKenna and Old Fitzgerald since it was founded in 1934.

**Historic Tom Moore Distillery** (300 Barton Rd., Bardstown; 502-348-3774). Founded in 1897, the Tom Moore Distillery produces a whiskey named for the year Kentucky became a state: Ridgemont Reserve 1792. Other brands turned out there include Ten High, Kentucky Tavern, and Very Old Barton. In 2008 the distillery became the eighth stop on the Kentucky Bourbon Trail; tours and a new visitor center demonstrate the craft of distilling while sharing a bit about the state's past.

**Jim Beam's American Outpost** (Highway 245, Clermont; 502-543-9877; www.jimbeam.com). They've been around for more than two centuries, and not a single day has passed without a Beam family member acting as master distiller in what many consider one of the greatest business dynasties in American history. The Beam tradition goes back to the late 1700s when large numbers of Germans began to arrive in this country. One of these immigrants, Johannes "Jacob" Boehm, settled the lush bluegrass hills of Kentucky to try his hand at farming, eventually changing the spelling of his last name to Beam. Like many farmers of the day, Beam also knew the art of distilling, and he sold his first barrels of corn whiskey around 1795. It was known as Old Jake Beam. Just a 30-minute drive from Louisville, this American institution is one of the most-visited sights in Kentucky.

**Maker's Mark Distillery** (3350 Burks Spring Rd., Loretto; 270-865-2099; www.makersmark .com). Mention Maker's Mark and the distinctive bottles sealed with red wax come to mind. The theme is carried over at the red-shuttered, black distillery buildings at Maker's Mark Distillery in Loretto. Another National Historic Landmark, this was originally built as Burks' Distillery in 1889 and claims to be the first in the country to actively use landmark buildings for distilling. The current recipe for Maker's Mark was developed in 1951, and since then it has developed a cult following among some whiskey enthusiasts.

Operating year-round on different schedules, My Old Kentucky Dinner Train features three beautifully restored vintage dining cars from the 1940s, pulled by two 1950s F-unit locomotives. Inside the elegant interiors, traditional tables that seat four provide space that's intimate enough for private conversation, yet open enough to chat with your neighbors. The two-hour excursion takes diners through beautiful Kentucky countryside as the executive chef prepares a delicious meal in the kitchen car. Lunch menus include three-course specials with a choice of entrees; for dinner there are four courses.

## MY OLD KENTUCKY HOME
**501 East Stephen Foster Avenue**
**Bardstown**
**(502) 348-3502**
http://parks.ky.gov/findparks/recparks/mo

One of the most popular tourist attractions in the Bluegrass, this Georgian-style mansion is just as endearing to visitors today as it was in 1852, the year Stephen Foster wrote what would become the official state song during a visit to his cousins, the Rowans. At My Old Kentucky Home, visitors can relive the days of the antebellum South as costumed guides escort them through the grand estate and formal gardens. The house and visitor center are open 9 a.m. to 4:45 p.m. Thursday to Sunday during the winter period (January 2 to February 28) and daily from March 1 to December 30.

**i** My Old Kentucky Home is one of 52 state parks. Here you can experience the tradition of the longest-running outdoor drama in the Bluegrass in a celebrated musical featuring colorful period costumes and lively choreography. In addition you'll hear more than 50 Stephen Foster songs, including his most famous ballad, "My Old Kentucky Home." For information about show times and ticket prices call (800) 626-1563 or visit The Stephen Foster Drama Association's Web site at www.stephenfoster.com.

## Frankfort

An hour's drive east on I-64 will take you from Louisville to the state capital of Frankfort. Although it's the center of government for the Commonwealth, it's not the largest city. In fact, with only around 30,000 residents, Frankfort is one of the smallest capitals in the nation. Despite its small population, there are a good number of attractions in this small town, including the capitol building. There's a large historic district, and the visitor center at 100 Capitol Avenue offers walking-tour brochures and more information

about area attractions. Call (800) 960-7200, or visit online at www.visitfrankfort.com.

**i** Lexington was chosen to host the 2010 World Equestrian Games—the very first time the Fédération Equestre Internationale decided to hold the games outside of Europe since they began in Stockholm in 1990. Held every four years, two years prior to the Olympic Games, the World Equestrian Games are composed of the world championships for eight different equestrian sports. The disciplines are dressage, driving, endurance, eventing, jumping, para dressage, reining, and vaulting. For more information, visit the Web site of the Fédération Equestre Internationale at www.horsesport.org.

## Lexington

Kentucky's second city, Lexington, enjoys an idyllic setting in the middle of some of the most picturesque scenery the state has to offer. The county seat of Fayette County, it takes about an hour and a half to drive there from Louisville. The scenic area is known for its world-famous race thoroughbreds, and the rolling hills are dotted with manicured horse farms and country estates surrounded by old stone fences. Keeneland Race Course is located on the fringes of Lexington, and it merits a visit not just to see the horses running, but also for its natural setting. (Go online at www.keeneland.com for details.) Also nearby is the Kentucky Horse Park, Lexington's tribute to the animal that has garnered so much fame for the Bluegrass State. (Visit www.kyhorsepark.com for more information.) But the Lexington area has much more than equine attractions that will make a day trip worth your while. White Hall, for example, the grand country estate of Henry Clay, is not too far away in Richmond; call (859) 623-9178 for more information. To find out about the wealth of attractions in and around Lexington, go online at www.visitlex.com, or call (800) 845-3959 for more information.

# CAVE COUNTRY

### MAMMOTH CAVE NATIONAL PARK
1 Mammoth Cave Pkwy., Mammoth Cave
(270) 758-2180
www.nps.gov/maca/index.htm

Located in the hilly country of south central Kentucky, this is the world's longest known cave system, with more than 367 miles explored. An early guide by the name of Stephen Bishop once called the cave a "grand, gloomy and peculiar place," but numerous vast chambers and complex labyrinths have earned it the name of Mammoth Cave. Since 1816, visitors have toured its subterranean labyrinths. In addition to its famous caverns, Mammoth Cave National Park contains more than 70 miles of backcountry trails through forested hills for hikers, horseback riders, and bicyclists. In addition to the Web site maintained by the U.S. Parks Service, you can find a lot of useful information at www.mammothcave.com.

# SOUTHERN INDIANA

### FRENCH LICK/WEST BADEN SPRINGS
8670 West SR 56
French Lick, IN
(888) 936-9360
www.frenchlick.com

A little more than an hour's drive from Louisville, out in the middle of the rolling countryside of southern Indiana, you'll find something you wouldn't expect: two old hotels keeping alive the grand resort tradition of the 1800s. On one end of the main drag is French Lick—hometown of NBA great Larry Bird—and its beautiful turn-of-the-20th-century grand hotel, which recently underwent a $500 million historic restoration; a mile down the road is West Baden Springs and a stunning circular hotel with an enormous dome and fanciful minarets that was touted as the "eighth wonder of the world" when it opened in 1902. Today the two hotels have joined forces to form a beautiful retreat with a scenic environment where visitors can stroll shaded walkways and visit the famous gazebo housing the Pluto Mineral Spring. Although a variety of activities can be enjoyed year-round,

the most popular draw is the new casino that has revived the local economy.

## Madison, Indiana

Few river towns are as pretty or as well-preserved as Madison, Indiana, situated on the Ohio River about 55 miles northeast of Louisville. It's a preservation-oriented town known for its intact Main Street and summer regatta that draws hydroplane enthusiasts from across the country. Virtually all of the downtown core—133 blocks of the city—have been listed on the National Register for Historic Places, so there's no shortage of eye candy for old-home enthusiasts and lovers of Americana. One of the biggest draws is the Lanier Mansion, a beautiful 1844 Greek Revival mansion designed by architect Francis Costigan for financier and railroad magnate James F. D. Lanier. For more information, call (812) 265-3526. To discover the other treasures this charming river town has in store, contact the Madison Area Convention and Visitors Bureau by calling (812) 265-2956, or go online at visitmadison.org.

### SAINT MEINRAD ARCHABBEY
200 Hill Dr.
St. Meinrad, IN
(812) 357-6611
www.saintmeinrad.edu

The Benedictine tradition arrived in the Midwest in 1854 when the Swiss Abbey of Einsiedeln sent two monks to Indiana to found a monastery. Today, the Saint Meinrad Archabbey is a thriving community where some 100 monks live, work, and pray together. Visitors are always welcome at the Archabbey, and guests are encouraged to join the monks in prayer or Mass in the church, or tour the historic buildings and peaceful grounds. The highlight of the visit is the Archabbey Church, a majestic stone structure that counts as one of only two Archabbeys in the United States, and only seven in the world. About a mile away you can also visit the beautiful Monte Cassino Shrine, the site where a novena to Our Lady of Monte Cassino is credited for saving the village from a smallpox epidemic in 1871. If you have more time, consider attending a retreat given by one of the monks.

# Close-up

## Two Bluegrass Favorites

The area around Frankfort and Lexington is known as the Bluegrass. Here are two of the most beloved Bluegrass destinations, in case you're looking for a traditional meal during your day trip from Louisville.

**Beaumont Inn** (638 Beaumont Inn Dr., Harrodsburg; 859-734-3381; www.beaumontinn.com). Considered the state's oldest family-operated country inn by most, the Beaumont Inn has a lineage of hospitality that goes back almost a hundred years, to when the Dedman family began inviting guests to enjoy their grand ambience and southern flair. And if you're not convinced that Kentucky is part of the South—at least as far as food is concerned—make this famous Harrodsburg inn your next destination, and you'll think otherwise. Stately white columns adorn the antebellum structure, which housed a girls' school in the 19th century, and costly antiques fill the parlors and sitting rooms. There are even portraits of Confederate generals hanging on walls in the entryway. Items such as country ham, yellow-legged fried chicken, corn pudding, and Robert E. Lee orange cake, a house specialty, are on the menu, and overnight guests can order biscuits and gravy, grits, and cooked-to-order, cornmeal batter cakes with brown sugar syrup for breakfast. The famous Duncan Hines—a native of Kentucky—said the Beaumont Inn was his very favorite place to eat, and it receives regular accolades from such national publications as *Southern Living* magazine today. Little wonder that the Beaumont Inn ranks high on the list of must-eat places in the Bluegrass State.

The spacious, parklike grounds of the Beaumont Inn are perfect for a leisurely stroll after their famous Sunday brunch or before turning in for the night in one the 33 guest rooms appointed with antique and period furnishings. Although the food in the main dining room alone is worth the trip, their Old Owl Tavern also offers casual dining, and a spa was recently added that allows visitors to pamper themselves even more. Since the drive from Louisville to Harrodsburg takes about an hour, the Beaumont Inn is a popular destination for diners in search of a taste of the Old South.

**Shaker Village of Pleasant Hill** (3501 Lexington Rd., Harrodsburg; 800-734-5611; www .shakervillageky.org). The Harrodsburg area is the perfect spot to experience the Shaker legacy in the Bluegrass State. Founded in the early 1800s by members of the United Society of Believers in Christ's Second Appearing, the community at Pleasant Hill thrived with more than 500 residents and 4,000 acres of land by the mid-19th century. They were a peaceful, highly innovative sect, and its adherents would come to be known as the Shakers because of their ritualistic dance. Today it is an open-air museum of living history that welcomes visitors all year long. From April 1 to October 31, admission to the village for self-guided tours is $15 (for visitors age 13 and above); from November 1 to March 31, it is $7.

Although the last of the Kentucky Shakers left their community at Pleasant Hill in the early 1900s, their sense of hospitality remains, and guests at this National Historic Landmark can enjoy hearty regional foods and original Shaker recipes at the Trustees' Office Inn. Breakfast features a hearty country buffet with specialties like pumpkin muffins and southern biscuits with sausage gravy, and the lunch menu offers open-faced sandwiches, salads, and ham biscuits served with Pleasant Hill coleslaw and homemade corn sticks, a popular variation on corn bread. Dinner entrees include sliced pork with apple cider sauce, rainbow trout poached in white wine, skillet-fried catfish, steak, and salt-cured country ham topped with traditional fried chicken and served with freshly baked rolls. Old-fashioned desserts such as Shaker lemon pie and chess pie are popular ways to end meals at Shaker Village. When possible, menus incorporate local ingredients and fresh seasonal vegetables grown in their historic farm garden.

# RELOCATION

In recent years, Louisville has received recognition and various awards highlighting the qualities that make it a city worth relocating to. To see the entire list, go to the rankings and recognitions link at the city government Web site (www.louisvilleky.gov/Mayor/IWantTo). In the meantime, here are some of them:

## 2009

- 21c Museum Hotel named the very best hotel in the nation by the readers of *Condé Nast* magazine
- One of North America's "Small Cities of the Future" by *Foreign Direct Investment Magazine*
- One of the "Top 25 Places to Retire" in America by *Money Magazine*
- One of the "Most Livable U.S. Cities for Workers" by WomenCo.com
- Among "America's Foodiest" Cities by *Bon Appetit*
- One of the "Cities to Watch" in the *Smarter Cities* environmental survey

## 2008

- A "Most Livable City in America" (large city category) according to the U.S. Conference of Mayors
- Ranked seventh in the "Best Towns of 2008" by *Outside* magazine
- Among the "25 Best Cities for Raising a Family" by *Best Life* magazine
- One of the "Most Improved Cities for Cycling" by *Bicycling* magazine
- Among the "Five Cheapest Places to Rent in America" by NBC *Today* show
- Best-tasting water in America by the American Water Works Association, which judged Louisville's water "Best of the Best"
- Among the 100 Best Communities for Young People according to America's Promise Alliance

## 2007

- Named one of the "Top 10 Safest Cities in America" by the Crime in Metropolitan America Report
- One of the "Top 10 Underrated Cities in America" by Sherman's Travel
- One of America's 50 "Hottest Cities" for business expansion and relocation by *Expansion Management* magazine
- Among the "Best Cities to Have a Baby" by *FitPregnancy* magazine

## 2006

- Best large city for relocating families, according to Worldwide ERC, Primacy Relocation, and Bert Sperling of Sperlings BestPlaces
- Eighth-Safest City in America by Morgan Quitno
- One of America's "Hottest Cities" for business expansion and relocation by *Expansion Management* magazine
- A bronze-level Bicycle Friendly Community, two years ahead of its targeted goal, according to the League of American Bicyclists
- Fifth-most-affordable city for family health insurance, according to eHealthInsurance
- Top city in the Southeast for manufacturing jobs by Manufacturers' News, Inc.
- Waterfront Park named one of the nation's Top 10 Urban Parks by the Urban Land Institute
- Ninth-Fittest City in America by *Men's Fitness* magazine

- Kentucky rated fourth-most-competitive state for attracting business by *Site Selection* magazine

## 2005

- Fifth-best large city for relocating families, according to Worldwide ERC, Primacy Relocation, and Bert Sperling of Sperling's BestPlaces
- Seventh-Safest City in America by Morgan Quitno
- Ranked ninth of the Top 20 Hot Headquarters Cities for the 21st Century by *Business Facilities* magazine
- Salary.com ranked Louisville the 15th-best city for building personal net worth in its "Salary Value Index"
- Louisville Slugger Museum ranked as one of the great tourist tours in the country by *Fortune* magazine

**i** According to the Greater Louisville Association of Realtors, prospective buyers of real estate in Louisville will find the highest median home sales prices north of I-64 in the East End. The lowest home sales prices are found west of I-65, in the West and South Ends, and the area between I-64 and I-65 in the South and East Ends is where you'll find the middle range of home sales prices. For more information about the Derby City housing market, in addition to a comprehensive list of area realtors, check out the Web site for the Greater Louisville Association of Realtors at http:// louisvillerealtors.com.

## REALTORS

**BILL STOUT PROPERTIES, INC.**
**1114 South Fourth St.**
**(502) 637-7368**
**www.billstoutproperties.com**
A leader in local real estate management services, Bill Stout is certified by the Institute of Real Estate Management of the National Board of Realtors. Providing professional management, as

### What is Meant by "the Ends"?

In some ways, Louisville has been divided up into three basic parts of town since the mid-1900s: the West End, the South End, and the East End. And, depending on who you're talking to, it could lead to some generalizations being made about who you are and what socioeconomic class you identify with. The South End has long been considered the white, working-class part of town, and for most—especially those in the East End—the East End has come to be seen as very white and very middle- and upper class. For many, the West End—that area north of Algonquin Parkway and west of Seventh Street—is a euphemism for the African-American part of town, and although a high percentage of black residents make up the population there, most African-American Louisvillians no longer live in areas where more than 80 percent of residents are black.

well as leasing and brokerage services, Bill Stout Properties specializes in single-family residential, multifamily, commercial, and condominium association developments.

**CATALYST REALTY**
**10507 Timberwood Circle**
**(502) 588-7929**
**www.catalystrealty.net**
Guiding buyers and sellers through the entire process, the people at Catalyst Realty want to provide the highest level of professionalism and service possible. Whether it's for residential, new construction, investment, multifamily, commer-

cial, property management, or international relocation, you'll probably find what you're looking for at Catalyst. They also have a branch office at 1235 South Fourth Street that specializes in the historic homes of Old Louisville and other parts of town.

**RE/MAX PROPERTIES EAST**
**10525 Timberwood Circle, Suite 100**
**(502) 425-6000**
**www.homesinlouisville.com**
RE/MAX has a strong presence in the real estate business of eastern Jefferson County and throughout the area. Several agents specialize in working with transferees from large corporations and offer other services to make a smooth transition to a new home in Louisville.

**SEMONIN REALTORS**
**4967 US 42, Suite 100**
**(502) 425-4760**
**www.semonin.com**
Not only is Semonin the largest real estate agency in the state, but it's also one of the largest in the country. With hundreds of sales associates scattered throughout locations in the Louisville area, this is the place many in Louisville call when they're looking to sell or buy.

**WALTON JONES REALTY, INC.**
**1731 Frankfort Ave.**
**(502) 896-4262**
**www.waltonjonesrealtors.com**
Specializing in historic properties in the Clifton, Crescent Hill, and Highlands neighborhoods, this small but savvy full-service real estate company was started by owner and principal broker Walton Jones III in Crescent Hill in 1986. A number of well-informed agents, both qualified and personable, are always on hand to help you find the commercial or residential property you're looking for.

## DRIVER'S LICENSES

If you are moving to Louisville from another state and your license has expired, you must take a

### Your Dream Home in Old Louisville

Like what you see in Old Louisville? With the abundance of old homes and Victorian mansions, this up-and-coming neighborhood is a popular relocation choice for out-of-towners moving to the area. And compared to what you'd find in most cities of comparable size, the homes here are a steal. Where else could you find 5,000 square feet of good-condition living space with six bedrooms, fireplaces, original hardwood floors, and lots of charm for $350,000? *This Old House* magazine recently named this charming neighborhood one of the top places to buy an old house in the United States, proving that in Old Louisville, your housing dollars go a long way. There are 48 blocks' worth of Queen Annes, Second Empires, and Stick Victorians with other styles such as Italianate, Tudor, and Georgian Revival. Many have been lovingly restored, but others still need work. "A rehabbed manse might run you about $275,000, and prices top out at $800,000."

Old Louisville resident Don Driskell of Catalyst Realty specializes in "historic homes and historic services," so if you're interested, call (502) 727-0280, or go online at www.dondriskell.com for more information. Mary K. Martin at Semonin Realtors will also help you get that dream house you've been looking for. Call her at (502) 637-4000 or go on-line at www.marymartin.semonin.com/

written test and an eye exam prior to receiving a Kentucky state license. There are five offices around Louisville that issue permits, driver's licenses, personal IDs, and commercial driver's licenses. Only the Bowman Field office, however, handles written and driving tests for new drivers and those relocating to Louisville. Find out more online at www.louisvilleky.gov/Residents/drivers_license.htm.

## ST. MATTHEWS / BOWMAN FIELD DRIVER'S LICENSE BRANCH
**3501 Roger Schupp St.**
**(502) 595-4405**
Office hours are Monday from 8 a.m. to 6 p.m., Tuesday through Friday from 8 a.m. to 4 p.m., and Saturday from 8:30 a.m. to 12:30 p.m. (renewals and duplicates only). You can also visit the Kentucky Transportation Cabinet Web site at http://transportation.ky.gov/drlic for complete details on getting a Kentucky driver's license. This includes information about enrolling in traffic school online, downloading driver's manuals, and learning about how the point system works.

# LIBRARIES

The largest public library system in the Commonwealth of Kentucky, the Louisville Free Public Library (LFPL) opened in 1908. The main branch library is housed in a neoclassical Carnegie library built around the turn of the last century and located just south of Broadway in downtown Louisville. Over time, other branches were added—including the Western Branch, the first Carnegie facility built exclusively for African Americans—and at one time some 30 outlets of the Louisville Free Public Library could be found throughout the city. Subsequent lack of funding has reduced that number to the current 16.

The Louisville Free Public Library became the first in the nation to put its own FM radio station on the air in 1950, and WFPK, the second one, was added several years afterward. The main library building was expanded from 42,000 square feet to 110,000 square feet in 1969 when the north building was added on

to the original Carnegie structure at a cost of $4 million.

Individuals who live, work, go to school, or own property in Jefferson County qualify for a free library card, as do the individual's spouse and minor children living in the same household. This library card is good at all Louisville Free Public Library locations. For more information, visit www.lfpl.org; to schedule an adult tour of the Main Library, contact Main Information Services at (502) 574-1616. For links to many useful community resources, go to www.lfpl.org/internet, or for information of particular interest to those thinking about relocating to Louisville, go to www.lfpl.org/internet/louisville.htm.

## MAIN LIBRARY
**301 York St.**
**(502) 574-1611**
Mon–Thurs: 9 a.m. to 9 p.m.
Fri, Sat: 9 a.m. to 5 p.m.
Sun: Closed

## BON AIR
**2816 Del Rio Place**
**(502) 574-1795**
Mon–Thurs: 9 a.m. to 9 p.m.
Fri, Sat: 9 a.m. to 5 p.m.
Sun: Closed

## CRESCENT HILL
**2762 Frankfort Ave.**
**(502) 574-1793**
Mon–Thurs: 10 a.m. to 9 p.m.
Fri, Sat: 10 a.m. to 5 p.m.
Sun: Closed

## FAIRDALE
**10616 West Manslick Rd.**
**(502) 375-2051**
Mon, Wed, Thurs: Noon to 8 p.m.
Tues: 10 a.m. to 8 p.m.
Fri, Sat: 10 a.m. to 5 p.m.
Sun: Closed

**FERN CREEK**
**6768 Bardstown Rd.**
**(502) 231-4605**
Mon–Thurs: 10 a.m. to 9 p.m.
Fri, Sat: 10 a.m. to 5 p.m.
Sun: Closed

**HIGHLANDS/SHELBY PARK**
**1250 Bardstown Rd.**
**(502) 574-1672**
Mon–Thurs: 10 a.m. to 9 p.m.
Fri, Sat: 10 a.m. to 5 p.m.
Sun: Closed

**YOUNG ADULT OUTPOST (AT HIGHLANDS /
SHELBY PARK)**
**1250 Bardstown Rd.**
**(502) 574-1640**
Mon–Thurs: 1 p.m. to 9 p.m.
Fri, Sat: 10 a.m. to 5 p.m.
Sun: Closed

**IROQUOIS**
**601 West Woodlawn Ave.**
**(502) 574-1720**
Mon–Thurs: 10 a.m. to 9 p.m.
Fri, Sat: 10 a.m. to 5 p.m.
Sun: Closed

**JEFFERSONTOWN**
**10635 Watterson Trail**
**(502) 267-5713**
Mon–Thurs: 10 a.m. to 9 p.m.
Fri, Sat: 10 a.m. to 5 p.m.
Sun: Closed

**MIDDLETOWN**
**200 North Juneau Dr.**
**(502) 245-7332**
Mon–Thurs: 10 a.m. to 9 p.m.
Fri, Sat: 10 a.m. to 5 p.m.
Sun: Closed

**NEWBURG**
**4800 Exeter Ave.**
**(502) 479-6160**
Mon–Thurs: 10 a.m. to 9 p.m.
Fri, Sat: 10 a.m. to 5 p.m.
Sun: Closed

**OKOLONA**
**7709 Preston Hwy.**
**(502) 964-3515**
Mon–Thurs: 10 a.m. to 9 p.m.
Fri, Sat: 10 a.m. to 5 p.m.
Sun: Closed

**PORTLAND**
**3305 Northwestern Pkwy.**
**(502) 574-1744**
Mon, Tues, Thurs: Noon to 8 p.m.
Wed: 10 a.m. to 8 p.m.
Fri, Sat: 10 a.m. to 5 p.m.
Sun: Closed

**ST. MATTHEWS**
**3940 Grandview Ave.**
**(502) 574-1771**
Mon–Thurs: 10 a.m. to 9 p.m.
Fri, Sat: 10 a.m. to 5 p.m.
Sun: Closed

**SHAWNEE**
**3912 West Broadway**
**(502) 574-1722**
Mon–Thurs: 10 a.m. to 9 p.m.
Fri, Sat: 10 a.m. to 5 p.m.
Sun: Closed

**SHIVELY**
**3920 Dixie Hwy.**
**(502) 574-1730**
Mon–Thurs: 10 a.m. to 9 p.m.
Fri, Sat: 10 a.m. to 5 p.m.
Sun: Closed

## SOUTHWEST
**10375 Dixie Hwy.**
**(502) 933-0029**
Mon–Thurs: 9 a.m. to 9 p.m.
Fri, Sat: 9 a.m. to 5 p.m.
Sun: Closed

## WESTERN
**604 South Tenth St.**
**(502) 574-1779**
Mon, Tues, Thurs: Noon to 8 p.m.
Wed: 10 a.m. to 8 p.m.
Fri, Sat: 10 a.m. to 5 p.m.
Sun: Closed

## WESTPORT
**8100 Westport Rd.**
**(502) 394-0379**
Mon–Thurs: 3 p.m. to 9 p.m.
Fri: Closed
Sat: 10 a.m. to 5 p.m.
Sun: closed

### Accessibility Services

- Adult Outreach Bookmobile: A wide variety of library materials are delivered to scheduled stops throughout Metro Louisville.
- Downloadable audiobooks: High-quality, free, unabridged, downloadable audio books via NetLibrary and OverDrive.
- Homebound Books to You: A program that delivers library material to patrons who are physically unable to visit their local branch library.
- Kentucky Talking Book Library items available at LFPL.
- Music CDs: A diverse collection of music from around the world.
- National Library Service books and playback equipment: A deposit collection available at the Main Library.
- Services for Blind and Visually Impaired Patrons: Free computer training, outreach, and more.
- Sign language interpreters at library programs or classes for patrons who are deaf and/or hard of hearing.
- Translation of print to alternative formats (Braille, audio, e-mail, or large type) for patrons who cannot read regular print.

## Pets

All dogs, cats, and ferrets in Louisville must be licensed at four months of age and have proof of a current rabies vaccination. It costs $9 to license a spayed or neutered pet and $50 for one that is unaltered, although a $35 voucher is included in the price. Senior citizens with no more than two altered pets per household only have to pay $4.50 for the licensing fee. For general information about owning pets in the Louisville Metro Area, or for specifics on local veterinarians selling licenses, visit the city Web site at www.louisvilleky.gov/animal services.

# EMERGENCY VETERINARIANS

**BLUE CROSS ANIMAL HOSPITAL**
**827 East Broadway**
**(502) 587-6677**
Located in the downtown area and within just a few minutes' drive of most hotels, Blue Cross Animal Hospital offers 24-hour emergency service. Their regular hours are Monday through Friday from 8:30 a.m. to 7 p.m. and Saturday from 8:30 a.m. to 4 p.m.; they are closed on Sunday.

**JEFFERSON ANIMAL HOSPITAL & REGIONAL EMERGENCY CENTER**
4504 Outer Loop
(502) 966-4104
http://jeffersonanimalhospital.com
Established in 1978 on the Outer Loop in Okolona, the Jefferson Animal Hospital & Regional Emergency Center has been operating 24 hours a day, every day of the year since 1980. A national leader in veterinary medical treatment and emergency trauma care, they are always fully staffed and open anytime of the day or night for emergencies, as well as routine care.

**LOUISVILLE VETERINARY SPECIALTY & EMERGENCY SERVICES**
13160 Magisterial Dr.
(502) 244-3036
www.lvses.com
Located in Middletown in the East End, not too far from the Gene Snyder, Louisville Veterinary Specialty & Emergency Services has been offering 24-hour emergency veterinary care since 1998; currently it is the only 24-hour animal emergency center in the area with boarded specialists in critical care.

# TOURISM BUREAUS, CHAMBERS OF COMMERCE, ETC.

**CLARK–FLOYD COUNTIES CONVENTION & TOURISM BUREAU**
315 Southern Indiana Ave.
Jeffersonville, IN
(812) 282-6654
www.sunnysideoflouisville.org

**EAST DOWNTOWN BUSINESS ASSOCIATION**
P.O. Box 406722
Louisville, 40206
(502) 587-8750

**FOCUS LOUISVILLE—A LEADERSHIP LOUISVILLE CENTER PROGRAM**
732 West Main St.
(502) 561-0458
www.leadershiplouisville.org

**FRANKFORT AVENUE BUSINESS ASSOCIATION**
2337 Frankfort Ave.
(502) 296-0091
www.frankfortave.com

**GREATER LOUISVILLE INC.—THE METRO CHAMBER OF COMMERCE**
401 South Fourth Ave. #555
(502) 583-1671
www.lca-inc.org

**GREATER LOUISVILLE SPORTS COMMISSION**
401 West Main St., Suite 2200
(502) 587-7767
www.louisvillesports.org

**HISTORIC MAIN STREET VISITOR CENTER**
627 West Main St.
(502) 568-2220
www.mainstreetassociation.com

**JEFFERSONTOWN CHAMBER OF COMMERCE**
10434 Watterson Trail, Jeffersontown
(502) 267-1674
www.jtownchamber.com

**KENTUCKIANA MINORITY BUSINESS COUNCIL**
614 West Main St., Suite 5500
(502) 625-0135
www.kmbc.biz

**KENTUCKY RESTAURANT ASSOCIATION**
133 Evergreen Rd., Suite 201
(502) 896-0464
www.kyra.org

**LOUISVILLE DOWNTOWN MANAGEMENT DISTRICT**
401 South Fourth Ave., #555
(502) 583-1671
www.lca-inc.org

**LOUISVILLE EAST—MIDDLETOWN CHAMBER OF COMMERCE**
12906 Shelbyville Rd., Suite 250, Middletown
(502) 244-8086
www.middletownchamber.com

**THE LOUISVILLE URBAN LEAGUE**
1535 West Broadway
(502) 585-4622
www.lul.org

**ONE SOUTHERN INDIANA—CHAMBER & ECONOMIC DEVELOPMENT**
4100 Charlestown Rd.
New Albany, IN
(812) 945-0266
www.1si.org

**ST. MATTHEWS AREA BUSINESS ASSOCIATION**
3940 Grandview Ave., #216
(502) 899-2523
www.smaba.org

**SALES MANAGEMENT & MARKETING ASSOCIATION**
1410 Bunton Rd.
(502) 587-5015
www.smalouisville.com

**VISITOR CENTER IN HISTORIC OLD LOUISVILLE**
218 West Oak St.
(502) 637-2922
www.historicoldlouisville.com

## VOTER REGISTRATION

To find out who your state and local representatives are and how to register to vote in the Commonwealth of Kentucky, visit the Web site for Jefferson County clerk Bobbie Holsclaw at www.jeffersoncountyclerk.org/voter-info, or contact her at:

**JEFFERSON COUNTY CLERK'S OFFICE**
527 West Jefferson St.
(502) 574-5700

# HEALTH CARE AND WELLNESS

Louisville has emerged in recent years as a major center for the medical sciences and health-care industries. In addition to being at the forefront of cancer treatment, it has been central to advancements in hand and heart surgery; among the many medical breakthroughs here were the first human hand transplant and the first transplantation of a self-contained artificial heart. Louisville's thriving downtown medical research campus includes a new $88 million rehabilitation center, as well as a health sciences research and commercialization park that has lured dozens of top scientists and researchers. Louisville is also home to Humana, one of the nation's largest health insurance companies. Given all this, it's not surprising that health care and wellness occupy prominent positions in Louisville.

## HOSPITALS

### BAPTIST HOSPITAL EAST
4000 Kresge Way
(502) 897-8100
www.baptisteast.com

At Baptist Hospital East, the slogan "Feel better" reflects the hospital's commitment to treating the whole person in mind, body, and spirit. Louisville's preferred medical center in the East End, Baptist offers specialized services for orthopedics, neurosciences, women's health, cancer, heart, emergency care, rehabilitation, sleep disorders, occupational health, and behavioral health, including chemical dependency and psychiatric care. Among its various facilities are the Baptist East / Milestone Wellness Center, Baptist Hospital Northeast, Baptist Regional Medical Center, Baptist Urgent Care, and Baptist Medical Associates. To get a complete list and more information, visit their Web site at www.baptisteast.com.

### CLARK MEMORIAL HOSPITAL
1220 Missouri Ave.
(812) 282-6631
www.clarkmemorial.org

Providing exceptional health-care services to southern Indiana and Louisville since 1922, Clark Memorial Hospital is located off I-65 in Jeffersonville, Indiana. With this long-standing tradition of care and a continuous expansion of new programs and services, Clark Memorial has evolved into a comprehensive medical center offering advanced medical care with a personal touch. Highly trained health-care professionals balance compassionate, friendly service with sophisticated medical technology to make this one of the region's premier health-care providers.

### FLOYD MEMORIAL HOSPITAL
1850 State St.
(812) 944-7701
www.floydmemorial.com

Floyd Memorial Hospital got its start in 1947, when community leaders in southern Indiana got together to address the need to expand the aging St. Edward's Hospital. Six years later, they dedicated the new Memorial Hospital of Floyd County in memory of community members who had served during wartime. The hospital has grown steadily over the years, and in January of 2006, it opened its new comprehensive Heart and Vascular Center with expanded intensive care and cardiovascular care units. In April 2006 they opened a new state-of-the-art emergency center that includes a Critical Decision Unit, Fast Track area, and a specialized Cardiac Unit and trauma rooms. In addition, Floyd Memorial's newly expanded Women's Imaging Center opened in July 2006. Other advances occurred in

December 2007, when a new 10-room pediatric unit opened, and in May of 2008, when Floyd Memorial began welcoming post-op surgery patients to its new 32-bed Surgical Inpatient Unit, with all private rooms and advanced telemetry monitoring.

## JEWISH HOSPITAL & ST. MARY'S HEALTH CARE
**200 Abraham Flexner Way**
**(502) 587-4011**
**www.jhsmh.org**

Without a doubt one of the best medical facilities in the region, this hospital traces its roots back to 1905. It has long been known for its groundbreaking work in heart disease, Kentucky's leading cause of death. Always making medical history, Jewish Hospital's main facility address commemorates medical pioneer Abraham Flexner, PhD. Flexner's book, *Medical Education in the United States and Canada,* revolutionized medical education when it was published in 1910, and the University of Louisville was among the many schools to heed his call for reforms. To learn about the many medical breakthroughs pioneered at Jewish Hospital, visit their Web site. Jewish Hospital has a number of branches beyond its main facility on Abraham Flexner Way. Some of them are:

## JEWISH HOSPITAL MEDICAL CENTER EAST
**3920 Dutchmans Lane**
**(502) 259-6000**

## JEWISH HOSPITAL MEDICAL CENTER SOUTH
**1903 West Hebron Lane, Shepherdsville**
**(502) 955-3000**

## JEWISH HOSPITAL MEDICAL CENTER SOUTHWEST
**9700 Stonestreet Rd.**
**(502) 995-2400**

## JEWISH HOSPITAL SHELBYVILLE
**727 Hospital Dr., Shelbyville**
**(502) 647-4000**

## KOSAIR CHILDREN'S HOSPITAL
**231 East Chestnut St.**
**(502) 629-6000**
**www.kosairchildrens.com**

Providing medical care for children when families cannot afford it, Kosair Children's Hospital is part of Norton Health Care. Although its primary mission is to serve the children of Kentucky and southern Indiana, Kosair Children's Hospital treats patients from all 50 states and abroad. The quality of the care it delivers is so good that it was named one of the 10 best in the nation by *Child* magazine.

Founded in 1892, it consolidated with Norton Hospital in 1969 and Kosair Crippled Children's Hospital in 1981, and then moved to its current location in 1986. Areas of care at Kosair include craniofacial disorders, poison control/toxicology, cardiovascular surgery, and psychiatry, among others; however, its reputation in the fields of oncology, diabetes, and burn treatment has earned it a spot among the best children's hospitals in the country.

## LOUISVILLE VETERANS ADMINISTRATION MEDICAL CENTER
**800 Zorn Ave.**
**(502) 287-4000**
**www.louisville.va.gov**

About a quarter of the nation's population, or roughly 70 million people, may be eligible for VA benefits and services because they are either veterans or the family members or survivors of veterans. In Louisville, many of them go to the Louisville Veterans Administration Medical Center on Zorn Avenue, which serves about 200,000 in Kentuckiana. Built in 1952 to accommodate the burgeoning patient population after World War II and the Korean War, the facility offers a wide range of services today, including substance abuse programs, ophthalmology, and the treatment of infectious diseases and post-traumatic stress disorder.

## NORTON HOSPITAL
**www.nortonhealthcare.com**

From its humble beginnings in 1886 as an infirmary at the corner of Third and Oak, Norton Healthcare has grown to be one of the region's leading health-care providers, with a well-trained team of physicians, nurses, and staff that has access to some of the most advanced technologies in the field today. Founded largely by women from St. Paul's Episcopal Church, Norton is known for its Women's Pavilion, which provides complete, caring services for women through all stages of life, from adolescence, pregnancy, and delivery through midlife and beyond. Today Norton Healthcare includes 4 large hospitals, 11 Norton Immediate Care Centers, and more than 60 physicians' practice locations. Three main locations are listed below; for a complete listing, go to their Web site.

**Norton Audubon Hospital**
**One Audubon Plaza Dr.**
**(502) 636-7111**

**Norton Hospital**
**200 East Chestnut St.**
**(502) 629-8000**

**Norton Suburban Hospital**
**4001 Dutchmans Lane**
**(502) 893-1000**

**ST. MARY'S & ELIZABETH HOSPITAL**
**1850 Bluegrass Ave.**
**(502) 361-6000**
**www.jewishhospital.org/healthnetwork/**
**stmary.html**
This hospital was created when CARITAS Health Services and Jewish Hospital HealthCare Services, two of the region's most well-established health systems, joined together in 2005. Today's merged company is a major regional health-care system, which includes 71 health-care facilities with more than 1,900 licensed beds and almost 100,000 emergency room visits per year. More than 8,000 people dedicated to providing quality care to the residents of Louisville and the surrounding areas are employed here; the array of health-care services they provide in Kentucky and southern Indiana includes hospitals, rehab medicine, behavioral health, home health care, assisted living, outpatient care, occupational health, and nursing home care.

**UNIVERSITY OF LOUISVILLE HOSPITAL**
**530 South Jackson St.**
**(502) 562-3000**
**www.uoflhealthcare.org**
The University of Louisville Hospital got its start when the General Assembly of Kentucky established the Louisville Hospital Company in 1817. In 1910 ground was broken for a new $942,000 hospital, which opened its doors in 1914, and by 1939 the hospital had become officially affiliated with the U of L School of Medicine. After further growth the name changed to Louisville General Hospital in 1942, and in 1978, construction began on a new hospital building. In 1979, this hospital was deeded to the University of Louisville. Today it's one of the most influential centers for medical research and health care in the nation. Whether it's trauma, cancer, high-risk obstetrics, stroke care, or any number of other specialties, University of Louisville Hospital offers the most advanced care available.

# MENTAL HEALTH FACILITIES

**BAPTIST HOSPITAL EAST**
**Center for Behavioral Health**
**4000 Kresge Way**
**(502) 896-7105**
**www.baptisteast.com**
Individuals requiring assistance for addictions and emotional problems will appreciate the comprehensive services available at the Center for Behavioral Health at Baptist Hospital East. In addition to psychiatric services that provide assessment, treatment, and education to adults suffering from emotional problems, there is also a chemical dependency recovery program that provides continuing care in the form of assessment, detoxification, treatment, and education to adults who are addicted to alcohol or drugs. These programs offer a wide range of treatment options, including inpatient, partial hospitalization, and intensive outpatient services. In addition, homebound individuals can receive mental health services through the Baptist Hospital East Home Health Agency.

## BRIDGEHAVEN MENTAL HEALTH SERVICES
**950 South First St.**
**(502) 585-9444**
**www.bridgehaven.org**
Founded in 1958 after the Louisville Section of the National Council of Jewish Women conducted a study that identified the need for local programs to help ease patients' transition from mental hospitals back to community participation, Bridgehaven was the first program in Jefferson County, and only the third of its type in the nation to serve people with psychiatric problems outside a hospital setting. Today, adults with severe and persistent mental illness are offered high-quality, community-based psychiatric rehabilitation and recovery services while acquiring the skills to live, learn, work, and socialize in their chosen environment. Bridgehaven is considered a 501(c)3 organization by the IRS.

## THE BROOK HOSPITALS
**8521 La Grange Rd.**
**(502) 426-6380**
**www.thebrookhospitals.com**
Realizing that mental health and substance abuse issues are complex problems that impact not just the individual, but also their family and friends, the Brook Hospitals provide a calm and safe setting for progressive, individualized treatment for all ages. Located on 97 landscaped acres in eastern Jefferson County, on the former site of the Kentucky Military Institute, The Brook conducts comprehensive evaluations to address past history and present level of functioning, as well as medical stability, chemical dependency history, and risk factors. In addition to the free assessments provided at The Brook, on-site mobile evaluations are also provided, performed at hospitals and emergency rooms, schools, and group homes. Besides the facility on La Grange Road, there is also another Brook Hospital at 1405 Browns Lane; call (502) 896-0495 for more information.

## OUR LADY OF PEACE
**2020 Newburg Rd.**
**(502) 451-3330**
**www.oloplouisville.org**
A service of Jewish Hospital & St. Mary's Health Care, Our Lady of Peace is one of the largest private, not-for-profit psychiatric hospitals in the nation; their qualified team consists of mental health workers, attending psychiatrists, nurses, social workers, chemical dependency counselors, behavioral analysts, chaplains, and art/activity therapists. Trained to address an array of emotional/behavioral/psychiatric disorders and substance abuse issues and dual diagnoses, the experienced staff offers a variety of psychiatric treatments, including inpatient, partial hospitalization, and outpatient services for children, adolescents, adults, and seniors.

## SEVEN COUNTIES SERVICES, INC.
**101 W. Muhammad Ali Blvd.**
**(502) 589-4313**
**www.sevencounties.org**
Seven Counties is not a government agency, but rather a private, not-for-profit corporation that is the state-designated regional behavioral health and developmental services center for Bullitt, Henry, Jefferson, Oldham, Shelby, Spencer, and Trimble counties of Kentucky. By state statute, it is responsible for comprehensive planning and resource allocation in community mental health, substance abuse treatment, and developmental services for its region. Aside from individuals abusing alcohol and drugs or those with developmental disabilities, Seven Counties specializes in the treatment of children with severe emotional disturbances and people with severe mental illnesses, such as schizophrenia, bipolar disorder, and chronic depression. A 24-hour crisis and information line is available at (800) 221-0446.

## WELLSTONE REGIONAL HOSPITAL
**2700 Vissing Park Rd.**
**Jeffersonville, IN**
**(812) 284-8000**
**www.psysolutions.com**
This 100-bed psychiatric hospital, the most-respected behavioral health center in Jeffersonville, Indiana, offers 74 acute-care beds for children, adolescents, and adults, and 26 residential beds for children and adolescents. Comprehensive outpatient services are also available for partial hospi-

talization and intensive outpatient programs. The goal of its many treatment options is to strengthen the spirit by identifying coping strategies and supporting each person's efforts. Psychiatrists and nurse practitioners offer medication evaluations and outpatient follow-up appointments via Wellstone's Physician Group Practice.

## URGENT CARE CENTERS

### BAPTIST URGENT CARE
**www.baptisturgentcare.com**
Baptist Urgent Care provides a dependable and convenient alternative for the treatment of minor injuries and illnesses close to home. Patients are served at a number of clinics in the Louisville area by a team of board-certified physicians and support staff, and no appointment is necessary. Most major health plans are accepted. Get more information by checking out the Web site above, or by calling the individual facilities at the numbers below.

**Baptist Eastpoint**
**2400 Eastpoint Pkwy.**
**(502) 210-4800**

**Baptist Medical Associates**
**10000 Brownsboro Rd.**
**(502) 426-3500**

**Baptist Promptcare**
**3215 Westport Green Place**
**(502) 412-1112**

**Baptist Urgent Care—Middletown**
**12010 Shelbyville Rd.**
**(502) 238-2800**

**BaptistWorx Urgent Care**
**7092 Distribution Dr.**
**(502) 935-9970**

**BaptistWorx Urgent Care**
**3303 Fern Valley Rd.**
**(502) 964-4889**

**NORTON HEALTHCARE IMMEDIATE CARE CENTERS**
**www.nortonhealthcare.com**

Most major health plans are accepted at nearly a dozen Norton Health Care Immediate Care Centers throughout the greater Louisville area. No appointmentss are needed, and most centers are open from 9 a.m. to 9 p.m. Immediate care centers provide a convenient alternative for the treatment of minor illnesses and injuries. Get more information by checking out the Web site above, or by calling the individual facilities at the numbers below.

**Clarksville**
**2051 Clevidence Blvd.**
**(812) 282-1720**

**Dixie**
**4420 Dixie Hwy.**
**(502) 449-6444**

**Dorsey Plaza**
**10284 Shelbyville Rd.**
**(502) 244-5827**

**Fern Creek**
**9340 Cedar Center Way**
**(502) 239-8431**

**Highlands**
**2450 Bardstown Rd.**
**(502) 459-3991**

**Jeffersontown**
**12615 Taylorsville Rd., Suite A**
**(502) 261-1565**

**Jeffersonville**
**3118 East 10th Street**
**(812) 280-9355**

**Lyndon**
**1321 Herr Lane, Suite 195**
**(502) 423-7911**

**Okolona**
**7626 Preston Hwy.**
**(502) 964-4357**

**Old Brownsboro Crossing**
**4950 Norton Healthcare Blvd.**
**(502) 394-6333**

**Shepherdsville**
**115 Huston Dr., Suite 2**
**(502) 957-6434**

# EDUCATION AND CHILD CARE

Education in Louisville mirrors the rest of the state and includes elementary school (kindergarten through fifth grade in most areas), middle school or junior high (in most locations, sixth grade through eighth grade), high school (generally ninth through twelfth grade), and postsecondary institutions. Most Kentucky schools and colleges are accredited through the Southern Association of Colleges and Schools (SACS). Along with many Southern states, unfortunately, Kentucky suffers from a negative stigma when it comes to education.

Some statistics—such as ranking 47th in the nation in percentage of residents with a bachelor's degree, or an estimated adult illiteracy rate of about 10 percent—seem to justify the stereotype. Others, however—like being ranked 14th in educational affordability and being named the 31st-smartest state using a formula by author Morgan Quitno, which placed Kentucky ahead of western states like California—suggest that the negative stereotype might be somewhat exaggerated. To bolster this assertion, Louisville's main rival, Lexington, ranks 10th among U.S. cities in the percentage of the population with college degrees, and most studies agree that, all in all, Kentucky is making progress in the area of education.

## PUBLIC SCHOOLS

### ANCHORAGE INDEPENDENT SCHOOL DISTRICT
11400 Ridge Rd.
(502) 245-8927
www.weeklywaves.com

A source of local pride for the bucolic, affluent community of Anchorage, Jefferson County's other public school system has an easier go at it with its small number of students and low student-teacher ratio. In addition, the high tax rate pours lots of resources into the school, a quaint white stucco building with a red tile roof that was started in 1912. Students consistently rank at the top of statewide tests, and emphasis is placed on a dynamic learning environment overseen by a committed instructional staff. Professional development and skills training is a focus and highly diversified teachers possess a wide assortment of instructional strategies and in-depth content knowledge. The staff strives for mastery learning and connectedness so students will be successful in their journeys through life as well as in their educational careers. In addition, writing and math mentor programs give teachers opportunities to share and reflect on different approaches that work in the classroom.

### BULLITT COUNTY SCHOOLS
1040 KY 44 East, Shepherdsville
(502) 869-8000
www.bullittschools.org

Despite its proximity to Louisville, Bullitt County has a rural atmosphere that makes it an inviting place for parents to raise a family. With 23 school facilities (12 elementary, 6 middle, and 4 high schools, and 1 area technology center) and educational services provided to more than 12,000 students, Bullitt County Public Schools ranks among the 10 largest districts in Kentucky—even though it's still much smaller than the Jefferson County system. There are over 750 certified and 600 classified employees meeting the needs of the student population, and education services are offered through the Bullitt County Day Treatment Center and the Bullitt County Area Technology Center as well.

Every 1 Reads is a community-wide literacy program implemented in the fall of 2003 as a joint venture between Jefferson County Public Schools, Greater Louisville, Inc. and the Metro Louisville government. The goal was to get every student at his or her appropriate grade level of reading by 2008. As of fall 2007, Every 1 Reads reports that 87.1 percent of all JCPS students are "reading at grade level," while the statewide system reports only 54.25 percent are at least proficient at reading. For more information, visit www.every1reads.com.

## CLARKSVILLE COMMUNITY SCHOOLS
200 Ettels Lane
Clarksville, IN
(812) 282-7753
www.ccsc.k12.in.us

The smallest of the three public school districts in Clark County, Indiana—there are approximately 1,400 students enrolled there—the Clarksville Community Schools system has four school buildings in the town that was the site of the beginning of the Lewis and Clark Expedition. There are two elementary schools, a middle school, and a high school. While striving to serve the educational needs of a diverse group of students, Clarksville Community Schools form part of a countywide special education cooperative, and high school students can participate in the Prosser Area Vocational Program. The Clarksville schools are presently overhauling the curriculum to include statewide standards considered by some educators to be the best in the nation, and these standards will soon be aligned with classroom practice.

## GREATER CLARK COUNTY SCHOOLS
2112 Utica-Sellersburg Rd.
Jeffersonville, IN
(812) 283-0701
www.gcs.k12.in.us

With more than 10,000 students in 20 schools, Greater Clark County Schools is the largest of the three school systems in the county and counts as number 19 in the state. Among others, it serves families in the southern Indiana communities, of Utica, Nabb, New Washington, Charlestown, and Jeffersonville, the county seat. The system includes educators who have won the State Teacher of the Year award in conservation, art, and physical education, in addition to Counselor of the Year. Experiencing rapid growth, particularly in the eastern segment of the school district, Greater Clark County Schools offers a variety of courses and academic atmospheres for students at all academic levels. It is currently in the process of building a new Charlestown High School and renovating Jeffersonville High School and New Washington Middle/High School.

## JEFFERSON COUNTY PUBLIC SCHOOLS
3332 Newburg Rd.
(502) 485-3949
www.jefferson.k12.ky.us

With nearly 100,000 students in 90 elementary schools, 24 middle schools, and 21 high schools, the Jefferson County public school system is one of the largest in the country. There are also 20 other learning centers where alternative or special education programs are offered. With a fleet of more than 1,500 vehicles, it also operates one of the 10 largest transportation systems in the nation. The JCPS is administered by an elected seven-member board of education, responsible for administering an almost $900 million budget. It additionally selects and hires a superintendent to act as the chief executive. Of the more than 6,000 teachers, 83 percent hold a master's degree or higher, and the average educator has 11.6 years of classroom experience. Given its large size and the number of poorer inner city neighborhoods included in its boundaries, a good percentage—more than 60 percent—of its students go on to college or other postsecondary schooling.

For the past several years, Jefferson County parents have consistently given JCPS high marks. On a recent districtwide parent survey, 58 percent of respondents graded their child's school with an A; 31 percent gave a grade of B. In addi-

# Close-up

## Kentucky Education Reform Act

For a state that has borne the brunt of more than one joke about its educational system and priorities, Kentucky has really made a big splash on the national school scene in recent years—and it's largely been a positive one. It's spelled KERA.

KERA—the acronym for the 1990 Kentucky Education Reform Act—came about when the state was accused of inadequately and inequitably funding its schools by a group of disgruntled school districts. The Supreme Court in Kentucky found the school system's allocation of funds to be unconstitutional, and instead of a simple redistribution of the funds, the General Assembly took drastic measures and overhauled the entire school system. This meant not only a restructuring of their finances, but also a shake-up in how they were governed, assessed, and held accountable. All at once, Kentucky became the national leader in education reform.

With over 1,000 pages, the law is a complicated one that strives to create a set of learning goals and outcomes in which the application of knowledge—and not merely the acquisition of knowledge—receives top priority. In addition, attention is paid to improving attendance and dropout rates, as well as increasing the numbers of graduates making a successful transition to work, college, or the military. To meet these goals, most schools have employed a number of reform ideas, such as cooperative learning in small groups and "whole language instruction"—an approach that involves real literature rather than readers, and implements much more writing than previous methods of teaching literacy.

The most significant reforms to the system entail periodic assessments to gauge the students' progress throughout their education. Pupils are evaluated in grades 4, 8, and 11, and tests combine multiple-choice questions with short essays and performance exams, where students have to demonstrate a capability to transfer the knowledge they've gained to new situations. In addition, individual schools are expected to show progress against a baseline that allows them to measure against themselves rather than other schools, and schools showing improvement are financially rewarded. Schools that show no improvement face the threat of takeover by the state or the dismissal of educators.

tion, Jefferson County public schools receive their fair share of praise at the national level: four area schools were included on the *U.S. News and World Report* 2008 list of America's Best High Schools, and three schools appeared on *Newsweek* magazine's 2007 list of Best American High Schools.

Because of its size, JCPS can offer a greater range of educational options than any other educational system in the area. From elementary to high school, there are dozens of options and magnet programs, including the Youth Performing Arts School. There are also career academies in a wide variety of subjects, something in which Jefferson County has been a leader.

In recent years, Jefferson County Public Schools received national media attention when

a Louisville mother filed a lawsuit on behalf of her son (*Meredith v. Jefferson County Board of Education*), whom she claimed was denied enrollment in a particular school because of his race. The 6th U.S. Circuit Court of Appeals ruled against Meredith in October 2005, but in June 2006, the U.S. Supreme Court agreed to hear the case, the first time the high court elected to rule on a school district's use of a voluntary desegregation plan. The case was heard with a similar one from Seattle, Washington, and in June 2007, the Supreme Court handed down a verdict in favor of the plaintiffs, maintaining that the school districts in Louisville and Seattle violated constitutional guarantees of equal protection. The far-reaching ramifications of this decision have not been seen

KERA has, of course, received its fair share of criticism. Some claim the testing system is flawed, and others—especially those who believe "the basics" are neglected in favor of more esoteric disciplines—claim that its learning goals undermine the role of the parents and attempt to instill values that should be taught at home. Nonetheless, it seems that the reform has been paying off.

Since the Commonwealth realigned its educational goals and made schooling its highest priority, student achievement has shown marked progress; and regardless of individual feelings about KERA, most would admit that the increased funding resulting from KERA has resulted in significant improvements in Kentucky's test scores. Most notably, the state has since scored well on national achievement tests. From 1992 to 2002, for example, Kentucky's average jumped six points in reading on the 4th Grade National Assessment of Educational Progress, with only five other states showing larger gains, and Kentucky also increased three points on 8th Grade NAEP reading, from 1998 to 2002; this exceeded the national average increase, and only nine other states had larger achievement gains. In addition, Kentucky's assessment results have showed sustained progress in reading, language arts, and mathematics, and Kentucky generally falls above the national average at all three testing stages.

State officials claim that although the law has hit some snags, the overall effect has been positive. More than 92 percent of the 1,400 schools in the state showed improvement in performance between 1992 and 1996, and 50 percent met or exceeded their performance goals. Moreover, these gains occurred at every income level, in every racial category, and in every region of the state. The reform act only affects public schools in Kentucky, however, and because of that, many private schools in and around Louisville have experienced rapid growth with an onslaught of students from families who fear the uncertainties of change. Most of them are, of course, unaware that private schools implemented many of these reforms years before KERA.

yet, but it is believed that hundreds of school districts across the nation might be affected by the outcome of the Louisville case.

**NEW ALBANY-FLOYD COUNTY CONSOLIDATED SCHOOLS**
**2813 Grant Line Rd.**
**New Albany, IN**
**(812) 949-4200**
**www.nafcs.k12.in.us**
Nestled among the rolling hills of southern Indiana, the public school district for New Albany has operated as a separate governmental unit since 1956. The New Albany-Floyd County Consolidated School Corporation considers itself a symbol of progressive and visionary excellence.

Located in Floyd County, Indiana, directly across the Ohio River from Louisville, the corporation serves the city of New Albany, and the towns of Georgetown, Galena, Floyds Knobs, and Greenville, in addition to Floyd County townships covering approximately 149 square miles. Floyd County is a community of over 71,000 residents with a variety of racial, ethnic, and religious groups and diverse economic levels that are represented in its student population.

**OLDHAM COUNTY SCHOOLS**
**6165 West KY 146, Buckner**
**(502) 241-3500**
**www.oldham.k12.ky.us**

Consistently among the highest-performing of Kentucky's 120 county school districts on state accountability tests of student learning, the Oldham County School District serves nearly 12,000 students in the rapidly growing communities located 20 miles northeast of Louisville. Student enrollment has more than doubled in recent years, and the latest results of the Kentucky State accountability tests shows Oldham County as one of the highest county districts in the state with a combined academic index of 99.47. Student academic results compare favorably to the best schools in the nation as well. The award-winning district consists of 1 preschool, 10 elementary schools, 4 middle schools, 3 high schools, an alternative school, a career center, and a center for the arts and community education, and it maintains the highest accreditation possible from the Southern Association of Colleges and Schools. With one of the lowest dropout rates in the state, *Money* magazine has selected Oldham Country Schools as one of its "100 Top Schools in Towns You Can Afford."

## SHELBY COUNTY PUBLIC SCHOOLS
**1155 West Main St., Shelbyville**
**(502) 633-2375**
**www.shelby.k12.ky.us**
Like Oldham County, Shelby County Public Schools has been a leader in the implementation of the Kentucky Education Reform Act, and it was a pioneer in the region for the use of computers in the classroom. It has a program for gifted and talented students that starts off informally in the lower grades and progresses to advanced placement in the upper grades. Located in Shelbyville, approximately 30 miles east of Louisville, the district lies in a rural community that has experienced progressive industrial growth over the past two decades. Some 1,800 students attend its flagship school, Shelby County High School, which is accredited through the Southern Association of Colleges and Schools; the average ACT composite score is 21.5, and the SAT average is 1100.

# PRIVATE SCHOOLS

## ARCHDIOCESE OF LOUISVILLE
**P.O. Box 1073**
**Louisville, KY 40201**
**(502) 585-3291**
**www.archlou.org/archlou/schools**
The Archdiocese of Louisville Catholic has 40 parish, regional, and special elementary schools serving more than 15,500 students in seven counties. In Louisville there are also eight secondary schools with some 6,000 students; three are boys only and four are for girls. Focused on the skills needed for today and tomorrow, students emerge from Louisville-area Catholic schools with a strong liberal arts background supported by technology and decision-making skills. Their education allows them to develop high levels of literacy in language arts and mathematics, as well as apply inquiry-based experimentation and problem solving. In addition, they gain an understanding of world history and cultures, participate in award-winning visual and performing arts programs, build lifelong habits of fitness, and engage in a variety of high-quality electives and extracurricular activities. Positive results for a recent secondary school report card included 98 percent of its graduates pursuing college/postsecondary training, 66 Governor's Scholars, 25 National Merit semi-finalists and 23 National Merit finalists. The average ACT score was 23.7 and the average SAT score was 1164. In addition, students in Louisville's Catholic schools performed 204,626 hours of community service and received college scholarships and other cash awards valued at $87.8 million.

## CHRISTIAN ACADEMY OF LOUISVILLE
**700 South English Station Rd.**
**(502) 244-3225**
**www.christianacademylou.org**
Committed to the application of biblical principles in the education of young people, the mission of Christian Academy is the spiritual, intellectual, and physical development of its students. They strive to accomplish these objectives by offering a traditional education in a

Christian environment with a focus on excellent and diverse academic, fine arts, athletic, and extracurricular opportunities. The Christian Academy School System serves over 3,000 students in preschool through 12th grade on four campuses in the Louisville and Southern Indiana area, and each offers attractive and well-maintained facilities specifically designed to enhance the students' educational experience. Although the same environment is fostered at each location, every campus has its own unique feel.

## KENTUCKY COUNTRY DAY SCHOOL
**4100 Springdale Rd.**
**(502) 423-0440**
**www.kcd.org**
Located on a spacious 85-acre campus in eastern Jefferson County, Kentucky Country Day School is an independent, JK–12, coeducational college-preparatory school that combines a rigorous academic program with a wide variety of athletic and extracurricular programs. Established in 1972, the school has an enrollment of about 900, and a faculty that strives to create an intimate learning environment that is both challenging and supportive, and which fosters honor and accountability. Through a schoolwide honor code and the student-run Honor Council in the Upper School, KCD encourages students to take responsibility and to conduct themselves with integrity. The result is undeniably impressive: Every KCD graduate has matriculated in a college or university. In addition, Kentucky Country Day School boasts a high percentage of its alumni enrolled in the most prestigious and selective universities across the country.

## LOUISVILLE COLLEGIATE SCHOOL
**2427 Glenmary Ave.**
**(502) 479-0340**
**www.loucol.com**
The tree-lined campus of Louisville Collegiate School lies in the historic neighborhood of the Highlands near downtown Louisville, located on Grinstead Drive just across from Cave Hill Cemetery. It was founded at 512 West Ormsby Avenue in 1915 as the first school in Kentucky dedicated to "preparing young women for college," and in

1927 the school was moved to its current location because of the increase in enrollment and a lack of space. Today, the independent, nonsectarian, junior kindergarten through 12th grade school has gone coed, and has an enrollment of approximately 650 students. The school prides itself on its long tradition and a safe and invigorating environment where students can expand their knowledge, widen their worldview, and express their inner selves. Small class sizes ensure one-on-one attention as students pursue studies in a traditional curriculum. A number of Collegiate School teachers have received the prestigious Presidential Award for Excellence in Teaching, in addition to National Endowment for the Humanities grants and fellowships from the Klingenstein Foundation.

## OUR LADY OF PROVIDENCE JUNIOR-SENIOR HIGH SCHOOL
**707 Providence Way**
**Clarksville, IN**
**(812) 945-2538**
**www.providencehigh.net**
Our Lady of Providence Junior-Senior High School is a coed Catholic high school in Clarksville, Indiana, in the Roman Catholic Archdiocese of Indianapolis. The school first opened on September 12, 1951. Recognized as a Blue Ribbon School of Excellence by the U.S. Department of Education in 2000, Providence also receives accreditation from the Indiana Department of Education and the North Central Association of Colleges and Secondary Schools.

With a classroom ratio of 14 to 1, Providence is well regarded for its art and theater departments, as well as its lineup of extracurricular activities. The school does not discriminate on the basis of religion, ethnic origin, or ability; however, attendance at worship services is mandatory. A dress code is strictly enforced, and financial aid is available at this, southern Indiana's only Catholic upper school.

## ST. FRANCIS HIGH SCHOOL
**233 West Broadway**
**(502) 736-1000**
**www.sfhs.us**

St. Francis is an urban school that takes advantage of its location in downtown Louisville. Twice a month the school closes down in the morning so students and faculty can go out and perform community service, and the Louisville Free Public Library across the street is the main resource center for its students. Branding itself as "the School of Thought" in advertising throughout the community, St. Francis challenges its students with critical thinking and intellectual academics to prepare them for college, and life.

### WALDORF SCHOOL OF LOUISVILLE
**8005 New Lagrange Rd.**
**(502) 327-0122**
**www.waldorflouisville.com**

Since the Waldorf School of Louisville opened its doors in 1993, enrollment has increased steadily. Aside from grades one through five, you'll find a mixed-age kindergarten for children who are three and a half to six years old, and a prekindergarten program for children from the ages of two and half to three and a half. There is also a parent-child program for expectant parents and families with children from birth through three years old. An independent, private school that offers a developmentally appropriate, experiential approach to education, the Waldorf School of Louisville integrates academics and the arts for children from preschool through grade five. The aim of the Waldorf education is to enable students to fully develop their capabilities while inspiring lifelong learning. Warm, inviting classrooms encourage a sense of beauty in harmony with the natural surroundings, while wooded play yards provide safe and ample space for exploration of the natural sciences.

# COLLEGES, UNIVERSITIES, AND TRADE SCHOOLS

### BELLARMINE UNIVERSITY
**4201 Newburg Rd.**
**(502) 452-8000**
**www.bellarmine.edu**

This independent, Roman Catholic, liberal arts university in Louisville's Highlands neighborhood is the largest traditional, nonprofit private university in the state. It is a small school with several thousand students. The institution opened in 1950 as Bellarmine College, established by the Archdiocese of Louisville, who named it after the Catholic saint Robert Bellarmine. In 2000 the board of trustees changed the name to Bellarmine University. While offering one doctoral degree, it is currently classified as a Masters-I university. Accredited by the Southern Association of Colleges and Schools (SACS), the school is perennially ranked as a top-tier master's degree university in the South by *U.S. News & World Report*, and the W. Fielding Rubel School of Business is one of the select few to receive accreditation from the Association to Advance Collegiate Schools of Business.

### INDIANA UNIVERSITY SOUTHEAST
**9201 Grant Line Rd.**
**New Albany, IN**
**(812) 941-2333**
**www.ius.edu**

Established in 1941, Indiana University Southeast is a regional campus of the Indiana University system, located in New Albany, less than a 15-minute drive from downtown Louisville. The campus is situated at the edge of southern Indiana's picturesque "knobs," a region of rolling hills that run parallel to the Ohio River. With some 6,000 students, IU Southeast has earned a good reputation for its bachelor's degree programs in nursing, business, and education. They also offer a variety of other bachelor's degree programs, in addition to six master's and various associate degree programs. A large percentage of the students at IUS are considered nontraditional students, and most of the student body take advantage of the school's convenient scheduling—there are lots of night classes, and generally no classes on Fridays—to study while they work full- or part-time.

### JEFFERSON COMMUNITY & TECHNICAL COLLEGE
**109 East Broadway**
**502) 213-4000**
**www.jefferson.kctcs.edu**

Located in downtown Louisville, Jefferson Community & Technical College is one of 16 two-year, open-admissions colleges of the Kentucky Community and Technical College System. JCTC was formed on July 1, 2005, when Jefferson Community College and Jefferson Technical College consolidated. The largest college in the Kentucky Community and Technical College System, JCTC is accredited by the Southern Association of Colleges and Schools and can average around 15,000 students in a given semester. Aside from offering a wide range of academic and technical programs to prepare students to study for a four-year degree or to enter a career, JCTC also offers associate degrees, pre-baccalaureate education, and diploma and certificate programs in occupational fields. There are also opportunities for adult, continuing, and developmental education, as well as distance learning and customized training for business and industry.

## LOUISVILLE PRESBYTERIAN THEOLOGICAL SEMINARY
**1044 Alta Vista Rd.**
**(502) 895-3411**
**www.lpts.edu**
The Louisville Presbyterian Theological Seminary has a heritage that stems from seminaries founded by two branches of the Presbyterian Church: the Danville Theological Seminary, which first opened its doors to students in 1853 in Danville, and the Louisville Presbyterian Seminary, founded in Louisville in 1893. In 1901, the two seminaries united, and for some 60 years, the Louisville Presbyterian Theological Seminary educated students at its neo-Gothic digs in the downtown area, at First and Broadway. The seminary moved to its current location near scenic Cherokee Park in the spring of 1963, and it has grown considerably since 1983, when after 122 years of separation, the northern and southern branches of the Presbyterian Church reunited. In recent years, the LPTS has joined with other Presbyterian Church (USA) schools to offer tuition grants to all students eligible for assistance based on need. Among its recent accomplishments are a Grawemeyer Award in Religion, and the

Louisville institute, a Lilly Endowment–funded program based at Louisville Seminary, supporting those who lead and study at American religious institutions.

ℹ️ Created by Louisville industrialist and philanthropist H. Charles Grawemeyer in 1984, the lucrative Grawemeyer Awards at the University of Louisville consist of five annual $200,000 prizes given in the fields of music, political science, psychology, education, and religion. They were founded to help make the world a better place, and since the initial endowment of $9 million to fund the awards, nominations have come in from around the world.

## SIMMONS COLLEGE OF KENTUCKY
**1018 South Seventh St.**
**(502) 776-1443**
**www.simmonscollegeky.edu**
Located in historic Old Louisville, this institution of biblical higher education is "dedicated to educating people in the urban context through strong academic and professional programs in order that they may become productive citizens and agents of change in society." A historically black college, Simmons College was founded in 1879 at its current location; during the 1930s, it moved to the West End after losing its property in a foreclosure. In 2006, the school was able to buy back the property and relocate to the original campus. Simmons College of Kentucky is in applicant status for accreditation from the Association for Biblical Higher Education and is working toward accreditation from the Southern Association of Colleges and Schools. A small school, it has a staff of some 60 individuals and an enrollment of around 230 students.

## SOUTHERN BAPTIST THEOLOGICAL SEMINARY
**2825 Lexington Rd.**
**(800) 626-5525**
**www.sbts.edu**
Founded in 1859 in Greenville, South Carolina, as the first seminary of the Southern Baptist Con-

vention, the Southern Baptist Theological Seminary is the oldest of the six seminaries related to the SBC. Often referred to as "the mother seminary" in Baptist circles, it relocated to Louisville in 1877 after the Civil War left the seminary holding worthless Confederate war bonds in a newly impoverished area. Despite shaky times, Southern was able to grow and prosper, becoming one of the first seminaries in the nation to offer a PhD program. During the 1970s and '80s, it had the largest accredited PhD program in religion in the United States. It was also the first in the nation to offer courses in church social work and religious education, and it counts as one of the few seminaries in the country to offer a full degree course in church music. Its department of missions is one of the oldest in the world, and the Billy Graham School of Missions, Evangelism and Church Growth opened in 1994. Today, men and women from around the world and across the United States study at its attractive campus near Seneca Park. Laid out in the 1920s, the campus features a number of neo-Georgian and Colonial Revival structures.

## SPALDING UNIVERSITY
**845 South Third St.**
**(502) 585-9911**
**www.spalding.edu**
Located between downtown Louisville and the Old Louisville neighborhood, Spalding University is a fully accredited doctoral level university that provides a number of opportunities for a diverse community of learners. A coeducational, independent institute of higher education that is open to all qualified students regardless of race, religion, color, age, gender, sexual orientation, national origin, or disability, Spalding offers day classes for the traditional student, in addition to evening and weekend classes for the career-oriented learner and graduate classes for the advanced degree seeker. Spalding University opened the first Weekend College in the Louisville area in 1980, adding the Adult Accelerated Program (AAP) in 1998. The Adult Accelerated Program continues to have an impact on the Louisville community today, with students

## For Visitors

Throughout the year, the Southern Baptist Theological Seminary hosts a variety of lectures, concerts, recitals, and events featuring church music and drama that are open to the public. The Chapel's 113-rank Aeolian-Skinner organ—a magnificent instrument with some 6,000 pipes—is always a popular draw.

On the campus of the Southern Baptist Theological Seminary you'll also find the Joseph A Callaway Archaeological Museum. This small museum houses the Nicol Collection of Biblical Archaeology and the Eisenberg Collection of Egyptian and Near Eastern Antiquities. There is also an art gallery with rotating exhibits of a religious nature. Visitation is free, but the museum is closed on Sunday.

In addition, there's the James P. Boyce Centennial Library, a large space with nearly a million cataloged items that attracts scholars and researchers from around the globe. Although they may not check items out, private citizens are encouraged to visit the library and use its resources. Apart from numerous recordings and books, the music collection has tens of thousands of scores. There's also a rare Bible collection with a third-century papyrus fragment. The library is open Monday through Thursday from 7:45 a.m. to 10 p.m., Friday from 7:45 a.m. to 7 p.m., and Saturday from 11 a.m. to 7 p.m. For more information, call (502) 897-4713.

and graduates employed by businesses such as Ford Motor Company, UPS, Norton Healthcare, Humana, YUM! Brands, and Brown-Forman. The Spalding community also places a great deal of emphasis on service learning and volunteerism.

ℹ️ Tucked away behind the façade of the Spalding University's administration building at 851 South Fourth Street is one of the few remaining examples of Louisville's downtown residential architecture from the 1870s. A veritable time capsule of Victorian splendor, the Spalding Mansion is one of only a handful of surviving structures designed by Henry Whitestone. Instead of tearing it down in the 1940s, school officials had the new administration building built to incorporate the sumptuous residence for use as offices and reception areas, preserving the home's original grandeur for the public today. When school is in session, you're invited inside (free of charge) to enjoy the public spaces and get a glimpse of a bygone era; use the north entrance to get in.

## SPENCERIAN COLLEGE
**4627 Dixie Hwy.**
**(502) 447-1000**
**www.spencerian.edu**
To look at the modern, concrete building that houses Spencerian College today, you wouldn't think that its roots go back very far. However, this vocationally centered school goes back to the 1890s. Spencerian offers education only for those careers that are in demand, and students can pursue certificate, diploma, or associate degrees in a variety of concentrations, including health sciences, business, graphic design, computer-aided design, and more. Unique features of study at Spencerian include programs taught in quarters, a career-first curriculum where students take only the classes needed for their professions, and a four-day school week, with Friday set aside as the "plus" day for meetings with professors, studying, or relaxing. In addition, accelerated day

and evening programs allow learners to work while pursuing an education, and the school offers lifetime, nationwide employment services that help graduates to prepare for interviews and find employment. Graduates may also audit free of charge classes previously taken at any point in their careers.

## SULLIVAN UNIVERSITY
**3101 Bardstown Rd.**
**(502) 456-6505**
**www.sullivan.edu**
What was started primarily as a business school in 1962 has since grown to an accredited institution that is considered the largest private university in the state. Today, Sullivan has gained a reputation for its graduate employment record, the high numbers due in no small part to the lifetime employment assistance that helps graduates secure employment nationwide and around the globe. Students can earn career diplomas or certificates from Sullivan University in as little as nine months, and they can attend college at a time that fits their schedules; classes are offered during the day as well as on evenings and weekends, and online courses are also available.

Sullivan University offers a variety of majors—accounting, pharmacy, and travel/tourism are just a few—and there are even courses for training paralegals, future law enforcement officers, medical assistants, and professional nannies. It's also the home of its flagship program, the respected National Center for Hospitality Studies, where future chefs and caterers hone their skills. Aspiring chefs in this country no longer need to worry about getting into prestigious cooking schools like Johnson & Wales or the Culinary Institute of America to earn a respected degree in the culinary arts; Sullivan's program is consistently ranked as one of the best in the United States. Students can also earn a degree in hotel and restaurant management, and several on-campus businesses—a bakery and catering operation, for example—allow students hands-on opportunities to hone their chops in the food service industry.

## Culinary Classroom

Since becoming a professional chef demands practical experience, it's important to put what you've learned in the classroom to the test. That's why senior culinary students at the National Center for Hospitality Studies at Sullivan University serve a practicum at Winston's Restaurant, a three-and-a-half-star on-campus restaurant just off of Bardstown Road. Under the leadership of executive chef John Castro, student chefs prepare and serve gourmet dishes for an extensive menu of brunch, lunch, and dinner items. Considered one of the foremost culinary training restaurants in the country, Winston's has received numerous awards for its service and wine selection. This is the place to try a "Not Brown," a tasty rethink of the original open-faced sandwich invented at the Brown Hotel in the 1920s. Instead of turkey breast, toast points, and tomatoes, you'll find a creation of fried green tomatoes, shrimp, crab, bacon, spinach, and Mornay sauce that's every bit as tasty as the original. Winston's is a member of the Kentucky Restaurant Association, Louisville Originals, and the Chaine des Rôtisseurs, and has been featured by the Food Network, Travel Channel, *Food and Dining Magazine,* and *Wine Enthusiast* magazine, among others. Winston's Restaurant is located at 3101 Bardstown Rd. (502-456-0980; www.sullivan.edu/winstons).

## UNIVERSITY OF LOUISVILLE
**2301 South Third St.**
**(502) 852-5555**
**http://louisville.edu**

The University of Louisville is a state-supported research university located south of the downtown area on the outskirts of the Old Louisville neighborhood. When founded in 1798, it was among the first universities chartered west of the Allegheny Mountains, and it was the very first city-owned public university in the United States. It was a municipally supported public institution for many decades prior to joining the state university system in 1970, and the university has three campuses today: the main 287-acre Belknap Campus, home to 7 of the university's 11 colleges and schools; the Health Sciences Center, situated in downtown Louisville's medical complex, which houses the university's health-related programs and the University of Louisville Hospital; and the 243-acre Shelby Campus, located in eastern Jefferson County.

With a student body of some 20,000, U of L enrolls students from practically every Kentucky county, in addition to all 50 states and 116 countries from around the world; almost 6,000 individuals comprise the faculty and staff. The University of Louisville offers bachelor's degrees in 70 fields of study, master's degrees in 78 fields, and doctoral degrees in 22 areas of concentration. *U.S. News & World Report* considers the school's admission standards among the "more selective" of American colleges and universities.

Among its accomplishments as a center for medical research, the University of Louisville participated in the development of a highly effective vaccine against cervical cancer in 2006 and was instrumental in the development of the Pap smear test. It also carried out the first fully self-contained artificial heart transplant surgery and the first successful hand transplantation ever. In addition to having one of the first blood banks in this country, U of L is also credited with the first civilian ambulance and the nation's first accident services, now known as an emergency room.

In addition to medicine, U of L has achieved a good reputation in other areas as well. Their program in English rhetoric and composition is ranked among the best in the nation, and *Success* magazine has named it one of the top 25 schools for entrepreneurs. The Speed Scientific School, the university's school of engineering, enjoys an excellent reputation across the country and offers a number of degrees, including those in civil engineering, computer science, and engineering mathematics.

Kentucky's oldest, and the fifth-oldest law school in continuous operation in the United States, the U of L School of Law was established in 1848. It is the repository for the papers of former Supreme Court justices John Marshall Harlan and Louis Brandeis. In 1990 the law school became one of the first in the country to make pro bono, or donated, service a mandatory part of each law student's legal education.

## CHILD CARE

Google the term "Louisville childcare" and you'll get thousands of hits. There are hundreds of religious institutions, locally run agencies, and private establishments offering babysitting, daycare and nanny services. Information about some of the more wellknown providers follows.

### COMMUNITY COORDINATED CHILD CARE
**1215 South Third St.**
**(502) 636-1358**
**www.4cforkids.org**
Dedicated to improving the quality, availability, and accessibility of child care and early childhood development programs in the Kentuckiana area, Community Coordinated Child Care, or 4-C, has been a point of contact for local child-care needs for more than 40 years. One of the oldest child-care resource-and-referral organizations in the United States, this private, nonprofit Metro United Way agency was established in 1969 as part of a pilot program, whose aim was, and continues to be, the development of a comprehensive approach to coordinating child-care services in the local community. It looks to support families by ensuring that high-quality early childhood care is available to all.

---

### For Visitors

Modeled after the Jeffersonian Rotunda at the University of Virginia, Grawemeyer Hall is U of L's hallmark building that faces Third Street. In front sits a statue of *The Thinker* by Auguste Rodin. Although numerous casts can be found around the world, the Louisville cast is the first that was made from the original. Nearby is the final resting place for former U.S. Supreme Court justice Louis D. Brandeis and his wife under the portico of the Brandeis School of Law. Other points of interest on the Belknap Campus include the Rauch Planetarium, the galleries of the Hite Art Institute, and the Speed Art Museum, a private institution not affiliated with the University of Louisville. The Confederate War Veterans Monument, located nearby in front of the Speed Art Museum, at the juncture of Second and Third Streets, honors Confederate Civil War dead. It was built there before the university grew and surrounded the city-owned land where it stands.

---

### THE PROFESSIONAL NANNY PROGRAM AT SULLIVAN UNIVERSITY
**3101 Bardstown Rd.**
**(502) 413-8607**
**www.sullivan.edu/Early_Childhood_Education**
Since 1989 Sullivan University has been training and placing graduates of their professional nanny program, one of only a select few programs in the country to be accredited by the American Council of Nanny Schools. The program has grown to include an associate degree in early childhood education, and graduates are known

nationwide for their professional attitude and dedication to the child-care industry. In addition to first aid, CPR, and water rescue, all graduates receive valuable training in nutritional cooking, child development, and etiquette. Participants must also be nonsmokers and have successfully undergone background checks.

## SITTERS SERVICE
P.O.Box 436354
Louisville, KY 40253
502.254.2999
www.sittersservice.com

Touting itself as Louisville's premier childcare and nanny placement agency, Sitters Service has been serving Louisville and the surrounding areas for over 50 years. They pride themselves on being able to give their childcare providers and client families lots of individual attention, going to great lengths to get to know the individual families; childcase providers are meticulously pre-screened through an intense one-on-one process prior to their initial interview.

## YMCA CHILD CARE
2411 Bowman Ave.
(502) 637-1575
www.ymcalouisville.org

Offering a variety of programs to help children of all ages to expand their imaginations and foster lifelong values, various branches of the Louisville YMCA provide child-care services. Meeting and exceeding state standards for licensed child-care facilities, the YMCA prides itself on its efforts to hire and develop caring, loving, and devoted staff committed to providing quality care. The Chestnut Street YMCA, the Northeast YMCA, and the Southwest YMCA have programs specifically designed for infants, toddlers, and preschoolers, and many branches offer popular day camps during the summer.

**i** Children of working families in Kentucky may be eligible for free or low-cost health insurance. KCHIP is the Kentucky Children's Health Insurance Program that was developed to ensure coverage for children of working families who are unable to afford health insurance. The YMCA of Greater Louisville has partnered with KCHIP to help educate, screen, and enroll eligible children in KCHIP. For more information, call (800) 578-0603, ext. 78573.

# WORSHIP

**L**ike the majority of American cities, Louisville is dominated by the presence of Christian churches. Visitors often remark on the number of churches they will pass in a given neighborhood, and many wonder at the variety of styles that define Louisville's houses of worship. Redbrick structures of Gothic proportions, shining megachurches, steeples rising over sanctuaries that seem to have been plucked from the New England countryside, limestone masterpieces that resemble baroque opera houses more than churches, Mission-style roofs with walls of glazed brick—these are some of the images conjured up by the mention of Louisville churches. It seems almost as if influences from all corners of the globe have shaped the spiritual landscape in this city, at least architecturally speaking. Louisville is, however, a Christian town.

Although a number of synagogues—and even a Hindu temple—dot the community, a drive through town reveals a variety of houses of worship dedicated to the city's two main religious groups: Roman Catholics and Southern Baptists. In 1781 the Baptists had their first church in Kentucky, in Bardstown, and Squire Boone, the brother of Daniel Boone, reportedly traveled to Louisville to spread the news soon thereafter. The city's first Baptist church—the Baptist Church of the Beargrass—was founded in 1784 by Reverend John Whitaker; since then, it has been the dominant faith in the Derby City. A year later Roman Catholics, branching out from Maryland, established the first parish in Bardstown in what was considered "the West" back then, gradually making their way to Louisville. Influxes of Catholic immigrants from Ireland and Germany in the mid-1800s would solidify the presence of Catholicism in Kentucky's largest city.

During its early years, Louisville was considered a rough-and-tumble town where, as one Episcopalian minister supposedly said in 1820, "much caprice and indifference toward religion prevailed." A number of brothels catered to the needs of itinerant frontiersmen and workers in the city's burgeoning industries, many of which would include a dedication to vices such as drinking, smoking, and gambling. Given the prevalence of whiskey distilling, tobacco farming,

and horse racing in Kentucky's history, it's hardly surprising that many came to see its largest metropolitan center as "America's Original Sin City." Long before Las Vegas, long before other naughty towns that developed a reputation for gratifying vices, there was Louisville.

Men of the cloth were needed to civilize the rowdy, morally lax river town. Louisville Presbyterians welcomed their first minister in 1800, and it would be a Presbyterian who officiated at the funeral of city founder George Rogers Clark in 1818. In 1988 the Presbyterian Church USA made their headquarters here in a huge renovated building on the waterfront. Asa Shinn, a roaming Methodist preacher, arrived in 1806 and took on the added challenge of converting Native Americans in the area. Methodists were largely successful in this endeavor, and also attracted large numbers of African Americans. Methodists, like Presbyterians, still constitute a sizable part of the population.

Their Protestant comrades, the Lutherans, didn't arrive to establish a church until after the Civil War, and it is one of the less-visible denominations in Louisville today. During the years leading up to the Civil War, the congregations of local churches reflected the political divisiveness that overwhelmed the nation. Many churches split along southern or northern lines, and this is when groups like the Southern Baptists were born.

This is also the period when Protestants and Catholics alike began erecting large-scale buildings that would reflect the region's ethnic heritage, as well as a desire to monumentalize their faiths. The neo-Gothic Cathedral of the Assumption was built downtown on Fifth Street in 1852, and with its towering spire, it was said to be the tallest cathedral in the country at that time. St. John's Evangelical Church (1867) at 637 East Market Street and St. Martin of Tours (1853) at 639 South Shelby Street have detailed interiors that are the product of German woodcarvers and artisans.

Not long thereafter, institutions dedicated to the education of religious men began to appear in Louisville as well. In 1877, a massive structure with Flemish spires and gables went up on Broadway to accommodate the faculty and student body of the Southern Baptist Theological Seminary. The school, one of the largest of its kind in the world, would later move to its current location at 2825 Lexington Road. Students graduate from this seminary with degrees in theology, Christian education, social work, and church music, but in recent years some students have been disappointed to see a distinct swing to the right in the seminary's leanings.

Some twenty years later, the Presbyterians would also use Broadway for the location of an impressive seminary building, one that still stands today as part of Jefferson Community College. They, like the Southern Baptists, moved to Lexington Road in search of more space. By the time the Presbyterian Theological Seminary was built, a number of synagogues could be found in downtown Louisville as well. Jews had already become a permanent fixture on the city's religious scene by the 1880s, when Eastern Europeans began arriving on the banks of the Ohio. It was said that at one time, Yiddish was heard more frequently than English on Preston Street, a main thoroughfare for Jewish commerce, and "going out Preston way" became local jargon for dying because of the Jewish cemetery located at the end of the street. There were also so many people of the Jewish faith in Butchertown that for a while, it was known as "Jerusalem." Today,

## Grotto and Garden of Our Lady of Lourdes

In the small, triangular-shaped neighborhood of St. Joseph's, named for the now demolished St. Joseph's Infirmary, you'll find the long-forgotten Grotto and Garden of Our Lady of Lourdes. Constructed in 1927 and designed as part of the original hospital complex, the grotto and gardens provided a secluded place of quiet contemplation for staff, patients, and visitors. The site, near Eastern Parkway and Bradley Avenue, also has a marker placed there by the Kentucky Historical Society. It was built by the architectural firm of D. X. Murphy and Brothers, the inspiration for the grotto at St. Joseph's Infirmary coming from the famous Grotto of Our Lady of Lourdes in southern France. It was there that young Maria-Bernada Sobirós—later known as Saint Bernadette—claimed that the Virgin Mary visited her and spoke to her on 18 separate occasions between February 11 and July 16, 1858.

the Jewish community consists of nearly 10,000 people served by five synagogues. Jewish immigrants founded Jewish Hospital, which was once the center of the city's Jewish district; today, it's considered one of the nation's best heart and lung treatment centers. In recent years non-Judeo-Christian religions have begun leaving their mark on Louisville. Kentucky's only Hindu temple opened in suburban Louisville in 1999, and has several hundred members and two full-time priests. There are an estimated 10,000 Muslims practicing in Louisville at the moment, with a total of six local mosques.

Modern Louisville is often seen as a model for interfaith cooperation among U.S. cities, and membership in the Kentuckiana Interfaith Community includes churches, synagogues, the Board of Rabbis, the Catholic Archdiocese, the African Methodist Episcopalian Church, Presbyterian Church USA, the Indiana-Kentucky Synod/Evangelical Church, and others. It remains nonetheless a predominantly Protestant community, and far from its days as a religiously indifferent and capricious town, Louisville has incorporated Christianity into the social and political life of its residents. African-American pastors in the West End drum up rallies whenever there's a case of perceived police brutality, and Catholic schools have come to be known for the quality education they provide. Southeast Christian Church, a megachurch in the East End known as "Six Flags over Jesus" to many locals, boasts weekly attendance of 18,000 members and has facilities that rival those of local universities. Having established two satellite churches in the Louisville Metro area, it is Kentucky's largest church—and the sixth largest in the nation—and its conservative brand of Protestantism always plays a significant role in local elections.

Given its sometimes turbulent past regarding religion—on "Bloody Monday," August 6, 1855, at least 22 Irish and German immigrants were killed in anti-Catholic riots in downtown areas—Louisville has come a long way as far as tolerance is concerned. Despite its location in the Bible Belt, Louisville is a place where people keep largely to themselves where religion is concerned.

**i** For more information about news and special events in local churches, read the *Courier-Journal*'s weekly religion column, located on the second page of the Metro section in the Saturday edition.

**ABDULLAH MUHAMMED ISLAMIC CENTER**
**1917 Magazine St.**
**(502) 772-1500**

**CALVARY EPISCOPALIAN CHURCH**
**821 South Fourth St.**
**(502) 587-6011**
**www.calvaryepiscopal.org**

**THE CATHEDRAL OF THE ASSUMPTION**
**433 South Fifth St.**
**(502) 582-2971**
**www.cathedraloftheassumption.org**

**CHRIST CHURCH UNITED METHODIST**
**4614 Brownsboro Rd.**
**(502) 897-6421**
**www.ccum.net**

**CONCORDIA LUTHERAN CHURCH**
**1127 East Broadway**
**(502) 585-4459**
**www.concordia-lutheran.com**

**FIRST UNITARIAN CHURCH**
**809 South Fourth St.**
**(502) 585-5110**
**www.firstulou.org**

**HIGHLAND BAPTIST CHURCH**
**1101 Cherokee Rd.**
**(502) 451-3735**
**www.hbclouisville.org**

**HIGHLAND PRESBYTERIAN CHURCH**
**1011 Cherokee Rd.**
**(502) 451-2910**
**www.hpc-lou.org**

**HINDU TEMPLE OF KENTUCKY**
**4213 Accomack Dr.**
**(502) 429-8888**
**www.kytemple.org**

**ISLAMIC CULTURAL CENTER OF LOUISVILLE**
**4007 River Rd.**
**(502) 893-9466**

**KENESETH ISRAEL SYNAGOGUE**
2531 Taylorsville Rd.
(502) 459-2780
www.kenesethisrael.com

**ST. LOUIS BERTRAND CATHOLIC CHURCH**
1104 South Sixth St.
(502) 583-4448
www.stlb.org

**SOUTHEAST CHRISTIAN CHURCH**
920 Blankenbaker Pkwy.
(502) 253-8400
www.southeastchristian.org

**TEMPLE SHALOM**
4615 Lowe Rd.
(502) 458-4739
www.templeshalomky.org

**UNITY CHURCH OF MIDDLETOWN**
11700 Main St., Middletown
(502) 244-9696
www.unitychurchofmiddletown.com

**WALNUT STREET BAPTIST CHURCH**
1143 South Third St.
(502) 589-5290
www.walnutstreet.org

**i** Visitors to Louisville looking for a place to worship while they're away from home often attend the Unity Church of Middletown, "which is open to all people of faiths." All individuals are welcome to join "in recognizing and celebrating the Divine in everyone and affirm our oneness with Spirit and each other."

## ETHNIC SERVICES

In addition to the following houses of worship accommodating specific ethnic and language groups, the Kentucky Baptist Convention has a list of churches catering to certain ethnicities in Louisville on their Web site at www.kybaptist.org. Among the churches and ethnicities listed are:

# Walnut Street Baptist Church

A Gothic masterpiece of stone and mortar, the Walnut Street Baptist Church in Old Louisville is one of the most magnificent houses of worship in the entire city. Although its history is mostly an illustrious one, it was the center of a scandal that received national coverage in 1900. In the September 12 edition of the *New York Times,* a correspondent reported about an ongoing feud between adjacent homeowners and the church's pastor, Dr. Eaton. Whereas all the neighbors had adhered to their deed restrictions and built their mansions 30 feet back from the sidewalk to preserve the feel of a public promenade, the church had decided to flaunt the restrictions and planned to have its front doors open right onto the sidewalk. When asked if he wasn't bothered that these actions would devaluate his neighbors' properties, Eaton replied that "the church would buy the land when it got cheap." Despite the boycott that followed, the church carried out its plans and currently owns much of the adjacent property. To this day many Old Louisvillians still refuse to attend services at the Walnut Street Baptist Church.

## Chinese
**LOUISVILLE CHINESE CHRISTIAN CHURCH**
6120 Lovers Lane
(502) 231-6113

THIRD AVENUE BAPTIST CHURCH
1726 South Third St.
(502) 634-3673

## Eastern European

BUECHEL PARK BAPTIST CHURCH
2403 Hikes Lane
(502) 452-9541

HIGHVIEW BAPTIST CHURCH
7711 Fegenbush Lane
(502) 239-7711

## Filipino

GRACE FELLOWSHIP CHURCH
201 Biltmore Rd.
(502) 741-1705

## Haitian

LYNDON BAPTIST CHURCH
8025 La Grange Rd.
(502) 425-7150

LYNN ACRES BAPTIST CHURCH
5007 Southside Dr.
(502) 368-9593

## Korean

BETHANY BAPTIST CHURCH
2319 Taylorsville Rd.
(502) 542-2681

FIRST KOREAN BAPTIST CHURCH
5937 Six Mile Lane
(502) 499-7916

HURSTBOURNE BAPTIST CHURCH
8899 Shelbyville Rd.
(502) 426-2444

## Laotian

MELBOURNE HEIGHTS BAPTIST CHURCH
3728 Taylorsville Rd.
(502) 454-4681

## Vietnamese

BEECHMONT BAPTIST CHURCH
4574 South Third St.
(502) 368-5806

# RETIREMENT

In 2009 *Money* magazine listed Louisville as one of the 25 best places to retire, citing the "huge bang you get for your buck—plus lots of other perks" as reasons to think about choosing the Derby City for your post-work home. It's a city where roughly a third of the population is over 50, the typical three-bedroom home goes for $155,000, and the state income tax is 6 percent. In addition, it ranked high for the Louisville Loop, the not-yet-completed 100-mile series of paths and bikeways that will allow retirees easy access to many of the town's parks and neighborhoods. Given its relatively mild temperatures, it's also a place where residents usually don't have to worry about digging themselves out after a good winter's snow, and although late summers can get humid, the warm weather doesn't impede people from getting out and enjoying activities such as golf and boating. The scenery in the other two seasons is such that an individual can't help but want to head outdoors and make the most of the beautiful days; parks and neighborhood streets sparkle with the bright blossoms of dogwoods and redbud trees in the spring, and in autumn the riotous backdrop of turning leaves and church steeples begs for an easel and paints to capture the image on canvas.

The vibrant arts scene makes Louisville an attractive destination for retirees, along with the variety and quality of health care and services. Preventive care is a strong point, and there are renowned centers devoted to specialties in heart and lung problems, cancer treatment, and geriatrics. Aside from women's treatment centers, there is also an assortment of adult day-care centers, nursing homes, and assisted living communities. And if volunteering is your thing, hospitals and shelters are always on the lookout for helping hands, as are places like the Brown Theatre, Iroquois Amphitheater, Actors Theatre of Louisville, and the Kentucky Center for the Arts; when you volunteer to usher at one of these locations, it's a great way to see the show for free.

## AGENCIES, ORGANIZATIONS, AND SERVICES

### AARP (AMERICAN ASSOCIATION OF RETIRED PERSONS)
10401 Linn Station Rd., Suite 121
(866) 295-7275
www.aarp.org/states/ky
AARP, formerly known as the American Association of Retired Persons, is a nonprofit, nonpartisan membership organization for people age 50 and over that is "dedicated to enhancing the quality of life for all as we age." It is one of the largest membership organizations for individuals 50 and over in the United States. Like its sister chapters around the country, the Kentucky branch of the

AARP provides a wide range of unique benefits, special products, and services for its members. With over 35 million members nationwide, it is one of the most powerful lobbying groups in the United States, and it also sells insurance, investment funds, and other financial products.

### AGING RESOURCE CENTER
900 South Fourth St.
(502) 589-4941
A phone call to this organization that acts as an umbrella agency to a large number of local organizations serving the aged will put you in touch with groups ranging from the Alzheimer's Association to medical centers for veterans. The center also hosts a speakers network and pro-

# Close-up

## Louisville Metro Human Services Senior Nutrition Program

The Senior Nutrition Program of Louisville Metro Human Services provides nutritional lunchtime meals to senior citizens throughout the area. Nutrition sites that are generally open Monday through Friday from 9 a.m. to 1 p.m. offer seniors the chance to meet at these neighborhood locations for socialization, activities, and a nutritious lunch. The Meals on Wheels program ensures that the elderly who are homebound receive home-delivered meals from the various nutrition sites. Anyone age sixty or older and/or homebound due to illness is eligible for these meals. To qualify, candidates receive an in-home visit from a social worker who assesses need; those in the greatest physical, social, and economic need are given priority as a vacancy becomes available. Waiting lists are maintained to accommodate the growing need in this community.

This program also allows seniors the chance to volunteer their time while providing a much-needed service in delivering meals to the homebound elderly. Currently, more than 300 meals are served each day on approximately 24 routes. Although the volunteer's primary role is to deliver a nutritional meal to senior citizens who aren't able to leave their homes, they are also instrumental in maintaining one-on-one contact with the recipients. For some homebound seniors, the volunteer delivering the meals is their only social interaction; the Nutrition Office therefore depends on volunteers to report any changes or information concerning the Meals on Wheels client. For more information, visit the Web site at www.louisvilleky.gov/HumanServices.

grams that explores issues relevant to the community. In addition, the Aging Resource Center has a helpful staff of friendly volunteers and a well-stocked resource library that specializes in publications dealing with the psychological and social aspects of aging. Interested parties can also sign up for a free newsletter that keeps you abreast of the various activities and opportunities provided by the center.

**KENTUCKY ASSOCIATION OF HOMES AND SERVICES FOR THE AGING**
**2501 Nelson Miller Pkwy.**
**(502) 992-4380**
**www.kahsa.com**
Founded in 1977, the Kentucky Association of Homes and Services for the Aging (KAHSA) strives to enhance the quality of life of its members by developing leadership, advancing sound public policy, providing education, sharing information, and facilitating networking opportunities. It represents a variety of not-for-profit community, church, proprietary, and government-sponsored health-care facilities, as well as retirement communities, assisted living, housing, and service programs for the elderly and the disabled. KAHSA members include assisted living facilities, independent housing units, nursing facilities, intermediate care centers for the mentally challenged continuing care retirement communities, retired seniors volunteer programs, and multifacility agencies offering direct care. KAHSA is affiliated with the American Association of Homes and Services for the Aging (AAHSA), the national organization of homes and services for the aging, located in Washington, D.C.

**LIFESPAN RESOURCES, INC.**
**33 State St., Third Floor**
**New Albany, IN**
**(812) 948-8330**
**www.lsr14.org**
Established in 1973, LifeSpan Resources, Inc. has as its mission the promotion of independent living for people of all ages. It is the designated local agency on aging for Clark, Floyd, Harrison,

and Scott Counties in southern Indiana. It is one of 16 regional agencies that serve the state, and its responsibilities include the development and coordination of programs and services which enable older adults and persons with disabilities of any age to remain independent in their own homes. Some services are provided directly from LifeSpan, and others are contracted with home health-care agencies, nonprofit entities, and private-sector businesses. Specific services include care management, outreach, counseling, legal advice, nutrition, and transportation.

## LOUISVILLE METRO OFFICE FOR AGING & DISABLED CITIZENS
**810 Barret Ave., Room 329**
**(502) 574-5092**
**www.louisvilleky.gov/HumanServices/**
**SeniorsAgingServicesResources**
The Office for Aging & Disabled Citizens is the city government's way to provide information on community resources to citizens who are aging and disabled, and to the community at large. It strives to educate about the needs of aging and disabled citizens while serving as a valuable resource of information and referrals to individual citizens. It also provides community groups with consultation on aging and disability issues and participates in community initiatives to sustain and improve funding and services for the aging and disabled. In addition to advocating for rights and policies that enhance the lives of seniors and disabled individuals, it also offers collaboration on housing, crime and safety, elder abuse, and issues that impact the quality of life of Louisville's aging population. For more information, contact the program coordinator at (502) 574-5092, or visit the Human Services link for Metro Louisville online at www.louisvilleky.gov/HumanServices.

# RESIDENCES AND COMMUNITIES

## BAPTIST TOWERS
**1014 South Second St.**
**(502) 587-6632**
Almost 200 subsidized apartments are available

for rent in this 17-story high-rise centrally located between downtown Louisville and the Old Louisville neighborhood. Efficiency and one-bedroom apartments come with one bath, and an average rent is about $340 per month. Floor area listed varies between 358 and 496 square feet, and amenities include a laundry, community room, van outings, and an activities building with pot-luck dinners, bingo, and arts and crafts.

## EPISCOPAL CHURCH HOME
**7504 Westport Rd.**
**(502) 736-7800**
**www.echky.org**
Providing senior living since 1881, the Episcopal Church Home is an interdenominational Christian community retirement and care facility, dedicated to providing a full range of high-quality resident services. From long-term Alzheimer's/memory care to short-term rehabilitation, individual residents and couples of all faith traditions are served. Located in the East End, the Episcopal Church Home offers on-site independent living options as well: Dudley Square allows for independent living in individual patio homes with convenient access to friends, activities, and emergency medical care.

## HILLEBRAND HOUSE
**1235 South Third St.**
**(502) 634-4878**
Consisting of subsidized efficiency and one-bedroom apartments, 240 independent living units are offered at this high-rise in the heart of the Old Louisville neighborhood. In addition to sponsoring many activities, including pancake breakfasts, birthday parties, and cookouts, the Hillebrand House has a beauty shop and a lunch nutrition program. In-house groceries and van outings are added perks, and residents are encouraged to grow flowers and vegetables in an assigned garden plot.

## JEFFERSON MANOR
**1801 Lynn Way**
**(502) 426-4513**
This swanky East End nursing center features

an outdoor courtyard, semi-private and private rooms, and Medicare certification. In addition to physical therapy, occupational therapy, respiratory therapy, and speech therapy, restorative nursing services are available. A daily menu allows residents to select their favorite foods and eat in their rooms, the lounge that overlooks the courtyard, or in the formal dining room, which features waitress service. Housekeeping services are provided as well, and there is assistance with bathing and dressing if needed. A range of organized group activities is offered, and all areas of the building are sparkling clean and tastefully furnished. Named Kentucky Facility of the Year, Jefferson Manor has also received national awards for their interior design.

## LOURDES HALL
**735 Eastern Pkwy.**
**(502) 569-3902**
**www.lmha1.org**
Built in 1984, Lourdes Hall is a senior living site located off of Eastern Parkway in the St. Joseph neighborhood near the University of Louisville. There are five floors with 62 efficiency and one-bedroom units, in addition to two community rooms and a television room for resident use. Trash compressors and two laundry rooms are located on each floor. Key card access is needed to move around within the building. Conveniently located on one of the main bus routes, Lourdes Hall is also located near a grocery store, drugstore, and a walking track.

## PURITAN APARTMENTS
**1244 South Fourth St.**
**(502) 634-4731**
**www.beaconproperty.com**
Once the most prestigious hotel in Louisville, the old Puritan was restored and updated in 1978 to accommodate today's seniors and handicapped population. The magnificent entry and front lobby still remind residents of its days as a grand hotel in the 1920s, and its corner location ensures that most of the rooms get lots of sunshine and fresh breezes. Located just five minutes from downtown, the Puritan offers its residents lots

of amenities, including a nondenominational chapel, a game room, a recreational area with exercise machines, and an in-house grocery. In addition, pets are welcome.

## ST. CATHERINE COURT
**1114 South Fourth St.**
**(502) 569-3759**
**www.lmha1.org**
Built in the 1970s, this building on the southwest corner of Fourth and St. Catherine in Old Louisville underwent a comprehensive $12 million modernization in 2003. The 15-story high-rise has 159 efficiency and one-bedroom units serving a clientele of elderly and non-elderly alike. Features include exterior seating areas, raised panel doors, and entrances designed for accessibility; a door-entry system and additional lighting ensure increased security. St. Catherine is located next to a grocery store and is only a short distance away from downtown Louisville.

## SHALOM TOWER
**3650 Dutchmans Lane**
**(502) 454-7795**
**www.jewishlouisville.org**
Owned and managed by Urban Innovations, Shalom Tower is a federally funded independent living facility with 144 one-bedroom and 6 two-bedroom apartments for older adults and handicapped persons. Located adjacent to the Jewish Community Center, it offers its residents the opportunity to participate in a wide variety of community activities that promote residents' physical, mental, spiritual, and social well-being. An entire floor is dedicated to its residential activities and programs. English as a Second Language classes are offered on-site, and residents often use the Jewish Community Center's 14-passenger van for theater excursions and shopping trips. Located directly on a major bus line, Shalom Tower sits very near a number of shopping centers as well.

## TREYTON OAK TOWERS
**211 West Oak St.**
**(502) 589-3211**
**www.treytonoaktowers.com**

Located at the corner of Third and Oak in the heart of Old Louisville, Treyton Oak Towers offers an elegantly traditional lifestyle for senior adults looking for the company and security of a retirement community. However, this is a cut above the typical such community with its beautiful decor, spacious high-rise apartments, and luxury living. In addition, a full-service salon and an in-house bank cater to the needs of residents, and guests are often entertained in high style in the dining room, where waiters take their orders and serve them with aplomb.

## SENIOR CITIZEN CENTERS

**ALMOST FAMILY**
**4545 Bishop Lane, Suite 201**
**(502) 893-1661**
**www.almostfamily.com**
Almost Family has been a national leader in personal care services, home health nursing, and rehabilitation for over 30 years, providing skilled care in local communities under a variety of respected company names. With the goal of promoting personal independence so as to allow seniors to age in place for as long as possible, Almost Family has a clinical team that looks beyond the obvious needs of the patient in an effort to become advocates in all dimensions of their physical, mental, and emotional well-being. Since the home is the ideal setting to promote healing, comfort, and support of those facing the challenges of aging, they take their expertise to the clients, where they live. In addition to in-home care, they also offer adult day-care services where clients are picked up at their residences and then shuttled to a location for an activity-filled day of recreation and stimulation.

**ARTHUR S. KLING CENTER**
**219 West Ormsby Ave.**
**(502) 636-3424**
**www.neighborhoodlink.com**
Since 1978, the Arthur S. Kling Center has provided seniors 55 and older with a safe and convenient meeting and activity center in the heart of Old Louisville. Offering a host of activities

designed to help older people maintain a full and active lifestyle, the Kling Center has many opportunities for education, recreation, fellowship, and local travel. Inside, you'll find a pool table, exercise equipment, card games, puzzle-making, weekly bingo, exercise classes, monthly birthday parties, and more. The Kling Center also hosts informative weekly and monthly guest lecturers that afford attendees the opportunity to learn about topics of special interest to seniors, like health and legal matters, community affairs, aging issues, social security, Medicare, and Medicaid. Hours are Monday through Friday from 8:30 a.m to 4:30 p.m.

### Recreation for Senior Citizens

Metro Parks Senior Services offer a variety of social and athletic programs for senior citizens, including dances and card games. The Senior Services staff also conducts the annual Fifty and Over Games, and provides programs for senior citizens in the Kentucky State Fair's Heritage Hall. Interested seniors meet at one of two locations, the Flaget Senior Center or the Wilderness Road Senior Center, which are open Monday to Friday from 8 a.m. to 5 p.m. Hours for the fitness room are 9 a.m. to noon. For more information, go online at www.louisvilleky.gov/MetroParks/recreation/seniors.htm.

**Flaget Senior Center**
4425 Greenwood Ave.
(502) 574-2831

**Wilderness Road Senior Center**
8111 Blue Lick Rd.
(502) 964-5151

## JEFFERSONTOWN SENIOR CITIZENS CENTER
**10631 Watterson Trail**
**(502) 267-9112**
**www.jeffersontownky.com/srctr.html**
Well known throughout the region, and regarded as a model center by other cities across the country, the Jeffersontown Senior Citizens Center is noted for a wide variety of activities, programs, and services. Located in a historic building in downtown Jeffersontown in the East End, its setting makes it a popular gathering place for its 2,400 members. Attractive interior decorating and pleasant color schemes add to the draw. In addition to a 4,200-square-foot ballroom for dances and parties, the first floor has a kitchen-dining area, a meeting room with plush furniture and fireplace, and an activity room; on the second floor seniors have access to a computer classroom, a craft and sewing room, an exercise and fitness room, hair salon, a quilting room, and more. Welcoming seniors Monday through Friday, the Jeffersontown Senior Citizens Center is open from 8 a.m. to 3 p.m.

# MEDIA

One of the best ways to get a feel for the community—what it's all about, what's going on, what is important to the residents—is to pick up a newspaper. It's a good way to feel like a native, as well. Sitting with the local daily over a cup of coffee in a neighborhood diner or entrenched in a comfortable chair in the hotel lobby—this is the way to take the pulse of the town. Louisville has a variety of newspapers and magazines that make it easy to keep abreast of happenings and goings-on in town, but there are other sources of news and information as well. A goodly number of television and radio stations make use of the spoken word, and, increasingly, more and more people are turning to the Internet for local sources that inform and entertain.

All in all, the Louisville media has enjoyed a solid reputation among its counterparts across the nation, and this is backed up by regular recognition of its quality and accomplishments. WHAS Radio was a pioneer in broadcasting, and its clear-channel signal allows it to be heard in most of the United States today; the *Courier-Journal*—even since Gannett took them over—has consistently ranked as one of the best newspapers in the country, winning numerous Pulitzer Prizes over the years. In recent decades, a number of upstarts such as *Business First* and *LEO* (*Louisville Eccentric Observer*) have managed to become fixtures on the regional news scene as well. Even local television stations are reported by those in the industry as being more serious and less sensationalistic than stations in other parts of the country.

That having been said, Louisville radio often leans to the conservative side, and a healthy number of stations are devoted to religious talk and gospel music. Louisville public radio—there are three separate public radio stations in town—has really distinguished itself and has become the envy of larger cities that cannot claim the same number of stations, not to mention the same quality of programming.

Obviously, you will have no trouble staying up-to-date on local happenings in the Derby City; whatever you decide on—newspaper, magazine, online publication, radio, or TV—this list should have you feeling like one of the locals in no time at all.

## ALTERNATIVE WEEKLIES

### LOUISVILLE ECCENTRIC OBSERVER
640 South Fourth St.
(502) 895-9770
www.leoweekly.com

The *Louisville Eccentric Observer*—most widely known as *LEO*—is a free newspaper that is distributed every Wednesday in over 800 locations throughout the Louisville area. You can pick up a copy at most bookstores, coffee shops, colleges, shops, etc. The 'Ville's most popular urban weekly, it was founded in 1990 by now-U.S. Representative John Yarmuth and then University of Louisville men's basketball coach, Denny Crum, among others. It claims a readership of almost 200,000. Not one to take itself too seriously, *LEO* is a mainstay for the younger crowd and those in the arts. Needless to say, most consider it a rather liberal publication, something that has always balanced the relative journalistic gravity of the *Courier-Journal (CJ)*.

### VELOCITY
525 West Broadway
(502) 582-4011
www.louisville.metromix.com

# Close-up

## The *Courier-Journal*

Without a doubt the "main" newspaper in the Derby City, the *Courier-Journal* (525 West Broadway; 502-582-4011; www.courier-journal.com), traces its roots back to the 1860s when several city papers merged. According to the 1999 *Editor & Publisher International Yearbook*, the *CJ*, as it's known to locals, is the single largest daily in Kentucky and counts as the 48th-largest daily paper in the United States. Its editorial voice has generally shown a liberal bent, relatively speaking; however, it's swung a bit to the right since the days when it encouraged readers to take to the streets and protest the second inauguration of Richard Nixon.

In recent years, the biggest shake-up occurred when the Bingham family—the Kentucky stalwarts of journalistic excellence—sold the daily to the Gannett chain. Most saw the sale as the demise of the newspaper's glory days, when the arts and literature occupied a revered position in the *CJ* lineup. Nonetheless, most journalists agree that the *Courier-Journal* still cuts the mustard when stacked up against the dailies in other cities of a comparable size. In 2005 cartoonist Nick Anderson became the most recent member of the *CJ* to win a Pulitzer Prize.

As might be expected, however, an abundance of sports coverage reflects local tastes, and lifestyle and food columns in the Features section garner faithful readers, though many complain that the weekly "Travel" section falls short of the mark. The *Courier-Journal* also owns the alternative weekly paper *Velocity*, which is provided free of charge.

It is estimated that some 500,000 people read the *Courier-Journal* daily, and almost 700,000 read it on Sunday. Like many of the nation's established newspapers, the *Courier-Journal* has been suffering the effects of a poor economy and the trend away from print media. On July 8, 2009, it was announced that 44 employees would be laid off, reducing the workforce to only 575 workers.

First published in December of 2003 by the *Courier-Journal*, *Velocity* is a free full-color tabloid that is distributed at some 1,800 locations through a 13-county area that encompasses Louisville and parts of southern Indiana. It has been widely seen as an attempt by the *CJ* and its parent company, Gannett, to snatch some of the market away from the *Louisville Eccentric Observer*. Although most consider it consciously nonpolitical, *Velocity* has on occasion covered hot-button issues such as gay life, the Iraq War, and the ban on public smoking in Louisville. The target demographic is readers in their 20s and 30s, and regular weekly features include columns about the town's nightlife and entertainment scene. "Rock This Town" profiles a local band or musician, and "The Party Crasher" features a photo-story about big parties that were held over the weekend. "The Bar Hopper" always spotlights a local tavern, and "All I'm Saying Is" ponders a reader-submitted essay. Another popular part of *Velocity*'s lineup is "The Big Screen." The latter is a movie section detailing movies playing locally with humorous one-paragraph reviews.

## DAILY NEWSPAPERS

**THE *EVENING NEWS***
**221 Spring St,**
**Jeffersonville, IN**
**(812) 206-2187**
**www.news-tribune.net**

Serving Jeffersonville and Clark County, Indiana, the *Evening News* comes out six days a week. It is published in the morning on the weekends and in the afternoons on weekdays; there is no Monday edition. It is owned by the Birmingham-based Community Newspaper Holdings, Inc., and it shares a publisher, editor, staff, and other resources, with the *Evening News* of Jeffersonville in neighboring Floyd County, Indiana. The daily circulation is around 7,000, and for a small-town newspaper, many readers think it takes a harder approach to news than many of its contemporaries.

## THE TRIBUNE
**303 Scribner Dr,**
**New Albany, IN**
**(812) 206-2192**
**www.news-tribune.net**

This six-day daily primarily serves Floyd County and New Albany, Indiana. There is no Monday edition, and it publishes in the morning on the weekends and in the afternoons on weekdays. It is owned by Community Newspaper Holdings, Inc., a company based in Birmingham, Alabama. The newspaper shares a publisher, editor, staff, and other resources, notably its Web site, with the *Evening News* of Jeffersonville in neighboring Clark County, Indiana. The daily circulation is between 5,000 and 10,000, and most of its coverage tends to the nonconfrontational. Local high school sports is a mainstay.

# INTERNET

## LOUISVILLE MOJO
**www.louisvillemojo.com**

Based on the Web standard of total engagement (number of visits multiplied by the average session length), this site is the most popular in the state. They serve over 600,000 visits a month, with the average session lasting 26 minutes. At Louisville Mojo, there's coverage of local media, politics, issues, food and dining, regional events, and more.

## 'VILLE VOICE
**www.thevillevoice.com**

Folks at the 'Ville Voice like to provide a "critical take on Louisville news." An examination of regional politics, as covered in the city's major media outlets, forms the bulk of the online postings; however, current events and items of local interest make an appearance as well. A sister site, 'Ville Voice Eats, covers the food and dining scene in town.

# MAGAZINES

## FOOD & DINING LOUISVILLE EDITION
**P.O. Box 665**
**Louisville, KY 40201**
**(502) 493-5511**
**www.foodanddiningmagazine.com**

With all the production values of a national publication and the focus and sensibility of a local magazine, *Food & Dining* is a Louisville-based metropolitan lifestyle trimonthly that focuses on the experience of dining out in and around Louisville. Apart from food and cooking, the enjoyment of wine and spirits figures prominently in the mix, and every issue features tips and recipes from the top restaurant chefs in the city. There are also compelling articles and personal interest stories that introduce readers to the food growers and artisans that make the Louisville dining scene as rich and vibrant as it is. Included in each issue is a restaurant section and dining guide to help you navigate your way through the hundreds of locations featured; in addition, there's a map directory that pinpoints more than 1,000 restaurants. Another plus is the beautiful photography by Pulitzer Prize–winning photographer Dan Dry.

## LOUISVILLE MAGAZINE
**137 West Muhammad Ali Blvd., #101**
**(502) 625-0100**
**www.loumag.com**

Started in March 1950 by the Louisville Chamber of Commerce as a quarterly publication, the magazine quickly evolved into a monthly journal of the most interesting happenings in the Derby City. Today the general interest magazine is owned by Louisvillian Dan Crutcher and includes regular features on dining, arts, entertainment, and local personalities. Every year readers vote on the Best of Louisville awards for everything from the top restaurants to the best places to buy a Derby dress, and the coveted awards are often prominently displayed throughout the city. Widely recognized as the city's best and most influential magazine, *Louisville Magazine* has won hundreds of awards for writing, photography, and design from the Society of Professional Journalists.

## TODAY'S WOMAN
**9750 Ormsby Station Rd., Suite 307**
**(502) 327.8855**
**www.iamtodayswoman.com**
Provided free of charge to its readers through the support of its advertisers, *Today's Woman* is a monthly magazine with a distribution area that includes Jefferson, Oldham, Shelby, Nelson, and Bullitt counties in Kentucky, and the Indiana counties of Clark, Floyd, Scott, and Harrison. It has grown over the years since its first issue in December 1991, and now counts as one of the premier regional women's magazines in the country. By providing information on current issues, future opportunities, and successful women, *Today's Woman* strives to motivate women to make positive changes. Read by women (and men) from all walks of life, it is available in more than 200 major outlets. Pickup sites include all Louisville-area and Southern Indiana Kroger, Whole Foods, and Valu-Market grocery stores, as well as libraries, liquor stores, YMCAs, Paul's Markets, Panera Bread cafes, Rainbow Blossom stores, Curves, hospitals, and other medical facilities.

## TRAVELHOST OF GREATER LOUISVILLE
**7202 KY 329**
**(502) 241-2643**
**www.travelhostlouisville.com**
The oldest, largest, and best-known visitor services publication in the United States, *TravelHost* is published bimonthly and represents Greater Louisville and southern Indiana to visitors and guests from around the world. Packed with tour guides, maps, and lists of the region's best restaurants, art galleries, day-trip destinations, historic places, performing arts, shopping, and museums, TravelHost also features relocation tips and comfort services.

## UNDERWIRED MAGAZINE
**P.O. Box 5128**
**Louisville, KY 40255**
**www.underwiredmagazine.com**

Pick up this this monthly magazine for and about women free of charge at locations primarily in downtown and the East End of Louisville. Distributing some 20,000 copies a year, they make sure there are always stacks of the magazine at a multitude of local groceries, gift shops and cafes. Underwired's goal is to support women in "their pursuit of meaningful work, creative passion and other spirited adventures," and they accept submissions of personal essays and artwork for publication.

## WELCOME TO GREATER LOUISVILLE
**812 South Third St.**
**(502) 584-2720**
**www.kytravel.com**
This is Louisville's complete visitors' guide, updated every other Wednesday since 1951. In addition to useful information about restaurants, shopping, accommodations, and points of interest, readers can also find out about the sightseeing tours, conventions, and special events that make the Derby City an interesting place to live and visit. There are also good recommendations for vacation rentals, spas, theater, and sports. The publisher, Editorial Services Company, also puts out a yearly *Kentucky Travel Guide* that will help you navigate the Bluegrass State.

# REGIONAL PUBLICATIONS

## KENTUCKY LIVING
**4515 Bishop Lane**
**(502) 451-2430**
**www.kentuckyliving.com**
*Kentucky Living* is a magazine devoted to Kentucky people, places, history, and events. Published by the Kentucky Association of Electric Cooperatives, it strives to support electric cooperatives in Kentucky by creating a community of people "who take pride in thinking of themselves as Kentuckians and as knowledgeable electric co-op members in order to improve their quality of life." Travel and annual events, cooking, homes, and gardens are just some of the topics covered. *Kentucky Living* magazine is the largest-circulation publication in the state; each month it is received

by 487,000 homes and businesses, and is read by more than 1.26 million people.

### KENTUCKY MONTHLY
**106 St. James Court, Frankfort**
**(502) 227-0053**
**www.kentuckymonthly.com**
A general interest magazine about all things Kentucky, *Kentucky Monthly* was founded in 1998 by Stephen Vest, Kay Vest, and Michael Embry. Based in Frankfort, the state capital, the magazine features all aspects of contemporary Kentucky culture and presents an annual Kentuckian of the Year award. In 2005 *Kentucky Monthly* was featured in the Stu Pollard film, *Keep Your Distance*, in a scene where the main character was presented with the award. In the same year, *KM* also received the "Governor's Awards in the Arts" for media, the Commonwealth's highest prize in the arts. In addition to regular columns about regional history, sites of interest to travelers, and sports, patrons can also read up on the trends in Bluegrass cooking, dining, arts, and literature. Famous Kentuckians are profiled as well: George Clooney was featured on the very first—and the 101st—cover.

### THE LETTER
Your respected source for GLBT news, information, and community updates since June 1990, the *Letter* is published in Louisville and provides a gay and feminist perspective on the regional news of the day. Although it caters to the gay community, it has a faithful following of straight readers as well.

## WEEKLY PUBLICATIONS

### AL DÍA EN AMÉRICA
**P.O. Box 206275**
**Louisville KY 40250**
**(502) 451-8489**
**www.aldiaenamerica.com**
The only Spanish-language newspaper in Louisville, *Al Día en América* is a growing biweekly publication that plans on going weekly soon. With an estimated 65,000 readers, it is a free newspaper that is distributed to over 320 different locations in key traffic areas throughout southern Indiana and north central Kentucky, where people in the community live, work, and play. Most of the readers are native speakers of Spanish and come from Mexico; however, there are significant numbers of immigrants from Cuba, Puerto Rico, and Central America as well. Many are refugees who were located in Louisville through federal resettlement programs.

### BUSINESS FIRST
**455 South Fourth St., Suite 278**
**(502) 583-1731**
**http://louisville.bizjournals.com**
One of 42 subsidiaries of American City Business Journals, the nation's largest publisher of metropolitan business newspapers, *Business First* serves its market well, staying clear of controversial subjects and focusing on commerce, trade, and the movers and shakers of the Derby City. It's sold at newsstands, in street boxes, and by subscription. A popular resource for local businesspeople is the *Business First of Louisville Book of Lists,* which provides the rankings for hundreds of the hottest area companies in their fields, in addition to the names of key decision makers, their titles, and complete contact information.

### THE LOUISVILLE DEFENDER
**P.O. Box 2557**
**Louisville, KY 40201**
**(502) 772-2591**
Published weekly every Thursday, the *Louisville Defender* has been the voice of the black community in the Derby City since 1933. Aside from pieces centering on local events and personalities, it also runs Associated Press stories of particular interest to African Americans that often get overlooked in the mainstream media. Available at local retail outlets and by subscription, copies cost 50 cents.

### VOICE TRIBUNE
**130 St. Matthews Ave., Suite 300**
**(502) 897-8900**
**www.voice-tribune.com**

Published on Thursday, the former *Voice of St. Matthews* has been covering happenings in the East End for over 50 years now. With a circulation of some 8,000, it counts as one of the state's largest paid weeklies. Heavy on the society end, it's a community paper with obituaries and lots of photos of weddings and charity galas. In addition to two society columns by veteran columnists Lucie Blodgett ("The Social Side") and Carla Sue Broecker ("Party Line"), readers of the *Voice Tribune* can read regular pieces by Angie Fenton ("The Dish"), Ashley Medley ("Style File"), and Shari Baughman ("Around the Town"). A number of columns written by nationally syndicated columnists are also included.

## Louisville Television Stations

| Station | Channel |
|---------|---------|
| WAVE | 3 |
| WBKI | 7 |
| WHAS | 11 |
| WKPC | 15 |
| Metro TV | 25 |
| WLKY | 32 |
| WDRB | 41 |

## Louisville Radio Stations

**AM Stations**

| Call Letters | Frequency | Format |
|--------------|-----------|--------|
| WTUV | 620 | Spanish |
| WKRD | 790 | Sports |
| WGTK | 970 | News/Talk |
| WLCR | 1040 | Christian |
| WKJK | 1080 | News/Talk |
| WLLV | 1240 | Christian |
| WLOU | 1350 | Christian |
| WQKC | 1450 | Sports |
| WNDA | 1570 | News/Talk |
| NOAA/ Trimarc | 1610 | Traffic/ Weather |

**FM Stations**

| Call Letters | Frequency | Format |
|--------------|-----------|--------|
| WJIE | 88.5 | Christian |
| WFPK | 89.3 | News/Talk |
| WUOL | 90.5 | Classical |
| WFPK | 91.9 | Alternative |
| WTFX | 93.1 | Rock |
| WLCL | 93.9 | Oldies |
| WULF | 94.3 | Country |
| WFIA | 94.7 | Christian |
| WQMF | 95.7 | Rock |
| WAMZ | 97.5 | Country |
| WZKF | 98.9 | Top 40 |
| WDJX | 99.7 | Top 40 |
| WAKY | 103.5 | Oldies |
| WRKA | 103.9 | Country |
| WAYI | 104.3 | Christian |
| WLRS | 105.1 | Alternative |
| WLVK | 105.5 | Country |
| WRVI | 105.9 | Christian |
| WSFR | 107.7 | Rock |

# INDEX